States and Social Evolution

States and
Social Evolution

Coffee and the Rise
of National Governments
in Central America

Robert G. Williams

The University of North Carolina Press

Chapel Hill and London

The paper in this book meets the guidelines for
permanence and durability of the Committee on
Production Guidelines for Book Longevity of the
Council on Library Resources.

Library of Congress Cataloging-in-Publication Data
Williams, Robert G. (Robert Gregory), 1948–
    States and social evolution : coffee and the rise of national
governments in Central America / by Robert G. Williams.
        p. cm.
    Includes bibliographical references and index.
    ISBN 0-8078-2154-3 (alk. paper).
    ISBN 0-8078-4463-2 (pbk. : alk. paper)
    1. Coffee industry—Central America—History—19th century.
2. Central America—Politics and government—1821–1951. I. Title.
HD9199.C42W54 1994
338.1′7373′09728—dc20   93-44709
                                     CIP

Robert G. Williams, Voehringer Professor of Economics at
Guilford College, is author of *Export Agriculture and the
Crisis in Central America.*

Frontispiece: "Coffee Plantation at Las Nubes," Department
of Suchitepéquez, Guatemala, 1875. (Department of Special
Collections, Stanford University Libraries)

98 97 96 95 94   5 4 3 2 1

For Deb

Contents

Maps

Figures

Tables

Illustrations

Preface

I first stumbled on the puzzle entertained in this book when doing fieldwork in Central America in 1972, before widespread unrest swept the region. My own naïveté regarding the diversity of political cultures and government structures of the isthmus led to many humorous encounters and more than one unpleasant experience that summer.

The purpose of the research was to investigate the treatment of foreign investment in the Central American Common Market, a project that required interviews with government officials and business executives in all five Central American capital cities. Preparation for the field trip included having my most conservative suit dry-cleaned, setting up contacts for interviews in Central America, studying available documents at the Stanford University Library, reading theoretical articles on foreign direct investment and common markets, and brushing up on my Spanish. A research grant from the Center for Latin American Studies at Stanford gave ample resources to pay my travel expenses and those of a fellow graduate student, who not only knew Spanish as a native language but could also repair a Volkswagen. Neither of us had traveled through Central America, and as first-year graduate students, we were wide open for adventure.

Although José knew more about Central America than I did, it became clear on the bumpy drive down that he held a blurred vision of the region as simply more primitive than Mexico, both politically and economically. Neither of us was prepared for the dramatically different political contexts we found as we drove from one country to another.

The state of Chiapas in southern Mexico has a noticeable Indian population that can be seen riding buses and walking along the sides of the road wearing traditional garments and carrying heavy loads. Across the border in Guatemala, ethnic differences became even more pronounced, and in the public markets we visited, Spanish was rarely spoken. In addition to being overwhelmed by Indian culture, I felt as though I had entered a police state. Guards carried submachine guns, and Indians passed by with their heads bowed in fear. In the countryside, however, the Indian people and their communities displayed a profound sense of integrity and independence. There also seemed to be some mutual respect, though a cold distance was kept, in individual interchanges between Indians and non-Indians regardless of whether an armed guard was close by. This apparent civility gave us a feeling of safety in Guatemala despite the menacing glances of uniformed men.

We desired to keep that feeling of security after leaving Guatemala, a notion that proved to be bad judgment in El Salvador. Just over the border, the change from Guatemala was undeniable. At dusk, the roadways teemed with barefoot people and mangy dogs, and an occasional scrawny cow halted automobile traffic. Beyond the road right-of-way, vast fields could be seen, but the people appeared to be herded onto the great river of the road. Their features, clothing, and movements looked more like those I had observed in the cities of central Mexico than in the Indian centers of neighboring Guatemala. Men wore store-bought shirts, hats, and trousers, and women wore single-fabric dresses devoid of the colorful weavings and needlepoint of Guatemala. Instead of clay pitchers, the women carried lighter and more durable plastic water jugs on their heads. Everyone spoke Spanish.

After several days of collecting documents and completing interviews in San Salvador, José and I drove toward Honduras on the coastal road. Near La Unión we took a detour on an unpaved road that led toward the sea. We gave a ride to a wrinkled woman, who carried a child so yellow and tired it could not blink its eyes fast enough to keep back the flies. The woman pleaded for money to buy medicine to save the child. We dropped her off at a group of shacks at the top of the ridge before the road descended to the beach. The peasant community below had built palm-frond shelters in a coconut grove; their canoes were pulled up on the beach, and their nets were spread out to dry. We parked several hundred yards from the settlement, changed into our bathing suits, and followed the winding path to the section of the beach unprotected from the wind and waves. As we body-surfed, we reflected on our good fortune to have found this tropical paradise when just hours before we were fighting traffic in crowded, polluted San Salvador. After riding one wave all the way in, I looked up at the car and saw a crowd peering into it, examining its contents. Children were crawling on the hood and standing on the rear bumper to get a better look. José thought I was paranoid to keep such a close eye on the red bug until I spotted a young man prying open the rear window and reaching in. As we returned to the vehicle, we ignored the violated window and conversed with the people in as relaxed a manner as possible. They had spotted José's guitar and my flute and requested a song. The sun was setting, and they invited us to stay the night. We thanked them and told them we had time for one more tune and then we had to return to La Unión to meet with some friends. I noticed that José's guitar-playing was unusually stilted. On the road back, José told me he had overheard the men at the fringe of the crowd behind him planning our demise.

On returning to El Salvador several weeks later, we learned that the incident at the beach was not unusual. We were invited to stay at the home of a family that owned a small dairy farm and cheese processing business, and through this contact we met wealthier individuals who owned coffee farms and cotton plantations. At the entrance to every home we visited, where one might expect to find a coat or hat rack, stood a gun rack, and whenever a trip was planned to the countryside, people habitually strapped on a pistol. I inquired about this practice (which I had not encountered anywhere else in Central America), and the dairy man told me that outside of the police-patrolled towns, it would be crazy to go without protection from a machete attack. He described the situation in the countryside as open hunting season on the haves by the have-nots. I also learned on this return visit that in conjunction with some wealthy businessmen the military president of the country had staked out an area of the coast to build a tourist resort; one obstacle the corporation faced in developing the resort was the peasant occupation of the site.

We arrived in Tegucigalpa late in the afternoon and promptly found a hotel in a busy commercial section. We parked the car out front. Later that night we heard noise in the street and looked out the window to see the car being burglarized. We yelled out the window, and the young men, who were armed only with coat hangers, scurried off. The hotel keeper did not have a weapon, but he flashed on the outside lights. We brought in all of our valuables, including the documents I had collected that were stowed in a duffle bag. The car was ransacked four more times that evening, and each time the unarmed robbers left when we yelled at them from the window. Although we felt vulnerable enough to hire an overnight car keeper and buy a lock for the trunk, we never felt personally threatened in Honduras either in the cities or the countryside. Nevertheless, the robbery did inconvenience me. Among the missing items were my black wing-tip shoes, which I needed for an interview that morning with an official in the Central American Bank for Economic Integration. I borrowed José's shoes, which were four sizes too large. Although I felt like Bozo the Clown and tripped over door steads, the interview went well, and I secured some relevant data and established contacts with Honduran government officials and corporate executives. Several days later, after all my planned interviews had been completed, José and I visited the national university outside of town, where I was able to photocopy some documents from the archives and speak with students and professors. One of the most thought-provoking conversations was with the editor in chief of the student newspaper, who gave a Maoist analysis of Honduran politics and social conditions. He also presented us with the latest copy of his paper, which had a large front-page picture of a machine gun with its barrel propped on a stack of red books. The bold-lettered caption read, *Estudiar y Luchar* (Study and Struggle).

That afternoon we drove to the Nicaraguan border at El Espino. After passing through the Honduran side without a snag, we entered a slow line. The vehicle two cars ahead was pulled aside by the Nicaraguan customs agents; the long-haired occupants had been removed, and a search crew was pulling off every door panel and hubcap. When our vehicle rolled up, a guard with a rifle began shouting, waving his weapon nervously through our rear window. The chief of customs was called to the scene and ordered a thorough search. In addition to the Honduran student newspaper that we had tossed in the back hours before, the guards found a package of nopal incense wrapped in corn husk, and they began a close inspection of every document in my briefcase and the large duffle bag. Although they overlooked some radical books that had been published in Honduras, they did pull aside as evidence against us three items that José had acquired in Mexico in preparation for a popular course called Challengers to Capitalism that Jack Gurley would be teaching in the fall. These pamphlets were *Wages, Prices, and Profits* by Karl Marx,

Imperialism by V. I. Lenin, and *Three Essays* by Mao Tse-tung; all had been printed in Spanish in Havana. Two twenties slipped in José's passport did not do the trick as it would have in Mexico. The chief of customs ordered our car locked and put us under armed guard for the night. The next morning I dressed in my interviewing suit, and guards drove us to the central customs house in Managua.

We explained to the minister of customs the reason for the trip and presented him with official letters from Stanford University and the Ford Foundation authorizing the project. We told the origin of the newspaper and the purpose of the three pamphlets, but the minister felt that this was a matter of national security and sent us to the minister of internal security, located at the fortresslike central prison in the center of Managua. It was ninety-eight degrees, the humidity was oppressive, and they placed us in a hot box with bright lights and a one-way mirror wall. We were pulled out separately and questioned extensively on exactly where in Cuba we were from. It was difficult for me to fathom that they would believe that I, a red-haired, light-skinned graduate student with a U.S. passport, a modest command of Spanish, and a gringo accent was a native of Cuba. It was almost as unlikely that they would consider José, a tall, athletic figure with straight black hair, high, chiseled cheekbones, a bronze complexion that belied some Indian heritage, and an accent with the unmistakable song of Mexico in it, was actually a Cuban in disguise. After our individual investigations, we were subjected to a group interrogation. After explaining in great detail once more precisely where we were from, that we had never traveled to Cuba, and that we were just passing through for a couple of interviews on our way to Costa Rica, a large interrogator with a pockmarked face picked up the nopal incense from the Indian market in Guatemala and said, "hashisha." A young, handsome officer in a white uniform laughed, explaining that he had been trained as a catechist and that the dense gooey substance was incense used in religious ceremonies. We were then sent back to the hot box.

I had been told before by a minor functionary that I could make a telephone call, and after sitting for another thirty minutes I opened the hot box door and asked again. He said that would be fine and he would notify me when the lines were clear. I had the telephone number of a Nicaraguan colleague from Stanford, whose grandfather had been president of the country and whose uncle had not only married President Somoza's sister but had served for many years in Washington as Nicaraguan ambassador to the United States. I thought that a short call might spring us from the clutches of this paranoid bureaucracy. When José was returned to the hot box from another round of interrogation, I used the open door as a third opportunity to request access to a telephone. A major who was standing out of sight in the corner of the switchboard room erupted, shouting "*al bote*" (to the clink).

In seconds, we were marched at gunpoint out of the office section and toward the fortress gate, which creaked open. The guards prodded us to the first wing of cells on the right, where a functionary sat behind a plain table with a drawer below and a guest list on top. We signed in and were told to leave our personal belongings there. I left a fountain pen and a note pad but decided that my watch and the fat wad of dollar bills in my pocket were safer left on my person. The hallway behind the table led through two rows of cells. The first one on the right was large and makeshift, and some fifty women with unkempt hair and soiled faces clutched the chicken wire and peered hungrily at us, making occasional catcalls and whistling as we were ushered by.

A guard unlocked a heavy gate, and we were shoved into the second cell, which was very narrow with walls three feet thick, allowing us to stand in the doorway with our backs against the bars. A nauseating stench belched from the hole in the floor in front of us, and male figures, dressed in grungy briefs, rushed from the bunks lining the wall. I was glad that I had removed my tie and placed it in the pocket of my jacket, for it would have made an excellent pulling device for the inmates. José talked fast and with his arms pushed off the advances of the bully of the cell, who pressed José with his fat belly. Two skinny prisoners made their way around the bully and toward me. One tried to grab my suit jacket while the other asked for cigarettes as he reached for the wad in my trouser pockets. Protected from the flank by the portal walls, José and I fended off their attacks. I winced in anticipation of what we would have to do to defend ourselves when night fell on the prison. Among other thoughts, I envisioned the dollar bills flying as inmates fought over them, for in Nicaragua at that time, one could buy one's freedom at the rate of fifty cents per day of sentence.

The commotion attracted the attention of a group inspecting the prison. Leading the group was the officer in white, who had interviewed us before. He asked the guards, "What are *they* doing in *that* cell?" He promptly had us removed. He told us he did not have the immediate authority to release us, but he arranged for our valuables, including the wad of bills, to be checked at the desk and a receipt drawn up listing all items and affixed his signature as witness to the transaction. He asked if we knew anyone in Managua. I wrote down my friend's telephone number and name. When the officer read the name, he gasped, hesitated, and said he would do what he could. At least one person believed our story. He ordered the guards to place us in the large cell on the end.

The octagonal cell was in one of the corners of the old fortress, which could have been built during the colonial period, judging from the age and thickness of the walls and the architectural style. The great door clanked shut, but we were not attacked by the inmates, who were seated in orderly fashion with legs dangling from four shelves of scaffolding that followed the perimeter of the octagon and rose toward the thirty-foot ceiling. A man in his twenties stood in the center and pointed with a stick to the spots where we were to sit. We were allowed to converse with those next to us for ten minutes, when the young man banged the stick on the scaffolding, calling for silence. He then ordered José to come to the center. At first it was unclear whether resistance or obedience was the correct response, but the old man sitting next to us, who had been a tenant in these quarters for sixteen years on a murder charge, urged José to obey. A second young man of muscular build searched José and took from his person some small change, a pocket notebook, and a bottle of eye drops, which José protested to no avail. All items were placed in a communal box, which contained a collection of money, jewelry, and other valuables. They found nothing of value on me. We were seated in different places, and every half hour thenceforth the seating arrangement was changed at the orders of the two men in charge, allowing for entertaining conversations. In Nicaragua at that time, the prison system did not provide food for the prisoners, who had to fend for themselves or have family members deliver food from outside. Late in the day, a bucket of rice and beans arrived for one of our cellmates. The bucket was immediately expropriated by the cell leaders, who announced that "our guests" should receive food first. He placed two wooden spoons in the bucket and offered it to José and me for dinner. My stomach was still churning from the day's excitement, but more out of gratitude than hunger, I managed to down two spoonfuls. After we were asked two or three times if that was all we wanted, the remainder was distributed to the fifty or so others.

The old man warned me not to talk of politics in the cell. I asked why not, and he pointed to his ear and to a couple of the inmates around the room. I tried to follow his advice, but my curiosity was too great, especially regarding the cluster of cell leaders, who as it turned out were all said to be political prisoners. I asked one of them what he thought about multinational corporations in Nicaragua (the subject of my research project), and he whispered that all of the companies entering Nicaragua had to provide Somoza with shares in the company and that there were close ties between the Somoza dictatorship, the imperialist corporations, and the U.S. military. He also told a story about a leader from the past called Sandino, who had offered up his own life in the struggle against this unholy trinity.

Before dark set in, sleeping locations were arranged, and I was given a spot on the third tier, a good place, according to the old man, who offered me the use of his pillow, which was a rolled-up piece of cardboard. After about three hours of relative quiet, the action began, and by midnight the floor of the cell was filled with fresh detainees of all ages, some of them less than twelve years old, who had been pulled from the streets of Managua. On more than one occasion, the strong man had to wield the stick to break up fights on the floor and usher drunks to the hole. At dawn, the entire cell was awakened by the sound of the stick banging against the scaffolding. The cell leader ordered the figure on the floor, who was crumpled up in a pool of vomit, to begin cleaning the cell and handed him a broom, a bucket of water, and a can of detergent. The figure stumbled to his feet and began a lackluster effort of moving the mess around with the broom. The leader said, "Clean harder," but got no noticeable change in effort, at which point the leader dealt the drunk a series of blows that left him in a heap below the closest bunk. The leader then rapidly cleaned a section of floor, quickly swirling the broom and sopping up the foam with an old rag. After this demonstration, the leader asked for volunteers and pointed to a young man on the top tier, who in trepidation climbed down and cleaned the entire floor.

The second in command held a short conference with José and me and informed us that he knew of cases when North Americans had been detained for months before being released. That morning, he was to be allowed four hours' parole to look for a job, and he requested our passport numbers so that he could leave them for us at the U.S. and Mexican embassies. Shortly after he and several others were allowed out, the guards moved us to a holding cell across from the women, and after several hours the officer in white arrived and made sure we received all the items on our list. He then wished us well and handed us over to four National Guardsmen who drove us in a van toward the border.

The conversation centered around automobiles, television sets, and other consumer durables, and the lieutenant told of a recent trip to Miami that General Somoza had paid for. We stopped at a restaurant along the way, and it was strongly suggested that José and I pay for the guards' meals. After lunch, as we drove through a small town, a group of peasant women was crossing the road with babies strapped on their backs and water jugs on their heads. Instead of slowing down, the sergeant stepped on the accelerator, veering toward the women as they fled. Even though the corporals were but one step out of the peasantry themselves, all four men laughed heartily, and for the remainder of our trip, they laughed several more times in reference to the incident. At the border we recovered our Volkswagen and drove to the Honduran checkpoint. The lieutenant had crossed the border ahead of us and had spoken with the Honduran customs agent, who sent us to the chief's office. The chief informed us that the telephone line to Tegucigalpa was down and that we would have to be sent there for investigation. I imagined what the jail there must be like and reasoned with him, telling him we did not wish to stay in Honduras or cause any trouble and that we would gladly pay for an armed escort to the Salvadoran border. On the short drive to the border, I imagined being regurgitated from Central America. This did not occur because of the hiatus of communication between the Hondurans and the Salvadorans, a product of the so-called Soccer War between the two countries in 1969.

In El Salvador, we spent a week recovering from our sojourn into Nicaragua and planned an alternative route to Costa Rica, where I had interviews scheduled for the following week. At that time, Salvadoran vehicles could not pass through Honduras but had to take a ferry from La Unión to Poneloya to travel south. We booked passage on the ferry, which was a salvaged Staten Island vessel Somoza had acquired when this commercial opportunity arose following the 1969 war. Fortunately, our names and passport numbers had not yet made their way to the undesirable aliens list at the customs shack at Poneloya so once again we found ourselves on Nicaraguan soil. The Pan American Highway passed through the center of Managua, and our hearts raced when a National Guard van pulled up behind us and the traffic light turned red directly across from our accommodations of the week before; I tried not to make eye contact with the old man peering through the bars, and I refused to glance at the rear view mirror. When the van turned left toward the central office, we drove straight to Costa Rica without stopping.

In San José we stayed with José's second cousin, who was a native-born Costa Rican. Mario's extensive library collection contained several volumes that would have made him a prime candidate for Somoza's central prison if he had been a resident of nearby Nicaragua. Mario was a member of a political group called Vanguardia Popular, and he did not seem worried about people knowing his affiliations, even at his job in the government. On the lapel of his suit jacket, where a businessman might tack a Rotary Club pin, Mario placed a discrete bust of Lenin. I had some good interviews in Costa Rica, including one with an economist who had written extensively about the Central American Common Market and who later served as head of the central bank and minister of the economy, but the most lively discussions took place in the homes of Mario's friends, who were social scientists and historians with widely ranging perspectives and who taught at the university but held other jobs as well. What amazed me was that they were able to walk the streets and speak openly without fear of being abducted or gunned down. In fact, the only police I observed carrying weapons in Costa Rica that summer were those stationed in the lobbies of banks.

During that thin slice of time—before the great earthquakes struck Managua and Guatemala City, before Hurricane Fifi flooded the north coast of Honduras, before worldwide oil crises engulfed the area, and before civil wars broke out—personal experiences piqued my curiosity about an aspect of Central America that citizens of the region tend to take for granted. Central Americans who travel are adept at shifting social gears when crossing borders. When we told Central American friends about our summer adventures on their isthmus, instead of empathizing with us over our difficulties, they laughed at our foolishness for not knowing the facts of political life, but when asked why political cultures were so different from one country to the next, they gave most inadequate answers either along the lines of "that's just the way things are," or they gave belabored accounts of the nature of individual national leaders. Over the following fifteen years, when I made return visits to research a variety of subjects, the deeper enigma continued to stir my curiosity, and I finally decided to grapple with it head-on using comparative history as a method. Even after having lost my political naïveté of two decades before and after having worked directly on the issue for half a decade, I still find it remarkable to visit a place where one can drive such a short distance and pass through such a wide variety of political climates.

Acknowledgments

Because Central American political diversity has puzzled me for so long and because the evolution of my own thought on the subject has been influenced by so many others, acknowledging sources of insight and support is a difficult task. During my half a dozen or so field trips to Central America over the years, people of many walks of life have shared their experiences and knowledge with me, sometimes making it hard to pinpoint exactly where, when, and from whom a fresh perspective was generated. Central and North American scholars and librarians, too numerous to account for fully, have generously opened their collections to me; colleagues have steered me to the most promising sources and have read drafts of the manuscript in various stages of its development; others have encouraged the project with moral or material support. The following supporters of this endeavor stand out, and I apologize for any omissions.

My introduction to the structural differences in Central America's coffee sector came in 1980, when I began preliminary research on agriculture in the region. Among the most influential secondary sources that I read at the time was a 1975 article by C. F. S. Cardoso titled "Historia económica del café en Centroamérica (siglo XIX): Estudio comparativo," which sketched the development of coffee in Guatemala, El Salvador, and Costa Rica during the nineteenth century. I remember this article making good sense to me at the time, and after more than a decade of attention to Central American agriculture, I dust off my photocopy of it and once again appreciate the spadework done by the author. Other secondary works that have enabled me to build this comparative study pulled together diverse primary materials on coffee and nineteenth-century political processes for individual countries. Of special importance in this regard are the works by David McCreery and Julio Castellanos Cambranes on Guatemala, David Browning and Héctor Lindo-Fuentes on El Salvador, Jeffrey Gould on Nicaragua, and Carolyn Hall, Lowell Gudmundson, and Mario Samper on Costa Rica. Other works that have helped me visualize the colonial roots of nineteenth-century economic and political structures include those by Ralph Lee Woodward, Jr., Héctor Pérez Brignoli, José Antonio Fernández, Mario Rodríguez, and Miles Wortman.

Constructing a clear picture of nineteenth-century processes required collecting photocopies of agricultural surveys, government financial statistics, and other primary materials that were scattered about Central and North America. Fortunately for scholars, there exist some outstanding collections of Central American archival materials. Throughout the research for this book, the keepers of these archives assisted me, speeding my access to appropriate materials. My base collection came from more than a month of combing the stacks of the Latin American Library at Tulane University, where Tom Niehaus, Kathy Burke, Martha Robertson, Ruth Olivera, and others went out of their way to promote my project; of special importance was a personal tour of the Dieseldorff collection by its scholarly curator, Guillermo Nañez Falcón, who is currently director of the Latin America Collection. Of the centralized collections in Central America, the most important—especially with respect to early nineteenth-century land documents—was the Archivos Generales de Centroamérica in Guatemala City, where don "Goyo" Concoha, whose personal knowledge of the archives, became invaluable to my pursuits. Also of great assistance was doña "Lucky" Muralles, who led me through the CIRMA collection in Antigua. In addition to personal visits to collections, I have continued to benefit from the assistance of Jim Breedlove, curator of the Latin America collection at Stanford University, and Deborah Jakubs, curator of Duke University's Latin America Collection. Elizabeth Place-Beary and Malone Stimson of the Guilford College Library have been outstanding in patching the holes of my personal collection through the networks of interlibrary loan. In the final phase of the project, Linda Long and the staff of the Special Collections Department of Stanford University Libraries went out of their way to send inventory lists and copies of the Muybridge prints that were selected as illustrations for this book.

Sometimes the great collections do not have copies of the rarest documents, but scholars who have visited research sites and sleuthed through private libraries have unearthed valuable primary sources unavailable elsewhere. I continue to be grateful to the scholars who have so generously offered items from their personal collections. I especially thank Julio Castellanos Cambranes, William H. Durham, Marc Edelman, Dario Euraque, Richard Grossman, Lowell Gudmundson, David Kaimowitz, Edouard Fabrice Lehoucq, Stan Potter, Mario Samper, Regina Wagner, and Lee Woodward, Jr.

Without having visited the coffee zones of Central America, it would have been extremely difficult to read historical documents with a critical eye. Some of the most informative experiences came when I visited Central American coffee farms, processing mills, and export houses, first in 1982–83 and again in 1987–88. During these field trips I witnessed a wide diversity of cultivation and processing technologies, some employing nineteenth-century methods and equipment alongside others using the most recent agribusiness technologies. Helping me sort through and interpret these observations were independent coffee farmers, government agricultural technicians, coffee workers, and managers of coffee plantations, processing mills, and export houses, to all of whom I am indebted. During the first round of fieldwork, I was accompanied by Alan Hruska, who traveled with me through Costa Rica, Nicaragua, Honduras, and El Salvador, enlivening interviews, collaborating in note-taking, and providing technical assistance from his background in biology. During the second phase of fieldwork, I visited coffee enterprises and labor supply zones of Guatemala. Among the most helpful experts in Guatemala was don Rodrigo Chong, who shared his twenty-two years of experience as an agronomist for the national coffee association (ANACAFE) with me as he took me on his rounds of coffee farms, processing mills, and export houses in the department of Santa Rosa. In addition to facilitating interviews with numerous coffee farmers, processors, and exporters in the zone, don Rodrigo took time from his workday to give me a lesson in the art and science of shade management, which was his widely recognized area of expertise. A second guide in Guatemala who deserves special mention was Rodolfo Pérez Arrivillaga, manager of one of the oldest—and, undoubtedly one of the most beautiful—coffee plantations in Central America, El Capetillo, which lies at the foot of El Fuego Volcano near Alotenango. This was an unusual plantation for Guatemala in that the manager refused to have armed guards at the gate because such an action would "alienate the nearby community," which was a source of supply for temporary workers on the estate and a social support for the 150 permanent workers who lived on the plantation. This day on the *finca* Capetillo was one of the richest, not only because of the manager's scientific approach to coffee cultivation but because of the remarkably long-range perspective of don Rodolfo, whose decisions were governed not only by questions of short-term yield but by a deep sensitivity to the history of the estate, the application of ecologically sound methods of pest management and fertilization, the origins, beliefs, and customs of the various groups of people who worked the estate, and the aesthetics of planting flowering trees along the avenues and gardens in front of the work buildings. I left El Capetillo with the odd feeling that I had spent a day with Thomas Jefferson.

Various steps of this project were made possible through financial grants and other tangible support. In 1987, a library fellowship from the Andrew W. Mellon Foundation helped finance a month's work in the archives at Tulane University's Latin American Library, and while I was in New Orleans, Roger and Raymond Weill generously welcomed me as a guest in their home. In 1991, the Economics Department at the University of Utah funded a summer conference, "Labor, Development, and Economic Stability," where I received valuable criticism from Salem Ajluni, Gail Blattenberger, Michael Carter, Jens Christiansen, Ken Jameson, Peter Philips, Chiranjib Sen, Gita Sen, Sandy Thompson, and other participants. Similarly, in 1993, the History Department of the University of Costa Rica in Heredia hosted a summer conference, "Crisis in the Coffee Economy," where I received helpful critiques from Victor Hugo Acuña, José Antonio Fernández, Lowell Gudmundson, David Kaimowitz, Héctor Lindo-Fuentes, Jeffery Paige, Héctor Pérez Brignoli, Mario Samper, and other scholars. Over the years, the greatest financial support has come from Guilford College, where Kathy Adams, William Rogers, Sam Schuman, Carol Stoneburner, members of the Faculty Development Committee, members of the Computer Committee, and others have looked favorably on this endeavor and have encouraged it in many ways, including funding for computer needs, field trips to Central America, visits to library collections, and travel to related conferences.

Over the years, students, colleagues and friends have read chapter drafts and have responded in ways that have helped move the project along. At the risk of omission, I would like to thank Jefferson

Boyer, Ed Burrows, Marc Edelman, Dario Euraque, José Antonio Fernández, Joe Freeman, David Hewson, Alice Owens Johnson, Megan Keiser, Fabrice Edouard Lehoucq, David Perry, Carol Smith, Keith Strange, Marna Bromberg Williams, and Robert B. (Bob) Williams. For the final reading of the manuscript and for the writing of insightful comments, I am indebted to the two reviewers for the University of North Carolina Press, Ralph Lee Woodward, Jr., and Lowell Gudmundson. Of course, blame for any remaining errors or misinterpretations belongs to me.

One last word of thanks goes to my wife, Deborah Dunn Williams, who sometimes claims she married this project. For her patience in staying the course, I dedicate this book to her.

Robert G. Williams
Kernersville, North Carolina
August 10, 1993

Note on the Illustrations

The photographs that appear as illustrations in this book were taken by Eadweard Muybridge, the nineteenth-century photographer who is best known for his sequence studies of animals in motion. In 1875, the Pacific Mail Steamship Company sponsored Muybridge's field trip to Central America, where the artist spent approximately two months in Panama and six months in Guatemala. Upon returning to San Francisco in early 1876, Muybridge published five or six limited edition albums of photographs from his journey, two of which are now in the safekeeping of the Department of Special Collections of Stanford University Libraries under the title "The Pacific Coast of Central America and Mexico; the Isthmus of Panama: Guatemala; and the Cultivation and Shipment of Coffee." These albums are loaded with primary observations of transport technology and infrastructure, coffee cultivation and processing, social scenes and public buildings, and landscapes and cityscapes from a time when Central America was undergoing a profound transformation. The Department of Special Collections of Stanford University Libraries has generously permitted the reproduction of selected photographs, which provide the reader with visual images captured by the camera of a keen observer precisely in the middle of the historical period (1850–1900) explored by this book. Unfortunately for comparative purposes, Muybridge did not travel to Costa Rica or Honduras, and he did not venture inland from the Pacific ports of Nicaragua and El Salvador. His six months in Guatemala, however, yielded a treasure of social documentation in locations that appear to have been chosen for their aesthetic splendor, their portrayal of the colonial past, or their depiction of Central America's economic potential from a commercial perspective.

Grants from the Dean's Research Fund, Faculty Development, **xxxvii**

and Intercultural Studies at Guilford College financed the printing
of copies for use in this book and in the classroom. For persons
interested in viewing a larger sample of the Guatemala images, along
with a careful examination of Muybridge's observations placed in
historical context, see E. Bradford Burns, *Eadweard Muybridge in
Guatemala, 1875: The Photographer as Social Recorder* (Berkeley:
University of California Press, 1986). Albums of original prints can
be viewed at Stanford University, the California State Library, the
Museum of Modern Art, and the State University of New York at
Stony Brook.

States and Social Evolution

Chapter I

Introduction

The peculiar differences in the political character of the five Central American states that I experienced firsthand in 1972 were revealed in full glory soon afterward. Social tensions that had been gradually mounting for two decades were pushed to extremes by natural disasters and shocks from the world system during the 1970s.

Natural disasters hit unevenly in time and space, the major ones being the Managua earthquake, which flattened the capital city of Nicaragua in December 1972; Hurricane Fifi, which flooded the North Coast of Honduras in September 1974; and the Guatemala earthquake, which leveled towns in the Central Highlands and sections of Guatemala City in February 1976. All caused losses of property and life, disruptions in communication and transport, shortages of food, water, and medical and building supplies, and a strain on the capacities of public institutions. In the zones affected, peasants and workers responded to economic stress by invading idle properties, protesting price increases, striking for higher wages, and working through nongovernment institutions to alleviate the worst results of the disasters.

Shocks from the world system initiated by runs on the dollar and vastly increased oil prices, first in 1973–75 and then in 1978–83, gripped the entire region, simultaneously deteriorating the purchasing power of wage earners and peasants, squeezing profits of elites, and provoking fiscal crises of governments. Throughout the isthmus, these shocks triggered social unrest as workers struck for higher wages, urban dwellers protested increased food, energy, and transport prices, and peasants invaded idle lands. Threatened internationally by declining crop prices, rising interest rates, and rapidly rising input prices, elites attempted to hold the line locally by resisting pressures from workers and peasants.

I

All governments mediated social conflict with combinations of reform and repression, but the particular mixtures used were not uniform across the isthmus. The governments of Nicaragua, El Salvador, and Guatemala more frequently responded to unrest with official violence, killing and torturing peasant leaders, labor unionists, priests, and anyone who took the side of the poor, while the governments of Honduras and Costa Rica responded more flexibly to demands from below, raising minimum wages and bending to pressure from peasants for land reform. At a deeper level, fundamentally different national dispositions to conflict resolution appeared to be operating, confirming on a grander scale casual observations made during fieldwork in 1972. In El Salvador, Guatemala, and Nicaragua, the intent of the authorities seemed to be to terrorize the population into submission through highly publicized acts of barbarity, while in Costa Rica and Honduras, though repressive measures were applied periodically by local authorities and by elements in the national state, segments of the highest levels of government would listen to appeals from peasants and workers.

How governments mediated social tensions during the 1970s affected what followed. The three countries whose governments applied the heaviest doses of repression during the early 1970s later experienced popular uprisings of unexpected magnitude. Applications of terror by Somoza's National Guard following the Managua earthquake in 1972 and later world system shocks united factions that had never worked together before, leading to a civil war that by July of 1979 had killed fifty thousand Nicaraguans and toppled the Somoza dictatorship which for four decades had been considered invincible. During the 1980s, a war between the Sandinista government and a counterrevolutionary force funded and trained by U.S. national security operatives resulted in more than thirty thousand additional deaths. The governments of El Salvador and Guatemala also responded to popular protests during the 1970s with overt acts of terror that, instead of dividing the opposition, resulted in the creation of broad-based coalitions, which included guerrilla elements that hoped to overthrow the governments of those countries. During the 1980s, the Guatemalan conflict killed more than forty thousand persons, and an estimated more than five hundred thousand fled the country, seeking asylum in Mexico and the United States. During the 1980s, the Salvadoran government was besieged by even greater popular opposition than that of Guatemala, prompting economic and military aid from the United States to prop it up. During the twelve years of civil war, death squad activity and fighting between military and rebel groups killed seventy-five thousand Salvadorans, and an estimated 1 million Salvadorans out of a total population of 5.5 million sought asylum in the United States, Canada, and Mexico. In Honduras and Costa Rica, where national governments behaved more flexibly in response to social tensions during the 1970s, explosions of violence that occurred elsewhere were avoided, though U.S. military aid to both countries during the 1980s strengthened the hand of repressive elements within the security forces.

Why did governments respond so differently to pressures from below?

During the 1980s, many policymakers in Washington and elsewhere seemed to believe that military dictatorships were responsible for the internal political problems in Central America. After all, Costa Rica, where elected officials ran the national government, survived the turbulent 1970s without political instability. According to this view, one key to solving the political problem in the other countries was to hold fair elections that would allow people to have a voice in selecting who was to preside over their governments, thereby dampening popular disaffection. The scheduling of democratic elections for president became a quid pro quo for governments to receive U.S. assistance, and more subtle international pressures, especially from Western Europe, encouraged the same. With international teams of observers present to discourage fraud, elections for president were held in every Central American country during the 1980s.

Although it may have been morally admirable to encourage governments to extend voting rights to their citizens, the theory behind the policy—that a central political reason for instability was dictatorship, as opposed to democracy—was flawed from the start. The case of Honduras in the 1970s presents an anomaly to the theory. During the first wave of regionwide unrest (1973–75), a military dictatorship—not a popularly elected government—raised minimum wages and ruled in favor of Honduran peasants in numerous land disputes; during those years some twenty-four thousand peasant families gained access to approximately two hundred thousand acres of land. Furthermore, after the U.S. government imposed electoral democracy in El Salvador and Guatemala during the 1980s, rule by terror continued in full force, and during the first period of electoral democracy in Honduras (1980–84), incidents of political torture, disappearances, and assassinations by security personnel surged, though they never approached the levels of El Salvador or Guatemala.[1]

The dictatorship versus democracy argument provides, at best, a shallow explanation for why peasants, workers, and slum dwellers had greater room to pressure their respective governments in Honduras and Costa Rica than they did in Guatemala, El Salvador, or prerevolutionary Nicaragua. The diverse political behavior seems equally paradoxical from a world systems perspective, considering that the economies of all five countries are connected into the world economy in much the same way, as exporters of tropical agricultural products and importers of finished and semifinished products. And if one examines internal economic changes during the decades before the outbreaks of unrest, one finds that all five countries experienced very similar transformations, including technification of agriculture using imported inputs, dispossession of peasants from their lands, increasing dependence on seasonal wage labor, rapid growth of the overall population, and even more rapid growth of urban areas.

Before resorting to an argument for each case based on the motivations of the individuals, political parties, and military men who held the reins of power in each of the countries, it makes sense to explore relationships between political institutions and structures in agriculture, the backbone of the Central American economy. In my agricultural fieldwork in Central America in 1982, I was impressed by how similarly cotton, sugar, cattle, and bananas were raised in different countries but how markedly different were the land tenure and labor relations in coffee production. In all five countries, small, medium, and large-scale coffee farms coexist, but the relative importance of each size class differs substantially from one country to the next. At one extreme is Honduras, where small peasant farms are scattered across the coffee landscape intermingled with less numerous medium-sized farms; it is very rare to find a large capitalist coffee farm in Honduras. At the opposite extreme is Guatemala, where huge coffee *fincas*, guarded by men with rifles, provide the bulk of the crop, while pockets of small and medium-sized growers survive as less important producers. Next to Guatemala on the size spectrum are the coffee sectors of Nicaragua (especially before the decapitalization that occurred during the 1980s) and El Salvador, where large capitalistic coffee farms dominate production but where there is a more active segment of small and medium-sized producers than in Guatemala. Next to the extreme case of Honduras in participation by small and medium-sized coffee producers stands Costa Rica, where family-sized coffee farms predominate, though in certain sections of the country there can be found large capitalist enterprises that typically own processing mills to service the smaller producers.[2] If a connection exists between agrarian structures and the highly diverse political institutions of the region, the most likely place to look for it is in the coffee sector, where agrarian structures diverge.

In his now-classic inquiry into the agrarian roots of dictatorship and democracy, Barrington Moore, Jr., argues that large plantation systems with subservient labor augur poorly for the development of democracy because the "landed upper class is likely to need a state with a powerful repressive apparatus and thus one that imposes a whole climate of political and social opinion unfavorable to human freedom. . . . Further, it encourages the preponderance of the countryside over the towns, which are likely to become mere transshipment depots for export to distant markets. Finally, there are the brutalizing consequences of the elite's relationship to its work force, especially severe in those plantation economies where the laborers belong to a different race." Moore argues that several agrarian structures are conducive to the development of democratic institutions, such as when the process of commercialization incorporates small producers, who maintain at least de facto control over the land they work.[3] Although Moore's theory of dictatorship, characterized by autocratic and arbitrary rule by a single individual, versus democracy, with officials selected for public office by regularly scheduled elections, is *not* the question posed in this book, a more general formulation of his thesis is central to this work, namely that agrarian structures influence the character of states in their behavior toward nonelites.

It should make intuitive sense that governments, regardless of whether officials are elected, are more likely than not to reinforce land tenure and labor relations in sectors providing most of the foreign exchange for a small, open economy. Import capacity, employment levels, total productive activity, tax revenues, and the ability to borrow on international capital markets all depend on exports. If large plantations provide the bulk of the exports, governments will tend to support those enterprises if called upon, and if small proprietors are the key producers, governments are likely to ensure their health. Furthermore, vested economic interests have the capacity to pressure states on their own behalf, providing a causal link between those who already prosper and the behavior of governments. This reasoning, combined with the evidence available on land tenure and labor relations in the coffee sectors of the five countries, supports the worthiness of the general formulation of the Barrington Moore thesis in its application to coffee and state behavior in Central America.

Application of the thesis to a single sector of the economy at a point in recent history, however, does not explain why governments behave in certain ways. First, focusing on a single activity, coffee, ignores other economic sectors of importance for the overall health of the economy that may have strong vested interests. Since World War II, there has been a significant diversification of economic activity in Central America, and the relative importance of the coffee sector has diminished. This raises a serious challenge to the simple agrarian structure/state behavior thesis. For example, it raises the quandary of why the beef barons in the provinces of Olancho, Honduras, and Guanacaste, Costa Rica, who are engaged in a perpetual struggle with peasants for land, have not been more successful in pressuring national governments to intervene on their behalf, especially considering the post-World War II boom in beef exports. Second, viewing current economic structures as the primary cause of state behavior ignores the relative autonomy of states in relation to economic elites. Once state machineries are intact, they become powers in their own right and develop the capacity to intervene in ways sometimes perceived by economic elites as inimical to their interests. Recent Central American history is rife with examples of states enacting policies that go against the interests of the coffee elite. Furthermore, political elites can use their positions in the state to develop their own empires, independent of traditional economic elites. One has to look only at the militaries of Guatemala, El Salvador, and Honduras to see how those institutions and their officer corps have claimed their own economic turf independent of private sector elites, using the leverage of the state to establish their own banks, insurance companies, real estate development trusts, and industrial enterprises. Finally, richer, more powerful states can influence poorer, militarily weaker states with threats and inducements, sometimes breaking traditional ties and pacts of domination between national economic elites and their respective states. The most salient example in recent Central American history is the case of El Salvador in the 1980s, where heavy U.S. military and economic aid was used as a lever in the expropriation of land, export houses, banks, and other assets of the Salvadoran oligarchy. Despite the looser connections in recent times between traditional coffee elites and the state, national institutions in Central America have continued to behave toward the poor in ways characteristic of an earlier epoch, suggesting a resiliency in habits of governance that transcends immediate pressures by powerful economic interests.

Douglass North has pointed to the path dependence of institutions, noting that "once a development path is set on a particular course, the network externalities, the learning process of organizations, and the historically derived subjective modeling of the issues reinforce the course."[4] In attempting to explain the persistence of behavior patterns of political institutions in spite of significant changes in economic structures, one cannot take an arbitrary moment in time, compare economic and political structures at that moment, and expect to find revealing answers. Rather, to understand these persistent patterns, one must look back to the period when the path was embarked upon, when the institutions were first constructed.[5]

In *States and Social Revolutions*, Theda Skocpol explores the moment of construction of national states in China, Russia, and France. Skocpol argues that in all three cases national governments emerged out of social revolutions, which she defines as "rapid, basic transformations of a society's state and class structures, accompanied and in part carried through by class-based revolts from below." She shows how the breakdown of all three old regimes was accompanied by world historical developments that strained the capacities of existing state structures at precisely the same time that peasant uprisings were under way in the countryside. Of critical importance for the very different states that emerged were the particular configurations of urban, rural, and international contexts during the breakdown of the old order and the rise of the new, leading to a "modern state edifice" in France, a "dictatorial party-state" in Russia, and a "mass-mobilizing party-state" in China. Skocpol concludes that characteristics present at the beginning set patterns of governance that limited and conditioned changes in economic and political structures for many decades to come.[6]

Unlike the formation of national states in France, Russia, and China, Central American states did not emerge out of social revolutions in the sense that they were not accompanied by what could be called class-based revolts from below, though struggles there were. After the fall of the Spanish empire in the early 1820s, chaos reigned in Central America while local strongmen fought for control against strongmen from neighboring locales. Civil wars were not peculiar to Central America at this time. E. Bradford Burns has argued that throughout most of the nineteenth century Latin America was involved in struggles over how best to adapt to the rapidly changing world system, with "part of the elites and most of the middle class wishing to reshape Latin America in the image of Northern Europe," while "patriarchs, the Roman Catholic Church, and some intellectuals questioned rapid and unselective modernization and looked more to the Ibero-American past for guidance," and "the common people drew heavily on their own rich folk cultures" and life-styles, which "they were reluctant to abandon." Miles Wortman distinguishes between the Hapsburg mode of governance, characterized by controls over trade and decentralized rule, which permitted local power structures to flourish along with a strong role for the Catholic church in providing education, hospitals, and other public goods, and the Bourbon mode of centralized rule, with attitudes promoting "free trade and the sanctity of the market place" along with a strident anticlericalism. Wortman argues that from the Ibero-American past, these two distinct inclinations of governance provided an ideological basis for civil wars following independence and for political disputes thereafter.[7] Whether imported or inherited, abundant materials were available in 1850 for building governments in Central America, and the remainder of the century was spent doing just that.

Although the process was highly uneven and Honduras lagged behind the other four countries, by 1900 national states had formed out of the earlier chaos. More regular patterns of succession and longer terms of presidential officeholding reflected a greater legitimacy of national government than was true during the first half of the nineteenth century. During the latter half of the nineteenth century national legal institutions provided fundamental laws concerning marriage and divorce, labor contracts, property rights, and grievance procedures that were to remain intact during most of the twentieth century. Coercive institutions with their own officer training schools were founded, giving greater coherence to national authority and greater capacity to enforce laws within national jurisdictions. Although far from twentieth-century standards in advanced states, national governments in Central America improved their capacity to collect taxes during this period, and most governments were able to raise their international credit ratings, giving them greater borrowing power from world capital markets. In most of the Central American countries, during the latter half of the nineteenth century national governments took over hospitals, schools, and other charitable institutions that had formerly been the exclusive domain of the church. On the economic front, during this same period of political institution building the basic patterns of property ownership, land tenure, labor relations, and social classes were formed that have been extended and modified during the twentieth century. Finally, it was during the latter half of the nineteenth century that governments were able to project onto their citizens an identity of belonging to a nation; as Steven Palmer has put it, nations were "invented" in Central America in the late nineteenth century.[8] If one wishes to understand the foundation from which Central American structures evolved during most of the twentieth century, one must look to the latter half of the nineteenth century, when those structures and ideologies were forged.

A key element that changed the day-to-day material lives of Central Americans and accompanied the construction of national states was the rise of coffee as the region's most important export.[9] Along with the expansion of coffee came changes in trading networks, international financial connections, patterns of immigration and investment, and international political relations, but coffee also reached back into the structures of everyday life of ports, capital cities, inland commercial centers, and the countryside, altering the activities of merchants, moneylenders, landowners, shopkeepers, professionals, bureaucrats, the urban poor, and the peasantry. Because of the coincidence in time between this grand economic transformation and the formation of national political structures, a careful look at this single commodity affords a lens through which to view the construction of Central American states. Because so much was at stake economically, the historical documents from international and local sources both public and private are far more numerous and thorough for coffee than for any other economic activity at the time, allowing a convenient basis for comparison between locations than would be possible using sketchier evidence available on some other activity. As a caveat, this focus on a single commodity leaves out geographical areas that were not directly affected by coffee, populations that were not engaged in coffee production or trade, local or regional

economic activities that undoubtedly accounted for a larger portion
of aggregate supply than coffee, and other aspects of economic or
political life that do not happen to pass under the lens being applied.
The purpose of this method of abstraction is not to paint a complete
picture of politics and economics in the age of state building but to
provide a critical angle for achieving some causal clarity from a far
more complex reality.

For sorting out the dynamics of institution building, it would be
difficult to find a better field for comparative historical analysis than
Central America. The five countries of Central America are squeezed
into an area approximately the size of the state of California. They
possess similar soil and climate conditions and are connected to the
world economic system in much the same way. Politically they experienced a unified colonial background as a single jurisdiction of the
Spanish Empire. Because of these strong similarities, the comparative
method can be applied to locate causes of differences in economic
and political structures as they have evolved on the isthmus.

The starting place for the analysis is the world capitalist system.
Chapter 2 explicitly views causation as spinning outward from the
centers of industrial accumulation, thereby altering the opportunities for economic adaptation in peripheral Central America. The key
issue is why Central America came to specialize in the production
of high-grade mild coffee during the late nineteenth century. The
chapter traces the causes of the expansion in the demand for coffee
in Europe and North America at this time, the conditions that gave
Central America a competitive advantage as a low-cost, high-quality
supplier, and the technological changes in transport that permitted
an economically viable link between demand in the center and supply
from the periphery. The chapter investigates the major commodities exported from Central America before coffee took hold, and
it examines what happened in the markets for those commodities
that diminished their relative attractiveness to exporters as the century progressed. Because zones within Central America specialized
in production of different exports before coffee and because those
traditional exports suffered marketing setbacks at different times,
a world systems analysis can partially explain the timing of coffee's spread across the isthmus. To explain the very different rates
of growth of the coffee economies of the region and why different
structures of production took hold, one must examine local contexts
in close detail. To see why Costa Rica's coffee expansion was grad-

ual and steady, why Guatemalan and Salvadoran production, once begun, quickly surpassed that of Costa Rica, why Nicaraguan performance lagged far behind that of the other three major exporters, and why Honduras did not become a significant exporter until after World War II, we must go beyond the world system and take a careful look at the local conditions of land, labor, and capital, the factors governing the supply of coffee.[10]

All economies and especially agricultural ones are dependent on the natural environment for their sustenance, so that economic change is best visualized as development in geographical space. Chapter 3 identifies the soil, altitude, and climate conditions necessary for the healthy growth of the coffee plant and surveys the region to determine the location of the highest-quality coffee lands. It then explores the geographical and social conditions that facilitated or impeded the planting of coffee groves in those areas. In particular, the chapter examines how potential coffee lands were used before coffee, who had access to those lands, what social arrangements governed access to them, and what natural barriers stood between potential coffee lands and ports. On a zone-by-zone basis within countries, the chapter maps the geographical extension of coffee cultivation and determines how previously inaccessible areas were linked to the world market by the building of roads, railroads, bridges, and port facilities and how land tenure arrangements were transformed to favor coffee cultivation. Of particular interest is the way social groups and public institutions at local, departmental, and national levels intervened in the distribution of potential coffee lands. By using comparative historical analysis within and between countries it is possible to uncover the degree to which state interventions in providing access to land delayed or hastened the development of the coffee economy. Furthermore, the analysis shows how preexisting social customs combined with state policies of land access shaped the size distributions of coffee farms in different locales.

By definition, commodities require human labor for their production. Chapter 4 investigates the labor requirements of coffee production in its various phases, from preparing the soil, to planting, pruning, and cultivating the trees, to harvesting and processing the ripe berries. Total population sets an abstract limit on coffee production, but long before demographic limits are approached there appear social limits of labor provision that stand as obstacles to further expansion. For example, a large peasant population in the proximity of a potential coffee zone does not guarantee that coffee growers will be able to engage the labor of that population; it will be especially difficult to obtain labor if peasant communities have large reserves of fertile land or lucrative activities other than coffee production. Broad surveys of coffee production in Latin America have underlined the repeated complaint by coffee growers of "labor shortages" even in coffee areas where large populations are nearby; the complaint is especially strident during harvest season, when the greatest pulse of labor is required. Using cross-country comparisons, William Roseberry has shown how the ubiquitous *falta de brazos* problem was solved in highly diverse ways in the coffee economies of Latin America, resulting in plantation slavery in sections of Brazil, small proprietorships in parts of Costa Rica and Colombia, and various tenant farmer arrangements in different sections of Colombia.[11] The strong conclusion of this overview of the Latin American experience is that there is no technical connection whatsoever between the crop, coffee, and the social relations under which it is produced. Chapter 4 provides a comparative historical analysis of how the labor problem was solved in Central America. It examines on a zone-by-zone basis how populations and their location, the availability of land and alternatives to coffee production for peasant communities, and preexisting customs regarding labor access conditioned the rate of development of coffee cultivation. The chapter compares how social groups and government institutions at local, departmental, and national levels assisted or delayed a solution to the labor supply problem. The chapter then questions how the historical solutions to the labor supply problem in the nineteenth century established patterns of labor relations for the twentieth century.

Capital is a powerful lever of production, and access to it can greatly affect the rate at which an activity proceeds and the technologies employed. For example, it is technically possible for a single individual to develop a coffee grove using his or her own labor and no purchased inputs, but the rate at which the grove can be planted, its sustainable size, and the gross proceeds from the operation will be severely constrained. Access to capital, however, enables that same individual to command the labor of others, purchase commodity inputs, acquire processing equipment, and gain access to larger areas of already improved land, permitting the rapid formation of a larger operation. Chapter 5 explores the capital requirements of coffee in its various phases, from the initial establishment of a coffee farm to the working capital requirements of cultivation, harvesting, processing, and marketing the crop, and it compares the capital needs of coffee with those of previous commercial activities. The chapter examines the networks through which capital flowed into the coffee economy and the degree to which capital penetrated the growing, processing, and marketing phases in the different countries. By examining the capital dimension, the chapter seeks to determine who the primary investors were and to what extent the national coffee elites that emerged by 1900 were descended from a class of large landowners, merchants, and other precoffee elites, or to what extent newcomers, both foreign and local, were able to secure a foothold in this lucrative business. The chapter compares how public institutions intervened (or failed to intervene) to relieve the capital constraint and how private and public institutions were created to respond to the capital needs of coffee. By analyzing capital outlays, the chapter uncovers how the wealth generated in coffee production came to be distributed among growers, processors, exporters, and financiers, and how structures of distribution and the elites attached to these structures varied from one country to the next.

In the chapters on land, labor, and capital, public institutions are viewed as actors that facilitate or hinder the development of the coffee sector. In those chapters, several types of interventions are identified, including the provision of public goods to lower transport costs, the establishment of legal structures to lower costs and risks associated with labor, land, and capital transactions, and the building of coercive institutions to enforce labor contracts, discipline in the work force, and new property laws.[17] Chapter 6 inverts the direction of causation by asking how the expansion of the coffee economy shaped the development of public institutions. States, with their various capacities to intervene, are not built from scratch. The chapter examines government structures before coffee and probes into the ways the early expansion of coffee cultivation placed new demands on existing institutions. The chapter compares the ways emerging coffee elites pressured for public intervention through existing political institutions and the ways successes at a local level may have spilled over into a thrust for national institutions to be created, extended, and strengthened to carry out the perceived needs of the new elite. The chapter considers the political obstacles faced by the coffee interests, including those segments of the traditional elite, the peasantry, and the church that resisted some of the changes called for in the coffee elite's agenda. The chapter charts the struggles over public institutions in relation to the land, labor, and capital needs of the coffee sector and determines the degree to which members of the coffee elite directly participated in national institutions during this formative phase. After establishing how national institutions were built, the chapter briefly examines whether coffee elites continued to rule directly or whether they retired from the day-to-day administration of the state.

Chapter 7 summarizes some of the major lessons that can be learned from coffee and the rise of national states in Central America. Some of the higher-order questions that are addressed are, To what extent did world system forces shape the evolution of economic and political structures in the region and to what extent were these structures a product of local conditions? Does Barrington Moore's thesis on the relation between structures of landholding and the nature of states hold up to the historical record examined here? What were the forces of convergence that turned a situation of political chaos before 1850 into the order that emerged later in the century? Once national states had congealed, how important were they in organizing and shaping economic structures?

Chapter 8 takes some of the lessons distilled from the late nineteenth century and briefly projects them onto the twentieth. Questions of the relative autonomy of state structures and path dependence are returned to. Based on a glimpse at some of the forces that have shaped the evolution of Central American structures during the twentieth century, it is asked to what extent essential features of states present at the creation have been altered by or have been resilient to changes in the twentieth century.

Coffee and the creation of national states in the late nineteenth century should be of interest to Central Americanists who wish to apply the lens of history to reach a deeper understanding of the present. More generally, however, the Central American experience should fascinate historians and social scientists who, in other contexts, have sought to unravel the complex interplay between economic and political life, social classes and public institutions, states and social evolution.

Chapter 2

The Coffee Boom and the
World Capitalist System

Coffee became a major commodity in international trade in the seventeenth and eighteenth centuries, but consumption of the beverage exploded in the nineteenth century when the Industrial Revolution spread through Europe and North America. The increasing demand for coffee in the industrial and trading centers of the temperate zone stimulated the search for fresh sources of supply in the tropics. The adaptation of the steam engine to oceangoing vessels during the 1840s opened ports in Central America to regular shipping service by the early 1850s, permitting trade in bulkier cargo with lower unit value than was possible with sailing technology. By the mid-1850s, a railroad had been completed across Panama, and markets in California were booming from the Gold Rush, both of which enhanced the trade potential of the Pacific coast of Central America. During the second half of the nineteenth century, the discovery and diffusion of synthetic dyes in the industrial zones provided cheap substitutes, first for cochineal and later for indigo, thereby reducing the profitability of two traditional staples of the Central American export trade.

Originating from the centers of industrial accumulation, these world system changes raised the relative profitability of cultivating coffee in Central America, which had an absolute advantage in coffee production because of local conditions of soil and climate. The pressures of specialization were transmitted unevenly across the isthmus because of differences in existing networks of trade and credit. Costa Rican merchants discovered the commercial viability of coffee in the 1830s, followed by the Guatemalans and Salvadorans in the mid-1850s and the Nicaraguans in the 1860s. By the mid-1870s, capital was flowing heavily into coffee production, and by 1880 coffee had become Central America's most important export. At the close of

15

the nineteenth century, Central America was producing one-tenth of the world's coffee and had become the most important producer of the highly sought after "milds." Like no other commodity before it, coffee drew this peripheral zone into the orbit of international capital.

World Demand for Coffee

Before the Industrial Revolution, coffee was one of many luxury goods consumed by the wealthy in Europe. It was first introduced into Europe in the seventeenth century by merchants and adventurers who had contacts with the Muslim world, which had held a monopoly over the cultivation of coffee since the sixth century A.D.[1] In the early 1600s, coffee was a botanical and medical curiosity in Europe, but by the mid-1600s, the delights of the drug were fast becoming known, and the first coffee houses appeared in the great trading centers of Venice, Amsterdam, London, Marseilles, and Paris. As European markets expanded and worldwide colonization took place, monopoly trading companies that had already discovered the commercial potential of coffee began promoting its cultivation, breaking the Arab monopoly in the early 1700s by establishing plantations in tropical colonies.[2] The great trading companies such as the Dutch East India Company, the British East India Company, and the French Company of the Indies earned profits from their monopolies over the long-distance trade, while import merchants, roasters, and owners of coffee houses enjoyed the fruits of monopoly rights over internal markets granted to them by national governments.[3] Mercantilist practices contributed to the accumulation of capital by individual monopolists, but they inhibited the development of internal markets by maintaining high prices to the consumer.

As the Industrial Revolution spread through the manufacturing centers of England during the late eighteenth century and then on to France, Germany, and North America in the nineteenth, trade monopolies were successively destroyed, permitting greater competition in marketing and, therefore, a smaller markup between production costs in the tropics and consumer prices in the northern zones. The lowering of prices to the final consumer permitted more people to adopt the caffeine habit. Moreover, the Industrial Revolution increased the ranks of those who made their living solely through the

provision of wage labor, thereby expanding the market for traditional subsistence goods and opening a market for goods that had
previously been considered luxuries. Salt, sugar, tea, and coffee became basic necessities in the diets of most working people. Fernand
Braudel notes that in France in the late 1700s coffee had become
enormously popular among the workmen who "found more economy, more sustenance, more flavour in this foodstuff than any other.
As a result, they drink it in prodigious quantities, saying that it generally sustains them until the evening. Thus, they eat only two meals,
a large breakfast, and beef salad in the evening."[4] Likewise, employers learned that permitting a "coffee break" raised the intensity
of labor to such an extent that it more than compensated for the
five or ten minutes allowed for the ritual. Moreover, the Industrial
Revolution spawned shopkeepers, servicemen, and professionals of
all sorts, whose middle-class values dictated consumption of better
grades of the brew. In short, the frantic pace of the Industrial Revolution demanded a beverage that would keep the wheels of industry
moving, and coffee became one of the top commodities traded in the
world market system.

In England, tea became the stimulant of preference, but on the
continent of Europe coffee advanced in step with industrial growth.
Following the French Revolution, measures were adopted that broke
down centuries-old impediments to commerce, and the coffee trade
flourished along with industry. In 1853, the French consumed 50 million pounds of coffee. Twenty years later, consumption had tripled,
and by the turn of the century, 250 million pounds were consumed
annually. German industrialization was retarded by internal barriers
to trade, but under Prussian leadership a customs union was begun
in 1833 that quickly stimulated domestic commerce, industry, and,
as a sidelight, coffee consumption.[5] In 1853, Germans consumed 100
million pounds of coffee. Twenty years later, coffee consumption had
doubled, and by the turn of the century, 400 million pounds were
consumed annually. Similarly, in Holland, Norway, Sweden, Den-
mark, Belgium, and Italy, coffee consumption spurted during the
latter half of the nineteenth century so that by 1876 coffee consumption exceeded 5 pounds per person in each of those countries and
had reached 17.6 pounds per person in the Netherlands.[6]

The Industrial Revolution in the United States is generally considered to have begun when manufactured imports were blocked by the
War of 1812 (1812–15). The whole of the nineteenth century, espe-

cially the latter half, was a period of impressive industrial growth. As in Europe, coffee consumption paralleled industrial growth. In 1800, only 9 million pounds of coffee were imported into the United States. By the time of the Civil War, coffee imports had reached 180 million pounds, and by 1900, they had climbed to 750 million pounds. Part of this consumption was attributable to rapid population growth, including waves of European immigrants, but even discounting for population growth, annual coffee consumption increased from 3 pounds per person in 1833, to 6 pounds in 1868, 8 pounds in 1877, and 11 pounds in 1900–1904.[7]

Where did supplies come from to meet this massive increase in demand?

World Supply of Coffee

As demand for coffee grew in Europe and North America, import merchants searched the globe for new sources of supply. Early in the nineteenth century, the Dutch continued to expand production in preexisting colonies in the East Indies, and the British began cultivation in southern India in 1832. Later in the century, when expanding industrial powers joined the rush for empire, coffee was one of the commodities introduced in the colonies. The French carved out coffee estates in Madagascar, Indochina, and French colonial Africa; the Germans introduced it in German East Africa; North Americans began cultivating it in Hawaii; and the Belgians encouraged it in the Congo. Coffee production prospered in the age of imperialism, but the bulk of it did not come from Asia, Africa, and the Pacific but from Latin America and the Caribbean.

The first areas in the Western Hemisphere to be developed for coffee cultivation were selected more for their easy access to trade routes than for their terrain or climate. Square-rigged sailing ships, which dominated ocean cargo shipping until the mid-nineteenth century, had navigational limits. These vessels were best suited for traveling downwind. Sluggish, full-rigged ships experienced difficulty sailing closer than fifty degrees into the wind, and it was virtually impossible for them to sail closer than forty-five degrees into the wind. From Europe, cargo ships could catch the North Equatorial Current and Northeast Trade Winds off the coast of Portugal, where they would be thrust toward the lower Antilles and the coast of Venezuela and from there northwestward toward the Virgin Islands, Puerto Rico,

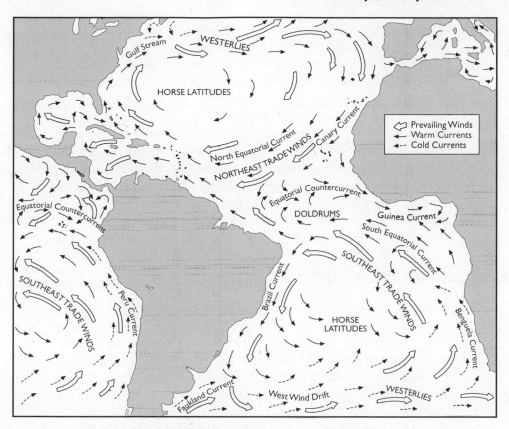

Map 2-1. Prevailing Winds and Ocean Currents
Source: Cathryn Lombardi and John Lombardi, *Latin American History: A Teaching Atlas* (Madison: University of Wisconsin Press, 1983), p. 7.

Santo Domingo, and Cuba. Leaving the West Indies, ships would be driven northward by southeasterly winds, which would carry them into the Gulf Stream off North America, where they could catch the westerly trade winds that would carry them back to Europe. The prime real estate in the Western Hemisphere was the islands of the West Indies, which were quickly claimed by European powers as ports along the Atlantic trade route. From these ports, irregular trade that depended on less reliable winds could be carried on with the inner islands and the mainland of middle and South America (see Map 2-1).

Because of their easy access to the Atlantic trade route, the outer islands were the first to become coffee producers. In 1715–16 the French Company of the Indies brought the first coffee plants from

Mocha to begin cultivation in the West Indies on the island of Bourbon, which was followed by cultivation in Martinique and other French islands. In 1730, the British introduced coffee cultivation in Jamaica, followed by the Spanish in Cuba (1748) and Puerto Rico (1755). For the remainder of the eighteenth century, the bulk of the coffee produced in the Western Hemisphere came from the outer islands, but these islands had insufficient land areas suitable for growing enough coffee to keep pace with the increasing demand in Europe. Venezuela, which had favorable access to the Atlantic route, began exporting coffee in 1784, a trade that expanded for the remainder of the colonial period and continued to thrive after independence from Spain in 1819; by 1830, Venezuelan coffee exports exceeded 25 million pounds, and by 1900 Venezuela was the second largest producer in the world behind Brazil.[8] The Portuguese introduced coffee into Brazil early in the eighteenth century (1732) in the Paraiba Valley of Rio province, and by the time of independence from Portugal in 1822, coffee was being successfully cultivated north of São Paulo, but after independence vast plantations employing slave labor were opened up to the crop. By the 1830s, Brazilian production surpassed that of the older producing areas of the Dutch East Indies and the islands of the West Indies, and by 1881 more than half of world output came from Brazil. After a decade of adjustment following the abolition of slavery in 1888, Brazilian production spurted once more, and by 1900 Brazil was producing more than two-thirds of the world's coffee.[9]

As ocean transport technology changed and less accessible areas such as Central America were drawn into coffee cultivation during the nineteenth century, one important fact about the world coffee market was already firmly established: there were much larger producers elsewhere. This meant that conditions of production in larger-volume areas like Brazil (and after World War II, Colombia) determined the general level of prices on the world market; when there was a freeze in São Paulo province, world coffee prices rose, and when bumper crops were reported in Brazil, world coffee prices fell. Central America, with a potential coffee-producing area one-seventh the size of Brazil's, had negligible influence on the world coffee price, no matter how good the harvest was.[10] Central American producers were relegated to the position of price-takers. Although they may have had no influence over the general level of coffee prices in the world market, Central American producers discovered that they could secure a favorable niche in the world coffee market by carefully controlling the quality of the product. As the century progressed, Central American "milds" became highly esteemed in the European market for their handsome appearance, fine aroma, high acidity, full body, and rich flavor, while the less attractive *robustas* from Brazil came to be used as filler coffee in the mass market. Because of their relative desirability, high-grown Central American coffees have commanded a premium of 5 to 10 percent over the price of Brazil Santos No. 4, the benchmark coffee in the New York market. Even in times of great glut, when all coffee prices have fallen and lesser grades have been left unsold, milds from Central America have been able to find a market.

Central America as a Potential Source of Coffee Supply

Central America has perfect soil and climate for growing *arabica* coffee, the most sought after of the three coffee species.[11] A chain of volcanoes runs from the state of Chiapas in southern Mexico all the way down the Central American isthmus into Panama. Over the centuries the prevailing winds from the Caribbean Sea have dumped volcanic ash onto the Pacific slopes and plateaus, where deep, rich pockets of earth have formed as tropical forests deposited abundant organic matter. The coffee plant thrives in a mixture of organic matter, which provides nitrogen, phosphorus, and other nutrients for plant growth, and volcanic ash, which provides good drainage, in addition to potassium, phosphorus, and trace minerals for strong stems, penetrating roots, a healthy immune system, abundant flowers, and good fruiting. Rainfall along this strip varies around the ideal for coffee of seventy inches per year, but even in drier places there is usually an abundance of rainfall during the period when the fruit is set (April through September), followed by a dry season (October through February) favorable for the final ripening of berries and the harvest. The temperature in this zone varies around the ideal for coffee of 68 degrees Fahrenheit, with danger of damaging frosts at elevations exceeding five thousand feet and low-quality berries because of excessive heat at elevations below a thousand feet. The slopes of this zone provide good drainage and protection from excessive sun, wind, and cold, and numerous rivers provide power to run the coffee mills and water to wash the berries. Although coffee can be grown in some of the wetter zones toward the Caribbean, there are few places in the world so blessed for coffee growing as the Pacific piedmont of Central America.[12]

The first recorded instance of the beverage being consumed in Central America was for dessert at a banquet in 1747 when the bishop of Guatemala was ordained as archbishop.[13] The beans could just as well have been brought over from Cuba for the event,[14] for there is no evidence of the plant being grown in Guatemala until the latter half of the eighteenth century, when the Jesuits are said to have tended some trees in their elaborate botanical garden in Antigua. It is from these trees that don Miguel Ignacio Alvarez de Asturias, a wealthy landowner from an aristocratic family, is recorded to have taken seeds and planted them in the shade of his cacao orchard on his hacienda, Soyate, in the department of Jutiapa.[15] Don Miguel's son-in-law, Juan Miguel Rubio y Gemmir, later took seeds from his father-in-law's estate and planted them on his farm near Guatemala City in 1808.[16] The first coffee trees in Costa Rica are also said to have been planted in the late eighteenth or early nineteenth century. One story claims the first seeds were brought from Panama and planted in 1791, a second tells of seeds being brought from Cuba by a priest in 1796,[17] and a third claims that Governor Tomás de Acosta acquired the first plants in 1808 from a native of the Atlantic coast, who most likely imported seed stock from Jamaica, with which the natives traded. By 1816, a map of San José showed the small coffee orchard of Father Felix Velarde located only four blocks from the central square.[18] Regardless of who grew the first trees and when, it is certain that by the time of independence from Spain in the early 1820s, it was known in Central America that the coffee plant could grow there, but it was considered little more than a botanical curiosity whose fruit could help relieve headaches.

Commercial Connections before Coffee

One reason why coffee may not have been viewed as a potential export of Central America before independence was the Spanish Crown's somewhat artificial set of mercantilist trade regulations, which designated Venezuela, Cuba, Puerto Rico, and some of the other outer islands as the producers of coffee for the empire. An economic rationale for the mercantilist division of labor that continued to deny Central America a major role in producing coffee after independence was related to transport technology. In the days of square-rigged cargo ships it was easy to sail to Central America's Caribbean ports from Puerto Rico, Cuba, Jamaica, or other islands on the Atlantic trade route because of the prevailing easterly winds. But once anchored in Central America, ships were sometimes pinned for months awaiting a countervailing wind from the southwest. As a result, shipping service was sporadic and costly. Furthermore, the land routes to Caribbean ports from the Pacific side of the isthmus, where the bulk of the population lived and the best agricultural lands were located, consisted of partially navigable streams and mule trails that were impassable during the rainy season. During the colonial period, legal import and export trade went on overland routes between Guatemala City and Caribbean ports of Guatemala, and illegal trade went through Belize and other British-controlled outlets along the Caribbean. The costly link-up with European markets favored the export of dyestuffs, first indigo and later cochineal, which were six to ten times more valuable per pound than coffee.

Mechanization and expansion of the textile industry in northern Europe during the late eighteenth and early nineteenth centuries increased the demand for dyestuffs, creating a favorable market for Central American growers, who had begun producing indigo much earlier. During the colonial period, the Spanish Crown designated Guatemala, El Salvador, and Nicaragua special status as indigo producers and attempted to regulate and tax the indigo trade through officially designated merchants in Guatemala City, who would transport the dye overland to Guatemalan ports on the Caribbean and then ship it on Spanish vessels headed first to Spain and afterward to textile manufacturers in northern Europe. El Salvador surpassed all other regions in Central America in the production of indigo. Although Salvadoran growers and merchants were hindered by tax levies from the Spanish Crown and by the dominance of Guatemala City merchants, Salvadoran production costs were low enough to support both a continuing indigo industry and payment of heavy tribute. Especially toward the end of the eighteenth century, when population expanded the labor force and smuggling enabled some merchants and growers to avoid mercantilist controls, Salvadoran indigo production boomed. Disruptions at the time of independence caused temporary setbacks to the industry in the early 1820s, after which merchants and growers in El Salvador were released from Spanish and Guatemala City controls and threw themselves into production, finance, and marketing of the dye. By 1860, Salvadoran indigo output was double that of 1793, the peak year of colonial production.[19]

In Guatemala, the major fortunes from the indigo trade during the eighteenth century were collected by Guatemala City merchants, who advanced money and goods to provincial merchants and growers located primarily in El Salvador and Nicaragua, who, in turn, cultivated indigo and lent to smaller growers, who were known to produce the highest-quality dye. Available statistics on the volume of this trade show that in 1797, indigo exports through Guatemala City peaked at 1,344,000 pounds, suffering a collapse in subsequent years so that by the end of the colonial period exports through Guatemala City had been reduced to 300,000 pounds, about one-fourth peak levels. No statistics are currently available that specify what portion of this trade was produced on farms within what later became the republic of Guatemala, though some large indigo plantations existed in eastern Guatemala in the eighteenth century, and some of the Guatemala City merchants also owned large indigo plantations in the provinces.[20] Robert Smith attributes this decline in the trade statistics to plagues of locusts, grasshoppers, and caterpillars, but the more recent work of José Antonio Fernández suggests that the decline is better attributed to the systematic breakdown of the mercantilist trading system, whereby provincial merchants in El Salvador and Nicaragua increasingly established direct contacts with British vessels, bypassing the control of Guatemala City merchants.[21]

Guatemalan merchants and growers sought numerous alternatives to indigo, but the one that received the most attention was another dyestuff: cochineal. The introduction of a new strain of nopal cactus from Mexico and an expanding market created by the booming textile industry in Europe and North America encouraged farmers and merchants to revive the cochineal industry, which had declined in the eighteenth century.[22] The cochineal insect feeds on a cactus that came to be cultivated in the highland valleys of Amatitlán, Antigua, Petapa, Villa Nueva, and Palín and to a lesser extent in Baja Verapaz. In 1820, approximately 4,000 pounds of cochineal were produced; by 1825 exports had expanded to 135,000 pounds. A decade later, production had grown to more than 600,000 pounds, and by 1837, cochineal had surpassed indigo as Guatemala's most important export.[23] During the 1840s, production continued to climb, peaking between 1846 and 1849.

Nicaragua's production of dyestuffs never reached the peak levels of El Salvador, but before and after independence, indigo was the most important outlet for merchant capital in Nicaragua. Toward the end of the colonial period the Crown had greater difficulty regulating and taxing Nicaragua's commerce than that of El Salvador because of the natural trade route across Lake Nicaragua and down the San Juan River to British-controlled Caribbean ports. Contraband trade with the British flourished, especially enriching the merchants of Granada, which was favorably located on Lake Nicaragua. After independence, indigo remained Nicaragua's most important export until the 1870s, but gold, cacao, and rubber also attracted merchant capital. Cattle and sugar were raised for regional markets, and hides were sold locally and in El Salvador for baling indigo.

Because merchants and growers in Guatemala, El Salvador, and Nicaragua were already connected with the world market for dyestuffs, because world demand for dyestuffs continued to grow after independence, and because transport technology at the time favored long-distance trade in higher value-per-weight commodities, it was difficult for coffee to break into the international networks of production and exchange that were restored following independence.

In contrast to the northern countries, Costa Rica had been officially banned from the production of dyestuffs during the colonial period, a status that was only partially compensated for by a license to produce tobacco and export it to Nicaragua, Panama, and Mexico. San José merchants who owned the tobacco-processing warehouse and small farmers who grew the crop prospered from the trade, especially between 1787 and 1792, when Costa Rica was granted a monopoly to produce for the entire kingdom of Guatemala. When the license expired after 1792, the tobacco industry suffered a decline that it did not fully recover from even after independence, though the tax on domestic tobacco sales remained a significant source of revenue for the new state of Costa Rica until the 1840s.[24] In addition to tobacco, there was some trade in brazilwood, wheat, cheese, hides, dried beef, and soap,[25] but during the final years of Spanish rule, the greatest attraction for merchant capital from the Central Valley was to stake claims in the gold mining district of Monte del Aguacate. After independence, the glitter of gold attracted an influx of British, French, German, Italian, and Spanish merchants. How many fortunes were made in the gold mines is debatable,[26] but it is certain that the activity of the mines forged important commercial ties between Costa Rican elites and foreign merchants. It also stimulated contact with merchant vessels from Europe, expanded the import trade, promoted improved warehousing and port facilities in Puntarenas, and encouraged the beginnings of a cart road between the Central Valley and Puntarenas. The mining boom may not have produced many fortunes, but it did establish a trading infrastructure that prepared the way for other exports.

Early Coffee Production in Central America

George Stiepel, a German merchant who came to Costa Rica in 1824, was the first to demonstrate the commercial viability of coffee.[27] In 1832, Stiepel made his first coffee shipment, which was sent to Chile and reexported to Europe as "Chilean coffee from Valparaíso." The following year the largest shipment went to Liverpool, thereby initiating direct export of coffee to England.[28] Others were attracted by Stiepel's success, including some of those who had invested in mining. Buenaventura Espinach, a Catalonian merchant who came to Costa Rica in 1824 and started a mining operation in 1825, began investing in coffee in the 1830s and by 1840 owned a plantation in Heredia with 170 acres planted in coffee and the largest, most modern coffee mill in all of Costa Rica. The Moras and Montealegres, members of the Creole merchant elite of San José, invested in mining in the 1820s and 1830s and later shifted their investments into coffee, becoming major coffee growers, processors, and exporters.[29] By the mid-1840s, thirty-five coffee export houses had formed, and some twenty-nine ships, most of them traditional square-rigged sailing vessels, were carrying Costa Rican coffee to European markets.

The news of Costa Rican successes in coffee cultivation encouraged elites farther north to consider coffee as a serious commercial venture. As early as 1835, Manuel Larrave and Marcial Zebadúa, both from aristocratic Guatemalan families,[30] and Carlos Klée, a German merchant who later became the largest producer and exporter of cochineal, began cultivating coffee,[31] and in the 1840s, cochineal growers began planting coffee trees as borders to their nopal cactus fields.[32] The Guatemalan coffee produced in those years,

"Loading Coffee for Shipment—Las Nubes," Department of Suchitepéquez, Guatemala, 1875. The Las Nubes coffee plantation is located in the upper range (3,600–5,300 feet above sea level) of the coffee belt along Guatemala's Pacific slopes. The owner's name, W. Nelson, and the destinations, London and N[ew]. York, are stamped on the bags of coffee. In 1875, William Nelson was the commercial agent for the Pacific Mail and Steamship Company in Guatemala. The bags of coffee were probably carried to the Pacific port of Champerico by the oxcarts shown here. (Department of Special Collections, Stanford University Libraries)

however, was not destined for export; the volume harvested was insufficient to meet the growing domestic demand for the beverage. During the late 1830s and early 1840s, several landowners in El Salvador began raising coffee as a commercial crop for local markets, and by the mid-1850s some Salvadoran coffee was being exported, but most of it went to the larger consumer market in Guatemala.[33] Coffee was first brought from Costa Rica and planted in Nicaragua

"Shipping Coffee at Champerico," Pacific coast of Guatemala, 1875. Regular steamship service allowed coffee from the Pacific coast of Central America to be shipped to expanding markets in California or to New York or European markets via Panama. Note that there is no dock facility; the coffee bags are first loaded onto a launch, which must then be pulled on the cable through the surf and rowed to the steamship. The foresail on the ship looks as if it is being used to steady the vessel at anchor. (Department of Special Collections, Stanford University Libraries)

during the late 1840s,[34] but as in Guatemala and El Salvador, it took several decades after the first commercial plantings for Nicaraguan coffee to move beyond domestic markets into the international arena.

The Switch to Coffee as a Major Export

The steam revolution in ocean transport stimulated Costa Rican coffee exports and created a favorable environment for the export of coffee from the other Central American countries. It took nearly eighty years for the steam engine, which was first patented by James Watt in 1769, to be effectively adapted for ocean transport. During the 1820s and 1830s, sailing vessels were fitted with cumbersome paddle wheels alongside, as were the *Savannah*, which made a North Atlantic crossing that took twenty-nine days in 1819, and the *Great Western*, which made a fifteen-day voyage under steam power alone in 1838. During the 1840s, ships began to be fitted with the more streamlined screw propeller, which was faster and less vulnerable in heavy seas. Steamships required larger initial capital outlays than sailing ships, and they also consumed large quantities of fuel, but de-

"Bay of Panama," 1875. All three ocean cargo vessels visible here are steam driven with auxiliary sails. The two closer ships have screw propellers, but the one in the distance appears to be fitted with a covered paddle wheel. Note also the makeshift service dock, built from the remains of a retired vessel, located in the left foreground. (Department of Special Collections, Stanford University Libraries)

livery took one-half to one-fourth the time that a sail cargo ship could achieve under the best wind conditions, and delivery dates were more reliable. The higher turnover achievable with steam lowered average transport costs, and by the 1850s steamships had begun to supplant sailing ships as the dominant mode of ocean transport. For Central America, which was in an unfavorable location for square-rigged sailing navigation, the introduction of steamship service during the early 1850s allowed for cheaper and more regular service between European and Caribbean ports. Furthermore, the California Gold Rush and the completion of the Panama railroad in 1855 activated commerce from the Pacific ports of Central America, reducing the

"Cactus Plantation for Cochineal—San Mateo," Department of Sacatepéquez, Guatemala, 1875. Fourteen years after this photograph was taken, no nopal cactus was reported being grown in San Mateo, only corn and bean cultivation on very small plots of land was reported. In the two Guatemalan departments (Amatitlán and Sacatepéquez) where cochineal production had been strongest, only seven small farms reported growing nopal in the 1889 survey; all seven claimed they grew "coffee and nopal" as their crops. (Department of Special Collections, Stanford University Libraries)

need to transport commodities over the costly land routes from the Pacific side to the Caribbean. In this rapidly changing context, Costa Rican coffee exports flourished, expanding from 2.5 million pounds in 1843 to nearly 7 million pounds a decade later. In 1853 Guatemala began exporting small amounts of coffee, followed by El Salvador in 1856, Nicaragua in the 1860s, and, finally, Honduras in the 1880s.[35]

The cheapening of ocean transport allowed for higher value-per-weight commodities to be exported, but it took a deterioration of profitability in dyestuffs to cause a decided shift of merchant capital from this traditional mainstay into coffee production. The profitability of cochineal collapsed before that of indigo, leading to an earlier switch to coffee in Guatemala than in El Salvador or Nicaragua. The apex of profitability of cochineal was in 1846–49, after which costs began to rise as a result of diseases among the insect population, excessive plantings on the same soil without fertilization,[36] and a disastrous flood in October and November of 1852 that drowned the insects from which the dye is made.[37] During the early 1850s, cochineal production increased in the Canary Islands, a more favorable location to supply the European textile market. In 1853, Guatemalan producers first entered the coffee trade with exports valued at 690 pesos.[38] The killing blow to the Guatemalan cochineal industry, however, came after the discovery of a mauve aniline dye by Sir William Henry Perkin in 1856, and other cochineal substitutes from coal tar began to be manufactured in the 1860s. Textile manufacturers began substituting the new synthetic dyes for cochineal, and the price of cochineal fell[39] just as coffee prices were in a secular trend upward that was to last until the mid-1870s (see Figure 2-1). Cochineal growers who had planted coffee trees as borders to their cactus groves extended their coffee plantings into these fields during the 1850s and 1860s, and new areas began to be opened up for coffee along the Pacific slopes of the volcanoes in Escuintla and Suchitipéquez. The decade of the 1860s witnessed a steady rise in the value of Guatemalan coffee exports, a stabilization of the value of cochineal exports at lower levels, and a blip in cotton exports resulting from the extraordinary price increases during the U.S. Civil War. As Figure 2-2 demonstrates, by 1870 coffee had surpassed cochineal as Guatemala's leading export.

Coffee got a much slower start in El Salvador because a synthetic close substitute for indigo was not discovered until the late 1860s. While the cochineal market was faltering during the 1850s and 1860s,

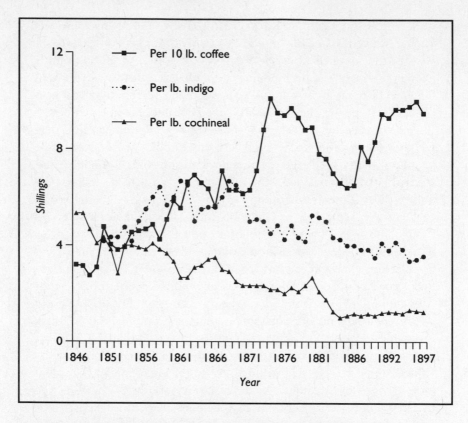

Figure 2-1. Prices of Coffee, Indigo, and Cochineal, 1846–1897.
Sources: Mulhall, *Dictionary of Statistics*, pp. 475–79, 792 (1854–97);
McCreery, "Rural Guatemala," chap. 4, pp. 27–28 (1846–53, cochineal prices);
Lindo-Fuentes, *Weak Foundations*, pp. 112–13 (1850–53, indigo); Commodity
Research Bureau, *Commodity Yearbook 1942* (1846–54, coffee).

indigo prices remained favorable so that Salvadoran merchant capital continued to be tied up in the production and exchange of the
dye. Coffee, which did not compete significantly with indigo for
land, was introduced slowly as an outlet for venture capital but did
not break the indigo circuit of capital until the 1870s, when indigo
prices followed those of cochineal in a secular decline that continued
for the remainder of the century (see Figure 2-1). During the 1870s
and even more forcefully during the 1880s, large indigo growers in
El Salvador began to mortgage their indigo haciendas and with the
proceeds established coffee farms in the volcanic highlands and piedmont areas of western El Salvador.[40] By the mid-1870s, coffee was

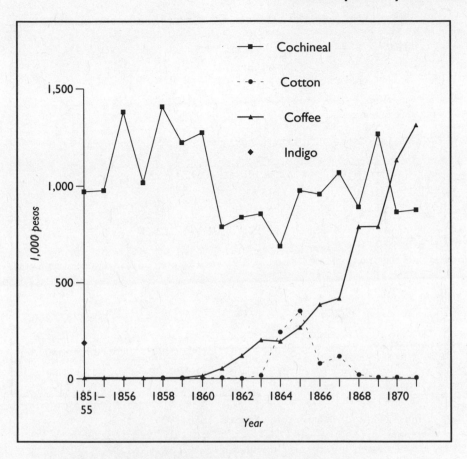

Figure 2-2. Composition of Guatemalan Exports, 1851–1871.
Source: Woodward, *Class Privilege*, pp. 48–52.

challenging indigo for the position of El Salvador's most important export, and by 1879, coffee forever surpassed indigo as an export earner for the country (see Figure 2-3). The boom was so rapid that by 1901, Salvadoran coffee exports consistently exceeded those of Costa Rica, making El Salvador the second largest Central American producer after its northern neighbor, Guatemala (see Figure 2-4).

As in El Salvador, Nicaragua's coffee boom lagged behind Guatemala's by almost a decade because of the continued favorable market for indigo until the early 1870s, when the price of indigo began its secular decline. Coffee was first brought to Nicaragua in the late 1840s, probably from Costa Rica. One account places the date at

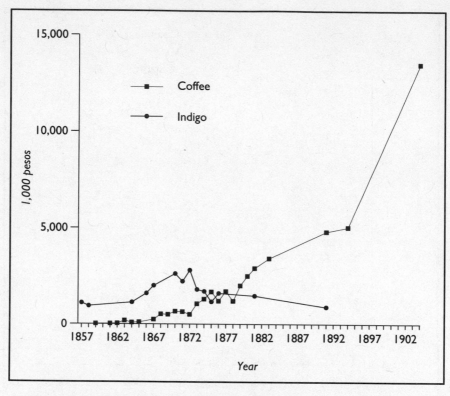

Figure 2-3. Value of Salvadoran Exports, 1856–1904.
Sources: Alvarado, *Tratado de caficultura*, p. 581; Walter, "Trade and
Development," pp. 16, 25; Browning, *El Salvador*, p. 162.

1845; another claims that in 1848 a Señor Matus cultivated the first
plants in Jinotepe, a town in the Carazo Highlands.[41] Between 1851
and 1855, approximately one-third of the passengers traveling by sea
to California for the Gold Rush crossed the isthmus through Nicaragua, stimulating the demand for locally produced coffee for in-transit
consumption. Furthermore, Cornelius Vanderbilt's Accessory Tran-
sit Company provided steamship service between New York and
Greytown on Nicaragua's Atlantic Coast, across Lake Nicaragua,
and between the ports of San Juan del Sur and Corinto on the Pacific
and San Francisco, stimulating traffic in such commodities as indigo,
hides, cacao, tropical hardwoods, gold, and coffee, in addition to
the primary traffic in passengers. This service was halted in 1855 because the Panama railroad was completed, Greytown was destroyed

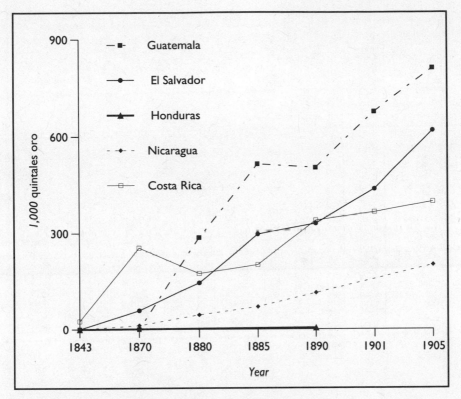

Figure 2-4. Central American Coffee Exports, 1843–1905.
Sources: Same as for Table A-1.

by floods, and William Walker invaded Nicaragua (1855–58).[42] Cotton was attractive as an export during the U.S. Civil War, and it provided approximately half of Nicaragua's export earnings at the height of the cotton famine in 1864 and 1865, though the cotton market crashed after the war ended.[43] Although coffee cultivation had a start during the 1850s and 1860s, by 1871 gold mining, rubber extraction, and indigo still provided greater export earnings than coffee, which had climbed to 9 percent of Nicaragua's export earnings that year for slightly more than one million pounds exported[44] (see Figure 2-5). With the relative decline of indigo prices, merchant capital began to be switched into coffee so that by 1880 Nicaraguan coffee export volumes had quadrupled to 4.5 million pounds, and by 1890 they had more than doubled again to 11.4 million pounds. The next two decades witnessed the opening of new coffee-growing

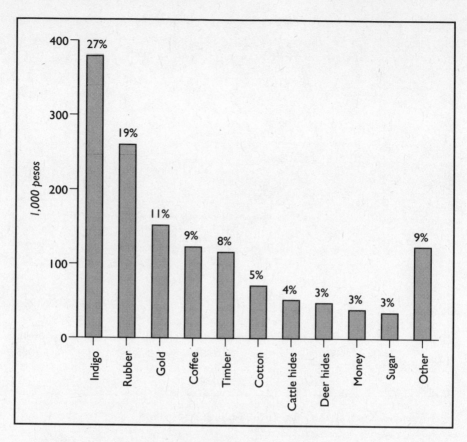

Figure 2-5. Composition of Nicaraguan Exports, 1871.
Source: Levy, *Notas geográficas*, p. 507.

areas in Nicaragua, and by 1910 coffee exports had soared to 26 million pounds, though Nicaragua was still in fourth place behind Costa Rica, and its sustained export levels were only one-third to one-fourth those of El Salvador and Guatemala (see Figure 2-4).

Honduras was the last Central American country to join the coffee export trade. E. G. Squier reported that high-quality coffee was being grown in Honduras in 1858, but none of it was exported. In 1875, some five hundred thousand pounds were produced, but evidence suggests that most of it went to local consumers.[45] In nineteenth-century Honduras, coffee was a crop much like sugar; it was grown and processed in local communities, but the road system was so bad and the areas suitable for cultivation were so scattered that transport costs made it unprofitable to send the crop to port. The coffee that did make its way out of the country followed the same paths that indigo had traveled. Small cargoes were carried to markets in El Salvador by occasional peddlers who serviced the dispersed mountain communities of southern Honduras. Merchants in El Salvador sometimes advanced money and goods for the following year's delivery of indigo, but the trade hardly attracted the attention of large merchant capital. A larger volume of trade was conducted in cattle from the eastern half of Honduras and the Pacific coastal plain. Following the pattern established during the colonial period, cattle were driven overland to markets in El Salvador and Guatemala, and during the 1860s through the 1880s oxen from Olancho were driven to the port of Trujillo, where they were shipped by steamer to Cuba to serve as draft animals in the expanding sugar industry.[46] By the late 1880s, Honduras, and especially the northern half of the country, had become firmly connected with the U.S. circuit of capital. Regular steamship service between the North Coast and New Orleans and Mobile supported a thriving trade in bananas and coconuts, which together accounted for 28 percent of Honduran export earnings in 1889. More important, U.S. mining companies extracted silver and shipped the semiprocessed paste to markets in the United States, accounting for 42 percent of Honduran export earnings in 1889 (see Figure 2-6). Large merchant capital, both domestic and foreign, was primarily absorbed by the items traded with the United States, which accounted for three-fourths of Honduran export value in 1889, while petty merchant activity continued with El Salvador, Guatemala, Belize, and other regional markets.[47]

For the most part, Honduran coffee remained in the petty commodity category well into the twentieth century. In 1912, when the Honduran government began to collect continuous data on the volume of coffee exports, only some 700,000 pounds were reported to have been exported, about the same level of Costa Rica's exports in the late 1830s. It is likely that more coffee was being produced but never made it to port. A 1914–15 survey of farms in Honduras measured some seventeen thousand acres of coffee under cultivation, which, under conservative estimates of yields per acre, would have produced 2.5 to 3 million pounds of coffee, but exports that year were reported at 264,000 pounds.[48] In the 1920s, when production statistics began to be collected, Honduras still exported only about one-fourth of the coffee produced, the lowest export ratio in all of

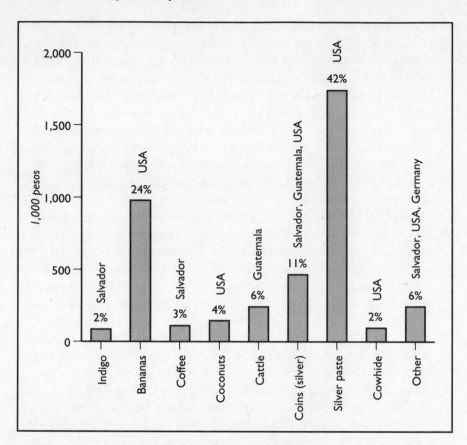

Figure 2-6. Composition of Honduran Exports, 1888–1889.
Source: República de Honduras, *Primer anuario estadístico de 1888–89*, pp. 290–92.

Central America. It was not until 1949 that Honduran coffee exports reached the levels of Costa Rican exports in the 1860s. During the post–World War II period, however, Honduras finally became an important exporter of coffee. In 1977, coffee surpassed bananas to become Honduras's most important earner of foreign exchange (an unusual year because of high coffee prices), and in 1978 Honduran coffee exports began to exceed those of neighboring Nicaragua.[49]

Conclusion

From the vortices of capital accumulation in Europe and North America, waves of change swirled outward during the nineteenth century, eventually reaching remote backwaters like Central America. As demand for commodities was transformed by industrialization in the center, price incentives to alter the mix of primary exports were transmitted to the periphery. The steam engine—the hallmark of the Industrial Revolution in manufacturing—was successfully adapted to ocean transport by the 1850s, permitting the ports of Central America to receive more regular shipping service at lower rates than was possible with sailing technology. Thus a change of technology from the center helped link peripheral Central America with the expanding markets of the center, allowing for lower-unit-cost commodities to enter the export trade alongside traditional exports. Technological change created fresh opportunities for alternatives to traditional exports, but changes in the center proved fickle. During the 1830s and 1840s, expansion of the North Atlantic textile industry raised the profitability of producing natural dyes in Central America, but when synthetic substitutes for those dyes were discovered in the 1850s and 1860s, profits collapsed, sending Central American producers into bankruptcy.

The timing of the introduction of coffee as an export crop in Central America had much to do with the ways certain areas were connected to the world trading system before coffee and technological changes in the center altered profitability conditions. Costa Rican merchants were the first to experiment with coffee on a commercial basis, because Costa Rica had been denied the right to produce and market dyestuffs during the colonial period. A brief attempt at mining attracted local and international investors in Costa Rica, but profits did not live up to expectations, and merchant capital was shifted decidedly into coffee very soon after independence. In both Guatemala and El Salvador, merchant capital continued to be tied up in the production and export of dyestuffs. El Salvador had proven to be the lowest-cost producer of indigo during the colonial period and expanded production to meet increased demand for the dye in the booming textile business of western Europe and North America, while Guatemalan merchant capital shifted out of indigo and into cochineal, which was made more profitable by the introduction of a robust strain of nopal cactus from Mexico. Chemical dyes replaced cochineal first, encouraging Guatemalan merchants and producers to shift into coffee before those of neighboring El Salvador, which experienced a flourishing indigo trade for another decade. Nicaraguan merchant capital continued to advance indigo production following independence, and trade in deerskins, gold, cattle hides, and other traditional products was more important than coffee until the last two decades of the century, the Nicaraguan coffee trade lagging a decade behind El Salvador's.

World system changes demonstrate how opportunities were altered for Central American merchants and farmers. When previous connections with the world system are added to the picture, a partial explanation of the timing of coffee's introduction can be achieved. But the focus of causation spinning in one direction—outward from the center—is woefully incomplete. It cannot, for example, determine why Honduras became a major coffee exporter a century after the other Central American countries, nor can it explain the intensity of the coffee boom as it made its way to different parts of the region. To see why coffee cultivation advanced slowly and steadily in Costa Rica while it swept like a hurricane through Guatemala and El Salvador, why the coffee boom took one area of Nicaragua swiftly while it met obstacles elsewhere, and why Honduran coffee production became geared to the world market only recently, one must look beyond the networks of international trade to the land itself, to the people who worked the land, to the investors who risked their capital, and to the social institutions that impeded or hastened coffee's march through the isthmus.

Chapter 3

Land and the Coffee Boom

Coffee cannot grow just anywhere. Without deep soil, taproots are unable to penetrate deeply enough to support the trunk and limbs, and without good drainage, the root system is susceptible to rot. Without sufficient nitrogen, foliage is inhibited, and without adequate phosphorus and potash, flowering and fruiting are retarded. At altitudes above five thousand feet, foliage and blossoms may be damaged by frost; at altitudes below one thousand feet, heat may cause damage, and beans lose richness of flavor and aroma. Every Central American country has areas of superior land and climate for growing coffee, but in the nineteenth century some of the best potential areas were difficult to reach and, therefore, difficult to develop commercially. Accessibility to land suitable for coffee varied across the isthmus, and governments built roads, bridges, railroads, and ports at different times, influencing the geographical spread and pace of the coffee boom.

Perhaps more important than physical access to land were the social relations of land tenure in the areas suitable for growing coffee. Coffee can be grown under a wide variety of land tenure systems, but because it requires a huge initial investment and three to five years to establish a mature grove, potential coffee growers were reluctant to risk capital and labor unless they had secure, well-delineated, private claims to land on which to establish groves. In the early nineteenth century, however, privately titled lands with carefully surveyed boundaries were the exception to the rule. Even haciendas with long-standing written "titles" rarely had clearly defined boundaries, and lands belonging to villages and Indian communities were even more vaguely defined. The coffee boom resulted in a transformation of traditional forms of land tenure into privately titled properties, but the traditional forms varied from one place to another, conditioning the structures of landholding once coffee was introduced.

Crucial in the transformation were the ways in which public institutions intervened in the process of land acquisition. The state's right to give and take away land was established early in the colonial period. At the conquest, all lands were declared royal, and the king granted lands (and populations) to finance the conquest. Shortly thereafter, royal lands were granted as an inducement to colonization. At any time, if lands given as grants were not put to use, the king's administrators could reclaim them as royal lands. By the final decade of the sixteenth century, the sale of royal lands to private individuals became an important source of revenue for the state and remained so throughout the colonial period. Both land grants and sales to private individuals stimulated the growth of large landholdings, but other colonial land policies worked in the opposite direction. The Crown not only granted latifundia to private individuals but also granted lands to Indian communities and to municipalities. In turn, the Indian communities provided tribute to the Crown and tithes to the church, and the municipalities became centers for tax and tithe collection.[1]

After independence, the Central American landscape was divided into large landholdings held by private individuals and by the church, communal lands held by Indian communities, municipal lands held by townships, and *tierras baldías*, unoccupied lands that were under the official jurisdiction of higher-order state institutions. None of these forms, even large landholdings in which vast areas were left idle, were naturally conducive to a rapid conversion to coffee, and in many places people held strongly to their traditional practices regarding land rights. As coffee became more profitable, a struggle over land rights began, and public institutions at various levels, from the township to the department and, finally, to the national state, became involved. The way state institutions at these various levels intervened in the land question differed from time to time and place to place, greatly influencing the timing of the coffee boom, the turbulence of the transition, and the ultimate structures of landholding associated with coffee.

"Clearing Ground for Coffee Plantation—Las Nubes," Department of Suchitepéquez, Guatemala, 1875. This 1875 photograph captures the forest-to-coffee sequence that would be repeated with the expansion of the coffee economy. Most large plantations, especially in Guatemala, gained access to substantial land reserves, which could be converted to coffee groves at a later date but which more immediately served as a source of lumber (see stack of timber drying on right) and firewood, cropland for the attraction of permanent workers and provisions for temporary harvest workers, pastures for draft animals and beef cattle, and an enhancement of the collateral base for obtaining credit. All of these reserve functions multiplied the exchange value of an estate beyond the capital tied up in coffee groves, buildings, and equipment. In an 1889 agricultural survey, Las Nubes is listed as having a total land area of 2,056 acres, though an 1890 coffee census records Las Nubes as having 150,000 coffee trees, which would have occupied approximately 260 acres. By 1930 the size of the total estate was still approximately 2,000 acres, but the area in coffee had expanded to 614 acres. (Department of Special Collections, Stanford University Libraries)

Coffee and Land in Costa Rica

During the 1820s and 1830s, when the coffee boom began in Costa Rica, most of the country's sixty thousand people were settled in the Central Valley, a fertile upland plateau approximately forty-five miles long and thirteen miles wide. The population was not evenly scattered in this valley but was concentrated in and around four major towns: San José, Cartago, Heredia, and Alajuela, each with outlying nucleated settlements. Much of the valley was still tropical forest at that time, and close to the towns were lands devoted either to pasture or to crops such as sugar, wheat, beans, corn, and vegetables. For the most part, smallholders worked these lands, which were either held in private (*tierras particulares*) or controlled by town governments (*tierras de legua*) and rented to users for a nominal fee.[2] Outside of the town's jurisdiction, which at that time was a radius of up to three leagues (one league equals approximately three miles), the national government officially claimed all idle lands (*tierras baldías*) and those lands not already claimed by private holders. Several Indian communities continued to control lands (*tierras comunales*) surrounding their villages.

The most appropriate lands for the development of coffee were those surrounding the commercial townships of the Central Valley, not the outlying areas, which had poorer access to capital, commercial establishments, and labor. Hence, during the first few decades of the coffee boom, municipalities took the lead role in privatizing land, and among the municipalities, the town government of San José was the first to introduce actions to speed the conversion, followed by Heredia, Alajuela, and Cartago. As early as 1821 the municipal government of San José passed an ordinance that granted municipal lands free to any person who fenced in land and planted coffee or other designated commercial crops.[3] Initially, the San José government provided free coffee seedlings to anyone who wished to begin a coffee grove. Shortly thereafter the other townships in the Central Valley passed similar land ordinances, some of which specified how many coffee trees constituted qualification for free land.

Throughout the municipal privatization process, the thrust of municipal land policy was to encourage the commercial use of land, not to restrict small farmers' access to it. From the very beginning, the procedure gave preference to those who already occupied a particular plot of land. The occupant would present to the town authorities a request for official recognition of private ownership along with evidence on boundary lines (ditches, hedgerows, and stone markers), any documents regarding improvements, including proofs of purchase or inheritance from former occupants, and testimony regarding the length of time the present occupant had worked the land. After the authorities reviewed the evidence and checked for any countervailing claims to the plot, a decision would be made on whether to grant recognition of ownership to the applicant. By the 1830s, the commercialization of land around the townships was well under way, and municipalities began charging for the transfer of lands to private individuals, using the proceeds of land sales to help finance public works projects. The prices charged for privatization procedures may have restricted access to land by the poorest members of society, but the prices were generally set below what equivalent land would sell for on the private market, creating an incentive for farmers to seek official recognition of ownership.[4] Payments could be made over a period of several years at low interest rates, making acquisition more affordable. This first round of privatization during the early years of the coffee boom favored those who had worked lands for several years, regardless of whether they held large or small plots, and provisions were made for others who may not have been so fortunate. During the 1830s and 1840s, municipalities continued the customary practices of allowing common access to public woodlands for firewood and pastures for grazing, and some cropland on the outskirts of towns was reserved for annual leases of small plots to those who wished to grow subsistence crops.

The process of privatization was highly uneven, beginning in the most active commercial centers and spreading outward, and some communities lagged considerably behind the commercial centers. An attempt to regularize and to project the process nationwide came in 1848 with the passage of National Decree 39, which legislated for all municipalities of the republic the practices that had already been established in San José, Heredia, Alajuela, and Cartago.[5] In addition to setting relatively easy terms for the private acquisition of land that had been worked for several years, the law contained provisions for public use of woodlands and grazing lands and for rental of small plots of municipal cropland by those who did not already have more permanent claims. During the 1850s, this law was used in contradictory ways by different actors: authorities in the more commercialized townships such as San José, Cartago, and Alajuela used the law as justification for pressuring neighboring villages (for example, Pavas, la Unión, and Turrúca, respectively) to submit to privatization, and poor farmers used it as a bargaining tool for the lower prices and better terms it provided compared to the charges imposed by the municipalities in the 1850s.

Although national lands outside the jurisdiction of townships were of little monetary value right after independence, they became more important as the coffee boom progressed. In 1828, the government of Costa Rica set the precedent of encouraging colonization and commercial use of outlying areas by awarding up to 110 acres of extra land for farmers who established permanent crops in under-populated parts of the country.[6] By 1839, national lands outside the jurisdiction of townships were being sold to occupants at prices one-third to one-fourth those charged by the townships, and payment could be waived if the occupant could show that improvements had been made equivalent in value to two to three times the value of the land. The procedure for establishing recognition of private owner-ship over national lands was similar to the early municipal practices, that is, if an individual could prove that he or she had worked the land for a stipulated period of time or had purchased or inherited the improvements from someone else, the government, after reviewing all the evidence, would sell or, in some cases, provide free official recognition of private ownership of the land. As relative availability of land within the commercial townships dwindled due to popula-tion growth and privatization, national lands became a convenient escape valve for social pressures, and the national government be-came an official mediator of these pressures, encouraging coloniza-tion and access to land for those who would take the initiative to work it. Of course, wealthy individuals did acquire large holdings of national lands for speculative purposes, but in an attempt to check this process the national government in 1854 placed a limit of ten *caballerías* (approximately eleven hundred acres) to the amount of land that could be sold to any individual.[7]

In addition to passing land laws favorable to commercial develop-ment, public (and private) institutions began to improve infrastruc-ture in an effort to open up new areas to coffee cultivation and to lower the private costs of transporting coffee. One of the first con-scious moves to stimulate the coffee trade in this way was by a private organization, the Sociedad Económica Iteneraria, which was com-posed of some of the wealthiest merchants and coffee growers from

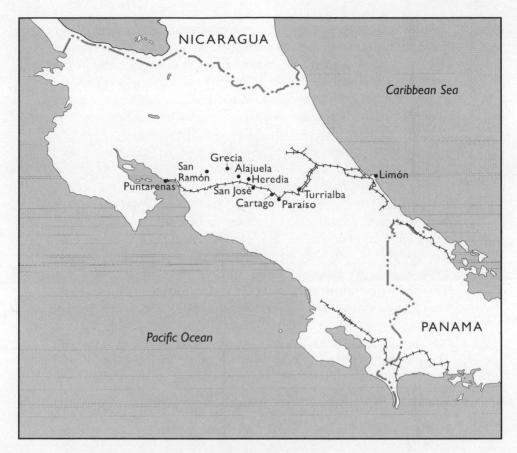

Map 3-1. Costa Rica

San José. Over a three-year period (1843–1846) this group raised enough funds to build a bridge over the Río Jesús María and to widen the Camino Real, a narrow mule trail used since 1601. The improved roadway linked San José in the Central Valley with the Pacific port of Puntarenas, permitting ox carts capable of carrying up to half a ton to replace mules capable of carrying one-fourth that amount, thereby cheapening coffee transport (see Map 3-1).[8]

The new ox cart road did not pass directly through undeveloped coffee areas, but the national government and homesteaders began constructing feeder roads into the more suitable area north of the Camino Real, opening up Palmares, Grecia, San Ramón, Sarchí, and Naranjo for settlement. After 1850, colonists flocked to this newly opened section; forests were felled, coffee trees were planted at the higher elevations, and sugar and basic grains were cultivated at lower elevations. Farther away from these villages and at higher elevations, grazing lands were established for cattle herds.[9] The older towns of the Central Valley such as San José and Heredia came to specialize in coffee production, while more recent settlements raised a variety of crops with coffee as a major cash crop.[10] By 1883, there were some eight hundred coffee farms in this westernmost section of the Central Valley, but the average number of coffee trees per farm was lower than in the older, more specialized coffee districts.[11]

The outskirts of Cartago along the road toward San José developed in a similar fashion to areas outside of San José. By the 1860s coffee cultivation had begun to extend east of Cartago into the *cantón* of Paraíso, but even by 1883 the bulk of Cartago Province's coffee was being raised to the west of the town toward San José. The full development of coffee cultivation to the east of Cartago was delayed until 1890, when the railroad to the Atlantic port of Limón was completed by North American venture capitalists, who obtained generous concessions from the Costa Rican government. The railroad charged high rates for transport, but shipping costs to Europe from the Atlantic were almost half the costs from the Pacific side. Thus, despite the railroad monopoly's high rates, much of the overland coffee traffic was diverted from the Pacific to the Atlantic. Furthermore, the railroad opened up the Reventazón Valley for commercial agriculture, and feeder roads were built along the tributaries of the Reventazón linking those rich valleys with the railroad line. During the 1890s coffee and sugar estates developed all the way past Turrialba, where a rapid descent to lower elevations permitted the establishment of banana plantations.[12] The area to the east of Cartago, where less than one-fifth of the province's coffee was grown in the 1880s before the completion of the railroad, boasted half of the province's coffee acreage by 1914, placing Cartago Province second behind San José Province in total coffee acreage.[13]

During the first phase of coffee expansion around the already established townships of the Central Valley, private holdings replaced traditional leases from municipalities, and coffee groves began to replace pastures and cropland. Within the jurisdictions and close suburbs of San José, Heredia, Cartago, and Alajuela the landscape remained dominated by small family farms of twenty acres or less, though merchants and other elites tended to have farms exceeding twenty acres. Nevertheless, out of eighty-nine large properties recorded in the judicial registry in the Central Valley in the 1840s, only eleven farms exceeded eighty-seven acres.[14] As the coffee boom intensified, the price of land near the old established settlements began to spiral upward. Small farmers who had made the switch to coffee and had obtained official recognition of their private holdings prospered, but poorer families who had been unable to take advantage of earlier land inducements found themselves for the first time without access to land. In 1849, lists of those in the suburbs of San José with and without planting lands were drawn up. It was found that "roughly one-third of those males listed were without planting lands for corn and beans."[15] The situation worsened in the 1850s, when the municipalities of San José, Cartago, and Alajuela began to repartition the common lands provided for in earlier legislation and sell them at auction to private individuals at higher prices than the poor could afford.[16] Wages increased, allowing some of those without land to survive as wage laborers in the major towns, but others chose to remain independent farmers by migrating to the newly forming settlements to the west in Alajuela Province. In progression, the tropical forests of the Central Valley were cleared and opened up for pasture, for basic grains, and, if the land was suitable, for coffee. The pattern of landholding in the newly settled areas to the west tended to reproduce the pattern around the older townships: private holdings around nucleated settlements with family-sized operations the norm. This pattern was reinforced by traditions of land access in the older townships from which the settlers came and by national colonization laws that permitted and encouraged small farmers to lay claim to national lands.

In contrast, the valley to the east of Cartago came to be dominated by much larger coffee holdings than those in the Central Valley. Before coffee, the area outside the jurisdiction of Cartago to the east was relatively sparsely populated. Valley areas were dominated by large cattle haciendas owned by elites from Cartago, unclaimed forested areas within the national domain, several towns (the largest of which was Paraíso) with attached town lands, and at least two Indian villages. Shortly after independence, land laws were passed to break up communal holdings, but it was not until later that pressures became great enough for communal lands to be privatized.[17] As coffee spread to the south and east of Cartago, by the 1870s outsiders had begun to move into the communal holdings of Indian communities. By the early 1880s, the conflicts over land and the intrusion of *ladinos* into the heart of the community reached the national state when the Indians of the community of Orósi, with the assistance of a local friar, appealed to the national government to overturn the actions taken on behalf of the *ladinos* by the municipal government of Paraíso. Despite the urgency of the petitions, the national government finally washed its hands of the matter in 1884, leaving the judgment in the hands of the local authorities, who proceeded to legitimate the outsiders' claims and privatize the remaining common lands.[18] Although the area to the east of Cartago was still an insignificant producer of coffee by 1883–84, the average holding there was larger than in any other district in Costa Rica, with three times the number of trees per farm than the average for the country.[19] When the railroad penetrated the Reventazón Valley farther to the east, the colonial pattern of land tenure in that area continued. Large coffee and sugar estates replaced extensive cattle ranches, and people who migrated to the area settled in enclaves of workers on these large estates or were able to stake small claims on undeveloped forest lands. By the time of the 1935 census, one-third of the coffee trees (34.5 percent) in Cartago Province were on large capitalist farms of more than one hundred thousand trees, and peasant and family farms had 25 percent and 16 percent of the coffee trees respectively, the smallest portions for these two size classes of any province in the country (see Table 3-1).[20]

Later in the nineteenth century some holdings around the earlier coffee-growing townships were centralized as elites tried to consolidate their fragmented holdings into single, geographically contiguous estates.[21] During the crises of 1897–1903, 1914–20 and 1930–35 the tendency toward greater concentration of landholdings was reinforced as smaller and less liquid growers were forced to sell their lands to owners of *beneficios* and other providers of credit.[22] One of several elite families that successfully consolidated holdings was the Rohrmoser family, which became one of the largest landholders in the Central Valley, acquiring fourteen coffee farms between 1892 and 1935. They held some fifteen hundred acres, eleven hundred of which were in coffee; many of their holdings were contiguous, facilitating management and harvesting.[23] Despite this tendency toward greater concentration, the older coffee areas around the major townships continued to reflect the general pattern of earlier development in which smallholdings were the norm. For example, by 1935 two-

**Table 3-1. Size Class Analysis of Coffee Farms by Province—
Costa Rica, 1935**

	Percentage of Trees in the Province by Size Class				
Province	100k+	60k–99k	20k–59k	5k–19k	<5k
San José	16.4	5.6	11.8	23.0	43.2
Alajuela	10.3	6.8	15.2	27.9	39.8
Heredia	11.5	5.9	18.2	21.6	42.9
Cartago	34.5	9.9	14.6	16.0	25.0
Costa Rica	17.8	6.9	14.6	21.9	38.7

Source: 1935 Coffee Census. Table from Samper, "Coffee Households and
Haciendas," Table 3.

thirds of the coffee trees in the province of San José were on peasant
farms of less than five thousand trees or on family-sized farms of less
than twenty thousand trees, and the remaining one-third of the trees
were on capitalist farms that required outside labor for the harvest
and year-round maintenance. The overall pattern of landholding also
continued to reflect early patterns in the second area of coffee development north of the ox cart road in western Alajuela Province.
By the end of the nineteenth century, a few large-scale operations
exceeding a thousand acres had been established there, but the landscape continued to be dominated by smallholders. In 1935, only 10
percent of the coffee trees of Alajuela Province were owned by large
capitalist enterprises of more than one hundred thousand trees, and
family-sized peasant farms had 68 percent of the trees in the province
(see Map 3-2).[24]

Costa Rican coffee growers first worked through municipal governments to promote road building and favorable access to potential
coffee lands, but as coffee cultivation proved its merit, the national
government began programs to build infrastructure and passed legislation promoting coffee. Despite the newness of the crop, structures
of access to land for coffee were heavily influenced by colonial patterns of landholding. The pattern of nucleated settlements spread
throughout the Central Valley, maintaining a structure of many small
and medium-sized holdings at the bottom with a diversified elite
involved in commerce, landholding, and public officeholding at the
top. In contrast, the area to the east of Cartago continued its colonial

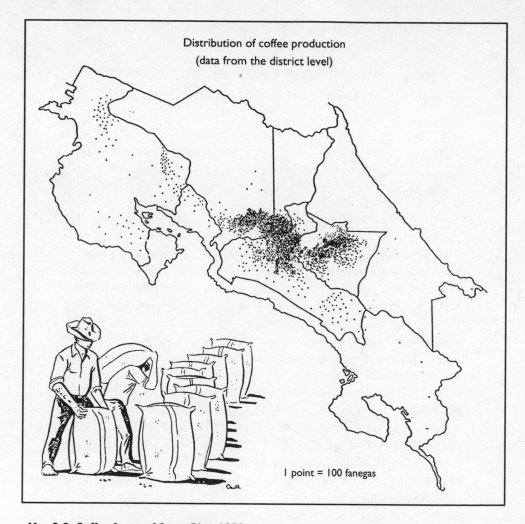

Map 3-2. Coffee Areas of Costa Rica, 1950.
Source: Dirección General de Estadísticos y Censos, *Censo agropecuario de 1950*, p. 69.

pattern of large estates. In all areas there was a shift to official recognition of private holdings with clearly delineated boundaries. In the Central Valley, municipal lands were converted to private property, while to the east of Cartago haciendas with vaguely defined borders were surveyed and officially processed.[25] Because the national state took a policy allowing for colonization in the form of smallholdings and because of high wages in coffee, the transition to coffee was relatively peaceful, and violence occurred mainly to the east of Cartago, where Indian communities resisted the takeover of their lands.

Land and the Coffee Boom in Guatemala

The first phase of commercial coffee growing in Guatemala (1840–71) began when wealthy merchant-landowners heard about commercial successes from the crop in Costa Rica. In the early 1840s the Economic Society of Friends of the Country, a private business organization, commissioned Licenciado Manuel Aguilar to write a practical manual on how to plant, cultivate, harvest, and process coffee based on the Costa Rican experience. In 1845, another business group, the Consulado de Comercio, published one thousand copies of the manual for free distribution and paid for the importation of processing equipment to be used as demonstration models.[26] The first areas to be developed were on already established cattle and sugar estates in the Pacific piedmont in the departments of Escuintla, Santa Rosa, Suchitepéquez, and Retalhuleu. An enterprising early grower was don José Tomás Larraondo, who began growing coffee on his sugar and cattle hacienda, Trapiche Grande, in the department of Suchitepéquez.[27] In 1856, Larraondo, who was also a lender to cochineal growers, received first prize from the national government for the largest number of coffee trees cultivated to the fruiting stage and collected twenty-five pesos per thousand trees.[28] Cochineal growers had begun to plant coffee trees as borders to their nopal cactus groves around Antigua and Lake Amatitlán, but most were reluctant to shift into coffee until the 1860s, when the cochineal market became depressed. The earliest statistics on geographical distribution of coffee trees (1862) show the largest concentrations of coffee in the Pacific departments of Suchitepéquez and Retalhuleu (31 percent combined) and Escuintla (23 percent) and in the highland cochineal districts of Amatitlán (20 percent).[29] At this time, some growers were experimenting with coffee in the northwestern portions of the Pacific piedmont in Quezaltenango and San Marcos and in sections of Alta Verapaz near Cobán, but the extension of coffee to these and other districts was hindered by extremely poor transport networks and by a national government that protected church, communal, and municipal holdings of land (see Map 3-3).

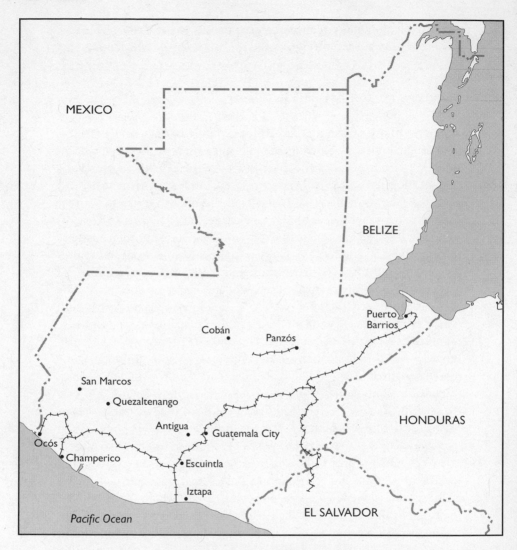

Map 3-3. Guatemala

The Conservative government of Rafael Carrera (1839–65) left the provision of most public goods up to private group initiatives (roads, bridges, and ports) or to traditional institutions like the church (hospitals, education). The only road-building project begun by the Carrera government was the cart road from Guatemala City to the Pacific port of Iztapa, built in the 1850s to stimulate cochineal exports and the import trade, which was still controlled by Guate-

mala City merchants. Coffee cultivation benefited indirectly from
this road, especially in the department of Escuintla and later in the
cochineal districts of Amatitlán. Elsewhere coffee growers got little
help from the national government, but they became increasingly
adept at pressuring political bosses at the department level. For example, in 1860 coffee growers persuaded the political chief of Alta
Verapaz to walk the treacherous road to Panzós, where coffee was
delivered on the backs of Indians for shipment by launch to the Atlantic port of Livingston. After seeing the life-threatening conditions at
one point of the road, the official recommended to the national government that an iron bridge be built over the Polochíc River at that
spot.[30] In other places, growers organized, pooled their resources,
and pressured their department governments to help secure labor
for road building in their districts. Some additional funds for road
projects were obtained from the same two national commercial organizations that promoted the coffee manual in 1845, the Economic
Society of Friends of the Country, composed primarily of Liberal
elites, and the Consulado de Comercio, a group of mostly Conservative elites. The Consulado de Comercio tended to support projects
that were perceived to be in the direct interest of the Guatemala City
merchant elite.[31] For example, when growers from the western district of Los Altos pushed for new port facilities in Suchitepéquez, the
Consulado de Comercio and the government turned the plan down
because the Guatemala City merchants feared it would erode their
monopoly on foreign commerce.[32] In 1871, when the Conservatives
were finally ousted by Liberals, the transport system of Guatemala,
though improved over what it had been in 1839, was still composed
of footpaths and mule trails, many of which were impassable during
the rainy season.

At the time of independence, religious orders in Guatemala had
substantial holdings of urban and rural property. As early as 1825,
the power of the church began to be questioned, and when Liberals
took control in 1829, the archbishop and priests were expelled from
the country and colonial privileges enjoyed by the church were dis-
mantled. Real estate owned by the religious orders was expropriated,
and between 1831 and 1835 the most valuable pieces of property were
sold at auction to private individuals.[33] When Conservatives regained
control of the national government in 1839, many of the privileges
of the church were restored, and some of the properties previously
expropriated were returned.[34] Much of the secondary literature on

the nineteenth century implies that sizable rural properties were returned to the church during the Conservative period, delaying their full-scale development as coffee estates until they were expropriated by the Liberals and sold to private individuals in the 1870s. Land records, however, reveal that only two of the many holdings of the church from the colonial period became important coffee estates by the end of the nineteenth century. These were San Andrés Osuna, a hacienda in Escuintla owned by the Order of La Merced, and Cerro Redondo, a sugar estate in Santa Rosa owned by the Dominicans. By 1890, San Andrés Osuna was the second largest coffee estate in Guatemala and Cerro Redondo was the fifth largest, but the archives show that both of these properties had been transferred to private investors before the Liberal land reform of the 1870s.[35]

Church properties may not have been a serious obstacle to coffee expansion, but communal and municipal lands were. In the 1860s, more than two-thirds of the land suitable for coffee cultivation were held by municipalities or Indian communities.[36] During the Liberal regime of Mariano Gálvez (1831–39), a series of laws was passed that allowed outsiders interested in cultivation of commercial crops to rent, and in some cases acquire, *ejidal* holdings of villages. This first attack on village lands was administered in an inept way by the Gálvez government, which provided inadequate military backing in the areas affected and offered little compensation to villagers and to small private farmers whose lands were taken. In eastern Guatemala the acquisition of municipal lands by cochineal producers and cattle ranchers provoked rural unrest, culminating in an armed uprising of *ladino* and Indian peasants in 1838 that brought the peasant leader Rafael Carrera to power in 1839.[37] One of the first actions of Carrera's government was to restore the lands taken from communities during the Gálvez regime. During its later years, the Carrera regime was pressured to reduce some of the privileges of the religious orders and to allow rental of community lands to outsiders, but the government did not cave in to pressure from growers to privatize village and community lands.

In the 1850s and 1860s, growers came to dominate department governments in the coffee zones and were able to influence some of the policies of the national government, but when the Liberals came to power in 1871, coffee growers finally had a national state of their own. That same year the Consulado de Comercio, which had narrowly supported public works that favored the interests of

"National Bank—City of Guatemala," 1875. Some of the start-up capital for this bank was obtained by auctioning assets expropriated from the church in 1873. Loans from the bank helped coffee growers start plantations on the Pacific slopes. (Department of Special Collections, Stanford University Libraries)

Conservative merchants, was replaced by Fomento, an activist government agency set up with a budget to build roads and ports and to promote coffee and other commercial ventures.[38] In June 1871, before Miguel García Granados had taken full control over the government, his first decree under a provisional government was for the improvement of the port facilities at Champerico, which would serve the expanding coffee economy of Retalhuleu and Suchitepéquez.[39]

García Granados was from an elite Creole family and had been a statesman for the Liberal cause for many years. He wanted to make reforms more gradually than some of the younger radicals led by General Justo Rufino Barrios, a prosperous coffee grower from western Guatemala. When Barrios came to power in 1873, a series of

"Coffee Carts at San José de Guatemala," 1875. San José (Iztapa) was Guatemala's most important Pacific port at this time, handling the commerce of Guatemala City, Amatitlán, Antigua, and Escuintla. Note the cattle hide covers on the oxcarts. (Department of Special Collections, Stanford University Libraries)

forceful decrees was enacted aimed at transforming the Guatemalan economy into an export dynamo.

In August 1873 Decree 104 called for the confiscation of all church property.[40] Urban and rural real estate that had been returned to the religious orders under the Carrera regime was seized along with silver, gold, artworks, and furniture. Convents and monasteries were turned into hospitals, jails, military academies, and government office buildings. City houses, haciendas, and valuables were sold at auction, and the proceeds became starting capital for the National Bank of Guatemala, which made loans to the national state and to coffee growers who wished to expand their holdings.[41]

In December 1873 Decree 109 taxed land at two pesos per 110 acres, and the revenue was used to build roads, bridges, and ports. Coffee growers continued to pressure municipal and department governments for roads to service their areas, and Fomento provided national assistance to these efforts.[42] Improvement of the port of Champerico was completed in the early Barrios years, and in 1878 a cart road between Champerico and Retalhuleu was finished, lowering the transport costs for the most important coffee-growing zone at that time.[43] Later, the port of Ocós to the west was improved, and roads were built to link that port with the rich coffee areas of the Costa Cuca (Quezaltenango) and San Marcos.[44] The Atlantic ports of Livingston and Puerto Barrios were also developed, and cart roads were completed to connect the ports with the expanding coffee areas of Alta Verapaz.

Travel on cart roads was slow even in dry weather, but during the rainy season cart wheels dug deep ruts and mud slides blocked roads in places. For the main transport routes, the Barrios government and successive Liberal governments contracted with foreign companies to construct all-weather railroads. Capital requirements were enormous, and delays were frequent. A project begun in 1874 to link the capital with the port of San José was completed in sections, first from San José to the coffee town of Escuintla in 1880, then the more difficult stretch from Escuintla to Guatemala City in 1884.[45] In 1884, a railroad between Retalhuleu and the port of Champerico was begun. In 1883, the railroad from Puerto Barrios to Guatemala City was initiated, but because of lack of funds and labor it was not completed until the early 1900s.[46] Infrastructure along the Pacific coast was built with Indian labor and North American capital, but in the Alta Verapaz German coffee growers solicited private capital from Germany to begin the railroad line between Tucurú and Panzós in 1895. By 1912, railroad lines linked the most important coffee zones of Guatemala with ports.

Potentially the most explosive obstacle to coffee expansion was the Indian population. For centuries, Indian communities from the Western Highlands had seasonally migrated to the Pacific piedmont to plant and harvest corn, taking advantage of differences in climate between the highlands and the piedmont. Piedmont forests also provided firewood, wild game, vines for making rope, and numerous plants and medicinal herbs, all of which were items of trade in highland markets. The borders of these communal holdings were poorly delineated, but communities considered certain sections of forest to be the domain of particular communities.

In addition to highland communities that used the forests on a seasonal basis, Indian villages in the piedmont had municipal claims (*ejidal* rights) to lands surrounding their villages and communal claims to forest areas farther away. During the 1860s, before the Liberals took control of the national government, *ladinos* began to encroach on village lands in the Pacific piedmont by renting lands from the municipalities to grow coffee, in effect replicating a process that had proved commercially successful in the cochineal districts of Antigua and Amatitlán, where cochineal growers obtained long-term (usually nine-year) leases on municipal lands in return for the payment of an annual fee or *canon* equivalent to a small percentage (usually 2 or 3 percent) of the estimated value of the land.[47] This procedure of *censo enfiteusis* had worked well for cochineal, allowing two cycles of cactus plantings before a new lease had to be negotiated, and a grower could sell the use rights to the land (*dominio útil*) and the improvements to a third party before a lease expired. The labor intensity of caring for the cochineal insects favored small and medium-sized holdings over large-scale operations, and there was widespread participation in the business, including Indians in the villages outside of Antigua. Perhaps for this reason, coffee growers were able to pressure the Carrera government to pass an order in 1862 encouraging Indian villages of the piedmont to open uncultivated lands for *censo* lease to coffee growers, but the decree protected the right of village officers to accept or reject *censo* requests by growers.[48] The potential profits from coffee growing led to political maneuvering and abuses of traditional Indian land rights. A frequent complaint of Indian communities was that once coffee groves were well established, growers neglected to pay the canon and treated the land as if it had been developed on *baldíos* instead of on community land, sometimes selling the improved lands to other *ladinos* without going through the municipality. When Indian communities protested to department governments, frequently the governor (*corregidor*) would favor *ladino* claims, though when the dispute was appealed to the national government, Carrera's ministers were more likely to back up Indian claims.[49] Some Indian municipalities in the piedmont refused to rent land to *ladino* coffee growers, maintaining a buffer of fallow land for the community to continue the practice of shifting cultivation, but *ladinos* protested that access to municipal land should be open to all citizens regardless of race. Department governments sometimes intervened by forcing communities to rent and demanding that growers pay rent to the municipalities.[50] Nevertheless, because the growers' legal claims to municipal lands were flimsy, the capital invested in a coffee grove was subject to political risk, especially when Indian communities were well organized and the Conservative Carrera government was the ultimate arbiter in land disputes. After the death of Carrera in 1865, it became more difficult for Indian communities to use the lever of the national state in resisting encroachment on their lands. Vicente Cerna, who replaced Carrera, had been the *corregidor* of the department of Chiquimula, where he had worked closely with large landholders; during his regime (1865–71) encroachments on Indian lands in the piedmont and in the Alta Verapaz escalated, though full privatization did not occur until the arrival of the Liberals.[51]

The Liberal agenda included the transformation of land tenure relations in potential export zones to favor capital investment in the land. This meant a move to privately titled properties with clearly delineated boundaries to minimize risk of investment from disputed claims. It also meant a transfer of Indian holdings in the Pacific piedmont to *ladino* growers. Justo Rufino Barrios had been brought up in that area (San Marcos), worked there as a notary registering land claims, and established a coffee farm on *censo* lands of an Indian community and thus was well aware of the struggles between *ladinos* and Indians over land rights. To avoid a mass uprising such as had resulted from Gálvez's earlier Liberal reforms, Barrios did not immediately expropriate municipal lands around villages but at first encouraged their rental to coffee growers, a continuation of the process started during the Conservative period. It was not until 1877 that *censo enfiteusis* was abolished and replaced by private property. Decree 170 declared all *censo* lands to be national lands, and those holding *censo* leases could pay the capitalized value of the *canon* to the national government and receive private title to the land in question; if the renter did not wish to purchase the land, anyone could denounce it and purchase it as if it were *baldío*.[52]

Claims to communal holdings were more vague than those to municipal holdings, and Barrios was able to act quickly in turning these lands into coffee estates. Following the colonial precedent of reconstituting as Crown lands any underused territory, the Liberal government defined as "idle" (*tierras baldías*) all lands that were not

"Reception of the Artist at Quezaltenango," 1875. The strengthening of the
military was a key ingredient in the success of Liberal land reform, which was
administered out of departmental government office buildings like the one in this
photograph. Barrios appointed his father-in-law, Juan Aparicio, as governor
of the department of Quezaltenango during the reform, which distributed land
in the department's coffee belt located on the Pacific slopes beginning fifteen
miles south of town. Quezaltenango soon became the largest coffee producing
department in Guatemala. In 1890 Juan Aparicio and Sons was reported as
owning a large capitalist plantation with 400,000 coffee trees in the neighboring
department of Suchitepéquez. (Department of Special Collections, Stanford
University Libraries)

"planted in coffee, sugar, cacao, or hay," claiming them as national
property.[53] In 1873, some 200,000 acres in the western piedmont
areas of the Costa Cuca and El Palmar were reconstituted as national
lands and divided into lots of 110 to 550 acres, which were then sold
at 500 pesos per 110 acres, with 100 pesos down and 100-peso in-
stallments per year. If those lands were already in coffee or sugar,
the occupants paid only 200 pesos per 110 acres.[54]

The requirement of making payments to the national government effectively excluded peasants from acquiring lands in the zones suitable for commercial agriculture, and it discouraged very large landholders from keeping their properties idle. Furthermore, it channeled land resources into the hands of those willing and able to invest capital in an enterprise that would yield profits. In this way, the rich lands of the Costa Cuca in Quezaltenango and the Pacific piedmont sections of San Marcos were turned into coffee plantations, and the new owners of these plantations were government officials, military officers, merchants, already landed elites, and foreign investors.

The Barrios government prevented a wholesale uprising of peasants by increasing repression in areas where resistance was strong and by increasing the military budget to 60 percent of total outlays.[55] In 1875, an uprising began in the Western Highland town of Momostenango, where some five hundred people took up arms. By 1877 this uprising had been brutally crushed by the Barrios regime.[56] In sections of the piedmont where communal lands were taken, Indians resisted in a variety of ways. In some cases large groups armed with machetes and bludgeons would show up at the *finca* and threaten administrators. In other cases coffee groves, *beneficios*, administrative buildings, and even quarters for temporary workers were mysteriously set afire. In areas where resistance was great, Barrios created peasant militias to keep order in the villages and on the plantations. Military presence in these areas was increased, jails were built, and leaders of the resistance were jailed, beaten, or assassinated.[57]

But repression alone does not account for the success of the coffee land reform. Barrios was careful not to force the privatization of lands in the highland Indian communities, and he showed genius in dividing the opposition and using concessions to stop unrest. Usually when villages complained that they had inadequate land for planting, Barrios received their petitions with respect, and he frequently granted villages land in areas unsuitable for coffee cultivation. When communities in the highlands complained of losing communal holdings in the lowlands, Barrios would grant them lands adjacent to the highland village, which gave them greater security than they had with the tenuous holdings in the lowlands. Sometimes the lands granted by Barrios were claimed by a rival village. The president thus gained allegiance of one village, which would soon have its own militia, and old rivalries between villages were revived. Similarly Barrios used concessions to accentuate differences between *ladinos* and Indians, preventing them from joining into an opposition force like the one led by Rafael Carrera in 1838. On rare occasions, in a political move, Barrios turned lands claimed by large, low-productivity haciendas over to municipalities. For example, shortly after coming to power, Barrios ordered neighboring hacienda lands to be turned over to the municipality of Mataquescuintla, which more than three decades before had been a stronghold of the peasant revolt of Carrera.[58]

By the time of Barrios's death in 1885, a successful land reform had been carried out that furthered a process already under way in the zones of early commercial development, extending it to politically sensitive areas traditionally within the Indian domain. The success of the Barrios land reform relative to the earlier land reform of Gál-vez can be attributed to several factors. For one, Barrios made sure he had at his disposal a larger and better equipped repressive appa-ratus able to crush rebellions before a move was made on Indian lands. Second, Barrios established a more effective administrative organization that reached down into the departments and munici-palities from the command center in Guatemala City, and an appeals structure was developed through which complaints of abuses at a local level could be heard by higher levels of authority. Third, by the 1870s Guatemala had a large class of agricultural entrepreneurs who supported the reform process, a situation not available to Gálvez. Fourth, Barrios avoided a frontal attack on lands of Indian com-munities and the Indian way of life, tampering with these only in localities where lands were suitable for commercial development.

By the time of the 1890 coffee census, the basic structures of Gua-temalan landholding that would last for at least another century had been established. The census shows that more than half of the coffee trees (53 percent) registered in the country were on large capitalist plantations with one hundred thousand or more trees, the highest concentration in large capitalist enterprises of any country in Cen-tral America. The 1890 census reveals both land tenure patterns that existed within Guatemala before coffee and the conscious actions of the Liberal state to transform traditional land tenure relationships (see Table 3-2).

Areas that had been previously carved out for cattle, sugar, and indigo haciendas may have changed hands in the transition to coffee, but lands that were suitable for coffee became large coffee estates. Thus, when coffee became recognized as profitable, the cattle and

Table 3-2. Size Class Analysis of Coffee Farms by Department—Guatemala, 1890

Department	Percentage of Trees in Department by Size Class				
	100k+	50k–99k	20k–49k	5k–19k	<5k
Guatemala	39.9	32.4	13.7	8.0	6.0
Sacatépequez	25.8	13.2	10.4	12.0	39.8
Chimaltenango	62.8	23.5	6.8	1.9	5.0
Amatitlán	44.4	16.0	12.8	14.8	12.1
Escuintla	90.9	6.9	1.9	0.3	0.0
Santa Rosa	81.0	4.4	5.7	4.1	4.9
Sololá	61.0	16.4	14.1	5.0	3.6
Totonicapán	0.0	0.0	0.0	0.0	0.0
Quezaltenango	49.8	20.1	20.9	6.0	3.4
Suchitepéquez	52.7	21.1	11.9	4.8	9.5
Retalhuleu	29.6	30.9	18.1	8.7	12.6
San Marcos	65.2	10.3	11.6	8.1	4.8
Huehuetenango	0.0	0.0	0.0	0.0	100.0
Quiché	0.0	0.0	0.0	0.0	100.0
Baja Verapaz	67.6	0.0	5.1	14.9	12.4
Alta Verapaz	17.5	26.6	10.0	10.0	36.0
Petén	0.0	0.0	0.0	0.0	100.0
Izabal	0.0	0.0	0.0	0.0	0.0
Zacapa	0.0	37.4	0.0	3.2	59.4
Chiquimula	0.0	0.0	3.8	18.6	77.7
Jalapa	0.0	0.0	0.0	0.0	100.0
Jutiapa	0.0	0.0	100.0	0.0	0.0
Total	52.7	16.1	12.1	7.0	12.2

Source: Gobierno de Guatemala, Memoria de fomento, 1892, "Estadística de Café, 1890."

sugar haciendas of Santa Rosa (along the road from Guatemala City to El Salvador) and Escuintla (along the road from Guatemala City to the port of San José) were planted in coffee above elevations of one thousand feet. Large haciendas predating coffee cultivation covered most of the potential coffee land in these departments, and the 1890 census reveals that these two departments had the greatest concentration of coffee trees in large holdings of any departments in the country; 91 percent of the coffee trees in the department of Escuintla and 81 percent of the trees in the department of Santa Rosa were on coffee plantations with 100,000 or more trees. In other departments precoffee haciendas did not control such a large percentage of potential coffee land as in Escuintla and Santa Rosa, but the pattern of the move from hacienda to plantation can be identified in particular cases. For example, part of the Dominican Order's sugar hacienda of San Jerónimo in Baja Verapaz shows up in the 1890 census as having 268,000 coffee trees, though the Dominicans' holdings were expropriated in 1835, and ownership in 1890 was registered under the name of "La Familia Harris." Similarly, in the department of Sácatepequez, where a high concentration of small coffee farms emerged, the precoffee sugar hacienda El Capetillo became one of the eight large capitalist coffee plantations in the department and is listed in the 1890 census as having 150,000 coffee trees.[59]

In the districts where cochineal was produced before coffee, the coffee farms that replaced cactus fields were most frequently smallholdings, reflecting land tenure patterns in cochineal production. Because of the meticulous care needed for successful production of cochineal, large plantations were difficult to manage, and small operations were favored. Thus in the department of Sacatepéquez (where Antigua is located), by the 1890 census 40 percent of the trees were still on peasant-sized operations having fewer than 5,000 trees, and another 11 percent were on family farms with 5,000 to 19,000 trees, the greatest participation by noncapitalist enterprises of any major coffee-producing department in the country.[60] In the department of Amatitlán some smaller operations apparently were consolidated into large holdings by 1890. The greatest concentration of trees ended up in the hands of J. M. Samayoa, an important lender to cochineal farmers during the 1850s and 1860s, who in 1890 owned five coffee farms with a total of 582,000 trees. Nevertheless, in the department as a whole greater participation by noncapitalist enterprises was still higher than the average for Guatemala; 27 percent of the trees in Amatitlán were on farms with fewer than 20,000 trees, whereas the average in this size class for Guatemala was 19 percent. Noncapitalist farms also had higher than average participation in the marginal coffee-producing areas of already *ladinoized* eastern Guatemala in the departments of Jalapa, Chiquimula, Zacapa, Baja Verapaz, and Petén though these departments were never major producers.

In the zones targeted for development by the Barrios regime, peasant farms and family-sized operations had a lower than average chance of participating in the land grab. In Guatemala as a whole, 81 percent of the trees were registered on capitalist-sized farms of twenty thousand or more trees, but in all of the departments of the Pacific piedmont where Indian lands were sold off to coffee growers, there was a higher participation by capitalist-sized enterprises.[61] In San Marcos, 87 percent of the trees were on capitalist-sized farms by the time of the 1890 census; in Quezaltenango, 91 percent; and in the upper piedmont sections of Sololá (now part of Suchitepéquez) and Chimaltenango, 91 percent and 93 percent respectively. Within these departments, there existed clusters of smallholders, usually within *municipios* at lower elevations. Most of these smallholders on the 1890 list have *ladino* surnames, but some Indian surnames appear on the list, suggesting that a few Indian communities were able to participate in the transition.[62]

The areas of the western piedmont that were mapped out by the national government as a real estate development project during the 1870s and 1880s did not reflect previous relations of labor and land tenure in those zones, which had been either low-use, off-season cropping areas for highland Indian communities or municipal lands of piedmont Indian villages. Rather, the land tenure and labor relations that emerged there reflected the conscious attempts by the Liberal state to establish capitalist plantation agriculture in the area. In the 1890 coffee census, the departments of Quezaltenango, San Marcos, Chimaltenango, and Sololá had significantly higher than national average participation rates by capitalist farms with twenty thousand or more trees (see Map 3-4).[63]

Conservative governments before 1865 did little actively to promote coffee, though growers were able to garner assistance from national commercial organizations. Also at this time growers began to influence departmental and local officials in the areas where coffee showed greatest potential. In this way, growers were able to encroach on village lands and communal holdings of Indians, though the claims remained uncertain because of the support given to Indian appeals by the Carrera government. After the death of Carrera in 1865, encroachment on Indian holdings through *censo* rentals intensified, though the Cerna government refrained from full privatization of these lands. Especially after Justo Rufino Barrios came to power in 1873, the Guatemalan government undertook a serious

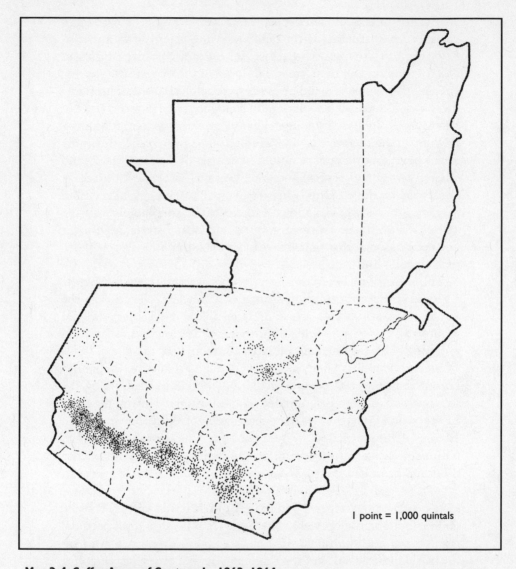

I point = 1,000 quintals

Map 3-4. Coffee Areas of Guatemala, 1963–1964.
Source: Dirección General de Estadístico y Censos. *Censo agropecuario de 1964*, p. 306.

land reform and an unprecedented infrastructure program with the express purpose of promoting coffee exports. To prevent a recurrence of a peasant revolt like that of the 1830s, Barrios applied a judicious mixture of repression, co-optation, and division of the peasantry. His government administered the land reform following precedents established in the colonial period, reconstituting lands deemed idle and then selling them to private individuals. Also following colonial practice, Barrios was careful not to present a public image of insensitivity to the plight of the peasantry. Indeed, coffee lands were removed from peasant control, but when communities pressured effectively, Barrios sometimes doled out lands to them in areas unsuitable for coffee cultivation. Firmly establishing private title as the ultimate form of land tenure in potential coffee zones lowered the risk of investing in coffee. Furthermore, the national government during the 1870s became directly involved in real estate development, carving out large lots for sale in the undeveloped western piedmont and providing roads, bridges, and ports to service this area. By the time of the first coffee census in 1890, the western piedmont had become the most important coffee-producing zone of Guatemala, with a higher than average participation rate by capitalist-sized enterprises, while areas that had developed as coffee centers before the Liberal reforms reflected precoffee structures of landholding.

Land and the Rise of Coffee in El Salvador

From a geographical perspective, El Salvador's coffee zones were the least difficult to develop in all of Central America. As the 1950 agricultural map shows, coffee production is concentrated in three major pockets, two in the western half of the country and one in the east (see Map 3-5). All three zones are within twenty miles of the Pacific Ocean. As in the other countries, the expansion of coffee in El Salvador depended on the development of ports, cart roads, and railroads, but because the prime coffee land was in compact zones of recent volcanics it was relatively easy to connect the farms with regional commercial centers, and because these zones were so close to the sea, the cost of linking the regional processing centers with the ports was lower than in the other countries.

The first areas to be claimed by coffee were the two western pockets shown on Map 3-5. In 1853, steamship service to Panama began, a warehouse was constructed at the Pacific port of La Libertad, and a twenty-mile stretch of road was started between La Libertad and San Salvador. The purpose of this infrastructure was to improve indigo exports and to facilitate imports, but the road passed through Santa Tecla, where some of the first commercial coffee farms

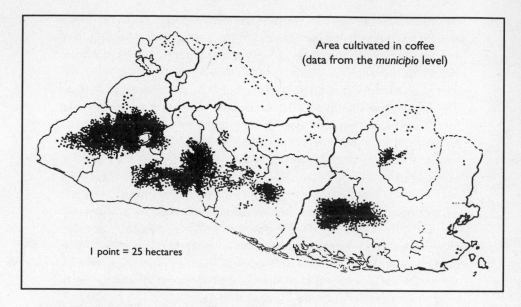

Map 3-5. Coffee Areas of El Salvador, 1950.
Source: Dirección General de Estadísticos y Censos, *Censo agropecuario de 1950.*

were started.[64] By the 1870s, Santa Tecla was a thriving coffee town. Also in the 1850s, a twelve-mile stretch of road was constructed between the Pacific port of Acajutla and the piedmont commercial town of Sonsonate. Coffee grown in the far western zone of Santa Ana and Ahuachapán passed through Sonsonate on its way to port. In the 1860s, the ports of Acajutla, La Libertad, and La Union in the east were greatly improved by the building of iron wharves.[65] These expenditures were probably intended to service indigo instead of coffee because at this time annual export revenues from indigo were ten times those of coffee. Nevertheless, these port and road improvements inadvertently stimulated the coffee trade (see Map 3-6).

After indigo declined and coffee became El Salvador's chief export earner in the late 1870s, more attention was paid to stimulating coffee production directly through infrastructure projects. Railroad building for the next twenty years was entirely aimed at promoting coffee. In 1885 a twelve-mile rail line between Acajutla, El Salvador's most important coffee port, and Sonsonate, an important coffee marketing center, was begun with the help of British capital. Eleven years later (1896), fifty-two more miles of track had been laid linking Sonsonate with Santa Ana, El Salvador's most important coffee-growing district. The following year (1897), twenty more miles of track had been laid linking the first line with San Salvador. This section passed through the important coffee district north and west of San Salvador. In addition to railroads in the west, roads to the eastern port of El Triunfo were constructed in 1894–98 to service the newly expanding coffee zone of Tecapa, Berlín, and Santiago de María.[66]

Physical geography may not have presented obstacles as serious as those in other Central American countries, but precoffee land use and land tenure relationships did. The mainstay commercial crop before coffee was indigo, which was raised throughout the country. In the northern zones bordering Honduras, where the soil is poor and acidic, indigo was raised primarily on small farms and then sold in the commercial centers, especially in the eastern towns of San Vicente and San Miguel in the heart of the two strongest indigo districts, where most of the country's large indigo plantations along with numerous medium-sized and small indigo farms were located.[67] Although indigo production peaked in 1872, Salvadoran production did not bottom out until the late 1890s, when synthetic indigo, a much closer substitute than the aniline dyes of the 1850s and 1860s, was discovered. In the low-cost indigo zones of San Vicente and San Miguel, land, labor, and capital continued to be tied up in the production of indigo until the close of the nineteenth century, postponing the development of the major coffee zone around San Miguel and the minor coffee pocket around San Vicente.

Before the Liberal reforms of the 1880s, land tenure relationships were by no means consolidated on a national basis in El Salvador but depended on customs, practices, and struggles at a local level. Colonial conflicts between haciendas with vaguely defined boundaries and municipalities with *ejidal* lands or Indian communities with communal lands continued with a passion after independence. The expansion of indigo production during the 1850s and 1860s intensified the use of *ejidal* lands by small and medium-sized *ladino* growers, who treated these lands as if they were private property, and cattle and indigo haciendas encroached on *ejidal* and communal lands in traditional fashion. In the 1850s and 1860s, *ladino* coffee growers began to intrude on *ejidal* lands of western El Salvador, especially around larger towns, where municipal governments were under the influence of local merchants, hacienda owners, doctors, lawyers, military officers, and other professionals and business

"La Libertad—Salvador," 1875. The Muybridge albums contain observations of port facilities in Panama, Nicaragua (Corinto), El Salvador (La Union and La Libertad), Guatemala (San José and Champerico), and Mexico. In the photographs, none of the ports appears to have facilities as modern as those of La Libertad, whose iron wharf was built in the 1860s with wealth generated from the indigo trade. (Department of Special Collections, Stanford University Libraries)

people who had independent sources of income and an interest in investing in coffee. Around towns such as Ahuachapán, Santa Ana, San Salvador, Sonsonate, and Santa Tecla municipal lands were increasingly rented or sometimes sold to coffee growers.[68] Other growers could still obtain private claims over uncleared forest areas by having the land surveyed and paying a fee to the national government, which had de facto claim to all lands (*baldíos*) not taken by municipalities, Indian communities, or private haciendas. By the 1870s, the sale of *baldíos* appropriate for growing coffee had reached a limit in the western districts, and much of the *ejidal* land around *ladino*-controlled towns had been rented to coffee growers. In more remote municipalities, *ladino* elites did not control local governments, and authorities took greater care to distribute lands equitably to members of the community.[69] Furthermore, there was a strip of prime

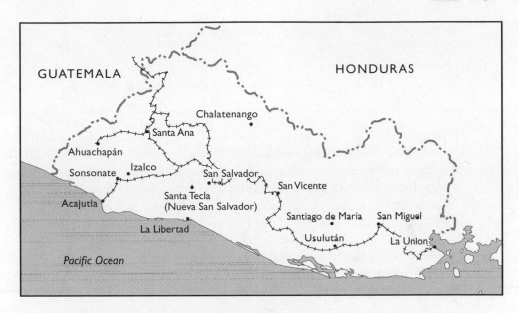

GUATEMALA

HONDURAS

Chalatenango
•

Santa Ana
•

Ahuachapán
•

Izalco
Sonsonate •
•

San Salvador
•

San Vicente
•

Acajutla
•

Santa Tecla
(Nueva San Salvador)
•

Santiago de María   San Miguel
•   •

La Libertad
•

Usulután   La Union
•   •

Pacific Ocean

Map 3-6. El Salvador

coffee land in the departments of La Libertad and Sonsonate that was
Indian communities jealously guarded from *ladino* encroachment. In
1875, when *ladinos* attempted to purchase *ejidal* lands from Izalco,
there was an uprising of Indians in the area.[70] Although this last
Indian stronghold produced such commercial crops as cacao, bal-
sam, sugar, and coffee alongside subsistence crops, *ladino* growers
were aware of the high quality of the upper piedmont lands and the
potential labor force living on those lands, and they viewed Indian
control over the zone as an obstacle to progress.

In addition to a strong cultural bias against Indian communities,
Salvadoran coffee growers more generally became hostile toward
traditional forms of land tenure. Rental of *ejidal* lands was prefer-
able to no access, but *ejidal* lands could not be mortgaged for further
coffee expansion, nor was it clear how municipal authorities even in
a *ladino*-controlled town might intervene if at a future date a grower
wished to sell rights to a grove that had been invested in. To secure
long-term credit and to reduce investors' uncertainty, growers increasingly pressured local governments to give private titles to those
who raised coffee. In 1878, the municipality of Mejicanos, a town in
the coffee district to the north of San Salvador, passed an ordinance
allowing for the use of municipal funds to purchase cocoa, coffee,

rubber, and agave seedlings and to distribute them free to citizens. If a grower planted one-fourth of the land area of a plot in one of these crops, the grower would receive freehold title to the entire plot.[71] Shortly afterward, four other highland towns passed similar legislation.

In 1879, the national government of El Salvador ordered that lands belonging to municipalities (*tierras ejidales*) and Indian communities (*tierras comunales*) be measured. Roughly one-quarter of the land area of the country at that time was claimed in these two traditional forms of land tenure, a situation growers wanted changed. In March 1879, a national law was passed requiring that municipalities set up nurseries and distribute plants and private titles to those who planted export crops on at least one-fourth of the land area claimed as private. Villages that did not comply would be fined. By September 1880, forty-three more local governments, mostly in the central highlands, had passed similar ordinances.[72] Some communities ignored the national legislation. For example, after the township of Coatepeque passed an ordinance treating its *ejidal* lands as prescribed by national legislation, the Indian community of Coatepeque ignored the national legislation and continued to raise corn and beans even though their communal holdings were deemed more suitable for coffee than the *ejidal* lands of the municipality.[73]

In February 1881, the national government decreed that the communal land system, "which impedes agricultural development, obstructs the circulation of wealth, and weakens family bonds and the independence of the individual," was abolished, and the leaders of the communities were instructed to distribute private titles to individuals who had lands under cultivation, after which those owners could legally sell the lands to third parties. In March 1882, the *ejidal* land system was legally abolished, and users of *ejidal* lands were ordered to apply for titles from the municipality. After payment of a lump sum, a private title was granted and the land was taxed for six consecutive years. Those who did not register for a title within six months and those who could not afford to pay lost all right to the land. Unregistered and uncultivated lands were then put up for public auction to the highest bidder.[74]

As a result of the national legislation, those with access to money were in a favorable position to acquire land, while those without money lost traditional rights to land. Distribution of land was left in the hands of communities and municipalities, leading to widespread confusion and irregularities in carrying out the law.

Especially in the coffee districts, the national legislation accelerated a process already taking place: subsistence farmers, both Indians and *ladinos*, lost land to coffee growers. This privatization of landholding was supported in 1881 by the creation of a national bank that lent money to private landowners; those with influence at the national bank were able to extend their holdings way beyond their own capital base. Furthermore, those with money and political influence had access to lawyers who could effectively petition for land, to surveyors who could measure boundaries, to mayors and judges who could be bribed, and to local police who could be called in to evict prior tenants.[75] In the western part of the country, where coffee growers were expanding most forcefully, peasants resisted by invading coffee estates, setting fire to coffee groves and processing plants, and even cutting off the hands of the agricultural judges in charge of transferring village lands to coffee growers.[76] In 1884, Indians revolted in Izalco and Atiquizaya and in 1885 and 1889 in Cojutepeque.[77] In 1888 municipalities began taxing coffee growers so as to expand and strengthen rural police forces,[78] and in 1889 the national government created a mounted police force to squelch unrest in the coffee departments of Santa Ana, Ahuachapán, and Sonsonate. Later, the mounted police were extended to operate throughout the entire country.[79]

As happened in Guatemala, the necessity of using military force to oust peasants from lands they had traditionally occupied resulted in coffee growers occupying the highest positions within the military and then moving to high positions in the national state. Furthermore, by directing the forces of eviction, military officers were in a key position to expand their own holdings. Some prominent examples of the military connection are General Gerardo Barrios, who was president of El Salvador from 1858 to 1863 and later became a coffee grower in the department of San Miguel; General Francisco Menéndez, who was a prominent grower and mayor of Ahuachapán and became president of El Salvador in 1885; and General Tomás Regalado, who acquired coffee properties in the Santa Ana region and became president of the country in 1898.[80] These cases are parallel to those of General Justo Rufino Barrios and General Manuel Lisandro Barillas, who owned large coffee plantations and were presidents of neighboring Guatemala.

In other respects, however, the coffee land reform was quite different in the two countries. In Guatemala, where a more centralized state accustomed to direct intervention in land tenure was inherited from the colonial period, reinforced by the Carrera dictatorship, and strengthened further after 1873, the land reform was carried out in a relatively organized manner by an agency of the national government that divided potential coffee properties into large lots and sold them, the national government pocketing the proceeds. The national state in El Salvador was slower to evolve into an effective, coherent force. National legislation was passed in El Salvador, but municipalities remained in charge of land auctions and kept the revenue from sales. It was not until 1889 that the national government took any responsibility for distributing *ejidal* and communal lands, and even this responsibility was revoked in 1896.[81] This relative weakness of the national state resulted in enormous confusion over land reform, and the groundswell of opposition from the dispossessed was more difficult to repress in El Salvador than in Guatemala.[82] Also, the Salvadoran land reform was more radical than the Guatemalan, which took land from communities in certain zones but did not make traditional Indian forms of land tenure illegal throughout the entire country. In Guatemala, communities that lost land in the piedmont were often appeased by the national government doling out land in noncoffee areas, but in tiny El Salvador such reserves of land were not available for redistribution. The process of breaking down Salvadoran Indian communities had progressed farther before coffee cultivation began than in Guatemala, but the impact of the coffee boom was more devastating in El Salvador because the remaining Indian population was most heavily concentrated in a zone that was optimal for coffee growing, whereas in Guatemala the Indian population was most heavily concentrated in the highlands, where it was too cold to grow coffee. Thus the Salvadoran land reform was more virulent and harmful to Indian communities than the Guatemalan version.

Precoffee patterns of land tenure and intervention by the national state during the coffee boom left a mark on twentieth-century structures of coffee holding in El Salvador, despite numerous forces of change during the twentieth century. For the country as a whole, the widespread cultivation of indigo, which allowed for small, medium, and large-scale enterprises to coexist, was partially reproduced when coffee became profitable.[83] This mix was reinforced by the decentralized nature of the Liberal reforms after 1880, which allowed greater room for small and medium-sized growers to participate than was generally true in Guatemala, where connections with the national

**Table 3-3. Size Class Analysis of Coffee Farms by Department—
El Salvador, 1939 (*ejidal* lands, 1879)**

Percentage of the Coffee Area in the Department by Size Class

Department	100+ mz.	50+– 100mz	10+– 50mz	1+– 10mz	Up to 1mz	Coffee Mz	*Ejidal* Mz 1879
Santa Ana	28	22	33	15	2	25,607	10,761
Ahuachapán	18	13	42	24	2	11,926	—
Sonsonate	42	11	27	17	3	13,601	50,023
La Libertad	58	15	15	10	1	23,264	58,102
San Salvador	36	17	20	22	6	5,575	23,628
Chalatenango	0	0	0	41	59	124	17,610
Cuscatlán	0	0	29	51	20	1,381	9,522
La Paz	12	29	25	29	5	4,344	—
San Vicente	0	28	43	25	4	926	9,984
Cabañas	0	0	23	60	17	466	8,155
San Miguel	27	19	37	15	2	6,961	—
Usulután	46	15	24	13	1	21,602	38,713
Morazán	31	8	23	27	10	1,184	49,442
La Union	43	22	23	11	1	256	24,172
Total	37	16	27	16	2	117,216	302,795

Sources: Asociación Cafetalera de El Salvador, "Primer censo nacional del café";
Menjívar, *Acumulación originaria*, p. 95.

government, not municipalities, were key in land acquisition. Thus
by the time of the first Salvadoran coffee census (1939), 37 percent
of land in coffee was on large capitalist farms with more than one
hundred *manzanas* (1 *manzana* = 1.73 acres) of coffee as opposed to
more than half of the trees in Guatemala in a similar size class when
the first Guatemalan census was taken; furthermore, peasants and
small family farms had a higher participation rate in coffee cultivation in El Salvador than in neighboring Guatemala (see Table 3-3).[84]

Precoffee patterns of land tenure and the late nineteenth-century
reforms also left traces on the structures of coffee holding within El
Salvador. In the northern zones of the country, where small *ladino*
farmers predominated in indigo production, the few coffee holdings
show up in the first coffee census as having significantly lower participation rates by large capitalist coffee farms and abnormally high
participation rates by peasant and small family operations.[85] Out of

a total of 198 coffee farms registered in Cabañas in 1939, none had more than fifty *manzanas* of coffee, and out of a total of 128 coffee farms in Chalatenango, none had ten *manzanas* or more. Similarly, 77 percent of Cuscatlán's coffee land was on farms with holdings of fewer than ten *manzanas*, reflecting both the precoffee pattern of peasant participation in commercial agriculture and the less suitable soils and climate there.[86] In the areas around San Vicente and San Miguel, where indigo had been grown on a mixture of large, medium, and small farms, the coffee holdings listed in the first coffee census show a similar mix, with lower than the national average participation by very large capitalist farms.[87] In the departments of Santa Ana and Ahuachapán, where *ladinos* gained control over municipal lands before the national land reform was imposed, the first coffee census showed that participation rates by very large capitalist farms were lower than the national average. In contrast, where Indian holdings were taken by force after the national land reform and force was applied (La Libertad and Sonsonate) in the late nineteenth century, large capitalist farms emerged with a significantly larger share of the coffee land than was true for the nation as a whole.[88]

El Salvador's geography made it much easier than elsewhere in Central America to develop transportation networks to link the most suitable coffee zones with the world market. Furthermore, the takeover of land by cattle and indigo haciendas and the intrusion by smaller indigo producers on *ejidal* lands were well advanced in much of the country before coffee came to be cultivated, allowing for a natural privatization of lands around the major towns when coffee became profitable. Coffee's further advance was impeded, however, by Indian communities that were located in some of the areas with the greatest coffee-growing potential. In the early 1880s, coffee growers were able to pressure the national government to enact a radical land reform that called for the abolition of traditional forms of land tenure and the wholesale institution of privately titled property, justified by the successes that had already been achieved in areas where private holdings had evolved. Local coffee growers who moved in to claim these lands were assisted by newly strengthened military and police forces, often under the growers' direct control. A bloody struggle ensued that ended in the privatization of land previously held by some of the country's Indian communities. Both the precoffee patterns of land tenure in the commercialized areas and a protracted struggle in some of the Indian-controlled areas left a lasting imprint on the structures of coffee holding within El Salvador.

Land and the Rise of Coffee in Nicaragua

The first phase of coffee expansion in Nicaragua began in the Southern Uplands, which includes the steeply sloped mountains south of Managua (Sierras de Managua) and the more gently sloped hills of the Carazo Plateau. This zone is composed of rich, recent volcanic soils, fifteen miles wide and thirty miles long, with 80 percent of the land between one thousand and twenty-five hundred feet above sea level and a climate of distinct wet and dry seasons, generally favorable for growing coffee except at lower elevations, where the dry season can become severe. Because of the area's compactness, it was easy enough to carve mule trails and ox cart paths linking coffee farms with commercial towns, though the slopes of more than fifteen degrees in the Sierras de Managua made transport more difficult than on the Carazo Plateau, where half the coffee land is flat and the other half is rarely sloped more than fifteen degrees.[89] In addition to the necessary conditions of soil and climate, this zone was favored for early coffee cultivation because it was located near the colonial commercial center of Granada and the cross-isthmian trade route of Lake Nicaragua and the Río San Juan. Although the entire zone was not developed for commercial use before coffee, commercial agriculture penetrated the area during the colonial period, and after independence a thriving trade in cattle, indigo, and cacao continued. Roads between the major towns had been built before coffee, and the population of the region was already exposed to commercial agriculture. Hence the Southern Uplands was the easiest region for developing coffee culture. In contrast, the North Central Highlands of Matagalpa, Jinotega, and the Segovias did not develop as a coffee zone until the end of the nineteenth century because of greater transportation problems, isolation from traditional centers of commerce, and populations that resisted being converted into a wage labor force.

By the late colonial period, commerce had penetrated southern Nicaragua, where many of the towns were controlled by Spaniards and *ladinos* and remaining Indian communities were a tiny minority. Don Domingo Juarros described Granada in the first years of independence as "a handsome and agreeable city. . . . Close to the lake, by which there is direct communication with the Atlantic, and its contiguity to the Pacific Ocean, affords the most advantageous facilities for carrying on extensive commerce." The population of Granada consisted of "363 European Spaniards and Creoles, 910 Mestizos, 4765 Ladinos, and 1695 Indians, who inhabit a village adjoining." The town of "Nicaragua" (Rivas, twelve leagues southeast of Granada) is described as a center of cacao plantations consisting of a town inhabited by Spaniards with an Indian village adjoining. The one town in southern Nicaragua that Juarros says was dominated by Indians was Masaya, where the population consisted of "6,000 individuals, of which only 83 are Spaniards."[90] After independence, wars disrupted commerce, but southern Nicaragua continued to engage in cattle ranching, especially across Lake Nicaragua in the department of Chontales and along the lower elevations of the Pacific coastal plain.[91] Indigo declined significantly immediately after independence but increased again after the Filibuster War (1855–57), exceeding colonial levels of production by 1865. In southern Nicaragua, indigo was particularly important in Rivas and to a lesser extent in Granada. It was in this context of prior commercialization of agriculture and claims on lands by both haciendas and small *ladino* holdings that southern Nicaragua became the cradle of coffee cultivation in the country (see Map 3-7).

Coffee was cultivated as an exotic plant as early as 1825 in the town of Jinotepe on the Carazo Plateau. When E. G. Squier passed through Nicaragua in 1849, he observed a few estates on the steep slopes of the Sierras de Managua and remarked on the coffee-growing potential of the area.[92] Political strife between the Conservative party, based in the highland town of Granada, and the Liberal party, based in the Pacific coastal plain town of León, retarded interest in long-run investments in crops such as coffee, and the incoherent national state did little to direct infrastructure development.[93] The North American capitalist Cornelius Vanderbilt invested in building a route across southern Nicaragua, and between 1851 and 1855, his company transported from five thousand to twenty-two thousand passengers a year across the isthmus headed to and from the California gold fields. Some researchers have suggested that the travelers who passed through the department of Rivas to the south of the Carazo Plateau stimulated the demand for Nicaraguan coffee. In addition, the increased transport activity gave Nicaraguan merchants contacts who enabled them to expand exports to North America.[94] This flurry of

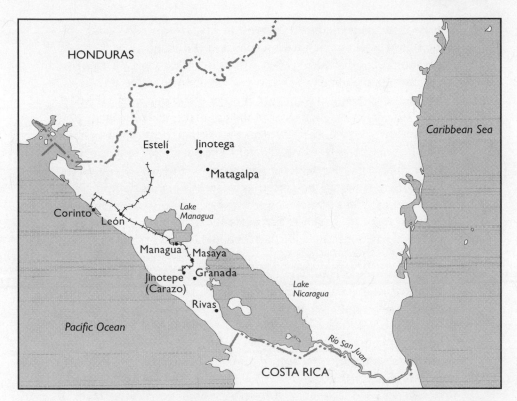

Map 3-7. Nicaragua

commercial activity was disrupted by the intervention of William Walker, who entered with the consent of the Liberals and occupied the Conservative-controlled highlands, burning to the ground the Conservative stronghold of Granada and imposing himself as president of the country. It was only after Walker was ousted and a period of relative political stability begun that the national government was able to take an active role in developing infrastructure that would promote coffee and other commercial crops. During the decade of General Tomás Martínez's rule (1857–67), Granada was rebuilt, a stagecoach road between the Pacific highlands and León was constructed, the Pacific port of Corinto was improved, and prizes promoting coffee cultivation were given. During the seven consecutive Conservative governments following Martínez (1868–93), the national government promoted coffee through further improvements in transportation and new land colonization laws.[95]

By 1867, coffee was being grown on a commercial basis on the

Carazo Plateau and in the department of Rivas (especially on the volcanic island of Omotepe), but the Sierras de Managua was the most important coffee-producing area with 149 coffee farms, 1,148,800 trees, and approximately 2,000 acres devoted to coffee growing.[96] When the road between Managua and León was improved, the port of Corinto came to handle most of the export trade from Managua, while trade from the Carazo Plateau continued to be shipped through Granada, making its way by boat over Lake Nicaragua and down the Río San Juan for Atlantic destinations or to San Juan del Sur on the Pacific.[97] Managua was enhanced as a transshipment point in 1886, when a railroad line was completed from Corinto to Momotombo, a port on Lake Managua thirty miles by steamer from Managua. This was the major route until 1903, when the railroad line was completed between Corinto and Managua. In 1898, Managua drew more of the coffee trade from Granada when a rail line was completed that linked Managua with the towns of Diriamba and Jinotepe on the Carazo Plateau.[98] When the Panama Canal opened, virtually all of Nicaragua's coffee came to be shipped through Corinto, which eclipsed Granada as a transshipment point.

Within Nicaragua, practices of land tenure differed substantially depending on local population pressures, the availability of virgin forests, and local custom. Before the 1870s national laws favored access to unclaimed lands by those who had money and could read Spanish. The process involved staking the boundaries of a claim and having the authorities post the claim publicly for a specified period. If no other claimants came forth, the authorities would grant the land to the person who made the claim after a fee was paid. Full title to the land was not granted in that if it went unused and someone else claimed it, the prior "owner" would lose all rights to it. Peasants in outlying areas where there was an abundant agricultural frontier usually did not go through the trouble or expense of posting a claim with the authorities.[99] Because of the heavy investment that coffee cultivation required, however, large and small growers alike sought the firmest form of land tenure available in an area at the time. Squier's 1849 account indicates that the steep slopes south of Managua were only partially in use before coffee was cultivated there. After Managua became the seat of state power in 1852, the process of claiming land in the Sierras de Managua most likely went through the legal procedure so that those without access to money or the state lost in the scramble; indeed, by 1867 the department of Managua had some 135 cattle haciendas, suggesting that private claims to large blocks of land were well advanced there. In portions of the Carazo Plateau, especially in the department of Masaya, it is unclear from the sources available to what extent Indian communities controlled the land areas suitable for coffee and how those lands came to be claimed by coffee growers, but by 1867 the transition had begun and the district of Masaya had twenty-one coffee farms with 185,000 mature trees and 138,000 saplings in nurseries.[100]

In some ways the north central zone showed greater potential for coffee than the Southern Uplands. The lands suitable for coffee in Matagalpa and Jinotega are at higher altitudes than those in southern Nicaragua so a higher grade of coffee could be produced there. Furthermore, an extended rainy season and numerous rivers and streams created favorable locations for wet-processing of beans and the use of water-driven processing machinery. But the soil in the north central zone consists of older, tertiary volcanic rocks, with only scattered pockets of soil rich enough to sustain coffee cultivation. These geological and meteorological characteristics created a formidable transportation problem. Unlike the Southern Uplands, where an almost continuous table of deep earth covers a land area of only 450 square miles, what became the coffee zone of north central Nicaragua stretches over an area of twenty-eight hundred square miles. The mountainous terrain made it difficult to connect the scattered pockets of coffee land with the merchant towns of Jinotega and Matagalpa, and heavy rains quickly washed out mule trails that were built. After being bagged, the coffee had to travel 115 miles by mule over broken mountain trails from Matagalpa until it reached León, where it could be put on a railroad car and shipped to Corinto.[101]

Far more difficult than the terrain were the people who occupied this area before coffee. Unlike the Southern Uplands, where *ladinos* from the commercial centers of Granada, Rivas, and later, Managua had extended claims over adjacent territories before coffee, the North Central Highlands remained the domain of Indian groups. A national assault on these lands began in 1877 following the Agrarian Reform Law promulgated by Pedro Joaquín Chamorro. The law required that those who worked *ejidal* and communal lands pay from two to five pesos per *manzana* of land to receive freehold title to those lands. If payment were not made, the land could be put up for auction. The law also provided for the sale of national lands in lots up to five hundred *manzanas* (865 acres) for potential cropland and up to two thousand *manzanas* (3,460 acres) for grazing lands.[102] To encourage commercial coffee development in Matagalpa, Jinotega, and the Segovias, in 1877 the national government offered subsidies of five centavos per tree to growers with more than five thousand trees, half of the subsidy payable when the trees were two years old and the other half when they began to bear fruit; this subsidy represented approximately one-half of the cost of planting.[103]

Despite these inducements, investors did not immediately flock to the area, though by 1881 some nine hundred acres had been planted in commercial coffee plantations in the department of Matagalpa, thirty acres of which were in mature coffee trees.[104] The political geographer David Radell cites poor transportation as the main reason for the slow development of this area, but Jeffrey Gould, who examined a wider spectrum of archival sources, argues that the social, economic, and political organization of the Indian communities made it difficult for the national state to control the area or for capitalist agriculture to establish itself there.

It is estimated that in 1881 the Indian population of Matagalpa numbered thirty to thirty-five thousand and held claim to approximately 175,000 acres of land on which many varieties of grains, vegetables, fruits, and livestock were raised.[105] Because the lands of the area were appropriate for coffee cultivation and a large potential labor force was already there, this area was targeted by the national government as a coffee development zone. The Indians were already cultivating some coffee and selling it in the local market, but because Indian production was based on long-run survival, not short-run profit, greater specialization in coffee would have been a slow process, resulting in a highly diversified agriculture, albeit with coffee as a cash crop on the side. As was happening in El Salvador and Guatemala, Nicaraguan elites were beginning to see the Indian communities as an impediment to their view of progress, which was synonymous with specialization according to comparative advantage in the international division of labor. As long as the Indian community remained politically organized, there would be social limits to the degree to which community land and labor could be harnessed for capitalist coffee production.

Although the lands taken into coffee production were not yet squeezing the Indian community of Matagalpa, by the early 1880s attempts by the state to attack the social organization of the Indian community and to draft Indian labor provoked a backlash from the community. On March 30, 1881, one thousand armed Indians attacked government headquarters in Matagalpa, demanding an end to forced labor and an amnesty. During the following five months, hostilities increased between Indians and *ladinos*, and in early August an army of five to seven thousand Indians (with some *ladino* allies) attacked Matagalpa once more. The national army retaliated, and after three months of fighting and one to two thousand Indians killed in battle or executed, the uprising was squelched.[106] Afterward, when the government attempted to bring the communities under military control, thousands fled to the agricultural frontier.

Despite the government's military victory in Matagalpa in 1881, Indian resistance to occupation remained strong, and only late in the decade was the national government able to establish a working relationship with the Indian community that outside investors considered credible. In 1889, when the government of Evaristo Carazo reenacted subsidies to coffee growers (five centavos per tree to those who planted more than 5,000 trees) and offered lots of up to 865 acres of national lands free to those who planted more than 25,000 trees in the region, the response of investors was stronger than it had been to previous promotional efforts. Within two years, some 14,000 acres of national land had been privatized, and several foreign investors were attracted to the region. By 1892 sixteen foreigners had some 700,000 coffee trees out of a total of 3,138,000 trees in Matagalpa and Jinotega, but the production zone was limited to the area controlled by the government, a strip fifteen miles long and two to three miles wide along the road connecting the two towns. Thus, after a decade of supposed domination, capitalist coffee production had only begun to encroach on Indian land and labor in north central Nicaragua, a zone that accounted for only 12 percent of the trees in the country in 1892.[107]

In 1893, thirty-six years of Conservative rule ended and General José Santos Zelaya, son of the Managua coffee planter Santos Francisco Zelaya, took power.[108] During his sixteen-year rule (1893–1909), Zelaya passed land and labor codes designed to promote coffee, and the military cracked down on Indian resistance, which included sporadic acts of violence such as the assassination of the largest coffee grower in the area, William Jericho, and the resurgence of a mass political movement in 1895. Land claims in Matagalpa had averaged 1.6 per year under Conservative rule, but under Zelaya they rose to 6.1 per year. Those who received land were primarily members of the Liberal elite loyal to Zelaya, though some Conservative families were awarded land. In 1898, the national government finally took control over administrative divisions of the Indian community, replacing elected officials and captains by the department governor's appointees. The presence of political appointees weakened the ability of communities to resist the takeover of lands, though resistance continued under Zelaya, finding other means of expression. By 1900, there were some seventy coffee farms in Matagalpa, and in the following years this number increased. Gould estimates that between 1895 and 1911, the Indian community of Matagalpa lost more than 10 percent of its holdings to expanding coffee plantations.[109]

When the first coffee census was taken in 1909, the northern departments of Matagalpa, Jinotega, Nueva Segovia, and Estelí had 29 percent of the trees in the country, and the old coffee region of the Southern Uplands (Managua, Masaya, Carazo, and Granada) had 68 percent, with Managua maintaining its lead role with a 38 percent share.[110] The portion of the land area devoted to coffee on the farms surveyed was 20 percent on the average for the country, but in the Southern Uplands, where the land is more homogeneously suited for coffee, specialization was greater than in the rest of the country, with 42 percent of the farm area devoted to coffee in Carazo, 41 percent in Masaya, and 36 percent in Managua (see Table 3-4).[111]

A size class analysis reveals that for the country as a whole, capitalist farms (those requiring hired labor for permanent maintenance and picking) had 81 percent of the trees in the census sample, while family-sized farms (those requiring outside workers only for the harvest) had 16 percent of the trees, and peasant farms (those requiring no outside labor either for maintenance or the harvest) had only 3 percent.[112] Fifty-three large capitalist farms, each with more than one hundred thousand trees, had 30 percent of the trees in the country, according to the census figures.

The structures of coffee holding by size class varied significantly by department. The greatest concentration of trees on large capitalist farms was in the department of Managua, where 40 percent of the trees were in farms with more than one hundred thousand trees each, while noncapitalist farms had only 6 percent of the department's trees, the lowest participation rate by small producers in the country. Granada had the second highest concentration of trees on large capitalist farms (37 percent) and lower than average participation by noncapitalist farms (16 percent). This high concentration in capital-

**Table 3-4. Size Class Analysis of Coffee Farms by Department—
Nicaragua, 1909**

Department	Percentage of Trees in the Department by Size Class				
	100k+	50k–99k	20k–49k	5k–19k	<5k
Granada	36.8	32.4	14.8	8.4	7.6
Rivas	0.0	23.6	47.7	19.0	9.7
Nueva Segovia	0.0	10.8	9.8	41.1	38.3
Estelí	0.0	0.0	56.7	36.7	6.7
Jinotega	28.0	27.4	26.5	16.9	1.1
Masaya	0.0	7.7	28.2	44.9	19.1
Chinandega	0.0	19.5	40.6	34.4	5.5
León	0.0	0.0	0.0	66.7	33.3
Jeréz	28.1	0.0	38.6	27.0	6.3
Matagalpa	26.1	32.3	31.0	10.1	0.3
Managua	40.1	30.0	23.7	6.0	0.2
Carazo	28.1	21.0	19.6	28.9	2.4
Total	30.1	25.7	25.1	16.1	2.9

Source: República de Nicaragua, "Censo Cafetalero de 1909."

ist enterprises, however, was not true for the Southern Uplands as a whole. Masaya had only 9 capitalist-sized farms out of a total of 129 coffee farms, and the noncapitalist coffee growers controlled 64 percent of the trees in the department. Carazo had farms in all size classes but had lower than average participation rates by capitalist farms; noncapitalist farms controlled 31 percent of the trees in the department. David Radell reasons that because of the steep slopes of the Sierras de Managua larger capital expenditures were required to construct water collection facilities and terraces for processing coffee than on the gentler slopes of the Carazo Plateau; this gave the larger units a competitive advantage over smaller units. Furthermore, because of better transportation on the flatter Carazo Plateau, small producers could avoid the high capital costs of water processing by hauling their ripe berries on ox carts for sale to central processing facilities on the larger farms and in nearby towns.[113]

This geographically determined explanation suffers from several problems. For the argument to be supported, the major source of scale economy, the water collection tank, should have been the dominant technology at the time when the large Managua plantations formed, but most of the coffee from the Southern Uplands was processed by the "dry" method when the census was taken in 1909, obviating the need for expensive water-holding tanks; even by World War II only half of the coffee from the Sierras de Managua was being processed by the "wet" method.[114] If flatness of land favored small producers, the explanation cannot account for the very high concentration of holdings in Granada, which has similar coffee land to that of neighboring Masaya, where noncapitalist farms predominated in 1909. Conceptually, the argument of steepness of slope and scale economies in processing makes sense in the theoretical framework of a perfectly competitive market for land. Historically, such a free market for land did not exist anywhere in Central America; as this chapter has documented, the market for land in Nicaragua and elsewhere was highly conditioned by precoffee land use and land tenure relationships and by political struggles as the coffee boom progressed. To explain the variegated structures of coffee holding on the Southern Uplands, a study of the region needs to be done along the lines of Jeffrey Gould's study of Chinandega, which incorporates published documents along with oral testimonies to establish the evolution of land tenure and labor relations in that area.[115]

Without such careful documentation, we can only hypothesize that the Indian community of Masaya, through resistance and adaptation to advances of capitalist agriculture, played a significant role in shaping the outcome of landholding structures in that department. It is known that colonial administrations had accommodated to the Dirian Indian–controlled communities of Monimbó (Masaya), Nindirí, Ticuantepe, and Niquinohomo, all in what later became the department of Masaya. Sections of the Carazo Plateau, starting in the department of Masaya, was and still is referred to as the "Meseta de los Pueblos," which implies that Indian communities occupied the plateau at one time, and artisans from the community of Monimbó still produce a variety of traditional crafts for the market in Masaya. When the Matagalpa Indians rose up in arms against state intrusions in 1881, there were simultaneous uprisings by the Indian communities in both Masaya and Subtiava (near León). Perhaps because of the deeper history of Conservative accommodation to the Indian community of Masaya, there is no record (to my knowledge) of the sort of slaughter that occurred in distant Matagalpa, and the carving

of Masaya as a separate department from Granada in 1883 may have been in response to Dirian resistance in 1881.[116] Even after the Liberal reforms of the 1890s, in 1898 Masaya was an Indian town of 15,000 persons, a larger population than that of Granada (12,600).[117] In the 1909 coffee census, with few exceptions, the owners' surnames in Masaya appear to be common *ladino* names, but this is not a good indicator because, unlike Guatemala, Indians in Nicaragua at this time frequently had Spanish surnames.[118] There may have been a slow *ladino* encroachment on *ejidal* lands before the 1909 census, which would help explain the preponderance of smallholdings, but the massive assault that occurred in Matagalpa does not appear to have happened in Masaya.[119] In contrast, the concentration of large holdings in the neighboring department of Granada makes sense because previously Granada and environs had been controlled by a merchant-landowner elite. Before 1852, Managua was an old Indian town, but Squier's account indicates that much of the land on the Sierras de Managua was still in forest with a few coffee plantations already established; after Managua became the capital city in 1852, it is likely that the presence of a central state apparatus and the influx of *ladinos* would have overwhelmed an Indian community's ability to control the destiny of land use and land tenure around the town. The department of Carazo remained under the jurisdiction of Granada until 1891; some of the largest coffee farms in the country were located there by 1909, but the precoffee patterns of land tenure probably allowed smallholders to continue to farm when coffee moved in.

When the military occupation of Matagalpa and Jinotega occurred following the 1881 war, capitalist coffee farms were favored over peasant and family-sized holdings; Jeffrey Gould, who is familiar with the family names of Indians in the Matagalpa region, found no Indian names listed in the 1909 coffee census for that area, though some Indians who were growing coffee for home use and sale in the local market could have escaped the census takers. One area of the country where the state was unable to penetrate effectively was in the Segovias near the Honduran border (now Nueva Segovia and Madriz), an area with poorly developed infrastructure and scattered small farms. In 1909, the census takers registered 161 coffee farms in the department, 86 percent of them peasant-sized operations with fewer than five thousand trees. The non-capitalist farms with fewer

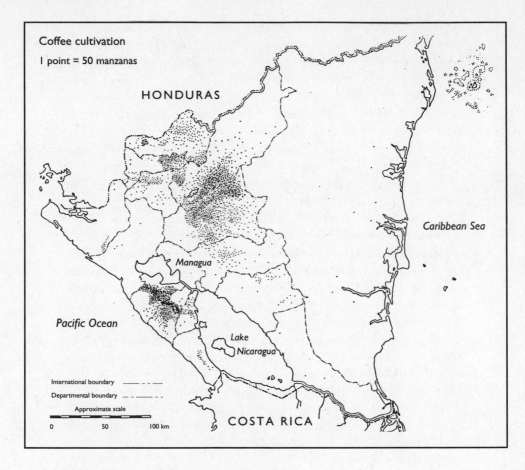

Map 3-8. Coffee Areas of Nicaragua, 1962–1963.
Source: Dirección General de Estadísticos y Censos, *Censo agropecuario de 1962–63*, Graph 9.

than 20,000 trees had 79 percent of the trees in the department, the greatest participation by small farms of any important coffee department in the country.[120]

As elsewhere in Central America, coffee and private titles with carefully delineated boundaries went hand in hand, leaving a lasting legacy on patterns of land tenure in the country. By the time of the 1962–63 agricultural census, coffee cultivation had spread through sections of Matagalpa, Jinotega, Madriz, and Nueva Segovia departments, which accounted for 57 percent of Nicaragua's coffee production that year. In the *municipios* of Matagalpa and Jinotega, where the bulk of the coffee was grown, *ejidal* properties had been virtually wiped out by the time the census was taken, while in low coffee-production departments such as Boaco and Chontales, *ejidal* holdings still accounted for more than one-fifth of the land in farms (see Map 3-8).[121] In the non-coffee-producing eastern *municipios* in the departments of Matagalpa and Jinotega, where peasants eked out a living on the agricultural frontier, much of the land was occupied without title. In contrast, the area of the Southern Uplands, including Masaya, was almost completely privately titled by the time of the 1962–63 census, with very low rates of *ejidal* land tenure and 2 percent or less of the land occupied without title.[122]

The development of coffee production in Nicaragua took place unevenly, beginning in the Southern Uplands in the 1860s and spreading to the north central highlands by the late nineteenth century. In the Southern Uplands the coffee boom took place smoothly without major transportation problems or social unrest because of the previous development of commercial agriculture in the area, but in the north central region, Indians resisted intrusions by the national state, whose leadership in the early 1880s consciously sought to develop the area for coffee production. After a war and a decade of military occupation to pacify the area, capital began to move into the north central region in the late 1880s and 1890s, claiming Indian lands and labor for coffee production. Everywhere coffee spread, the dominant tendency was for national, *ejidal*, and communal lands to be converted into privately titled property, and the national government assisted in the transformation through a series of land laws, production incentives, and coercion. The structures of private holdings that emerged with coffee, however, reflected both the precoffee patterns of land tenure and the way the state intervened in the process. Nicaragua emerged as second only to Guatemala in concentration of coffee in large capitalist plantations, but in certain areas of the country peasants were able to maintain control over lands and participated heavily in coffee growing.

Land and the Rise of Coffee in Honduras

Of the five Central American countries, Honduras faced the most formidable geographical obstacles to the development of coffee. As in Nicaragua's north central section, the lands suitable for growing coffee in Honduras are not recent volcanics but have a base of tertiary volcanic rocks. Especially in high valleys, where organic matter has collected over the ages, there are some excellent lands for growing coffee, but these pockets are scattered over an area of twenty-four thousand square miles, mostly in the western half of the country. Deep canyons and rocky peaks divide coffee areas from each other and make transportation to ports extremely difficult. Until the 1960s and 1970s the Honduran state was unable to develop a road network that would adequately service the coffee economy.

Geography only partially explains why the Honduran government was so late to develop an infrastructure for coffee. The pattern was set in the colonial era for functionaries of the state to enrich themselves by granting mining and timber concessions to foreign enterprises. Furthermore, the merchant class of Honduras was more accustomed to collecting deer hides, sarsaparilla roots, gold dust, vanilla, bananas, and indigo from hunter-gatherers or peasant cultivators than investing capital directly into the cultivation of items for export. What capital was invested in agriculture was in herds of cattle, which roamed over vast areas of untended grassland. When railroads were being constructed through the coffee zones of the other four countries, there was no class of young coffee entrepreneurs in Honduras to pressure the state to serve its interests. Instead, government officials granted vast tracts of land in the north of the country to railroad companies and in return were able to skim personal fortunes from the British loans that flowed in for the railroad. By 1912, Honduras had less than twenty miles of railroad track and the highest per capita national debt in the world.[123] When railroads were finally built, they serviced the fruit company concessions in the north of the country, not the coffee sector in the western and central highlands (see Map 3-9).

As in other countries, Liberals took control in Honduras, and they passed laws intended to stimulate commercial agriculture. With the help of General Justo Rufino Barrios of Guatemala, Ramón Rosa and Marco Aurelio Soto came to power in 1876. That same year church property was expropriated, and *diezmos* were abolished. On April 29, 1877, the Decree for the Development of Agriculture was passed, exempting from military service anyone who cultivated five *manzanas* (8.65 acres) of coffee, ten *manzanas* (17.3 acres) of sugarcane, or eight *manzanas* (13.84 acres) of cacao or indigo. Tax ex-

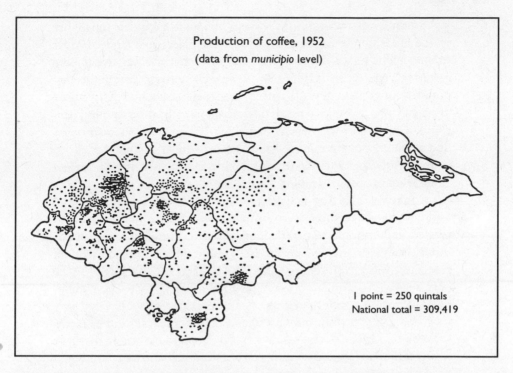

Production of coffee, 1952
(data from *municipio* level)

1 point = 250 quintals
National total = 309,419

Map 3-9. Coffee Areas of Honduras, 1952.
Source: Dirección General de Censos y Estadísticas, *Censo agropecuario de 1952*, p. 23.

emptions were granted on imported tools, fertilizer, seeds, and other agricultural inputs, and the law included an incentive to cultivate land. National lands that had been acquired as private property and *ejidal* and communal lands that had been rented to individuals were to be returned to the national state, the municipalities, or the Indian communities if they remained uncultivated one year following the passage of the law.[124]

The Honduran land law differed from Liberal legislation elsewhere in that it did not directly attack the rights of communities and municipalities to hold and distribute land; rather it encouraged them to make use of existing holdings, maintaining the same land tenure relationships as before. The national government continued to do what it had been doing since at least 1836: granting up to seventy-eight hundred acres free to municipalities that could prove the land would be used and selling national land to individuals as private property. Throughout the country municipalities, communities, and private individuals tended to register lands in a legal manner, but in the areas where coffee cultivation took place, this tendency was greatly accentuated. The two most important coffee departments in 1914–15 were Santa Bárbara and Comayagua, which together accounted for 52 percent of the coffee acreage in the country.[125] Between 1850 and 1899 these two departments out of a total sixteen in Honduras accounted for 39 percent of the *ejidal* property registrations and 32 percent of the country's private property registrations.[126]

Because of poor transportation networks, it was difficult for the Liberals who occupied high government offices to transform agriculture in the manner they may have wished. Decisions regarding land and who had access to it were left to the local municipalities, which tended to preserve traditional rights. Thus the coffee boom was less intense and less oriented toward the export trade in Honduras than elsewhere in Central America, and small farmers participated in the coffee sector to a much greater extent than in El Salvador, Guatemala, Nicaragua, or even Costa Rica (see Table 3-5).

When a survey of farms was taken in 1914–15, 1,143 coffee farms were listed with an average of fifteen acres planted in coffee trees per farm. In a highly unusual situation for Central America, only one-fourth of Honduran coffee farms at that time were on privately titled properties, the great majority being rented from the *ejidal* holdings of municipalities, occupied without title on national lands, or distributed by Indian communities from communal holdings. Two-thirds of the land devoted to coffee in the survey was either peasant farms with fewer than five *manzanas* of coffee (11 percent of the land in coffee) or family-sized enterprises with holdings between five and nineteen *manzanas* (56 percent of the land in coffee). Of the 83 capitalist-sized coffee farms in Honduras, 70 were small capitalist enterprises with twenty to forty-nine *manzanas* of coffee, representing 19 percent of the land in coffee, the largest portion for capitalist-sized enterprises. In the entire country there were only 5 large capitalist coffee farms with one hundred *manzanas* (173 acres) or more of coffee; four of these estates were privately titled.

The general pattern of landholding in Honduran coffee production was reflected in Santa Bárbara and Comayagua, the first and second most important coffee departments in 1914–15. In Santa Bárbara, where 34 percent of Honduras's coffee land was located, only 13 percent of the coffee farms were privately titled and three of the five

Table 3-5. Size Class Analysis of Coffee Farms by Department—Honduras, 1914–1915

	Percentage of Coffee Land in Department by Size Class					
Department	100+ mz.	50–99 mz.	20–49 mz.	5–19 mz.	<5mz.	% total coffee
Tegucigalpa	0.0	0.0	45.1	45.5	9.5	2.4
El Paraíso	0.0	24.0	17.5	38.0	20.5	5.5
Choluteca	53.9	5.6	11.9	24.4	4.7	14.4
Valle	0.0	0.0	0.0	0.0	100.0	0.0
Comayagua	0.0	0.0	36.2	51.7	12.1	17.7
La Paz	0.0	0.0	0.0	68.1	31.9	2.5
Intibucá	0.0	0.0	0.0	28.0	72.0	0.9
Santa Barbara	4.4	6.6	17.7	71.1	0.2	34.3
Grácias	0.0	0.0	0.0	54.3	45.7	2.7
Copán	0.0	0.0	0.0	24.0	76.0	2.2
Ocotepéque	0.0	0.0	0.0	45.5	54.5	2.3
Yoro	0.0	7.4	28.9	60.0	3.7	7.1
Cortés	0.0	0.0	5.3	87.7	6.9	3.8
Atlántida	0.0	0.0	0.0	0.0	100.0	0.2
Colón	0.0	0.0	0.0	100	0.0	0.2
Olancho	26.4	0.0	5.3	66.8	1.6	3.8
Islas de la Bahía						0.0
Total	10.3	4.9	18.7	55.5	10.6	100.0

Source: República de Honduras, *Memoria de fomento, 1914–1915.*

largest farms were still under the *ejidal* form of land tenure; family-sized farms controlled 71 percent of the department's coffee land. One of the large farms on *ejidal* land, operated by Herbert Howard, was the second largest coffee farm in Honduras with 150 *manzanas* (260 acres) of coffee. Similarly, in Comayagua, where 17 percent of the country's coffee land was located, only one-fifth of the coffee farms were privately titled, and the four largest farms, each with about 70 acres of coffee, were under the *ejidal* form of land tenure. In less important coffee departments in western Honduras, peasant and family-sized farms had greater overall participation than in Santa Bárbara and Comayagua. In Ocotepeque, Gracias (now Lempira),

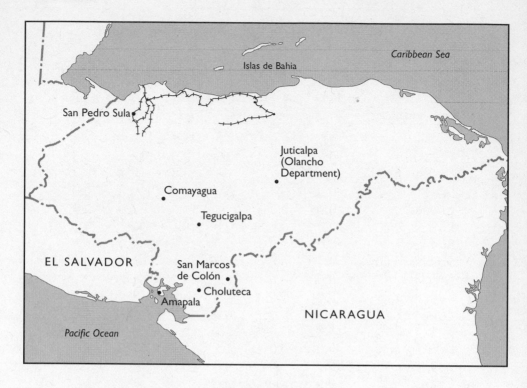

Map 3-10. Honduras

Intibucá, La Paz, and Copán, (each with approximately 2 percent of the country's land in coffee), all of the land in coffee was on peasant or family-sized holdings (see Map 3-10).

Choluteca, the third most important coffee department in 1914–15, is an anomaly for Honduras in the degree to which capitalist relations of production penetrated the coffee sector. When the 1914–15 farm survey was taken, three-fourths of Choluteca's coffee farms were privately titled holdings, the highest proportion in Honduras at that time, and the average sized holding was thirty acres of coffee, twice the national average. In Choluteca, 54 percent of the coffee land listed in the survey was controlled by large capitalist enterprises with one hundred *manzanas* or more of coffee, a concentration in large plantations more characteristic of Guatemala than Honduras, though peasant and family-sized farms made up a higher percentage (28 percent) of the land in coffee than the average for Guatemala. Although small farmers still controlled certain *municipios* in Choluteca, the structure of landholding in the important coffee *municipios* more resembles the pattern of neighboring El Salvador or Guatemala with large private holdings and merchants directly involved in the cultivation phase than it does for the rest of Honduras. One reason why capital could more easily penetrate the coffee sector of Choluteca was the proximity of its best coffee lands to port. San Marcos de Colón, Choluteca's most important coffee *municipio*, is thirty miles and El Corpus, the second most important, is only fifteen miles from the commercial center of Choluteca, where coffee could be shipped on the Choluteca River to the port of Amapala on the Gulf of Fonseca. More important, commercial agriculture had already been established in this area before coffee. In the seventeenth and eighteenth centuries, San Marcos de Colón and El Corpus had haciendas that supplied mules, oxen, and beef to the gold mines in El Corpus. Gold mining declined in the late eighteenth century, but in the late nineteenth century this area became one of the richest in Honduras as a community of enterprising landowners and merchants began investing in improved pasture grasses, dairy and beef cattle, sugarcane, rubber, cacao, and, finally, coffee. In addition to sales through Amapala, export commodities, including several types of cheese, were shipped north to El Salvador and south to Nicaragua.[127] In neighboring *municipios*, land continued to be held in communal and *ejidal* forms in 1914–15, but in these two capitalist *municipios* there were only four farms on *ejidal* or communal lands out of a total of sixty-seven farms listed in the survey. The largest coffee farm in Honduras, located in San Marcos de Colón, had 500 *manzanas* (865 acres) of coffee and was owned by Pedro Abadíe, a merchant with stores in San Marcos de Colón and the port of Amapala. The third largest farm in the country, located in the neighboring *municipio* of El Corpus, had 140 *manzanas* (242 acres) of coffee and was owned by Enrique Köhncke, a German merchant whose investments included a soft drink factory. Another merchant from San Marcos de Colón, Hipólito Agasse, had invested in 30 *manzanas* (52 acres) of coffee. The other large coffee farms in this area were owned by older landholding families, all of whom had private titles to their lands.[128]

Capitalist agriculture penetrated the Honduran coffee economy during the nineteenth century, but it did best in areas that had already been carved out for haciendas. Most of the land suitable for coffee, however, was located in areas previously dominated by peasant agriculture. In the richest coffee areas (Santa Bárbara and Coma-yagua) capitalist farms found a minority niche within the peasant economy. Because the national state was unable (and, perhaps, un-willing at times) to intervene on their behalf, capitalists investing in coffee had to go through local institutions to gain access to land. This meant, among other things, renting land from the *ejidal* hold-ings of municipalities, a situation that capitalist farmers in the rest of Central America had been able to change many decades before with the assistance of national land laws and enforcement agencies.

Comparisons and Conclusions

The lay of the land is crucial for understanding the geographical spread of coffee cultivation, which required adequate rainfall and well-drained, fertile soils at elevations between one thousand and five thousand feet. These conditions were met both in areas of re-cent volcanic activity and in older mountainous zones where de-posits of organic matter had accumulated. The areas blessed by re-cent volcanic activity had certain advantages over other potential coffee lands, and throughout Central America, these were where cof-fee cultivation developed first. The key advantage was not so much superior fertility of the soil. Rather, the areas of recent volcanic ac-tivity tended to have larger concentrations of suitable soil, allowing for the continuous planting of coffee groves without major breaks, facilitating access and lowering costs of transport. In such areas a single road could serve many coffee farms, and growers could pur-chase supplies and obtain labor from nearby towns. Furthermore, at harvest time it was easier in the concentrated districts to transport mature beans to centrally located *beneficios* and to ship dried cof-fee from *beneficios* to export houses. This provides one explanation why coffee cultivation developed much sooner in the Central Valley of Costa Rica, the Carazo Plateau and hills south of Managua, and the Pacific piedmonts of Guatemala and El Salvador than in areas of northern Nicaragua and Honduras, where it developed later on the disconnected patches of older volcanic soils.

Even in the more easily accessible areas, geography was an ob-stacle, and growers began to take collective action to improve infra-structure between high quality coffee lands and commercial centers and between commercial centers and ports. The task was easiest where prime coffee land was located close to already established merchant centers and ports, and in those cases commercial interests worked together to lower transport costs by fostering better roads, bridges, railroads, and docks. Sometimes collective action took the form of a voluntary organization that financed the construction, but as the century progressed major townships, department governments, and, ultimately, national states began to intervene to surmount the geographical obstacles to coffee's advance. At first, coffee growers and exporters benefited indirectly from public goods that had been constructed with other commercial interests in mind, but after coffee became the most important export, infrastructure projects were planned with coffee as the prime motivation. Except for Honduras, the major coffee-growing zones came to be serviced by roads, bridges, and railroad networks to the neglect of areas unsuitable for coffee.

Sometimes the social customs surrounding rights to land created obstacles more difficult than geographical constraints. Because of the heavy investment required and the long delay between planting a grove and the first harvest, investors desired the most secure form of land tenure possible, one that would allow for eventual sale of the property before capital and effort were put into establishing a coffee farm. The traditional form of land tenure that was most amenable to long-term capital improvements was the hacienda, a private claim on a land area the rights to which could be sold to another individual. Before coffee, however, the boundaries of haciendas were often vague and rarely surveyed, leading to disputes between hacienda owners and between villages and neighboring haciendas. Because of the large investment required to establish a grove, coffee's introduction raised the stakes in boundary disputes. Therefore, if a section of an hacienda was suitable for growing coffee, it behooved the owner to make sure that the land was surveyed and duly registered with the authorities before investing. The transition from hacienda to privately titled coffee farm was relatively easy because it involved a minor modification to a preexisting social practice. The key problem for haciendas was not in establishing a secure claim to the land but in obtaining a labor force to work it.

The potential coffee lands close to established population centers were the most favorable with respect to access to labor and other commodity inputs, but securing private, long-term claims to these lands was encumbered by townships and villages that traditionally controlled their distribution. The amount of land under municipal control varied considerably depending on size of population and previous grants from higher authorities, but the rule of thumb was control over a radius of approximately 1.5 miles from the center of town. Thus during the early phases of the coffee boom, obtaining title to some of the most attractive potential coffee land was a political act at the township or community level. The ease with which the act could be accomplished depended on structures of governance in the particular locale and the individual grower's access to those structures. The municipalities where coffee growers faced the fewest social obstacles to land access were those where commercial agriculture was already well advanced and commercial elites were involved in town governance. Every country in Central America (including Honduras) had examples of highly commercialized townships that transferred land to private individuals during the late nineteenth century. Some townships topped the transfer with free coffee seedlings and tax exemptions to encourage investment in coffee.

Growers faced greater difficulties securing land in communities where commercial relations were poorly developed and political structures were protective of traditional customs regarding access to land. If lands were particularly suitable for coffee, outsiders could sometimes rent idle *ejidal* or communal holdings from a township or an Indian community, providing a source of income for local government institutions, but the grower's claim was subject to the whims of the local power structure. As more idle lands were taken, the traditional practice of shifting cultivation, which requires periodic fallowing, was threatened, and when growers bypassed local authorities by selling coffee lands to other private individuals,[129] clashes sometimes occurred between outsiders and members of a community. Capitalist coffee growers sought assistance from higher levels of government, either at the departmental or national level, to validate their existing claims. Thus a political struggle over land rights began at the municipal level and proceeded to departmental and national levels of government. Growers could lobby at the national level for legislation that would invalidate claims by traditional communities, at least in the areas where coffee potential was greatest, and work for legislation favoring the commercial development of outlying areas that fell within the national domain. Where the new laws met with resistance, growers pushed for the development of a coercive apparatus that would impose penalties on those who operated outside of the new law.

The nature of the struggles over land differed. In Costa Rica, the transition was generally peaceful. The town of San José initiated municipal legislation, which was later followed by national legislation that favored privately titled holdings in newly colonized areas. In Honduras, the national government was incapable of carrying out a land reform throughout the nineteenth century, and local political structures continued to govern land tenure relationships. Because commercial elites were an ineffective minority throughout most of the coffee-growing region, developers of capitalist farms had to abide by local customs and rent *ejidal* lands from municipalities. The exception in Honduras was in the department of Choluteca, where capitalist agriculture preceded the introduction of coffee, and the more commercialized townships privatized the surrounding lands. In Guatemala, El Salvador, and Nicaragua, struggles over land took on a strong ethnic dimension. Previously commercialized areas converted to coffee cultivation in a smooth, peaceful fashion, but when coffee extended into areas controlled by Indian communities, conflicts erupted. Early in the period, national governments were unwilling to intervene on behalf of growers, but later in the century national laws were passed that were designed to give commercial interests the upper hand. In Nicaragua and El Salvador, Indian resistance was strong and the conversion process was bloodier than in Guatemala, which by the mid-1870s had a greatly strengthened military, a situation not shared by El Salvador until the 1880s or Nicaragua until the 1890s. Furthermore, in Guatemala many of the Indian claims in the coffee piedmont were distant from highland communities, and the Barrios government, wishing to prevent a repetition of the revolt against Liberal reforms in the 1830s, judiciously traded highland communities more certain claims closer to their villages for the traditionally looser claims those communities had in the coffee belt, thereby avoiding a frontal attack on the Indian way of life. In El Salvador and Nicaragua, potential coffee lands surrounded Indian population centers, and the reforms in both countries directly attacked traditional Indian rights, provoking a more violent response by the communities involved than in Guatemala.

The extremely varied structures of landholding that emerged in Central American coffee production depended primarily on precoffee customs regarding land use in particular locales. In all the countries, haciendas with suitable land were generally kept intact as large plantations when the conversion to coffee occurred. When coffee censuses were taken later, the areas within countries where hacienda agriculture preceded coffee had more top-heavy distributions of coffee holdings than the national averages. This pattern occurred in every country, and it is especially striking in Choluteca, Honduras, and the *cantones* to the east of Cartago (and smaller sections of the provinces of San José and Heredia), Costa Rica, which were pre-coffee hacienda zones that resulted in abnormally top-heavy coffee distributions within countries where the national average distributions of landholding in coffee were less top-heavy than elsewhere. Where coffee superseded previous commercial crops, the size distributions of landholding in coffee reflect the size distributions in the previous commercial crops. In sections of El Salvador where indigo was raised on a mixture of large, medium, and small farms, a similar configuration of coffee holdings emerged later, whereas sections in the north of the country, where peasants raised indigo on small plots, coffee holdings came to be dominated by peasant and family-sized farms, an anomaly to the national average. In Guatemala, the districts around Antigua and Amatitlán, where cochineal was grown on small and medium-sized farms before coffee, there emerged a much higher participation of peasant and family-sized coffee holdings than became the norm for Guatemala. Likewise, around the townships of the Central Valley of Costa Rica and the Western Highlands of Honduras, where *ejidal* lands were rented to households, peasant and family-sized farms emerged as the norm when coffee was introduced, though in Honduras they retained their *ejidal* form while in Costa Rica they were privatized.

Although the overall record points to the resilience of local customs and structures of land distribution, once national states developed the capability to intervene, landholding structures in the areas targeted for action were imprinted by the state policies, sometimes overcoming local traditions. The land colonization laws of Costa Rica set upper limits on the amount of land a single individual could obtain and later allowed title to smallholders based solely on "peaceful occupation" for a certain number of years, thereby projecting into unsettled areas the landholding patterns that existed around San José. In Guatemala, El Salvador, and Nicaragua, the coffee zones previously controlled by Indian groups became real estate development tracts, and national governments played the role of developer, dividing the area into lots exceeding one hundred acres, providing infrastructure, offering police protection, and selling the lots to private capitalists. Thus areas previously controlled by Indian communities were turned into privately titled coffee plantations with a more top-heavy distribution of holdings than was true on average for the three countries.

Geographical conditions, preexisting land tenure relationships, and the uneven ability of governments to provide infrastructure, favorable land laws, and an enforcement apparatus influenced when and where coffee cultivation took hold. Both precoffee patterns of landholding and the way governments intervened to promote the crop influenced the structures of coffee landholding, relationships that persist in only slightly altered form today. As the next chapter will demonstrate, labor in the nineteenth century was in much shorter supply than land; how the labor problem was solved had even deeper consequences.

Chapter 4

Labor and the Coffee Boom

Without people to work the land, Central America's coffee boom could never have happened. Coffee is more labor-intensive than subsistence crops and most alternative export crops, requiring approximately five times the labor per acre needed for beans, three times that for corn, and twice that for sugar or cotton.[1] These comparisons are for cultivation, maintenance, and harvesting of already established farms and do not include start-up expenditures (see Figure 4-1).

To get a coffee farm to a mature state takes an enormous amount of work for five or six years, a longer gestation period than for other Central American crops. At the start, cherries from the best existing trees are selected, pulped by hand, and left in the shade to dry. Later, these seeds are germinated and planted thickly in a seedbed, where they are kept moist and protected from the sun. After three months, the seedlings are taken to a nursery, where they are separated and planted in a sandy soil with manure or compost added. If rainfall is inadequate, the seedlings are watered, and they are protected from excessive sunlight, winds, and damaging pests. Approximately 15 percent of the labor costs of setting up a plantation are typically spent germinating seeds and caring for seedlings in the nursery.

After a year in the nursery, the seedlings are ready to be transplanted. The fields are prepared by clearing the land of trees and rocks and drawing grids marking the places where holes are to be dug. Where necessary, shade trees are planted. Holes are dug and compost is added. Seedlings are taken from the nursery with root balls intact and planted in the holes with great care to ensure that the taproots go straight down into soft soil. If there is no rain, the saplings are watered. Throughout the first year in the fields, weeds must be controlled and shade must be managed to guarantee healthy

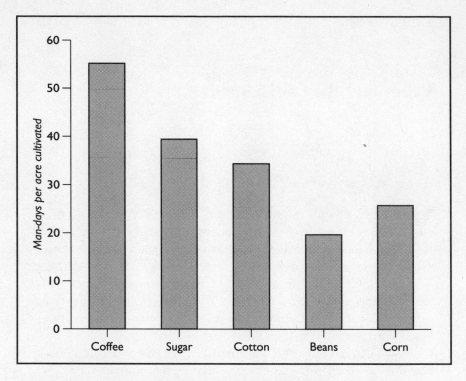

Figure 4-1. Average Labor Requirements for Different Crops in Central America, 1960s.
Source: SIECA, *Desarrollo integrado*, vol. 5, table 30, p. 74.

growth of the young plants. Because of the heavy labor involved in preparing the fields and planting, the first year out of the nursery takes almost 40 percent of the total labor to establish a coffee plantation (see Figure 4-2).

During the following four years, weeding requires the largest labor outlay, though some labor is expended fertilizing, controlling diseases and pests, and replacing unhealthy trees. In the third and fourth years, small harvests can be expected, and by the fifth year, almost as much labor is spent picking the crop as weeding the groves. It is estimated that to establish a mature coffee farm, approximately 278 man-days of labor are needed for each acre of trees planted.[2]

Once coffee trees mature, the greatest amount of labor is spent picking the crop, which can account for between one-third and one-half of the total labor needs for the year. In addition, groves should be weeded once or twice a year, coffee trees should be severely

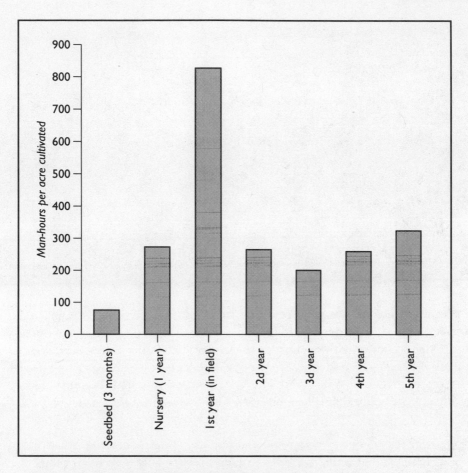

Figure 4-2. Labor Required to Establish a Coffee Farm.
Source: United Nations Food and Agriculture Organization, *Coffee in Latin America*, Table 16, p. 122.

pruned every sixth or seventh year, shade trees should be pruned to maintain a homogeneous canopy, fertilizer should be applied, low-productivity trees should be replaced, and pests should be controlled. It was estimated that in El Salvador in 1954 normal maintenance and picking required seventy-eight man-days per acre on an average mature coffee farm, though the amount of labor expended varies depending on relative scarcities of labor, land, and capital.[3]

If the labor needs could be spread evenly over the year, the problem would not be so severe. Along the Pacific slopes, where there are distinct wet and dry seasons, the harvest is concentrated in the

"Weeding and Protecting the Young Coffee Plant from the Sun, Antigua"
Department of Sacatepéquez, 1875. In my fieldwork in 1987, I toured a nursery
for coffee seedlings within ten miles of the spot where this photograph was
taken. A shade screen identical to the one in this photograph was being used,
though an irrigation system with an electric water pump had been installed.
(Department of Special Collections, Stanford University Libraries)

dry season between October and January, requiring a huge pulse of
labor at that time.[4] Pruning, replanting, fertilizing, and other maintenance, which require less labor than picking, can be spread more
evenly over the year. From the beginning of the coffee boom, labor,
and especially harvest labor, was the key constraint to the expansion
of the coffee economy (see Figure 4-4).

The development of coffee was limited by the absolute size of
the human population, which amounted to approximately 2.6 million persons during the 1870s and 1880s. This population, however,
was unevenly distributed over the isthmus. The most populous country was Guatemala with approximately 1.2 million people in 1880,
followed by El Salvador with 0.5 million (1878), Nicaragua with
373,000 (1875), Honduras with 307,000 (1881), and Costa Rica with
182,000 (1883).[5] Because of the labor-intensity of coffee, coffee farms
could be established more easily in densely populated regions than in
sparsely populated ones. The most densely populated country at the

time of the coffee boom was El Salvador with 69 persons per square mile in 1878, followed by Guatemala with 29 persons per square mile (1880), Costa Rica with 9.3 persons per square mile (1883), and finally Honduras (1881) and Nicaragua (1875) with 7 persons per square mile. The location of these populations relative to potential coffee zones influenced the timing and intensity of the development of the coffee economies of the region.

How human labor was harnessed for coffee production was in no way predetermined by the crop itself. Previous successes elsewhere in Latin America showed that coffee could be grown under a wide range of social relations of production, from huge slave plantations

"Planting Seed for Coffee—Las Nubes," Department of Suchitepéquez, 1875. The workers in this photograph are planting seedlings taken from the nursery, not seeds as Muybridge's inscription indicates. Because of the relatively high altitude of Las Nubes (3,600–5,300 feet above sea level) and the favorable cloud cover there (Las Nubes means "The Clouds" in Spanish), heavy shade was not so crucial as on plantations located at lower altitudes. (Department of Special Collections, Stanford University Libraries)

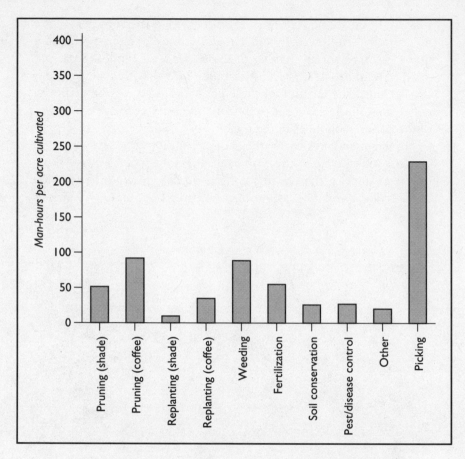

Figure 4-3. Labor Requirements by Activity on a Mature Coffee Farm.
Source: United Nations Food and Agriculture Organization, *Coffee in Latin America*, Table 16, p. 122.

in Brazil to small private farms using family labor in Venezuela.[6] In Central America, slavery was abolished by Liberal decrees shortly following independence from Spain, thereby eliminating one possibility. Small peasant proprietors using the labor of family members to care for the groves and harvest the crop became the most numerous producers in Central America, followed by family farms using their own labor for the permanent care of the groves and engaging in labor exchanges or contractual hiring for assistance at harvest time. Less numerous but far more important in production were capitalist enterprises of different sizes that hired labor under a variety of

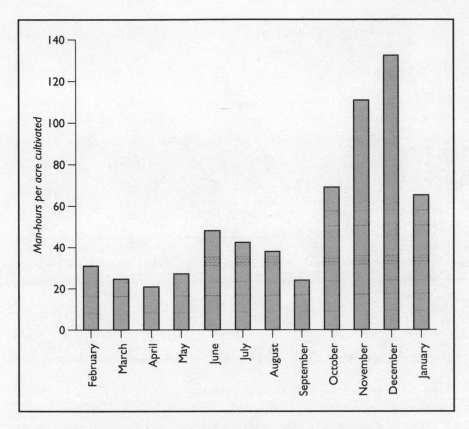

Figure 4-4. Seasonal Labor Requirements on a Mature Coffee Farm.
Source: United Nations Food and Agriculture Organization, *Coffee in Latin America*, Table 16, p. 122.

contractual relations for both the harvest and year-round care of the groves.

Peasant holdings, family farms, and capitalist plantations of all sizes emerged in every country's coffee economy, but the mix between the different types of enterprises and the particular labor relations they engaged in varied considerably between countries, between zones within countries, and over time. How people became involved in coffee production and the social relations under which they worked depended on preexisting patterns of land tenure and labor relations, the alternatives for survival in noncoffee zones, and the forging of new labor relations through state intervention in labor and land markets. How the labor problem was solved during this

"Village of Coffee Pickers—Las Nubes," Suchitepéquez, 1875. These were most likely barracks for temporary workers at harvest time. Permanent workers typically lived in smaller, family-sized dwellings on an estate. (Department of Special Collections, Stanford University Libraries)

formative period had profound implications for Central Americans for many generations to come.

Labor and the Rise of Coffee in Guatemala

Guatemala, with the largest land area suitable for coffee and the largest population, had the greatest potential for becoming the leading coffee producer in Central America. Nevertheless, certain areas that had perfect soil and climate could not be readily developed if a population of laborers was not available in the vicinity. As one German planter from Alta Verapaz put it: "Someone who wants to establish a coffee farm should, before anything else, search for a combination of lands not only with appropriate soils and climate, but also with a population of Indians, from which the necessary labor force can be obtained. Without a labor force living on the land, an enterprise does not have a chance."[7] Even when an adequate population was nearby, growers often encountered difficulties securing sufficient labor, especially when there were alternatives to plantation work.

It is not surprising that the Guatemalan coffee boom began in areas where land and labor were already claimed by commercial agriculture. The first coffee plantations were established on haciendas in the Pacific departments of Escuintla, Santa Rosa, Suchitepéquez, and Retalhuleu, where *hacendados* had already established claims to lands and had attracted a permanent labor force for raising sugarcane and cattle. Later, during the 1860s, lands near Amatitlán and Antigua that had been used for cochineal production were converted into coffee groves, and people who had once worked in the dye industry began to work the coffee farms. The permanent workers on the piedmont haciendas and the more mobile wage labor force around Amatitlán were mostly *ladinos*, while the labor force around the higher elevations of Antigua was composed primarily of Indians who lived in villages whose lands had been encroached on by rentals to *ladinos*, producing a population of workers that needed wages to supplement subsistence production on meager lands still held by the communities. Especially in the cochineal districts, coerced labor was unnecessary because there was an abundance of free wage labor (see Map 4-1).[8]

Growers in other areas of the country did not have such an easy time securing labor. In Alta Verapaz there was a large population of Kekchí and Pocomchí Maya, but complaints of labor shortages began to be heard in the 1860s despite the takeover of Indian lands for coffee around the population centers of Cobán, San Pedro Carchá, Tactic, and Tucurú. Indians adapted to the land squeeze either by moving to the abundant agricultural frontier outside of the coffee zone or by raising coffee themselves; both adaptations reduced the supply of labor available to the capitalist farms. Despite the Conservative state's claim that it was a protector of the Indians, growers were able to pressure the *corregidor* and local officials to execute labor drafts on Indian communities, though one result of the draft was to disperse the Indians out of central villages and into the forest.[9]

Before the Liberal reforms of the 1870s, coffee growers in the

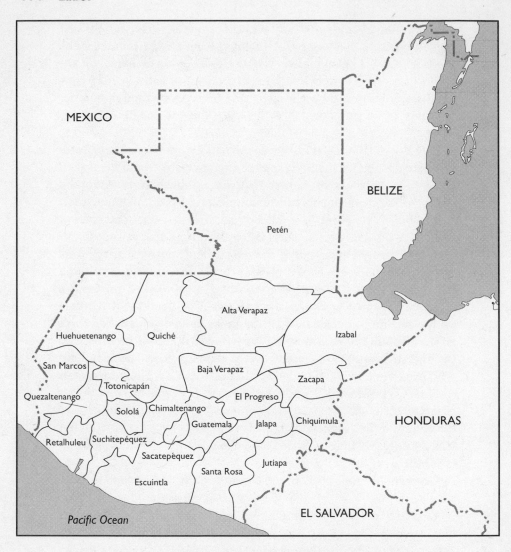

Map 4-1. Guatemala: Departments

Pacific piedmont had greater difficulty than the growers in Alta Verapaz in securing a labor force. Most of the Indian population lived
in communities in the Western Highlands, where they had adjacent
lands for growing subsistence crops, and they also claimed communal holdings in the piedmont or on the coastal plain, where they
could tap forest reserves and plant additional cornfields. Few had an
economic incentive to work voluntarily for wages. Many growers at

this time attempted to induce Indians to work by advancing wages during times of duress and later demanding that the Indians fulfill their labor contracts. This *habilitación* system was subject to numerous abuses by the laborers.[10] Some workers would get advances from several growers at once, and when the time came to provide labor services, workers would flee to the mountains or to a neighboring village. Growers and government officials played with the notion of importing "coolie" labor from Asia,[11] but the only pragmatic solution was to break the Indians' resistance to plantation work.

The last chapter showed how the government of Justo Rufino Barrios carved up communal holdings in the Pacific piedmont and distributed them to potential coffee growers. The loss of land was not evenly distributed among villages. By organizing effectively, some villages were able to hold on to Pacific piedmont lands, and others were able to gain highland lands at the expense of neighboring communities. Favored communities were organized into militias for enforcing the programs of the Barrios government.[12] In this way the Barrios regime intensified ancient struggles between Indian groups, while claiming lands for the export sector. The net result for the highland Indian population was a loss of access to "surplus" lands in an ecological zone substantially different from the cold highlands, making it more difficult for the highland formation as a whole to obtain off-season corn and the fruits of the piedmont forests. Those villages most severely squeezed by the loss of lands became a potential labor reserve for the plantations, but the transition from potential labor reserve to actual provider of labor was not smooth because the Indian population in these areas was unaccustomed to wage work.

After the death of Carrera in 1865, coffee growers found it much easier to work with department *corregidores* to solve the labor shortage problem. In 1867, growers in the department of Sololá successfully petitioned to set up a new Indian community in the vicinity of the plantation area to provide labor for nearby *fincas*. The growers promised officials that they would give the community its own corn lands, a church, and a clinic as an inducement for potential laborers to migrate from villages in Los Altos, where growers argued that such amenities were unavailable. By 1868, *corregidores* in Los Altos and Alta Verapaz were serving as labor supply intermediaries between Indian communities and growers, and by 1870 the *corregidor* of San Marcos was providing growers with a means to enforce debt servitude on plantations there.[13] A relationship between coffee growers and departmental officials that began in the 1860s became explicit national policy when Liberals took over in the 1870s. A national circular issued on November 3, 1876, empowered department chiefs to do everything possible to assist growers in obtaining a labor force, including enforcement of labor contracts and soliciting from fifty to one hundred workers from a single village, depending on the size of the village and the importance of the enterprise requesting labor.[14]

Decree 177 of April 3, 1877, spelled out in great detail the obligations between employers and employees and the legal position of the state in enforcing these obligations. Laborers were required to carry a *libreto*, or work pass, at all times. Employers were required to inspect the work passes of all incoming laborers to make sure that no outstanding debts were owed to other employers. At the end of each week, employers were required to update debits and credits to the worker's account and enter the results on the *libreto* card and on the plantation's balance book. Periodically, plantation owners were required to submit to local authorities a list of all laborers. Except in extreme cases such as an epidemic, workers were required to obtain written permission from the owner of the estate to leave the plantation in search of work elsewhere.[15]

An individual caught without a work pass or a debt contract for future labor would be subject to *mandamientos*, labor drafts similar to those used during the colonial period. Plantation owners in need of additional labor submitted requests to the department chief, who would send the requests to local authorities, who drafted able-bodied men (and sometimes women) not protected by labor contracts. The draftees received an advance of less than half the value of the labor contract, and the municipal governments received a payment from the grower for the service rendered.

In the late 1870s and 1880s, the forced draft of laborers became a common practice but declined in relative importance as Indians and poor *ladinos* became increasingly indebted to coffee growers. Several forces pushed peasants into debt contracts. The 1877 labor code stipulated that if a peasant could not pay the yearly road tax, an employer could pay the tax and the peasant would become indebted by that amount to the employer,[16] who would issue a *libreto* card to the peasant showing the number of days of labor owed. Furthermore, a peasant without a valid work contract could be drafted into military service or forced to labor on the detested road gang. From a peasant perspective, it was far better to be indebted to a known employer than subject to a labor draft, and from the perspective of an employer, it was better to have a labor force that was reasonably assured than to rely on a last-minute draft. By the turn of the century, so many peasants were indebted to plantation owners that the state had great difficulty supplying the *mandamientos* demanded by other growers.[17]

The system of labor contracts was adapted to the needs of the coffee economy. A permanent labor force living on the farm year-round was needed to weed, fertilize, prune, replace old coffee trees, care for the nursery, and maintain roads and buildings on the estate. Peasants who became heavily indebted found themselves bound by long-term labor contracts of up to four years, after which time they were free to leave the estate only if they had no residual indebtedness. Frequently, at the end of the period the contract would be rolled over for another four years. The debts of husbands or fathers could be passed on to women and children, and when a farm was sold, the laborers' outstanding debts, an important portion of the total assets of an estate, were transferred to the new owners, thereby guaranteeing the permanent labor force necessary to maintain the estate. By law, growers were required to provide these permanent *colonos* with shelter, a garden plot, a primary school, and subsistence allotments of food.[18] Because of the costs of maintaining a permanent labor force, plantations located near villages could sometimes hire *voluntarios*, or free wage laborers, to do specific tasks. Afterward, the workers would return to their homes in the nearby villages where they would care for themselves.

It was too expensive for landowners to maintain a permanent labor force large enough to meet the needs of the harvest, and the number of *voluntarios* in the towns of the piedmont was insufficient to make up the difference. The bulk of the seasonal labor was provided by Indian villages in the highlands. During July and August, when corn supplies were at their lowest levels, and on Saint's Days, when Indians needed cash for rituals, *habilitadores*, or labor contractors on the payroll of the plantations, advanced cash to individuals in return for a labor contract for one to three months of work beginning at harvest time. Sometimes *tratistas*, labor contractors working independently, would advance money or goods to Indians in return for a contract for a specified number of days of labor in the future. If there were a critical shortage of labor at harvest time, the *tratista*, who was

"Coffee Plantation—Las Nubes, Guatemala," Suchitepéquez, 1875. Most of the coffee pickers in this photograph are women. A solitary male worker with a full basket, possibly a posed figure, appears in the right foreground, and a male overseer appears in the lane on the left. (Department of Special Collections, Stanford University Libraries)

often a highland merchant, could then sell the contract at an inflated price to a grower under stress, thereby making a windfall profit. It is estimated that by the 1880s, some one hundred thousand Indians were regularly migrating to the piedmont for the coffee harvest, most of them falling under one of the above forms of enticement.[19]

Because of the huge labor needs at harvest time, growers competed for Indian labor. The labor code attempted to lessen the competition by fining growers who hired laborers already indebted to other growers.[20] The overall effect of the system, however, favored large plantations over medium-sized ones. Large growers tended to have greater access to capital, which enabled them to pay contractors in advance for harvest labor. Furthermore, large planters had an easier time than less important planters in pressuring the municipal and departmental governments in charge of enforcing labor contracts.

Some of the largest plantations in Guatemala were able to avoid the competition for harvest workers by acquiring *fincas de mozos,* estates in the highlands, where lands were rented to Indians in exchange for labor at harvest time. Thus General Manuel Lisandro Barillas, the largest coffee grower in Guatemala in 1890, owned five coffee farms in the Pacific piedmont along with a 70,000-acre labor reserve called Choacorral in the highland *municipio* of Joyabaj, Quiché.[21] Erwin Paul Dieseldorff, one of the most important growers of Alta Verapaz, had acquired at least fifteen properties by 1937, eight of which were farms for the provision of labor to his coffee estates.[22] In 1930, Schlubach, Sapper, and Company cultivated 980 acres of coffee on its Pacific piedmont farm in San Marcos and owned a 7,200-acre labor reserve in the highland department of El Quiché; the Nottebohm family cultivated some 4,000 acres of coffee on its farms in the piedmont and had a 555-acre labor reserve in the highland department of Huehuetenango; the Compañia Cecilia had some 2,700 acres of coffee in the piedmont and a 3,000-acre labor reserve in Huehuetenango; the Herrera Brothers cultivated some 1,300 acres of coffee in the piedmont and had a 3,800-acre labor reserve in El Quiché.[23]

Labor drafts and debt servitude affected the highland Indian population unevenly. Villages located along the roads between the highlands and the coast were most vulnerable during the early days of the *mandamientos*; residents of remote villages found it easier to escape the drafts. Over the years, some villages adapted to the influx of cash from wages by specializing in the production of cloth, clothing, pottery goods, straw goods, or some other commodity for the Indian market, granting them the luxuries of being able to pay the road tax, buy exemptions from labor drafts, and avoid entering into labor contracts with *habilitadores*. Other villages with poorer land and unfavorable access to central marketplaces, found themselves in a deficit situation and, therefore, unable to avoid being sent to the piedmont every year to pick coffee. Within Indian communities, those who held public office, who acquired private landholdings, or who had an independent source of income could afford to pay off the state and avoid labor drafts and debt contracts, whereas poorer community members found themselves bound every year for the coast. In certain *municipios* of the coffee zone, some individual Indians were

"Coffee Picking—San Isidro," 1875. This coffee plantation is at a lower elevation than Las Nubes, requiring more extensive shade for the groves and providing a less comfortable work environment for the laborers, who are scantily clad. These posed figures suggest that the women specialized in picking, while the men assisted by transporting ladders and harvested berries (see wheelbarrow at center). In the wheelbarrow is a wooden box (*caja*), which was probably being used to measure the volume of berries picked by each worker, who would be paid according to the number of *cajas* picked. The fully clothed male figure in background may be tallying the number of *cajas* picked. The "San Isidro" pictured here is probably a 460-acre plantation listed in the 1889 agricultural survey located in Suchitepéquez, one league from the departmental capital of Mazatenango; in 1890, San Isidro is listed in a coffee census as having 195,000 coffee trees. In 1889, Gustavo Boy owned both Las Nubes (altitude 3,600–5,300 feet) and San Isidro (altitude 1,200–1,600 feet); by 1930 both plantations were owned by Enrique Boppel, a German. These farms escaped expropriation during World War II; they both appear on a 1952 list as owned by Francisca Rosa *viuda de* [widow of] Boppel, who, by 1967, had passed them on to a son, Enrique Fernando Boppel Rosa (San Isidro), and daughter, Yolanda Gertrudis Boppel Rosa de Felman (Las Nubes). (Department of Special Collections, Stanford University Libraries)

able slowly to build up small coffee groves for cash needs, interplanting the groves with beans, squash, bananas, and other food crops.[24]

Throughout the Liberal period and lasting to the present day, Guatemalan elites and government officials have lived in fear of a general uprising of Indians. Following colonial precedent, any attempt by Indians to organize outside of the established channels had to be crushed in brutal fashion as a public lesson for the rest of the Indian population. A peasant uprising that began in the highland town of Momostenango in 1875 was put down in 1877, when Barrios sent troops into the area, killing or jailing suspected insurgents and burning peasants' houses. Similarly, in 1884, when Indians in the village of Cantel protested the seizure of village lands, federal troops retaliated by shooting every local official.[25] In 1896, when workers in San Marcos organized a strike, those who participated were sentenced to a month in jail and hard labor.[26] Troops executed those considered to be leaders of the strike.[27]

Brutality alone could not control the Indian population. Indians and poor *ladinos* had to be encouraged to work through the established channels of power. No matter how dictatorial the government might be, it had to give the appearance that it was dispensing authority in a just manner. For example, the 1877 labor code outlawed abusive behavior on the part of employers and specified several measures aimed at improving plantation conditions for the workers.[28] Even though the system was clearly stacked in favor of the plantation owners, peasants learned to use loopholes in the law as a means of resistance. If a plantation foreman was abusive, workers might escape the plantation and return to their home communities before they had fulfilled their contracts. The contractor, of course, knew where to find the escapees, but a legal appeal would have already been entered detailing the foreman's abuses. If several complaints had been entered, the peasant might have a chance at a favorable judgment from the authorities.[29] As long as the state could project the double image of flexibility and absolute coercive authority, it could maintain rule over a potentially explosive laboring population.

By the time of the 1890 coffee census, the basic structures of Guatemalan landholding and labor relations had been firmly established. The areas that were developed for coffee production before the Liberal reforms of the 1870s tended to reflect previous social relations of production. The zones that had once produced cochineal, which was raised on small plots, had a much higher percentage of peasant holders and small family farms than the average for Guatemala.

In Sacatepéquez (where Antigua is located) 40 percent of the trees
were on peasant farms with fewer than five thousand trees; lacking
enough trees to sustain a family year-round, some of these peasant
growers also worked as wage laborers on larger family-sized or capitalist farms.[30] In addition to peasant farms, another 11 percent of
the trees in the department of Sacatepéquez were on family farms
with five thousand to nineteen thousand trees. In Amatitlán 27 percent of the trees were on farms with fewer than twenty thousand
trees.[31] Both of the previous cochineal areas had a relatively abundant
wage labor force and did not have to rely heavily on government-
assisted labor drafts in the Liberal period. In the departments of
Escuintla and Santa Rosa, where large haciendas had dominated
the landscape before coffee, large capitalist farms with one hundred
thousand or more trees had 91 percent and 81 percent of the trees
in those departments respectively, the greatest participation rates by
large enterprises in the country. Family and peasant farms had abnormally low participation rates with less than 1 percent of the trees
in Escuintla and 9 percent in Santa Rosa. The areas of the western
piedmont that were mapped out by the national government as a real
estate development project during the 1870s and 1880s did not reflect
previous relations of labor and land tenure, which had been either
low-utilization off-season *milpa* areas for highland Indian communities or municipal lands of piedmont Indian villages. Rather, the
land tenure and labor relations that emerged there reflected the conscious attempts by the Liberal state to establish capitalist plantation
agriculture. In the 1890 coffee census, the departments of Quezaltenango, San Marcos, Chimaltenango, and Sololá had significantly
higher than national average participation rates by capitalist farms
with twenty thousand or more trees, which required both permanent
and seasonal laborers.[32]

The rise of coffee ushered in Guatemala's current system of plantation labor with a permanent work force living on the farms for
general maintenance and a migratory work force to harvest the crop.
The seasonal portion of the labor force in the Pacific piedmont and
Alta Verapaz was provided largely by Indian communities in the
highlands. The symbiotic relationship between the highland system
of small farms and the plantation economy of the piedmont did not
take place smoothly but required direct intervention by the state.
Land taken from the Indians squeezed the highland formation as a
whole so that poorer individuals and communities needed alterna-

tive sources of income to survive. Labor drafts were resurrected as an enforcement procedure, and a system of debt servitude emerged that tied individuals to particular plantations in the piedmont. Similar to the case of land policy, the Liberal state borrowed selectively from colonial labor practices, embellishing them with modern trappings and backing the new labor codes with a combination of military repression and legal mediation between employers and employees. The result was the emergence of two interdependent economies: the plantation economy dependent on the highland economy for harvest labor, and the highland economy dependent on the plantation economy for hard cash. Although the capitalist plantation using Indian labor became the dominant mode of organization of the Guatemalan coffee economy, in the eastern departments capitalist plantations made use of a predominantly *ladino* labor force. Furthermore, while capitalist farms with twenty thousand or more trees came to own more than 80 percent of Guatemala's coffee trees, a much more numerous group of noncapitalist producers (88 percent of the farms listed in the 1890 coffee census) claimed the rest, suggesting that within the capitalist-dominated economy, enterprising peasants and owners of medium-sized family farms, most of whom were *ladinos*, participated in the coffee boom. The 2,564 peasant coffee producers in the 1890 census had an average of approximately two thousand trees per farm, an inadequate number to support a family year-round or to absorb all of the family's labor; it is likely that many of the peasant farms provided labor, especially at harvest time, for larger family-sized farms and capitalist enterprises.[33]

Labor and the Rise of Coffee in El Salvador

In the first decades of coffee expansion, Salvadoran growers had great difficulty securing labor. Some of the best volcanic soils of the western piedmont were occupied by Indian communities, and until the late 1870s most *ladinos* living in towns had access to *ejidal* lands on which to grow food crops. Corn and bean yields were so high and the lands attached to villages and municipalities so abundant that early growers found it hard to entice people to work on the newly forming coffee estates. Some growers were able to attract *colonos* to their estates from the population of peasants who were unattached to a village by allowing them to cultivate food crops on small plots of land and paying them wages in return for labor in the coffee groves. If growers became too demanding, however, *colonos* would flee the estate, and because there was no highly organized military, growers could do little to apprehend runaways. The abundance of subsistence crops and the labor shortage in commercial agriculture caused real wages to approximately triple from 1807 to 1858, and the competition for laborers became so severe that during the 1850s public works projects were forced to a halt during harvest season.[34] Growers responded to shortages of harvest labor by offering workers advances on future labor, but without a strong state to back up contracts, the system was subject to abuses. Labor laws were passed penalizing violators with imprisonment, but enforcement was lax. In 1861, the penalty was changed from imprisonment (at public expense) to three to eight days' labor on public works, creating a direct incentive for authorities to apprehend violators.[35]

When coffee growers came to power in the 1870s and 1880s, they began to solve both their land and labor problems. National legislation in the early 1880s abolished *ejidal* and communal rights to land, reinforcing a process of encroachment that was well under way. Coffee growers acquired private titles to lands traditionally cultivated by peasants, and with funds from a coffee tax, militias were created with the power to evict previous tenants from the land. Agricultural judges were posted in the towns of the coffee zone to implement the land reform. Sabotage to coffee farms, evasion of labor contracts, and illegal squatting were so rampant that a national mounted police force was created in 1889 and stationed in the coffee zones of Santa Ana, Ahuachapán, and Sonsonate.[36] Through the use of force, squatting was held in check and the landless who did not move to less controlled areas became dependent on coffee growers for survival.

On larger plantations, nucleated villages of workers sprang up under the direct control of the landowner. Unlike *colonos* on the haciendas of the past, the workers in these nucleated villages were not allowed access to land to grow crops but were given rations by the grower and paid a money wage in return for labor year-round on the estate. Policemen were usually stationed in these settlements to keep order.[37] For labor needs in excess of those provided by the permanent work force, growers hired landless peasants from the nearby towns, where agricultural judges kept lists of all available day laborers. A seasonal labor force for the harvest was imported from outside the coffee zone. Often these migrant workers still had access

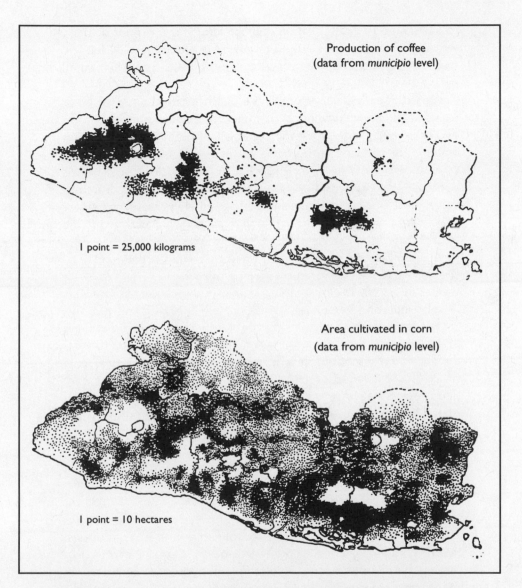

Map 4-2. El Salvador: Geographical Distribution of Coffee Production and Area in Corn, 1950.
Source: Dirección General de Estadísticos y Censos, *Censo agropecuario de 1950*.

to some land to grow corn on, but the land was too poor or there was too little of it to sustain a family year-round, making harvest wages a necessary supplement to corn and beans from their small plots of land.

A pattern of land use emerged in El Salvador that suited the labor needs of the coffee economy. This pattern is reflected in the coffee and corn maps taken from the 1950 agricultural census. The areas suitable for growing coffee came to specialize in that crop alone, cultivating almost no corn. Corn had to be imported to feed the permanent laborers on the coffee farms. Dense rings of corn cultivation developed around the coffee zone, where peasants who were dependent on seasonal wages in coffee became concentrated (Map 4-2).

Because El Salvador lacked the agricultural frontier common to all the other Central American countries, coffee growers had an easier time than anywhere else securing a cheap, hardworking labor force. A self-regulating labor market was created by squeezing peasants from a limited land base. Growers did not have to scour the villages and countryside in search of a potential work force because un-attached laborers would show up at the plantation site on a weekly basis. By 1885, the labor shortage of the 1850s was nearing an end, and growers began reporting that the supply of workers was adequate. Money wages for day labor remained the same from 1858 to 1885, but corn prices almost tripled, thereby lowering the real wage to 40 percent of what it had been in the 1850s.[38] Furthermore, with an abundant supply of people willing and able to work for wages, it was no longer necessary for the Salvadoran state to coerce laborers from peasant cornfields onto capitalist plantations, as was done for many decades to come in Guatemala and Nicaragua. Struggles over land were more severe in El Salvador than in neighboring countries, however, requiring constant vigilance and an army devoted to protecting the idle perimeters of coffee plantations from squatters. In the towns, larger police forces were needed to keep order over the mass of landless people who roved about in search of work. Thus the radical land reform, in the context of a growing population and a diminished agricultural frontier, created the pattern of Salvadoran labor relations that was to endure, with few modifications, for more than a century.

Labor and the Rise of Coffee in Costa Rica

Unlike Guatemala, El Salvador, and Nicaragua to the north, Costa Rica did not have a significant Indian population from which to draft labor. Nor did it have a local tradition of coerced labor that could be resurrected for the coffee boom. Moreover, the population of the Central Valley was small relative to the abundant reserves of land suitable for coffee, preventing the development of a mass of landless laborers, as occurred in El Salvador. In Costa Rica, coffee cultivation spread as population growth and competition for land in the already established centers led to colonization of the agricultural frontier, taking the form of nucleated settlements of primarily small and medium-sized producers. For these reasons, Costa Rica's coffee boom took place more gradually and with less social upheaval than the coffee booms of Guatemala, El Salvador, and Nicaragua.

Differentiation in landholding did occur when laws were passed that transformed municipal and national lands into private property holdings. Peasants who were accustomed to using common lands and those who did not have the financial resources to purchase private plots during the coffee boom lost out to peasants and townspeople who were able and willing to make the adjustment. A serious deterioration of living standards did not take place, however, because people could migrate to the agricultural frontier or work for wages on the newly forming coffee farms. Although most peasants preferred working on their own plots to working for wages, wage labor did not mean impoverishment during Costa Rica's coffee boom. Wages rose from 7.5 pesos per month in 1844 to 11.25 pesos per month in 1849, to 15–18.75 pesos in 1856, up to 25–30 pesos in 1869–70.[39] The underlying causes of the wage spiral were a buoyant demand for coffee and the relative abundance of land for colonization, but the shortage of available workers was intensified by a cholera epidemic in 1856 that killed off 7 percent of the Costa Rican population.[40]

The system of labor that emerged in the Central Valley was intricately connected with the structure of landholding in coffee. Small and medium-sized family farms dominated the landscape with a scattering of estates larger than one hundred acres. Family labor provided the bulk of the permanent labor force on these small and medium-sized farms, and the families of those with smaller holdings gained supplementary incomes working on the larger farms during the harvest. Further harvest labor was provided by petty traders and other people in the towns, who were lured to the coffee groves by high wages during the harvest. Because of higher wages and a more equal distribution of coffee lands in Costa Rica than in Nicaragua, El Salvador, and Guatemala, less of a social stigma was attached to harvest labor so that even the teenagers of middle-class families became accustomed to picking coffee. It is said that during the peak of the season San José would empty as people flowed to the surrounding countryside to pick coffee.[41]

Contrary to the pattern in Guatemala, small and medium-sized family farms in Costa Rica had an advantage over the largest farms in securing adequate labor.[42] A network of labor exchanges developed between neighbors and relatives who would promise to work on each others' farms during the harvest. Piece-rate wages were paid just as on the larger farms, but because of their greater labor needs, the larger farms were unable to participate in the exchange. Because of the excess demand for labor, this advantage in recruiting labor reinforced the vitality of the family farm and made it imperative that elites invest more heavily in processing equipment and marketing than in trying to control vast tracts of land as was the case in Guatemala, El Salvador, and Nicaragua. Furthermore, the dominance of family farms in Costa Rica meant that the land suitable for coffee was not entirely devoted to coffee as it was in El Salvador. Rather, staple crops such as beans, corn, plantains, and vegetables were grown alongside coffee, providing a family farm with sustenance as well as cash from the same plot of land. This difference from El Salvador can be seen in the 1950 agricultural census map, which shows corn peppering the coffee zone of the Central Valley (Map 4-3).

One exception to the family farm model in Costa Rica emerged in Cartago Province in the valley of the Reventazón and Turrialba, the area to the east of the Central Valley where very large farms with substantial permanent work forces came into being in the late nineteenth and early twentieth centuries after the railroad to the Atlantic was completed. This zone had a tradition of large haciendas during the colonial period, and when the railroad made coffee a potential commercial crop, large estates prospered. The population of Costa Rica grew from approximately eighty thousand people in 1844 to more than three hundred thousand by 1900, and 70 percent of that population was located in the Central Valley, where the agricultural frontier was all but exhausted by the turn of the century.[43] The extreme labor shortage of the early coffee boom was relieved by a crisis in 1897, when the price of coffee collapsed and credit dried up, forcing many family farms into bankruptcy. The large estates to the east offered relatively high wages, housing, schools, and the security of year-round employment. Because it had higher levels of rainfall more evenly distributed throughout the year, the harvest season in this zone was longer than that in the rest of the Central Valley. In addition, the large estates in this area typically raised a combination of coffee and sugarcane, and sometimes bananas, so that labor requirements were spread evenly throughout the year and these plantations could maintain a large permanent work force.[44] The coffee area to the east of Cartago along the railroad line to the Atlantic still boasts some very large plantations with thousands of acres of coffee and sugar and whole towns of resident laborers. As can be seen on the 1950 agricultural census map, the area devoted to corn in Cartago Province was concentrated to the northwest of that region's coffee zone, somewhat akin to the general pattern of land use that emerged in El Salvador. This zone, however, remains an anomaly in Costa Rica and produces less than 15 percent of total coffee output.[45]

By the 1970s only one-third of the permanent jobs and two-fifths of the harvest jobs in Costa Rica were generated by capitalist coffee farms exceeding 112 acres.[46] This structure of landholding and labor that came to fruition during the coffee boom created a larger class of moderately prosperous people directly engaged in the cultivation of coffee than was true for Guatemala, El Salvador, and Nicaragua, and in Costa Rica this class of relatively prosperous growers was connected by kinship ties with smaller growers who supplied occasional labor to their richer cousins, thereby reducing class antagonisms between those who worked for wages and those who did not. This peculiar labor relation became the material basis for an egalitarian ideology of a "nation" of coffee growers, despite increasing differentiation in relative wealth holdings.[47] Because a larger portion of Costa Rican coffee cultivation was in the hands of small and medium-sized producers, a vigorous local market emerged in the towns of the Central Valley, supporting numerous shopkeepers, petty commodity producers, and providers of services. Because the large plantation was not the dominant mode in coffee production, the Costa Rican state did not have to intervene directly to supply forced labor as was the case in Guatemala and Nicaragua, nor was

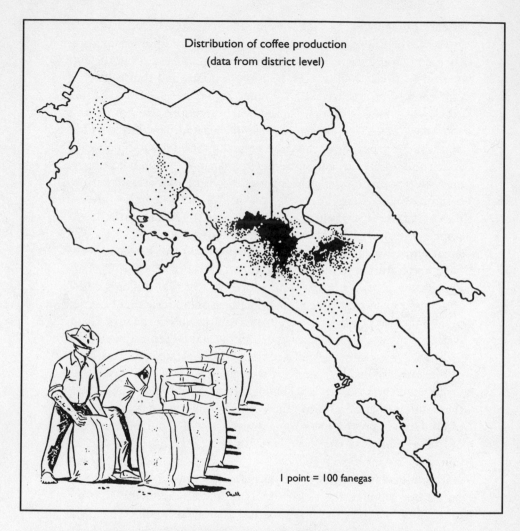

Distribution of coffee production
(data from district level)

1 point = 100 fanegas

Map 4-3. Costa Rica: Geographical Distribution of Coffee Production and Area in Corn, 1950.
Source: Dirección General de Estadística y Censos, *Atlas estadístico de 1950*, pp. 69, 70.

it necessary for the state to intervene to quell individual acts of violence as was the case in El Salvador. In Costa Rica's Central Valley, class struggles came to be fought more over the price of mature coffee berries when they were sold to the processors and exporters than over the wage rate for harvest labor.

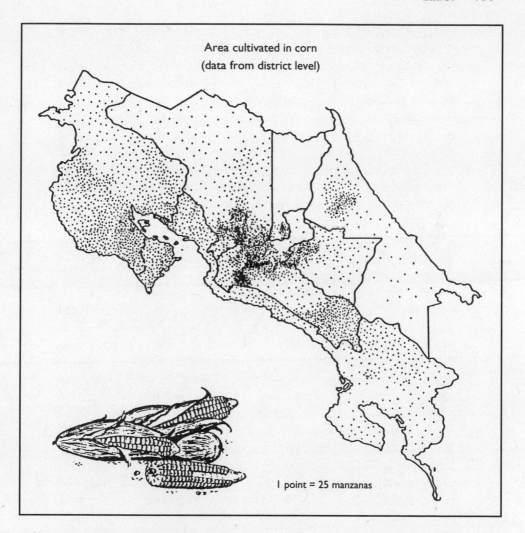

Area cultivated in corn
(data from district level)

1 point = 25 manzanas

Labor and the Rise of Coffee in Nicaragua

Like neighboring Costa Rica, Nicaragua had a small population and abundant land resources so that labor was a greater obstacle than land in the development of coffee. Peasant coffee farms with fewer than five thousand trees could solve the labor problem by using family labor to care for the grove year-round and harvest the crop, but family-sized farms with five thousand to fewer than twenty thousand trees would have either to arrange for labor exchanges with relatives and neighbors or hire wage laborers when heavy pulses of labor were needed at harvest time. By the time of the first coffee census (1909), the overwhelming majority of Nicaragua's coffee farmers (70 percent) worked peasant- or family-sized farms. More than 80 percent of the country's coffee came to be grown on farms with twenty thousand or more trees, requiring outside labor for year-round care and for the harvest. The key problem capitalist farmers faced was the abundance of unclaimed forest lands, which gave peasants an outlet for survival other than work on the coffee plantation. How the labor problem was solved varied geographically within Nicaragua and over time, depending on the size of the working-age population relative to available land, the proximity of the agricultural frontier, customary labor relations in an area before coffee, and the availability of state institutions capable of assisting growers in harnessing labor.

The area of the country where capitalist coffee farming had the greatest difficulty becoming established itself was in the far northern mountains of Nueva Segovia, where shifting cultivation by independent peasant farmers was the dominant mode of organization during the latter half of the nineteenth century.[48] Coffee cultivation was introduced there, but it was cultivated on farms of family size or smaller that required little wage labor. The mountainous terrain, the long distance from the central state apparatus in Managua, and the hostility of the peasant population to government intervention made it extremely difficult for the national government to draft labor for public works, the military, or capitalist farms.[49] By 1900, several cattle ranches had enclosed valley lands that had once belonged to peasants, and a few capitalist coffee farms had been started, but as one informant put it, "In that era, coffee from the mountain was raised by poor people."[50] By the time of the 1909 coffee census, peasant farms had 38 percent of the coffee trees in the department of Nueva Segovia, and family-sized farms had another 41 percent, the highest participation rates by noncapitalist farms in the country; only one medium-sized capitalist farm and two small capitalist farms were registered in the entire department at that time.[51] A less extreme version of the Nueva Segovia pattern appeared in the department of Estelí, where peasant coffee holdings along with family-sized farms had 43 percent of the trees and small capitalist farms with fewer than fifty thousand trees had the remaining 57 percent.

For very different reasons, the other coffee-producing department with abnormally high participation by peasant and family-sized farms was Masaya, where 64 percent of the coffee trees was on farms with fewer than twenty thousand trees. This department appeared to be a likely candidate for capitalist development because it had the highest population density in the country, good roads, and a location within easy reach of national state institutions in Managua, sixteen miles away. Why this department differed from the neighboring departments of Managua and Granada, where capitalist farms dominated the coffee landscape, is not fully understood. Masaya had a long history of independent control by its Indian population, which had its own local government during the colonial period. Perhaps this community was able to sustain its own social organization in an adaptive fashion after independence and for the remainder of the nineteenth century. Without a local government under the control of capitalist farmers, it would have been more difficult for large capitalist enterprises to gain access to the land and labor of the Indian community there. By 1909, even after sixteen years of Liberal labor and land laws there were only 1 medium-sized capitalist farm in the department (owned by a Dutch immigrant) and 8 small capitalist farms, the remaining 120 coffee farms being either family-sized enterprises or peasant farms that together held 64 percent of the trees in the department (Map 4-4).

With the exception of the northern frontier area and Masaya, Nicaraguan coffee came to be dominated by capitalist farms that required a permanent work force living on or near the estate and a seasonal work force for the harvest (see Map 4-5). Because of the possibility of squatting on unclaimed forest land, permanent workers had to be offered plots of land to raise food crops to induce them to stay on the plantation year-round. In the Southern Uplands, where a portion of the population was accustomed to working on cattle, cacao, indigo, and sugar haciendas, permanent labor could be secured in this fashion, and growers with coffee plantations near towns could obtain occasional labor from the towns for planting, pruning, and weeding the coffee groves. In Matagalpa, however, where the Indian population tended to live in tightly knit communities, growers rarely could attract permanent *colonos* to live on the estates.[52] By the 1890s, inexpensive Indian labor could be obtained on an occasional basis in Matagalpa, but Indians could not be relied on to show up for work at the agreed-upon times or to stay on the plantations to complete tasks.

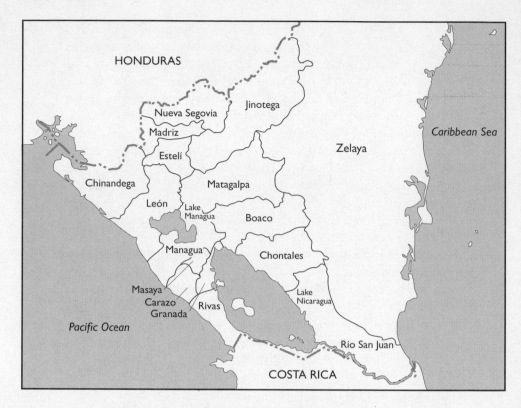

Map 4-4. Nicaragua: Departments

The greatest complaints of *falta de brazos* (labor shortages) came from capitalist growers at harvest time, when the permanent work force had to be supplemented with the labor of two to three times that many seasonal workers. Because of the intense competition for a limited labor force, growers would search the countryside and the towns for anyone willing to pick the crop. Although inexperienced workers were more likely to damage the trees, the piece-rate system prevented growers from having to pay in excess for low labor productivity. Attracted by relatively high pay, men, women, and children were pulled into the coffee zones from the towns and the agricultural frontier; those from afar lived for the duration of the harvest in makeshift barracks called "chicken-coops," where sanitary conditions were poor.[53] In addition to piece-rate wages, limited rations of beans, corn, and rice were offered to workers. On large plantations a commissary would sell soft drinks, cigarettes, candy, and extra pro-

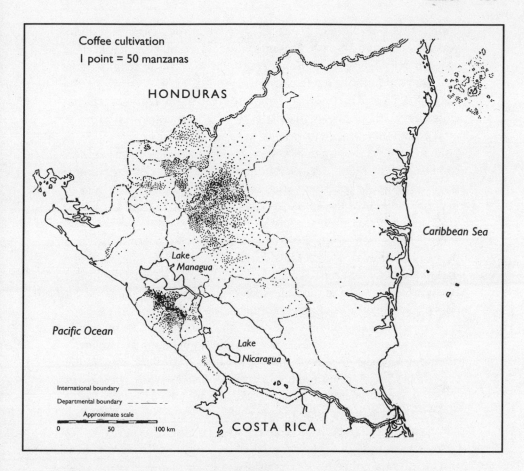

Coffee cultivation
1 point = 50 manzanas

HONDURAS

Caribbean Sea

Lake
Managua

Pacific Ocean

Lake
Nicaragua

International boundary
Departmental boundary
Approximate scale
0   50   100 km

COSTA RICA

Map 4-5. Nicaragua: Area in Coffee, 1962–1963.
Source: Dirección General de Estadísticos y Censos, *Censo agropecuario de 1962–63,*
Graph 9.

visions to workers at prices three to four times wholesale, thereby
recouping some of the cash outlay for wages and enabling debts to
accumulate on the more profligate workers, who might thereby be
ensnared into permanent labor status.[54]

The greatest fear of capitalist growers was that the berries would
rot for lack of a labor force to pick. To guard against this disas-
ter, Nicaraguan growers, like their Guatemalan counterparts, advanced money to workers in anticipation of the harvest season. Some
growers owned stores in town primarily to advance goods to peasants in return for labor contracts. Other growers would send labor

contractors (*habilitadores*) into villages when the peasant economy was most starved for cash. Peasants who had exhausted their *bodega* of corn and beans, or those who needed to pay for religious festivities, could obtain ready cash by signing a labor contract for the harvest season. The timing of labor contracting was important because in much of Nicaragua the coffee harvest coincides with the final corn harvest, when peasants have ample stores of food. As in Guatemala, the Nicaraguan system of labor contracts was subject to abuse by workers. Because of abundant land on the agricultural frontier and poor road networks, indebted workers found it easy to flee the controls of the coffee grower; workers with no intention of abiding by their contracts could sometimes get cash advances from several growers at once. An estimate of the costs over a three-year period of setting up a coffee farm in the 1870s included losing a normal amount on deserters. This amount was equivalent to the outlay for developing and maintaining a nursery for the young plants or the cost of clearing the land and planting shade trees.[55]

Also similar to Guatemala, where the agricultural frontier was difficult to close off, the Nicaraguan government made numerous attempts to assist growers in the apprehension of workers who deserted. In 1881, agricultural justices were posted in the coffee towns to help round up field workers and arrest those who refused to abide by labor contracts. In 1883, the government began issuing a catalog listing all field hands in the country and posting a monthly list of deserters. In 1886, a decree was issued permitting coffee growers to recruit private police forces to put down labor disputes. From 1862 to 1891, Conservative governments passed a new labor law almost every three years, but growers grew disenchanted because little was done to enforce these codes. At no time during the period was there a general labor draft, though partial drafts at harvest time were undertaken at the bequest of large growers, especially in areas targeted by the state for coffee development such as north central Nicaragua.[56]

In Matagalpa and Jinotega, Indians were an overwhelming majority of the population throughout the nineteenth century,[57] but because of their community organization and their communal and *ejidal* claims to land, heavy state intervention was required to turn this potential labor force into an actual supply of labor for coffee plantations. In 1881, government attempts to conscript Indian labor for public work on the telegraph line to Managua and the government building in Matagalpa triggered a rebellion, the principal demand of which was an end to forced labor. After six months of fighting and the death of one to two thousand Indians, the rebellion was crushed. Despite the victory by government forces and the military occupation of the area afterward, the government had great difficulty throughout the decade in its attempts to carry out the March 1881 law calling for forced labor and the abolition of the Indian communities. Only in 1889 did capital begin to penetrate Matagalpa. That influx suggests that coffee growers finally felt it safe to invest in the area.[58] Their ability to secure Indian labor and land, however, was enhanced during the Liberal regime of Zelaya (1893–1909).

Growers throughout the country found relief when the Liberal government of Zelaya passed a labor code in 1894. Similar to the code passed in Guatemala two decades earlier, the Zelaya code required all working-class or peasant men and women above the age of fourteen to carry a *libreto* card showing outstanding indebtedness, and a vagrancy law required all insolvent persons above the age of fourteen to work or face imprisonment. Those who were caught without a card could be drafted into the military, and those who were sufficiently indebted or working as permanent laborers were exempted. Falsification of a card was considered a felony. Before signing a contract, workers had the right to bargain over the terms, but once the contract was signed, it was illegal to form unions or to resist in any way. The new law made it obligatory for growers to crush any outbreak of labor unrest on their plantations. In 1899, the number of agricultural justices stationed in the countryside increased dramatically, and a special corps of agricultural guards was created to enforce the labor code. By the turn of the century, a regular duty of the army, the civil guard, the local police, the mountain guard, and the cavalry guard was to apprehend laborers who had fled the plantations.[59]

Conditions for coffee growers improved, but laborers continued to resist by fleeing to neighboring departments or to zones inaccessible to the military. Often it was difficult to force draftees in the military to apprehend their fellow peasants, with whom they empathized. It is estimated that in 1900 there was a less than 10 percent chance of capturing runaways. In 1900, seventy-five coffee farms in Matagalpa reported that out of a permanent work force of 2,246, 407 had decamped. In 1901, a new labor code declared as "vagrant" anyone with less than five hundred pesos. Vagrants who failed to obtain masters within three days after leaving a job were fined and put to work on the road gang. In an attempt to lower the high level of indebtedness, which encouraged decampment, the new law allowed for garnishments of up to half a laborer's salary for the payment of old debts, and any new loans extended to an already indebted laborer were to be interest free.[60] Still, some workers were able to secure advances from two or more growers, obtaining the five hundred pesos that exempted them from the new law. Vagrancy laws, *libreto* cards, increased military force, and a military draft for those who did not work on the plantations enabled the Zelaya government to counterbalance some of the labor-absorbing effects of an abundant agricultural frontier.

The labor problem in Nicaragua was more severe than that in El Salvador or Guatemala, the other two countries where the large plantation model was established. Nicaragua's situation was less akin to that in El Salvador, where the takeover of Indian lands and the extremely limited agricultural frontier created an unattached labor force that would show up at the plantations when it expected that hiring would take place. The labor situation was more akin to that of Guatemala, where a seemingly limitless agricultural frontier was a natural haven for fugitive workers, but Nicaragua's coffee boom came several decades later than Guatemala's, in large part because the Nicaraguan state was much less effective than the more developed Guatemalan state in enforcing labor discipline. Similar labor laws to those passed in Guatemala in the 1870s were passed in Nicaragua a decade later, but it was not until the 1890s, when the military was strengthened under the Liberal government of Zelaya, that the Nicaraguan government was able to enforce a draft and apprehend runaway laborers, and even when it did so, many workers were able to escape state controls. In Nicaragua a system emerged of cash advances from coffee growers to individual workers and a sporadic, albeit brutal, state enforcement apparatus.

Honduran Labor and the Delayed Coffee Boom

In Honduras, lands suitable for coffee were primarily located in areas where peasant communities maintained the *ejidal* form of landholding. In the rest of Central America governments were able to transform older forms of land tenure into private holdings, encouraging long-term investment in coffee groves and stimulating the development of a credit system based on coffee land as collateral. In Honduras, poor transportation networks and a weak national state allowed peasants in the more populated highlands to exercise influence at a local level and resist outside pressures to change. When coffee became a commercially viable crop, Honduran peasants began raising it in a piecemeal fashion alongside the traditional corn and beans but without shifting the manner in which the land was held. By 1914–15, only one-fourth of the coffee farms in Honduras were private holdings, comprising one-third of the land in coffee; the rest of the coffee farms were on communal, national, or *ejidal* lands, which accounted for two-thirds of the land in coffee.[61]

The meaning of ethnic categories given in population censuses is difficult to decipher, but according to the 1887 census, approximately one-fifth of the Honduran population was considered to be Indian, and the departments with the highest percentage of people in the indigenous category were La Paz (50 percent), Gracias (42 percent), and Intibucá (41 percent).[62] By the time of the 1914–15 agricultural census some coffee was being raised in all three departments, but none of it was being raised on capitalist-sized farms with more than twenty *manzanas* of coffee. This evidence suggests that the Honduran state either did not attempt or was unable to convert its Indian population into a labor force for capitalist coffee plantations as occurred in Guatemala, El Salvador, and Nicaragua. In two of those departments (La Paz and Gracias) all the land in coffee by 1914–15 was on *ejidal* holdings. The most important coffee-producing departments in 1914–15, however, had lower than average concentrations of Indians listed in the 1887 population census, suggesting a possible link between *ladinoization* and development of coffee as a cash crop. Despite lower than average Indian populations in the late nineteenth century, the top two coffee-producing departments in 1914–15 (Santa Bárbara and Comayagua) had 86 percent of the land in coffee under the *ejidal* system of land tenure (Map 4-6).

The maintenance of *ejidal* lands around towns and villages allowed peasants greater access to land than anywhere else in Central America and inhibited the development of the class of landless or land-poor laborers necessary to harvest coffee on a grand scale. This was possibly the cause of the phenomenon E. G. Squier observed in the early 1850s, when he reported "neglected patches [of coffee] at various places in the Department of Gracias, in all of which the bushes were heavily laden with the berries."[63] Although the popula-

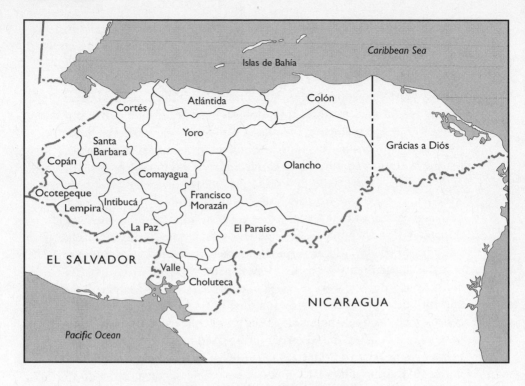

Map 4-6. Honduras: Departments

tion of Honduras grew from approximately two hundred thousand in 1826 to approximately four hundred thousand in 1890 to five hundred thousand in 1905, a critical shortage of wage labor continued because of the extension of *ejidal* holdings during the late nineteenth century and a de facto laxness on the part of the national government in preventing peasants unattached to villages from settling on national lands. Between 1850 and 1900 the Honduran state extended rights to 213 new *ejidal* claims, the largest number for any fifty-year period in the history of the country.[64] Furthermore, the government of Honduras was unwilling or unable to counteract the absorption effect of the agricultural frontier on the supply of wage labor by passing vagrancy laws and labor drafts, policy solutions that were applied in a similar situation in Guatemala and Nicaragua. These conditions gave a certain advantage to peasant farms and family-sized operations in recruiting labor at harvest time through labor exchanges with extended families and within communities. By 1914–15, two-thirds of the land in coffee was on peasant or family-sized farms, and in the most important coffee department (Santa Bárbara), even some of the large and medium-sized capitalist farms were operated on *ejidal* lands, suggesting both the difficulty of securing private title to municipal holdings and the desirability of locating coffee farms near a town where labor could be hired (Map 4-7).

Coffee did develop on a capitalistic basis in the department of Choluteca, where large cattle haciendas had existed during the colonial period. In 1887, Choluteca had the greatest number of merchants in the country, the second largest number of *hacendados* (after Olancho), the largest number of land surveyors, and the second largest number of laborers (*labradores*) (after Tegucigalpa).[65] In the late nineteenth century commercial crops, including coffee, began to be raised in Choluteca. By 1914–15, Choluteca was the third largest coffee producer, the largest rubber producer, the largest commercial hay producer, the largest indigo producer, and had lands devoted to bananas, cacao, and other commercial crops. Capitalist farms with twenty *manzanas* or more of coffee had 72 percent of Choluteca's coffee land, the highest concentration of large holdings in the country, and large capitalist enterprises with one hundred *manzanas* or more of coffee had 54 percent of the department's coffee land. Furthermore, 96 percent of the land in coffee was on private property, more than triple the national average and the highest proportion in Honduras.[66] The privatization of land in Choluteca put pressure on the peasantry, allowing for the development of a labor force for coffee and other commercial crops.[67]

Elsewhere in Honduras, the lower degree of privatization of land impeded the development of a credit system to service coffee, slowing the rate of capital investment in the cultivation phase. Peasant and family-sized farms slowly expanded their holdings through personal savings and extra labor of family members. Large numbers of people became direct producers of coffee, but their holdings were small and they typically marketed the product locally. The lack of any national class of capitalist producers strong enough to pressure the national government to build roads and railroads that would link highland coffee areas with ports reinforced the tendency for Honduran coffee to be a commercial crop for domestic, not international, markets. Even as late as 1948, less than one-third of Honduran coffee production was exported.

Before the end of World War II, Honduras accounted for less than

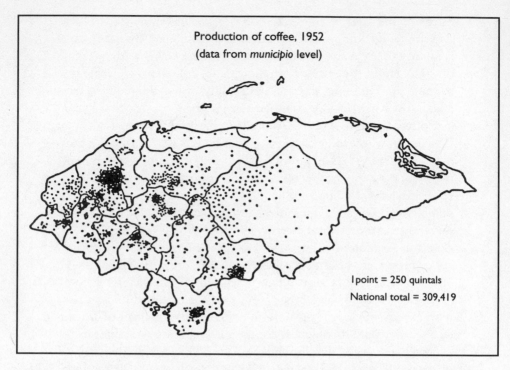

Production of coffee, 1952
(data from *municipio* level)

1 point = 250 quintals
National total = 309,419

Map 4-7. Honduras: Geographical Distribution of Coffee and Corn Production, 1952.
Source: Dirección General de Censos y Estadísticas, *Censo agropecuario de 1952*, pp. 25, 23

2 percent of total coffee exports from Central America. By 1952, only 27 percent of the coffee acreage in Honduras was privately-held, and 45 percent was in *ejidal* holdings; the rest had a mixture of *ejidal* and other forms (see Map 4-8).[68] In the three decades that followed, several forces worked together to turn Honduras into an important coffee exporter. Roads were built into previously inaccessible areas, government agencies with backing from the U.S. Agency for International Development provided finance for the coffee sector, and technical assistance programs with United States support were established to improve coffee yields. Moreover, a migrant labor force of Honduran origin was finally created by a combination of rapid population growth and an unprecedented expansion of investment in cattle ranches, sugar plantations, cotton growing, and other capitalist ventures that closed off the agricultural frontier and dispossessed peasants.[69] The number of workers in the coffee economy rose from

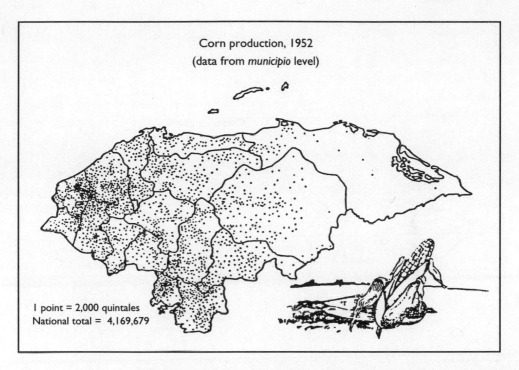

Corn production, 1952
(data from *municipio* level)

1 point = 2,000 quintales
National total = 4,169,679

an estimated 54,923 in 1960 to 66,634 in 1970 to 100,962 in 1977.[70] From 1948, when the export boom began, to 1987, Honduran coffee exports rose twenty-six-fold from 70,547 quintals to 1,805,760 quintals, making coffee Honduras's second most important export earner after bananas.

When the coffee export boom finally hit Honduras, it was accompanied by an increase in private holdings, an increased use of wage labor, and an extension of the use of credit, changes that occurred nearly a century earlier in other Central American countries. Honduran peasants, however, had prior experience growing coffee, and they continued to dominate the cultivation phase when the coffee sector went international. A USAID project paper written in 1981 estimated that 80 percent of the national area devoted to coffee was in groves of less than twenty-five acres each.[71] According to the study, the predominant source of labor on the average Honduran coffee farm was still family labor, but at harvest time, even small coffee farms hired wage labor from the pool of migrants that flowed through the coffee zones at that time of year.[72] Thus, although coffee as a major export crop was delayed for a century because of

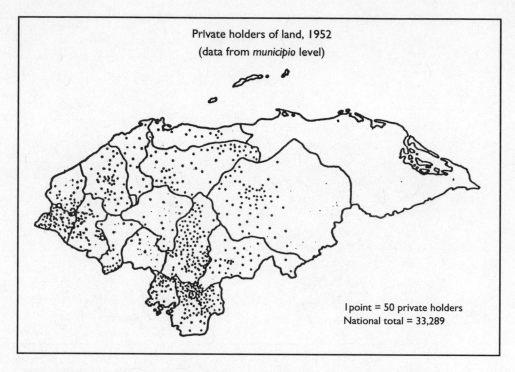

Private holders of land, 1952
(data from *municipio* level)

1 point = 50 private holders
National total = 33,289

Map 4-8. Honduras: Geographical Distribution of *Ejidal* and Private Holders of Land, 1952.
Source: Dirección General de Censos y Estadísticas, *Censo agropecuario de 1952*, p. 20.

land and labor conditions in Honduras, when coffee exports did expand, they did so from a production base that developed for local markets during the late nineteenth century. Land, labor, and credit conditions changed after World War II to stimulate coffee exports, but Honduran coffee cultivation has retained the nineteenth-century characteristic of peasant farms using predominantly family labor despite the recent trends associated with export growth.

Comparisons and Conclusion

Labor was critical in the development of coffee in Central America, and the labor problem was solved differently in each. In Guatemala, El Salvador, and Nicaragua, where large capitalist plantations became the dominant form, expropriation of peasant lands

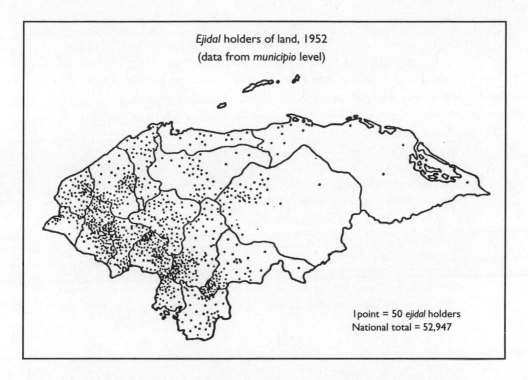

Ejidal holders of land, 1952
(data from *municipio* level)

1 point = 50 *ejidal* holders
National total = 52,947

helped solve the labor supply problem. Those who lost land became a potential work force for the plantations. In Guatemala and Nicaragua, where peasants could move to an agricultural frontier instead of working on coffee plantations, large growers ensnared permanent and seasonal workers through debt contracts, and permanent workers were allowed to plant gardens on small plots of land as an inducement to stay on the estate. In both Guatemala and Nicaragua, the state played a direct role in the labor supply process by enforcing debt contracts, issuing *libreto* cards, passing vagrancy laws, and drafting individuals into the road gang, the military, or for service on the plantations. In El Salvador, the only country that lacked an abundant agricultural frontier, a wage labor market obviated the need for the state to intervene directly in the labor supply process, but the large pool of landless and land-poor peasants required even greater vigilance by the state to prevent land invasions, curb individual acts of violence, and police the towns where squatter settlements formed. In Honduras and Costa Rica, the family farm became the dominant form of coffee cultivation, and transition to coffee was smoother and less violent though much more gradual than in the other three countries. In Honduras and Costa Rica, family labor provided the bulk of the permanent work done on the farm, supplemented at harvest time with wage labor. Nevertheless, the way the family farm model developed in the two countries differed greatly. From the start, Costa Rica's coffee boom was petty capitalist in nature. Farms developed on privately held properties, and an intricate system of credit emerged that was connected with the processing and marketing of the crop, which was export-oriented. In contrast, Honduran coffee production took place on *ejidal* holdings of land, and until the 1950s production was oriented more toward the domestic market than for export. These conditions impeded the development of a credit and wage labor system and helped delay Honduras's coffee export boom for more than a century compared with Costa Rica. For all of the countries except Honduras, the solutions found to the labor problem during the nineteenth-century coffee boom formed the basis of labor relations for the twentieth century, and in Honduras family labor continues to be the predominant mode employed in coffee cultivation.

Chapter 5

Capital, Commerce, and the Coffee Elite

Central America's coffee boom required considerable capital. Compared to most other crops before it, coffee required larger initial capital outlays to establish a working farm. Once coffee groves were mature, substantial expenditures were needed for year-round maintenance and even greater outlays to harvest the crop. At first, processing of the fruit was done crudely with large labor expenditures and very little capital equipment, but this method yielded an inferior grade of bean. Soon water processing was introduced, requiring large expenditures on plant and equipment but yielding a superior product that commanded a premium on world markets. Because of the large capital requirements for establishing and operating plantations and building improved processing facilities, the coffee boom placed a strain on traditional sources of finance. How the capital constraint was relieved brought lasting changes in the structure of elites, the role that small scale producers could play, the nature of financial institutions, the role of foreign investment, and the involvement of governments in economic activity.

Capital Requirements of
Establishing and Operating a Farm

The capital outlay required to establish a coffee farm in the nineteenth century was not owing to a scarcity of appropriate land but to the labor needed to turn virgin forests into mature coffee groves. After the initial labor was expended for clearing the land, establishing a nursery for seedlings, and planting the coffee saplings and shade trees, the young grove had to be kept properly pruned and weeded for at least three years before the first fruit could be harvested and for **147** approximately five years before commercially viable harvests could be achieved. Because of the five-year gestation between sprouting a seedling and receiving adequate revenues from the harvest and the heavy labor requirements throughout the waiting period, coffee cultivation tied up capital longer than indigo, cochineal, sugar, tobacco, and other commercial crops that preceded it, and once a mature farm was established, large amounts of labor were needed for pruning, weeding, and caring for shade trees, and even larger pulses of labor were needed to harvest the crop. Thus to establish a coffee farm on a capitalistic basis, hiring labor at each step of the way, an individual needed to have significant personal savings or access to the savings of others. To operate and maintain a mature farm, access to short-term finance was needed.

For peasants the route to establishing a coffee grove was a much slower process that consisted of planting a few trees at a time while maintaining adequate plantings of food crops. Over many years, a hardworking family of five could establish a coffee farm of up to five thousand trees without having to call on outside labor even at harvest time, thereby avoiding the problem of securing cash reserves in advance. A farm of this size would yield net revenues approximately equal to the money that could be earned if family members were able to find year-round work as day laborers. The advantage of owning a grove was independence from the labor market, though families with small groves would have to supplement income from their own coffee by working the harvest of growers with larger holdings. If a family ran out of corn and beans or needed cash for an emergency, it could get an advance on the coffee crop instead of having to sign a labor contract, though implicit interest rates on such advances were typically high. Some families could become relatively prosperous by gradually extending coffee groves beyond five thousand trees. A grove of fewer than twenty thousand trees could be built up over time and maintained adequately by the labor of a family of five, but at harvest time outside labor would have to be hired, requiring accumulated savings, labor exchanges with neighbors, or cash advances. Peasant and small family farms participated in coffee cultivation throughout Central America to varying degrees, but only in Honduras and Costa Rica did they come to dominate the cultivation of coffee. In both of these countries the coffee boom was slow and gradual compared with Guatemala, El Salvador, and Nicaragua, where capital more thoroughly penetrated the growing phase.

Capital Requirements of Coffee Processing

After the coffee cherries are harvested they must go through elaborate processing. The inner pair of coffee beans is protected by four layers: a rubbery outer skin that turns red when mature, a thick, gelatinous pulp that has a grapelike texture and sweetness, a tough parchment shell that becomes brittle when dry, and a thin, closely fitting hull that serves as the ultimate shield for the bean inside.

The first method used to remove the outer two layers was to spread the cherries on a dirt or cement patio in full sun to hasten the fermentation of the pulp and break down the outer skin so that the inner beans could be separated out by hand and left to dry more thoroughly. After adequate drying, the beans would be placed in a hollowed-out log or a stone mortar, and the parchment shell would be crushed with a wooden pestle and separated from the beans. This method required little capital so that even the smallest coffee grower had processing facilities, but it required approximately four times the human labor of the more capital-intensive wet method.[1] Furthermore, the quality of the coffee produced by the dry method is inferior because the gelatinous pulp undergoes excessive fermentation before it can be removed, imparting a sour taste and sometimes a foul aroma to the beans inside the parchment.

The alternative wet method generates a finer product, but it requires heavy capital outlays. A plentiful water source is needed, and washing tanks must be constructed for cleaning the ripe cherries and separating them from immature berries, stones, twigs, and other debris that may come from the fields. Pulping machines must be purchased for removing the outer skin and most of the pulp, and fermentation vats must be built to remove the sweet gelatin that sticks to the parchment. Sluices must be constructed for washing off the fermentation, separating out empty and immature beans, and carrying the clean beans to the drying patios. Expansive concrete floors are poured so that the damp beans can be exposed to sun and fresh air; sometimes huge mechanical dryers, heated by wood, gas, or coffee hulls, are acquired to assist in the drying phase.

During the early days of the coffee boom the dry method was universally employed, but consumers in Europe and North America became more discriminating, and importers were willing to pay a premium of approximately 10 percent for coffee that was washed or had been processed by the wet method. The development and adop-

"Coffee Plantation—San Isidro," 1875. Male laborers are being employed to spread the coffee beans to dry, and female workers are being used to transport the beans to and from the drying patio. Three drying platforms and four thatched roof buildings are pictured. In the 1889 agricultural survey, San Isidro had forty thatched roof buildings (probably the majority of these to house the labor force) and three tile roof buildings. (Department of Special Collections, Stanford University Libraries)

tion of improved processing technology was gradual and uneven and depended on the availability of water as well as capital. Costa Rican investors were the first to take advantage of the opportunities, and by 1900 practically all of the coffee exported from Costa Rica was washed, giving Costa Rican coffee a decided advantage in world markets. Costa Rica was followed by Guatemala, El Salvador, Nicaragua, and finally, after World War II, Honduras.[2] As Central American producers invested in the more sophisticated wet method, the dry processors had increasing difficulties marketing their crop. The wet method gradually displaced the dry method, and coffee processing evolved from petty manufacturing on backyard patios to a modern industry with giant factories and heavy machinery.

Once the beans are dried, they must be threshed and the parchment removed. After that they are sorted by size, and damaged or inferior beans are separated from those of higher quality. Finally, the tough, closely fitting membrane must be removed without damaging the bean. At this point, the coffee is ready to be roasted and ground. In the nineteenth century, most coffee from Central America was exported with the parchment still on the beans, and coffee importers or wholesalers in Europe would remove both the parchment and the hard film that adheres to the bean. This made for bulkier, heavier shipments, raising transport costs. As the boom progressed, more threshing machines were acquired by Central American mill owners, and greater pains were taken to sort and classify the beans so they

"Las Nubes Coffee Mill—Guatemala," 1875. William Nelson's state-of-the-art processing mill is shown here, complete with water wheel on the far right and a coffee husking machine in the center. Lumber strewn around the mill and stacked on its second floor suggests that it is still under construction. (Department of Special Collections, Stanford University Libraries)

"Spreading the Coffee Crop to Dry—Las Nubes," 1875. Washed beans are transported by water canal (right) to the drying patio, where male workers spread them in the sun to dry. If rain were to threaten, the crop could be quickly raked into the triangular shed (at center) to await the return of the sun. The large building was probably used as a storage space for the dry beans in *pergamino* form (husks still intact). Water-processing facilities like those of Las Nubes greatly improved the flavor and marketability of the product. (Department of Special Collections, Stanford University Libraries)

would fetch a higher price on the world market. At first, threshing and sorting were done in a primitive fashion, using much labor and little capital, but as in other phases of coffee processing, science was applied and new techniques were introduced that almost invariably substituted machines for the labor of human beings. For example, coffee sorting in 1900 was done exclusively by hand, usually employing women who were paid piece rates for discarding damaged beans and sorting by size. Today most coffee-processing mills in Central America have washboard gravitational devices to sort beans by size,

"Husking Coffee—Las Nubes," 1875. This piece of heavy equipment was used to thresh the dry husks from the beans, lowering the cost of transport. In 1875, most Guatemalan coffee was exported with the husk on (*en pergamino*), but as threshing machines like this one were introduced, more beans were exported in husked, but untoasted, form (*oro*). (Department of Special Collections, Stanford University Libraries)

and the most modern mills own laser sorters that detect color and remove the darker, damaged beans. Even the most modern mills, however, have as yet been unable to substitute completely for the precision of the human eye; after the gravitational devices and lasers have finished with preliminary sorting, the beans are spread on a conveyor belt and women cull the damaged beans overlooked by the laser.

After the beans are processed, sorted, and bagged, they are delivered to export houses. These companies must have clean, dry warehouses, a qualified staff to test and store the incoming cargo, access to port facilities, and trustworthy relations with shipping firms and import houses in Europe or North America. Because of the long time lags between investment and return in coffee cultivation and the heavy equipment outlays in coffee processing, capital shortages constrained the development of Central America's coffee economy.

Financing and the Coffee Boom

In the early days of the coffee boom, long-term mortgage lending was impeded by uncertainties about title to land, though long-term loans were sometimes arranged between individuals when personal ties of friendship, kinship, or established commercial relations were strong enough to lower perceived risks. The most regular source of finance followed the colonial pattern of short-term loans, using future crops, not improved land, as security. Some of the very merchant families who had made short-term crop loans during the colonial period made loans to coffee growers when the coffee export trade began, advancing funds from their own hoards of liquid wealth. As trade ties with Europe and North America were regularized, however, a more abundant source of short-term finance began to be tapped. The major importing countries had already undergone an industrial revolution and were flush with capital seeking profitable outlets. Finance capital began to flow into Central America through trade channels. Coffee import houses in the industrialized countries would borrow from banks or advance their own funds to export houses in Central America. The export houses would then advance funds to large growers or merchant intermediaries, who would make loans to smaller growers. As modern processing mills were built, they became a conduit for credit to growers. The collateral at each step was coffee to be delivered at harvest time, and implicit interest rates notched upward at each successive step away from the source of financial capital. Banks in Europe or North America would lend to coffee import houses at, say, 6 percent; the import houses would lend to Central American export houses at 8 percent; the export houses would lend to large growers or processing mills at 12 percent; and the latter would lend to growers at 14 to 24 percent depending on relative financial power and perceived risk. Upon delivery of coffee, debt contracts would be settled between growers and processors, processors and export houses, export houses and import houses, and finally, import houses and banks. If promised deliveries of coffee were not met, a commission penalty would be exacted for payments in cash, and additional penalties would be charged for late delivery or late payment. Thus trade channels provided the bulk of short-term finance to growers, and the provision of credit reinforced the delivery of coffee through a particular channel at harvest. Those with favorable access to international buyers could not only earn merchant profits from moving the crop but could also collect financial profits from growers by borrowing at low rates of interest and lending to growers at high rates.

The coffee trade attracted to Central America immigrants who had business contacts in Europe and North America. Usually the first business activity was to set up a commercial enterprise, importing hardware or luxury goods from the country of origin and exporting coffee to that country. This insertion of foreigners into the ranks of the national elites of Central America deepened over time. Owners of export houses, whose clients were coffee growers and processors, gained an intimate knowledge of the financial side of coffee processing and cultivation, and they were the first to know of their clients' financial difficulties. When a processing mill or plantation came under duress, the exporter, who had records of clients' past production levels, was in a position to judge the future profitability of the enterprise. Furthermore, the export firm, whether owned by Central American nationals or foreigners, had direct access to capital from the importing country, allowing it to purchase processing mills and plantations when other potential buyers may have been short of cash. After acquiring an enterprise, the exporter could secure finance for capital improvements. A system that began as strictly short-term credits attached to crops sometimes developed into direct investments by owners of export houses, who obtained long-term finance through their personal business relations with importers and banking houses in the industrialized countries.

In addition to strengthening the flow of capital from Europe and North America, the coffee boom spawned new instruments of domestic finance. Growers' need for long-term loans created an incentive for mortgage lending. As older forms of land tenure were replaced by clearly delineated properties with titles, a market developed for already established coffee farms, increasing the liquidity of capital tied up in coffee groves. As the purchase and sale of mature coffee farms became a regular feature of economic life, new sorts of debt contracts were created with longer-term maturities using improved land as security. New debt instruments with coffee lands as collateral took a variety of forms carrying different maturities, interest rates, and payment arrangements. As the coffee boom progressed, a process that had begun as direct long-term agreements between individual lenders and growers evolved into more institutionalized forms of financial intermediation. For the first time in Central American history, commercial banks were established that pooled scattered sources of savings and liquidity and made long-term loans to coffee growers and processors.

Governments helped relieve the capital constraint by stimulating the privatization of land, altering tax codes, abolishing the church's right to collect tithes, granting subsidies to coffee growers, providing inducements for foreign investment and immigration, creating government development banks, and establishing legislation favorable to private banking. The timing and intensity of government efforts varied from one country to the next, influencing the rate at which the coffee boom proceeded. Moreover, the methods governments and the private sector used to relieve the capital constraint conditioned the evolution of ruling elites in the different countries.

Capital and the Costa Rican Coffee Elite

During the early phase of Costa Rica's coffee boom (1834–50) municipalities and other colonial public institutions helped growers relieve the capital constraint at a time when metallic money and long-term loans from private sources were scarce. In an investigation of property transactions during this early phase, Iván Molina and Eugenia Rodríguez found that the coffee municipalities were a primary source of public lending to growers, but they also found instances of long-term loans with liens on coffee properties owned by two other public institutions, la Casa de Enseñanza de Santo Tomás and el Monte Pío de Agricultura. This period was characterized by privatization of municipal lands in the Central Valley, an increase in market transactions involving coffee land, and an upward spiral of land prices. Molina and Rodríguez discovered a high frequency of seller-financed coffee property transactions. Out of a sample of 280 transactions registered between 1834 and 1850, only 127, or 45 percent, were paid for in full at the time of purchase; the bulk of the transactions (153 or 55 percent) involved commitments to installment payments that were spread over periods lasting from several months to many years. Three-fourths of the seller-financed transactions carried no interest payments, 24 (16 percent) of the transactions carried annual interest rates of 4 to 6 percent, and 12 (8 percent) carried annual interest rates of 10 to 12 percent.[3]

As elsewhere, short-term finance with future crops as collateral was much more readily available in Costa Rica than long-term finance, and as the trade became regularized, short-term finance became closely attached to trade channels, primarily with Great Britain. By 1883 the United Kingdom was receiving 57 percent of Costa Rica's coffee exports, followed by the United States (17 percent), Germany (12 percent), and France (12 percent). This ordering continued throughout the remainder of the nineteenth century and into the twentieth, and the British further extended their control over the trade. In 1910 the United Kingdom's share of Costa Rica's coffee exports reached 84 percent, followed by the United States (8 percent), Germany (6 percent), and France (1 percent). Between World Wars I and II, the British continued to dominate the Costa Rican coffee trade, but their market share was weakened by competition from United States buyers. By 1939–40, the British share of Costa Rica's coffee exports had fallen to 47 percent while the U.S. share had risen to 37 percent.[4]

The rise of commercial banking was closely tied to the rise of coffee because of the long-term financing needs of coffee. Costa Rica was the first major coffee exporter in Central America, and it was the first to have a commercial bank. In 1858, President Juan Rafael Mora, one of the most important coffee growers and exporters in Costa Rica, assisted his friend Crisanto Medina, another important coffee exporter, in establishing the first bank.[5] This bank ran into problems when the Liverpool bank it was associated with failed, but in 1863 another important coffee producer, Mariano Montealegre (brother of the new president, José María Montealegre), founded the more substantial Banco Anglo Costarricense, also in partnership with British capital.[6] The importance of British capital in this bank prompted the government of Costa Rica in 1867 to found the Banco Nacional, which failed in 1877 and was replaced by the Banco de la Union (later the Banco de Costa Rica). After the turn of the century, several more banks, most of them with close connections to foreign banks, were formed: the Banco Comercial in 1904, the Banco Mercantil de Costa Rica in 1908, the Banco Internacional in 1914, and the Royal Bank of Canada in 1915.[7] Even though the long-term financing of coffee improved with the establishment of commercial banking, most small and medium-sized growers had trouble securing mortgages until after World War II, when the banking system was nationalized. For more than a century, then, small and medium-sized farms were restricted to short-term crop loans or longer-term loans from private lenders at sometimes usurious rates.[8]

The shortage of harvest labor limited the size of coffee holdings in Costa Rica, so the primary mode of accumulation for the elite was not so much the ownership of large tracts of coffee land as the ability to monopolize the coffee trade and the ownership of coffee-processing mills (*beneficios*). Frequently elites would own a coffee farm with one to two hundred acres of coffee and a coffee *beneficio*, but the bulk of their profits came from the fifty to one hundred small and medium-sized client farms nearby that were obligated by debt contracts to deliver mature berries at a prenegotiated price to the mill at harvest time. Debt connections, location, and tacit price agreements helped minimize competition between *beneficios* and created a local monopsony situation in the purchase of ripe coffee berries. The wealth generated in the cultivation of coffee was transferred to the owners of *beneficios* through a market transaction in which the price of mature berries was held below the equivalent value on the world market. Furthermore, mill owners exacted industrial profits from the forty to one hundred laborers who worked washing, drying, milling, and sorting the coffee beans, and they earned profits on the difference between the interest paid them by client growers and the interest rate charged them by the export houses.

Because of the higher rates of profit in processing as opposed to cultivation, Costa Rican capital was systematically drained from the cultivation phase (through price differentials and high interest rates) and flowed into the processing phase. As a result, Costa Rica had the best processing facilities and the strictest quality controls on exports in the region; by the mid-nineteenth century the wet method had displaced the dry method as the most important processing technique.[9] Quality controls set by the export houses made it difficult for growers to sell unwashed coffee except on the domestic market so that by 1900 virtually all of Costa Rica's export coffee was being processed by modern *beneficios*. Meanwhile, peasant and family-sized farms were starved of capital for reinvestment in their groves, and Costa Rican yields of coffee per tree and per acre fell behind those of El Salvador (and, to a somewhat lesser degree, Guatemala), where capital more thoroughly penetrated the cultivation phase because of the greater availability of labor and government supports for large plantations.[10]

In 1907, there were 221 coffee *beneficios* in Costa Rica. In the years that followed, the *beneficio* business became more centralized. Import houses, especially in England, sought the very finest coffees and paid substantial premiums for presorted beans that had been processed by the wet method. Larger outlays of capital were required both for wet processing equipment and mechanical sorters. Mills also began investing in mechanical dryers and threshing equipment. These capital outlays raised the capacity of *beneficios* so they had to process a larger volume per establishment. Between 1907 and 1964, the volume of Costa Rican coffee exports more than tripled, but the number of *beneficios* dropped almost in half to 122.[11] By 1981, the number of *beneficios* had dropped to 107 and coffee exports had risen 70 percent over 1964 levels.[12]

Export houses collected normal merchant profits with a smaller margin between purchase price and sales price than the *beneficios*, but there were fewer export houses so this thinner margin was spread over a larger volume of business. As the primary conduit of financial capital into the coffee business, export houses collected substantial profits on the differential between the interest rate paid them by *beneficios* and the rate charged them by import houses in Europe and North America. Both the *beneficio* owners and the owners of export houses could manage their risk by establishing set futures contracts for a certain portion of their business; they would be guaranteed a price differential between purchase and sale on that portion. Should coffee prices rise between the time of the futures contract and the harvest, however, the set contracts would prevent them from making windfall profits so *beneficios* and export houses would typically leave the price open in some contracts, especially when they expected the spot price of coffee to rise.

Who were the investors who came to own the export houses, coffee-processing plants, and larger farms of Costa Rica?

In the early days, Costa Rica's coffee elite was composed primarily of earlier elites who had access to capital from ownership of import businesses, urban and rural real estate, mining companies, and other investments. When coffee became a potential profit earner, members of these older families continued in a tradition established in the colonial period and diversified their holdings by investing in

coffee farms, *beneficios*, and export houses. Samuel Stone's list of
103 persons who bought or sold large coffee properties in the San
José area between 1820 and 1850 reveals that 29 of those listed were
descended from Antonio de Acosta Arévalo, one of the first Spanish colonists to arrive in Costa Rica. More than 90 percent of those
listed were descended from six other early settlers.[13] Fourteen of
those on Stone's list of coffee growers had invested in Costa Rica's
mines after independence.[14] Out of 80 important import merchants
before 1850, 19 were listed by Stone as important coffee growers in
San José, and 9 of these import merchants were listed as important
coffee exporters in 1846. In 1907, 47 of the 221 *beneficios* of the country were owned by descendants of the 80 import merchants prior to
1850, and 49 were owned by apparent descendants of the early coffee growers from Stone's list.[15] Lowell Gudmundson has shown that
between 1840 and 1860 coffee growers' wealth-generating activities
were highly diversified. Forty-one growers out of his list of 66 were
involved in commerce, 47 in politics, and 44 in two or more of the
following activities besides coffee: commerce, mining, cattle raising,
and politics.[16]

From the very beginning, foreigners with international connections were in a favorable position to share in the fortunes of Costa
Rica's coffee boom. One of the first important coffee growers was
Buenaventura Espinach, a Catalonian merchant who came to Costa
Rica to invest in the mines in 1824. In 1830 Espinach became a naturalized citizen of Costa Rica, and by 1838 he had acquired a coffee
farm in Cartago, where he installed the first wet method processing
mill in Costa Rica. Shortly thereafter he acquired a large farm in
Heredia with 170 acres planted in coffee, where he built a *beneficio*
even larger than the one in Cartago. By 1846, Espinach was listed as
an important coffee exporter, and he appears on the list of import
merchants before 1850.[17] The Frenchman Santiago Millet also came
to Costa Rica to invest in the mines but ended up as a coffee grower,
a *beneficio* owner, and an import merchant.

By 1846, one-fourth of Costa Rica's coffee exports were controlled
by foreign export houses, but the concentration of foreign ownership over coffee land and *beneficios* was much lower at this time.
Of the 103 San José coffee growers on Stone's 1820–50 list, only 7
were foreigners, including 3 Frenchmen, 1 Spaniard, 2 Germans, and
1 Englishman.[18] In 1850, only 5 percent of the coffee processing in
Costa Rica was carried out by foreign-owned *beneficios*.[19] The shal-

low penetration of foreign capital in the early years soon changed as foreign merchants who had established themselves in Costa Rica before 1850 began investing in coffee and came to own coffee farms, *beneficios*, and export houses. Examples are the Brealeys, the Dents, the Tournons, and the von Schrotters, all of whom were listed as import merchants before 1850. In 1907 each of these earlier import merchant families owned one or more coffee mills, and in 1915 they were listed as owners of coffee export houses.[20]

Earlier immigrants were joined by newcomers in the latter half of the nineteenth century. Although the coffee trade and short-term financial flows remained firmly attached to the British market, Germans began to make long-term investments far in excess of the share of Costa Rican coffee exports destined for Germany. At this time British investors such as the Inksetters and the Lindos were accompanied by German investors, including the Rohrmosers, the Kobergs, and the Niehauses. By 1907, all of these families had acquired coffee *beneficios*, and some had consolidated large farms from several moderately sized farms in the older coffee-growing areas near San José, while others bought large estates in the newly formed coffee zone toward Turrialba in the east. By 1915, these families along with the Lohrengels, the Steinvorths, the Rosings, the Orlichs, and several others had acquired export houses. That year 42 percent of the export trade was controlled by firms owned by foreigners and 58 percent by Costa Ricans. The British market absorbed 77 percent of Costa Rica's coffee exports in 1915, but British export houses in Costa Rica controlled only 19 percent of the export trade, German firms controlled 13 percent, French firms 5 percent, and North American and Italian firms 1 percent each.[21]

Coffee processing became more centralized as a result of the crises of 1920–21 and 1929–35. By 1935 one-third of the coffee *beneficios* in Costa Rica were owned by foreigners or descendants of those who immigrated to Costa Rica during the nineteenth century, and these *beneficios* processed 44 percent of the country's coffee. That year foreigners processed 44 percent of Costa Rica's coffee, but they owned only 14.5 percent of the land in coffee. They fit into the general pattern of the Costa Rican coffee economy by buying mature berries from small and medium-sized client producers and making a profit on lending, processing, and exporting.[22]

The coffee boom also created opportunities for some poorer farmers to enter the ranks of the social elite. For example, Florentino

Castro inherited a five-acre coffee farm and twelve acres of pasture in 1896 when he was twenty-one years old. With savings from those farms and from transporting coffee to port, he began to acquire more coffee land. By 1907, Castro owned numerous coffee farms and a first-class *beneficio* on his farm La Pacífica near San José, and by 1915 he had become the fifth largest exporter of coffee in Costa Rica. Similarly, Julio Sánchez Lépiz, a family of small farmers, worked hard, saved, and invested shrewdly in coffee farms. By 1907, he had acquired a first-class coffee mill on one of his farms in Heredia, and by 1915 he had become known as the "King of Coffee" with the second largest export house in Costa Rica. By 1930, Sánchez was the largest coffee exporter.[23]

After World War II, the organization of the Costa Rican coffee business underwent many changes. The 1948 revolution jolted the hegemony of the coffee elite by the nationalization of the banks, which, for the most part, were owned by coffee barons. The government-owned banks began lending to medium-sized producers, thereby diminishing some of the financial controls traditionally exercised by private *beneficios* and export houses. Furthermore, the government encouraged the formation of producer cooperatives, breaking the monopoly of the private *beneficios* and export houses. Finally, the development of coffee-processing technologies with economies of scale created conditions for further centralization of holdings. As a result, single proprietorships declined in both the export trade and the *beneficio* business, replaced by joint stock companies and cooperatives.

The formation of joint stock companies was the natural outcome of the necessity to maintain large, consolidated *beneficios* and export houses when the heirs to these businesses were the numerous grandchildren and great-grandchildren of the original proprietors. Unlike land, which could be split into ever-smaller holdings, the processing mills and export houses had to expand in size to remain competitive. Thus the heirs and heiresses were forced to accept small shares of the larger enterprise, which in good years provided them with dividends. Those who showed business acumen and an interest in working for the family business could sometimes become managers of the enterprise or represent their side of the family on the board of directors of the corporation.

The formation of cooperatives stemmed from the same necessity to compete in a world that required larger capital investments.

The first cooperative in Costa Rica was established in 1948 out of the expropriated assets of the Niehaus estate in Grecia. La Victoria includes a sugar refinery, a coffee *beneficio*, and several hundred acres of coffee groves and sugar fields adjacent to the processing complex. In 1974–75, La Victoria was one of the largest coffee-processing plants in Costa Rica with a diverse mixture of associate producers. Thirty percent of the coffee that year was supplied by 783 small member producers, 48 percent by 194 medium-sized producers, and 22 percent by 8 large producers, one of whom was the general manager of the enterprise and a descendant of the nineteenth century coffee elite.[24] In the 1960s, international coffee prices declined from their highs in the 1950s, forcing marginal enterprises into bankruptcy.[25] Some of the assets of these marginal processing mills were acquired by larger private enterprises, but some were consolidated into cooperatives, which received preferential credit from the government-owned banks. By 1981, 33 of Costa Rica's 107 coffee *beneficios* were operating as cooperatives. Their crop-lending practices were similar to those of privately owned *beneficios*, but the profits and risks were spread among the member producers. In addition, most of the cooperatives circumvented private merchants by buying fertilizer, pesticides, and equipment in bulk for member farmers. All of these cooperatives except La Victoria participated in a single, large export business. Ironically, the cooperatives did not form primarily to service the small producers. In 1974–75, 23 percent of Costa Rica's small producers were members of cooperatives, and 41 percent of medium-sized producers and 27 percent of large producers were members of cooperatives.[26] In part because of the changes after World War II in the structures of coffee processing and finance, family-sized farms in Costa Rica gained greater access to capital for reinvestment in cultivation. As a result, Costa Rican coffee yields rose dramatically during the 1950s so that by 1960 Costa Rica had surpassed El Salvador as the country with the highest yields per acre in the region.[27]

Increasing competition from the cooperative sector and within the private sector caused some of the traditionally strong coffee enterprises to lose their relative shares of the market, while those that reorganized their activities to fit the changing business environment increased their relative control over the coffee economy. Despite these changes since World War II and the influx of foreigners into the coffee elite in the late nineteenth and early twentieth centuries, the top of the Costa Rican coffee hierarchy today has a surprisingly high concentration of descendants from families that were elites during the first half of the nineteenth century.

An examination of the registry of *beneficios* in 1981 reveals that out of 107 private and cooperatively owned mills in operation, 65 had upper-level management or board members with the same surnames as those on the list of import merchants before 1850 and 75 firms had managers or board members with the same family names as those on the list of important coffee growers between 1820 and 1850.[28]

The turnover of elites in the coffee export business has been greater than that in the processing business, but the participation of descendants of earlier elites is still very high. Of the twenty-two coffee export houses in business in 1981, five had upper-level management with the same names as those on the list of import merchants before 1850, and seven had upper-level managers with the same surnames as those of important coffee growers between 1820 and 1850. The reasons for the unusual stability of Costa Rica's coffee elite can be better understood when compared with the evolution of the coffee elite in the other Central American countries.[29]

Capital and the Guatemalan Coffee Elite

Before the Liberals took power in 1871, there was no banking house in all of Guatemala. The credit system was still dominated by merchants in Guatemala City and Antigua, who supplied merchandise to farmers on credit in return for futures contracts on forthcoming crops. Prices of merchandise were set high and prices for crops low, enabling the merchants to exact high implicit interest payments on top of normal merchant profits. The crop lien system and favorable laws under Conservative rule permitted merchants to maintain in muted fashion some of the privileges enjoyed during the colonial period. The crop lien system in particular allowed them to influence farmers' decisions about what to grow and what inputs to use in the process.[30] For crops with a short growing season such as indigo or cotton, the provision of short-term crop loans was not excessively burdensome, but for long-term investments such as coffee cultivation, the system was inadequate. When the Liberals came to power in the 1870s, the Guatemalan state began an assault on colonial impediments to trade and capital formation.

The Liberal land reform with its emphasis on private titles created a basis for long-term lending with land as collateral instead of future crops. In 1873, the government used proceeds from the sale of expropriated church property to found the Banco Agrícola-Hipotecario, which allowed only agricultural property as security for loans. In 1881, the government established another long-term lending institution, the Banco Agrícola del Occidente, which channeled finance into the western piedmont and upper elevations of the central piedmont, which was being consciously promoted by government developers as a coffee export zone. These government banks were not always successful because they became open to government abuse when emergency finance was needed, but they broke from the crop lien system and paved the way for private banks to engage in long-term lending.[31] In 1878, the Banco Colombiano was established with private capital mostly from Colombians who had invested in coffee growing in Guatemala. By 1885, the merchant houses of Guatemala City were still the most important providers of agricultural credit, but they now competed with three private sector banks that had a total capital of five million pesos.[32] A decade later, there were six banks competing with merchant houses.[33]

In addition to financial reforms in the 1870s and 1880s, tax reforms released capital for investment and encouraged the commercial development of coffee. *Diezmos*, which had been a drain on private capital formation, were abolished, and the state instituted a two peso-per-*caballería* (110 acres) land tax that stimulated commercial development and sale of idle lands; the proceeds went to build roads. When prices of coffee were high, part of the windfall went to the government in the form of an export tax, but when prices fell these taxes were lowered. To stimulate the transfer of modern technology from Europe and North America, the duty-free importation of certain agricultural implements, processing equipment, and intermediate inputs was allowed.[34]

In an effort to attract international capital, an immigration society was formed in 1877. Foreigners were assisted in obtaining lands and were granted a ten-year holiday from local taxes, a six-year holiday from import duties on tools and machinery, and a six-month holiday on the importation of seeds, food, and personal belongings.[35] Licenses to establish import and export houses were granted to foreigners, and the Barrios government began to sign contracts with foreign firms for large-scale construction and colonization projects.

For most of the decade of the 1870s, world coffee prices exceeded fifteen cents a pound, and those who had invested in coffee reaped large profits. This success along with government programs to stimulate coffee created a speculative environment. Those with access to capital rushed to establish coffee farms and to import machinery for coffee processing. By 1880, Guatemala had some seven hundred pulping machines, more than two hundred threshing machines, and more than sixty steam engines. The expansion did not halt even in periods of low coffee prices. For the first five years of the 1880s coffee prices dipped below ten cents a pound, and this occurred again between 1897 and 1910, 1914 and 1918, 1921, and 1931 and 1933, each time bankrupting individuals and depreciating the market price of coffee farms. During these crisis periods, coffee estates were bought up, and when prices began to recover more processing equipment would be imported. By 1934 the number of steam engines used in coffee processing had doubled since 1880, the number of pulping machines had tripled, the number of threshing machines had nearly quadrupled, and many plantations had acquired mechanical dryers, water wheels, electric generators, centrifuges, ventilators, sorting machines, and mechanical polishers, some of which had not yet been invented in 1880.[36]

Who owned the great plantations of Guatemala and the modern processing plants? Who controlled the export trade and coffee finance?

Judging from the evidence available, the Guatemalan coffee elite was not a static group but experienced considerable turnover as the fortunes of individual families were subjected to cycles of boom and bust, penetration by foreign capital, and whims of changing governments. Even during the Conservative period, when official policies may have retarded rapid changes in landownership, labor relations, and access to capital, the collapse of the cochineal market sent shock waves through the old established commercial center of Antigua. With the Liberal reforms of the 1870s and 1880s, all sorts of opportunities emerged for those outside traditional elite circles to establish large capitalist enterprises in the country. In 1890, after two decades of Liberal coffee promotion, there were 112 Guatemalan farms listed with one hundred thousand or more coffee trees, representing only 3.5 percent of the coffee farms in the country but more than half (53 percent) of the coffee trees covered by the census.[37]

As might be expected, some of the owners of these large farms were descendants of wealthy Creole families who had ruled Guatemala before independence and had withstood land expropriations and exile afterward. For example, the Saravia family had intermarried with and become part of the extended Aycinena clan during the colonial period and were descendants of don Ignacio González Saravia, who served as captain general of Guatemala under Spanish rule; in 1890, José E. Saravia owned two large coffee farms, one with 150,000 trees and another with 215,000 trees. Similarly, the Urruelas and the Beltranenas, who had intermarried with Aycinenas and whose family members had served as priors and consuls of the Consulado de Comercio before independence, were among the coffee elite in 1890. Both families had large coffee farms with each family owning at least 250,000 trees. Others may not have been connected with the Aycinena clan, but their power and influence predated the rise of coffee. The Samayoas, Aguirres, Aparicios, and Matheus all had family members who served as priors or consuls of the Consulado de Comercio during the Conservative period of Rafael Carrera. By 1890, Juan Francisco Aguirre had a farm with 150,000 trees, Juan Aparicio had two large farms with a total of 500,000 trees, and Víctor Matheu had a coffee farm with 400,000 trees. Some of these earlier elites such as the Samayoas and Matheus had been heavily involved in the cochineal business before they invested in coffee.[38] For example, by 1890 José M. Samayoa, who had been a major lender during the cochineal boom of the 1840s and 1850s, had four large coffee farms with a total of 810,000 trees and several smaller coffee farms; most of these properties were located in the previous cochineal districts around Lake Amatitlán, suggesting a possible takeover of lands from smallholders when the cochineal market crashed in the 1850s and 1860s.

Some who appear on the 1890 list of large growers may have held land before coffee, but they greatly expanded their family fortunes through their connections with the Liberal state after 1871. For example, the Auyón family from San Marcos was one of the largest holders of hacienda lands in that district before the coffee boom, though they did not participate in national politics until Justo Rufino Barrios, whose mother was an Auyón, fought to overthrow the Conservative government; in 1890, the Auyón family was listed as owning a 300,000-tree farm named Siglo XIX in El Tumbador, San Marcos. Barrios himself had chafed under the Conservative land policy when he worked as a notary in San Marcos during the 1860s.

"Hacienda Serijiers—Guatemala," 1875. Returns from coffee investments supported European lifestyles for Central American elites. (Department of Special Collections, Stanford University Libraries)

In addition to notarizing land acquisitions for other growers, Barrios had invested in a medium-sized coffee operation in San Marcos before he came to power in 1873. After six years in power, Barrios had acquired several coffee plantations including El Porvenir, which by 1890 was listed as having 1,025,000 trees, the largest number of any plantation in the country at that time.[39] Barrios married Francisca Aparicio, whose father, Juan Aparicio, was an outspoken Liberal from the city of Quezaltenango. After coming to power, Barrios appointed his father-in-law governor of the department of Quezaltenango, placing him in charge of overseeing the distribution of properties in the Costa Cuca and El Palmar.[40] In 1890, Juan Aparicio and Sons owned the piedmont plantation Santa Cecilia with 400,000 coffee trees, and Barrios's brother-in-law Francisco Aparicio owned the plantation Casa Blanca, which had 100,000 trees. General Manuel Lisandro Barillas rose to power in the military under Barrios and became president of the country in 1885. By 1890 the Barillas family had the largest coffee holdings in Guatemala consisting of five coffee farms, three of them large capitalist plantations with a total 1,700,000 trees.[41]

Some of the earliest growers in Guatemala were immigrants. The news of profits from coffee and the enthusiastic welcome given foreign investors by the Liberals attracted many more to the country in the 1870s and 1880s. By 1890, one-fourth of the large coffee farms in Guatemala were owned by immigrants, including the largest coffee farm in the country. El Porvenir with its 1,025,000 trees in 1890 had been acquired from Barrios's widow by the German consortium Compañía Hamburguesa de Plantaciones. Indeed, German companies topped the list of foreign owners with fifteen large farms and a total of more than 4,000,000 trees, approximately 10 percent of all the coffee trees in Guatemala.[42]

In the four decades that followed, the flow of foreign capital intensified. Especially attracted to Guatemala were firms from the German ports of Hamburg and Bremen. Typically, a firm in Germany would set up a commercial house in Guatemala that would import hardware and other manufactured goods, make crop loans to growers, buy the crop at the end of the season, and export the coffee to Germany. Because of the financial connection with growers, these merchant houses became knowledgeable about the solvency of particular farms. When the owner of a farm came under duress, the merchant house, having access to commercial and finance capital in Germany, could acquire Guatemalan farms at bargain prices. It was rare for a merchant house to begin a plantation from scratch because lenders in Germany were unlikely to risk capital on a venture that would take five years before producing revenues; rather, the firm would buy up an already existing coffee farm with a reasonably assured cash inflow and then acquire contiguous lands for future expansion. Capital would be invested in improving existing groves, planting new ones, and renovating the processing mills on the plantation.[43]

In 1897, the world coffee market crashed. A combination of economic recession in the industrialized world and an enormous increase in Brazilian production levels[44] caused the world price of coffee to drop from sixteen cents a pound in 1895 to eight cents a pound in 1897, finally bottoming out at five and a half cents a pound in 1902.[45] This slump, which lasted until 1910, when the price of coffee rose above nine cents a pound for the first time in fourteen years, resulted in intense centralization of coffee production in Guatemala, with foreign firms, especially those of German origin, consolidating their holdings.

In 1897, 25 German individuals and corporations owned 66 coffee farms in Guatemala. By 1900, Germans had acquired 365,000 acres in Alta Verapaz alone, or about one-third of the land area of the department, where they produced between 60 and 70 percent of the coffee.[46] By 1913 there were 170 German-owned coffee farms that accounted for 36 percent of Guatemalan coffee production.[47] One example of a large buyout took place in September 1904, when Arthur and John Nottebohm, members of an important commercial and banking family in Hamburg, acquired from the Aparicio family for $731,095 some 29 properties in Guatemala, including 4 important coffee plantations, 9 lesser coffee farms, several *fincas de mozos* (labor reserve farms) with workers attached to them, a grand home in Quezaltenango, and several other urban and rural properties.[48] In the years that followed, the Nottebohm brothers bought more Guatemalan coffee farms and moved into banking, coffee processing, exporting, and importing.[49] Similarly, Erwin Paul Dieseldorff, also from an important commercial family in Hamburg, took advantage of this period of crisis to build a vertically integrated commercial empire in Alta Verapaz, with farms, processing mills, an export house, an import business, and several shops for the manufacture of wage goods and farm implements. In 1937, when Dieseldorff transferred the estate to his son, it contained at least 15 farms, some of them important coffee plantations and others that provided Indian laborers, food crops for wage supplements, and pasture for work animals.[50] Other important German acquisitions during this period were those of Schlubach, Sapper and Co. (Central American Plant Corporation), Sapper and Co., Buhl and Hochmeister, and others. Some of these German holdings were seized by the Guatemalan government during World War I, but many were returned to their original owners after the war, beginning a renewed expansion of German holdings in Guatemala. By 1932–33, five of the top eight coffee producers in Guatemala were of German origin, one was English, one North American, and one Guatemalan; together, these eight producers accounted for 17 percent of the Guatemalan harvest that year. All of these companies had their own modern processing plants, and most of them owned export houses and were involved in banking and crop finance.[51]

Even by Guatemalan standards, the process of elite turnover was hastened by the expropriation of Axis-owned assets during World War II. Following heavy U.S. government pressure in 1942, the Guatemalan government listed 139 farms as belonging to corporations or persons believed to be of German origin.[52] In 1944, 75 of these coffee farms and other German-owned assets were formally expropriated.[53] Unlike the expropriation of German assets in World War I, the majority of the properties expropriated in 1944 were not returned to the original owners after World War II but were held by the Guatemalan government, which managed them (usually poorly) or sold them (after 1954) to the private sector. In the early 1970s, the nationalized farms in Alta and Baja Verapaz that remained unsold formed into 22 producer cooperatives. In 1978, the remaining 20 government-owned farms were put up for sale to the private sector by President Romeo Lucas García.[54]

Despite the disruptions of World War II and the land reform of the decade that followed, the basis of Guatemalan coffee production, the large plantation, has been preserved since 1954 by a heavily militarized state that has been hostile to land and labor reforms. The 1979 agricultural census reported that 188 coffee farms larger than 2,200 acres accounted for approximately 20 percent of Guatemala's coffee production, while 3,463 farms with more than 110 and less than 2,200 acres accounted for 64 percent. The remaining 16 percent of the production was distributed among 94,028 small and medium-sized farms with less than 110 acres.[55]

The very largest coffee farms still have their own processing mills and export houses. Because of the move toward centralization in the processing business, however, during the 1970s and 1980s many large growers pooled their capital and invested in modern processing plants that take advantage of new technologies and economies of scale. These mills process the coffee of stockholders, who also benefit from the mills' processing of mature berries bought from small and medium-sized producers. An example of this is COGUASA, owned by large growers from eastern Guatemala. One of the COGUASA *beneficios* is Amate Blanco near Barberena, Santa Rosa, where a large wet processing plant is enhanced by a dry plant that has sun patios, mechanical dryers, threshers, hullers, mechanical sorters, and the latest laser technology for culling damaged beans. COGUASA also has its own export house.[56] In addition to grower-owned *beneficios*, there are several modern processing plants that are owned by Guatemalan industrialists who have not been involved in coffee growing. An example is one of the largest *beneficios* in Guatemala, San Lazaro in Antigua, owned by AGROPACIFICO Holding Company. San Lázaro buys half of the mature coffee berries it processes from small and medium-sized growers and about half from large growers. It also hulls and dries coffee that has already been processed to the *pergamino* stage (with the brittle shell still on); approximately 70 percent of this coffee comes from large growers, 20 percent from medium-sized growers, and 10 percent from small producers.[57]

Today's coffee elite in Guatemala continues to base its wealth on the ownership of large plantations and the control over vast numbers of poorly paid agricultural workers. This system has remained intact for more than a century, despite periodic upheavals. Nevertheless, those who occupy the top of the coffee hierarchy are not, for the most part, descendants of Guatemala's precoffee elite. Of the twenty-three surnames on José Cecilio del Valle's 1820 list of Guatemalan aristocrats, only three appear on the 1890 list of eighty-seven large coffee-grower families, and none appear as owners of the 125 largest coffee farms in 1933–34. Although they did not maintain positions at the top of the hierarchy, apparent descendants of nine of these preindependence aristocratic families did own coffee farms in 1984, but they owned only 1.2 percent of the farms on ANACAFE's list.[58] Of the sixty surnames on Ralph Lee Woodward's list of those who served as priors and consuls of the elite Consulado de Comercio between 1794 and 1871, only eight appeared as owners of large capitalist plantations (those with more than one hundred thousand trees) in 1890, when persons with these surnames owned 14 (12.5 percent) of the 112 large farms listed in that year's coffee census. By 1933–34 only 2 farms of the 125 largest Guatemalan farms were owned by persons with the same surnames as those on the 1794–1871 list. Of the broader list of 3,978 coffee farms in 1984, 423 farms (11 percent of the total) were owned by persons with the same surnames as those on the 1794–1871 list.

Even if we take 1890 as a starting point for analysis, there has been high turnover in the Guatemalan coffee elite. By 1933–34, only 9 of the 125 largest farms in Guatemala were owned by persons with the same surnames as those owning the 112 largest coffee farms in

1890. Apparent descendants of large growers in 1890 did continue to own coffee farms, but they did not maintain their position at the top of the coffee hierarchy. In 1984, 18.3 percent of the farms on ANACAFE's broad list of growers were owned by persons with the same surnames as those owning the top 112 farms in 1890.

What accounts for the higher turnover in Guatemala's coffee elite as compared to Costa Rica's? One economic explanation is the heavier investment of capital in Guatemala in the risky cultivation phase. During years of favorable coffee prices, Guatemala's plantation system yielded greater profits for the elite than Costa Rica's system of processing the coffee of small growers, but the profits claimed by Guatemalan elites were more vulnerable to world price declines than in Costa Rica. In Guatemala, a much larger share of the elite's capital was sunk into coffee groves than in Costa Rica, where capital was primarily tied up in processing equipment. Even during years of very low prices on the world market, Costa Rican elites continued to earn profits by purchasing mature berries from client farmers at prices low enough to guarantee a profit from processing. In Guatemala, losses could not be shoved onto the backs of small growers because the bulk of the coffee was grown on large farms owned by the processors themselves. Thus during years of depression Guatemalan coffee elites were forced to sell their plantations to newcomers while Costa Rican elites were better able to hold on to their coffee *beneficios*.

More important than economic vulnerability was the Guatemalan plantation system's political vulnerability. Coffee's rapid rise after 1871 was in large part a result of government intervention. The force of a highly centralized state was used to divert capital, land, and labor into the cultivation of coffee. Idle lands were taxed, merchant monopolies were broken up, church assets were expropriated, and land in potential coffee zones was seized by the state and doled out in large blocks to those with an inclination to invest. After 1871, descendants of the colonial aristocracy who had recovered some of their privileges under Conservative rule found themselves replaced either by aggressive upstarts who were connected with the Liberal state or by foreign capitalists who were invited in by the Liberal government. Some descendants of the colonial elite adjusted to the changing times and invested in coffee, but many lost land and commercial business to the politically connected newcomers.

The Liberal land reform built on the colonial precedent: the

Crown had the right to give and take away land. Despite the issuing of more carefully delineated titles in the late nineteenth century, the origin of the titles and the use of military force to establish and enforce them lingered in the minds of the laborers who worked the plantations, and the ease with which individuals connected with the Liberal state were able to acquire valuable properties lingered in the minds of displaced elites. The very size of the plantations made them a visible symbol of the power of capital and political connection, attractive targets for takeover either by purchase or by force. The primary mode of takeover between the 1890s and World War I was through market purchases, especially by foreign investors of German descent. During World War I, the state invoked its ancient privilege and took away properties of German nationals, only to return many of them to the original owners after the war. Again during World War II, a massive expropriation was carried out affecting one-fourth of Guatemala's coffee production and unleashing a decade of pressure for land reform from the peasantry. The order of the plantation system was reestablished after 1954 through the use of military force, and once again, those with capital and connections were favored in the grab for land. Because of the more firmly exercised precedent of the state giving and taking away land, there has been a higher turnover at the top of Guatemala's coffee hierarchy than in Costa Rica. Guatemalan elites today are aware of this history and their precarious hold on land, and they are strident in their demands that "land reform" not be uttered from the lips of government officials.

Capital and Coffee in Nicaragua

Although the coffee trade developed decades later in Nicaragua than in Costa Rica, Guatemala, or El Salvador, the pattern of first investments in coffee was similar to that in the other countries. At the opposite end of the spectrum from small farmers, who slowly expanded their groves by planting a few trees at a time, were elites, who from their previous commercial activities had access to capital that could be diverted into coffee growing, processing, and exporting. Precoffee elites were joined by professionals who had connections with local and national government and incomes sufficient to generate savings. As the trade developed, foreign investors with access to international markets and capital entered the business, setting up export houses and acquiring coffee farms.

A list of early coffee growers from Rivas suggests the pattern. Of the seven growers with twenty thousand or more trees in 1867, four had substantial holdings of cacao (Evaristo Carazo, General don M. Espinoza, José Antonio López, and Indalecio Maliaño), three were listed as major merchants (José Antonio López, Indalecio Maliaño, and Evaristo Carazo), two had large indigo plantations (Evaristo Carazo and José Chamorro), one was a cattle baron (Pedro Chamorro), one was a doctor (Dr. J. L. Colle), and one was an army general (General don M. Espinoza). Of the list of twenty-five Managua coffee growers with twelve thousand trees or more, six have the same surnames as those of cattle hacienda owners from Managua or Chontales (Francisco Aviléz, Francisco Bermúdez, Testamentaria de Ramírez A., José María Zelaya, Leandro Zelaya, Gordiano Zelaya), but for Managua there are no lists of merchants or investors in other sectors to make comparisons with.[59] Of the thirty-two early growers listed in Managua and Rivas, only one (Bruno Bone) has a surname that is not recognizable as Spanish, though three of the eighteen major coffee exporters in 1873 have non-Spanish surnames.[60]

Between 1871 and 1890, coffee exports expanded almost tenfold from 12,344 to 113,820 quintals.[61] Most of this development took place in the Southern Uplands, extending the ranks of the coffee elite to include both local and foreign investors, while at the same time promoting a class of small and medium-sized growers. A segment of the large growers specialized in raising coffee, but a significant element continued the pattern of diversification in commerce and other lines of business. Out of the thirty-four coffee growers listed in the 1892 directory, seven were wholesale import-export merchants with commercial houses in Managua, Granada, or Masaya, and nine growers owned coffee export houses. Five growers had both coffee export houses and general import-export businesses, while one family, the Chamorros, had members who were coffee planters, coffee exporters, wholesale import merchants, cattle ranchers, and bankers. The 1892 commercial directory shows an influx of foreigners into the Nicaraguan coffee business; out of thirty-five coffee planters in 1892, five have foreign surnames (Julio Baneki, Brown Hermanos, Daniel Frixione, Daniel Tritione, and Vaughan y Hermanos), and out of sixty-three exporters of coffee (hides, dyewoods, and so on), twelve have non-Spanish surnames (Otto

Blume, Pedro Burlet, and Ignatius Cardoza [Dutch]; Fred Derbyshire, Daniel Frixione, Groumeyer & Co., Pablo Giusto, Morris Hydne & Co., A. E. Pellas [Italian]; Alberto Peter, Alessandro Remotti, and Vaughan Brothers).[62]

As in other places in Central America, the rise of coffee in Nicaragua was accompanied by the development of new forms of finance. In addition to an expansion of traditional short-term crop loans, the coffee boom created incentives for long-term lending. As coffee lands were privatized, a market developed for already established farms, allowing growers to obtain longer-term loans using a lien on an existing coffee farm as security. One hybrid form of mortgage that became popular in the late nineteenth century was the *pacto de retroventa*, or repurchase agreement, whereby a grower would "sell" a farm to a lender, keeping use rights to the land in return for implicit or explicit interest payments to the lender over the term of the contract, at which time the grower would have the right to "buy back" the property at the original price; if the grower was unable to secure payment at the maturity date, the lender could take possession of the property. By examining the property records for what became the department of Carazo, Julie Charlip found some eighty-five cases of *pactos de retroventa* involving coffee properties between 1877 and 1901. This was the most common form of mortgage at that time and was used by large and small growers alike to obtain longer-term loans than was possible from traditional crop loans.[63] This early form of longer-term lending lasted into the 1930s in Nicaragua, but more conventional mortgages became popular as well, with payments sometimes designated in coffee and sometimes in money. In addition to long-term contracts between individuals, commercial banking institutions followed the rise of the coffee economy. By 1892, there were two banks in Nicaragua, the Banco de Nicaragua and the Banco Agrícola Mercantil, and seven private individuals in the coffee centers of Granada and Managua were listed as bankers. Charlip found that mortgage lending by banks in Carazo did not begin until 1913, when the Banco Nacional de Nicaragua made such a loan, followed by more numerous loans from the Compañía Mercantil del Ultramar in 1919.[64]

Conservative governments during the 1880s made a conscious effort to convert north central Nicaragua into a coffee export zone. Legislation was passed in 1877 and 1881 to abolish the political structures of the Indian communities, to extract forced labor from the communities, and to open Indian lands to outsiders; backlashes from the Indian communities were repressed with war in 1881 and a stepped-up military presence in 1885. In 1889, the government of Evaristo Carazo renewed the government subsidy of five centavos per coffee tree for growers who planted more than five thousand trees in the north central zone, and in an effort to attract foreign capital to the area, the government offered up to five hundred *manzanas* (865 acres) of unclaimed national lands free to foreign investors who planted more than twenty-five thousand trees in that region.[65]

The Zelaya regime (1893–1909) continued this program of subsidizing growers and passing land and labor laws favorable to capitalist farmers and decrees calling for the abolition of Indian community structures (1895 and 1906), but Zelaya created a stronger military apparatus for carrying out the transformation. Between 1890 and 1904 Nicaraguan coffee exports doubled in volume, and the north central zone became a major coffee-producing area. By the time of the 1909 coffee census, 23 percent of Nicaragua's coffee trees were located in what had been the Indian-controlled departments of Matagalpa and Jinotega. Abundant rainfall provided a cheap source of power, and producers in this zone could process coffee using the wet method, which enabled them to fetch a premium over Southern Upland coffee, where the dry method predominated.[66] Considerable capital was required for water processing, creating a barrier to entry for smaller growers, who became dependent on *beneficio* owners for financing and processing the crop. Out of twelve large capitalist enterprises in Matagalpa and Jinotega, nine had *beneficios* run by water power, two had steam engines, and only one was operated manually or with animal power in 1909.[67]

The Zelaya period witnessed a considerable influx of newcomers to Nicaragua's coffee elite. Of the fifty-two large capitalist growers in 1909 at the end of Zelaya's term, only twelve had the same family names found on a list of thirty-five important coffee growers in an 1892 commercial directory (before Zelaya entered office); eight of the large growers in 1909 were early growers or apparent descendants of those on a list of 1867 coffee growers. Only twelve of the large growers in 1909 had the same family names as those on a list of sixty-three coffee exporters in 1892. Some of the newcomers were from families involved in general merchant activities before Zelaya's term began, who were able to take advantage of the decline in plantation prices that resulted from the crash of the coffee market beginning in

1897 and from the incentives granted by the Zelaya government.[68] Others were foreigners who were attracted to the coffee business for the same reasons. Of fifty-two large capitalist growers in Nicaragua in 1909, twenty had foreign surnames and only three of those had invested in the Nicaraguan coffee business before Zelaya's term. In Matagalpa and Jinotega, where subsidies and free land were given as incentives, ten of the twelve large capitalist growers in 1909 had non-Spanish surnames.

Nicaraguan elites were less likely to pass down elite status to their progeny than were the Costa Rican coffee elites, though turnover among the elite appears to have been lower in Nicaragua than in Guatemala. Of the one hundred owners of Nicaraguan *beneficios* in 1957–58, only ten had the same surnames as those of the thirty-five growers listed in 1892. These notables were Rafael Cabrera, Agustín and Alberto Chamorro, Salvador and Joaquín Cuadra, Raúl Lacayo Montealegre, Ninfa Vega de Román, Arturo Vaughan, Franco Vega, and Ana María Zelaya. Only fifteen of one hundred *beneficio* owners were apparent descendants of the sixty-three coffee exporters of 1892, and twenty were apparent descendants of the fifty-two large growers of 1909.

Part of the explanation for the higher turnover in Nicaragua than in Costa Rica lies in the large plantation model that emerged there in the late nineteenth century. Indeed, the structure of coffee holding in Nicaragua is second only to that of Guatemala in the degree to which large plantations dominate the coffee landscape. As in Guatemala, this has made the Nicaraguan coffee elite more vulnerable to world market fluctuations, to labor unrest, and to land invasions. Furthermore, there has been a well-established tradition in Nicaragua (that is not so true for Costa Rica) for the acting president to distribute the fruits of power primarily to those closely related by kinship, friendship, or political party to the personalistic dictator. During the formative Zelaya period the government issued concessions primarily to those closest to the dictator. More than three million acres of land were sold, leased, or granted to private individuals or corporations during Zelaya's term, but not one sale was recorded to a member of the Conservative Chamorro clan, and only one member from each of the Conservative Zavala, Sacasa, Carazo, Arguello, and Solórzano families was sold a piece of land by the Zelaya government.[69] During the last ten years of Zelaya's rule there were no less than sixteen armed uprisings against him; during this time six members of the Chamorro family were exiled from the country. Toward the end of the period, when it became more and more difficult to collect taxes, the government resorted to borrowing heavily from abroad and issuing freshly printed money, much of it going to contractors close to the president.

This practice of using government funds to secure personal loyalties continued when Zelaya was replaced by a Liberal appointee, Dr. José Madriz, whose government was overthrown by Conservative General Juan Estrada less than a year later. Far from ending the practice, the Conservatives saw the opportunity to compensate themselves for seventeen years of hardship, doling out cash and land to those who had participated in the revolt. Total currency in circulation amounted to slightly more than 12 million pesos when Zelaya left office. After the next year of turmoil the total currency in circulation had risen to nearly 30 million pesos, and during the first four months of 1911, 15 million more pesos were issued by the Estrada government. According to an account from the U.S. banking perspective, "only a small portion of the new money went to defray legitimate government expenses, and the bulk of it was distributed among the friends of the new Government who presented various claims for payment."[70]

Stimulated by rising prices in the 1920s, coffee acreage was extended so that when the Great Depression hit, yearly exports were 30 percent higher than the peaks reached during the Zelaya period. Direct U.S. intervention in Nicaragua in 1912–25 and 1927–33 opened doors to foreign investors. Most notable in coffee was the firm Compañía Mercantil de Ultramar, established in 1912 by the banking houses of Brown Brothers and Seligman. This company came to dominate the financing and export of coffee from the region south of Managua. Although wet processing was more advanced in north central Nicaragua because of the abundance of water, until 1920 all of the coffee of Matagalpa and Jinotega was exported in the hull for lack of a hulling factory.[71] That year Englishmen David Dagnall and a Mr. Calley set up a threshing mill in Matagalpa and began buying coffee from growers in the area, offering advances on their crops. During the crisis of the 1930s, the firm of Calley-Dagnall acquired more than twenty-five large estates and numerous smaller ones, the total amounting to more than forty-five thousand acres.[72]

In 1933, the U.S. Marines were withdrawn and Anastasio Somoza García was appointed head of the U.S.-trained National Guard. He maneuvered himself into the presidency in 1936, where he remained until he was assassinated in 1956 and power in the National Guard and the presidency was passed on to his U.S.-educated sons, Tachito and Luís. From 1933 through 1979, the Somozas maintained control over the National Guard, and from 1936 through 1979, they acted as chief executives of the Nicaraguan government, except for a four-year period (1963–67) when a Somoza loyalist, René Schick, occupied the presidency. During four decades of rule, the Somozas continued the practice established during the nineteenth century, using their position in the National Guard and the national government to expand the personal fortunes of family members and those loyal to them.

During the Zelaya period, Anastasio Somoza invested in a coffee farm in the department of Carazo. By the 1909 coffee census the Somozas had ninety-four thousand coffee trees, a substantial farm just under the hundred-thousand-tree cutoff for a large capitalist plantation. After assassinating Augusto César Sandino in 1934, the National Guard swept through Matagalpa, Jinotega, and the Segovias, where Sandino's support had been strong, killing his followers and taking over lands that peasants had occupied under protection of his forces. Coffee lands and other properties that were taken in this counterinsurgency campaign were claimed by Somoza and either kept as Somoza properties or distributed to loyal officers in the National Guard and to others who had participated in the sweep. After seizing the presidency in 1936, Somoza began using state finance to acquire coffee properties from owners who were unable to pay off mortgages and from heirs anxious to liquidate estates they had inherited. During World War II, when Somoza came under pressure from the United States to expropriate coffee estates from German nationals, instead of offering them for sale to the elite, he kept them in the family trust. By 1944 Anastacío García Somoza had become the largest coffee grower in Nicaragua with forty-six coffee plantations, most of them in the north central zone but some in the older coffee area south of Managua.[73]

After Anastasio Somoza Debayle's fall in 1979, the Sandinista state continued the long process of turnover by expropriating assets of the dictator and those connected with his machine. In 1980, out of a total of fifty-two coffee-processing companies listed in the industrial directory, twenty-one had become the property of the state, including eight of the eleven large *beneficios* with one hundred or more workers and eleven of the twenty medium-sized *beneficios* with thirty to ninety-nine workers.[74] In addition to approximately half of the processing capacity, the Nicaraguan government acquired from the Somoza machine approximately 15 percent of the land area in coffee, including a large portion of the modern, higher-yielding plantations.[75]

The activist stance of the Nicaraguan state in the distribution of capital and land has benefited individuals who are closely connected with that state, but those who benefit during one era do not necessarily remain as elites in the following era. How a family might use state power to rise to elite status is remembered so that lands taken during one period become political spoils when that family loses political power. The colonial adage, "the king giveth and the king taketh away," remained in force in postcolonial Nicaragua, leaving the legacy of a higher turnover of that country's coffee elite than in neighboring Costa Rica.

Capital and the Rise of Coffee in El Salvador

The capital constraint in El Salvador was solved in a piecemeal fashion at first. Before 1880 El Salvador had no commercial bank. Early growers were obliged to raise capital wherever they could. Some were large landowners who were able to mortgage their indigo estates, diverting the proceeds into highland coffee lands. Others were professionals, military officers, or merchants from the larger towns who pooled their own savings and borrowed from friends and relatives. Once the coffee trade was established, coffee exporters advanced loans to growers, somewhat relieving the scarcity of capital. As coffee production expanded, growers were able to pressure municipalities to provide tax exemptions for those engaged in coffee production, lessening the drain of capital from growers.

By the early 1880s, coffee growers were able to consolidate a national state under their direction. At this time national land laws were passed declaring titled property the only legally valid form of land tenure, thereby legitimating a process of titling that had already taken place in the coffee districts and preparing the way for mortgage lending on an extended scale. In 1880, the Banco Internacional was established, making mortgage money available on a regular basis for coffee growers; it was followed by the Banco Particular in 1885, the Banco Occidental in 1890, and the Banco Agrícola Comercial in 1895.[76]

As was true in the rest of Central America, the capital requirements of coffee allowed foreigners to join the Salvadoran elite. Unlike Guatemala, where commercial ties with Germany permitted a single colony of foreigners to dominate coffee trade and production, El Salvador developed more diversified trading networks, exporting coffee to the United States, France, Germany, Italy, the United Kingdom, and other countries with no country taking an export share greater than 30 percent.[77]

Immigrants began import-export businesses, relying on existing connections in Europe and North America, but as they became knowledgeable of the coffee business, they invested in coffee-processing mills and plantations. An early example of this pattern is Emilio Belismelis, who arrived in El Salvador from Spain in 1868 to establish an import-export business in Santa Ana, where he served as consul for Spain. By 1875, Belismelis had acquired several coffee estates and a coffee-processing mill, and a century later his descendants were listed as important coffee producers and businessmen.[78] In 1887, the Italian partnership Borghi, B. Daglio y Compañía established an import-export business in El Salvador. By 1915, the company had become one of the most important merchant enterprises in El Salvador with additional interests in coffee and banking. For years B. Daglio served as the consul of Italy in El Salvador, and Borghi served on the board of directors of the Banco Salvadoreño, in which he was an important shareholder.[79] J. Hill, son of a wealthy Manchester industrialist, arrived in El Salvador at age seventeen in 1888. Soon thereafter he established an export business, which was later extended into cultivation and processing of coffee.[80] Similarly, in 1896 Herbert de Sola, a Spanish Sephardic Jew who came to El Salvador from Panama, established a luxury import business and soon began exporting coffee. The trade prospered as de Sola invested in coffee-processing mills and coffee farms. By 1974, H. de Sola and Sons was the largest coffee exporter in El Salvador with 14 percent of total exports going through the family business.

Examples abound of immigrants in the late nineteenth and early twentieth centuries who became members of the Salvadoran coffee elite. Immigrants sometimes received official welcomes, but because the Salvadoran state was so much less centralized than that of neighboring Guatemala, the official attraction of foreign investors was less coordinated and less directed toward a single country. Immigrants with capital, international connections, and expertise came to El Salvador from many places in Europe and the Americas. No single immigrant group was large enough to form its own cultural enclave as the Germans did in Guatemala. The British, French, Germans, Italians, North Americans, Spaniards, Lebanese, and Jews who were attracted by the coffee boom, mixed with the Salvadoran elite, adopted Spanish as their primary language, married Salvadorans, and became naturalized citizens of El Salvador. Fortunes rose and fell, and coffee plantations, processing plants, and export houses changed hands, giving some fluidity to the Salvadoran coffee elite, but if the early 1920s are taken as a base, more than half (55 percent) of those listed as major exporters in 1921 appeared in the early 1970s as large growers, coffee exporters, *beneficio* owners, and large landowners (see Appendix A, Table A.3). Most of those who remained at the top of the social pyramid in the 1970s had either descended from the precoffee elite or immigrated to El Salvador in the late nineteenth and early twentieth centuries. The following list of important coffee-producing families in the early 1970s reveals a scattering of names—Regalado, Salaverría, Alfaro, Palomo, and Quiñonez—that predate coffee, but these are mixed into a much more numerous group—Llach, Schonenberg, Drews, Sol, de Sola, Deinenger, Cohen, Cristiani, Belismelis, Battle, Harrison, Dalton, Daglio, Liebes, Borgonovo, Kriete, Duke, and Homberger—who arrived during the coffee boom (see Appendix A, Table A.3).

This list reveals a much greater concentration of control over the export trade than over coffee cultivation. In 1973–74, forty families controlled two-thirds of the country's coffee exports, the top seven families alone handling 44 percent of the country's exports, but in 1970–71, these forty families' farms produced only 29 percent of Salvadoran coffee and the top seven producers accounted for 14 percent of the crop. These figures suggest a continuation of the earlier pattern of participation in the cultivation phase by smaller capitalist producers and even peasant and small family holdings, with the elites having large coffee plantations and controlling coffee finance and the export trade. Elite control over processing came later to El Salvador than Costa Rica. As late as 1938, one-third of Salvadoran coffee was still being processed by the dry method, allowing some of the smaller growers to avoid relations with elite-owned *beneficios*.[81] At the insistence of the coffee growers' association that dry

processing be phased out, during the late 1930s the Salvadoran government offered subsidies to expand wet-processing facilities;[82] by
1953, only 15 percent of Salvadoran coffee exports bypassed wet-
processing plants, and this portion was further reduced during the
1950s and 1960s.[83] In addition to owning large coffee plantations
and having a virtual monopoly over coffee processing, export, and
finance, El Salvador's coffee elite has responded flexibly to new areas
of investment when opportunities have emerged. An examination of
other holdings of the top forty coffee families during the early 1970s
reveals highly diversified portfolios with investments in cultivation
and processing of such other agricultural products as cotton and
sugar and in Salvadoran industry, commerce, communications, and
real estate. Although there are other important Salvadoran families
who have not partaken directly of coffee profits, the great majority
of those at the top of the economic pyramid have as a basis of the
family fortune coffee holdings from the late nineteenth and early
twentieth centuries.[84]

Although peasant and family-sized farms have participated in the
cultivation of coffee in El Salvador more than in neighboring Guatemala, El Salvador's plantations have also become a symbol of power
and prestige, and the memory of how the large estates were taken
from peasant communities in the late nineteenth century has made
them a recurring target of peasant unrest. At least since 1906, however, the Salvadoran coffee oligarchy has not been nearly as divided
as Guatemala's (or, of course, Nicaragua's), and the Salvadoran state
has acted more in the interest of the oligarchy as a whole and not so
much as a vehicle for one elite group to accumulate at the expense
of another. This configuration of a united oligarchy has resulted in
a lower rate of elite turnover than in Guatemala (or Nicaragua),
even though it has had to share power with the Salvadoran military
since the 1930s. Until the 1980s the Salvadoran coffee elite was able
to withstand extreme pressures from below by presenting a united
front through the Salvadoran state, which during times of crisis has
traditionally acted in the oligarchy's short-term interests.

Capital and the Rise of Coffee in Honduras

Just as banks were established elsewhere in Central America to
provide long-term finance for coffee cultivation, the Liberal gov-

ernment of Honduras followed the lead of other governments and provided incentives for the founding of private banks in 1882.[85] But efforts of the weak central government could not immediately overcome the unfavorable business environment for long-term lending. Nineteenth-century Honduras had the poorest transportation network, the least developed wage labor pool, the least integrated national market, and the shallowest connection with the world economic system of any country in Central America. Hence Honduras was the last of the Central American countries to embrace the coffee boom and the last to have a commercial bank. Even after 1888, when the first Honduran bank was chartered, long-term lending to the coffee sector was impeded by the durability of a peasant-based land tenure system in potential coffee areas. Only privately titled estates could be offered as collateral for mortgages, and most of the land suitable for coffee was located in zones where *ejidal* rights to land were carefully guarded by peasant communities.

In 1889, some 422,089 pounds of coffee were registered as exported from Honduras, making coffee the sixth most important export that year behind silver, bananas, silver coin, cattle, and coconuts. The merchant connections for coffee were not like those for silver, bananas, and coconuts, which were shipped directly to importing countries. Rather, the bulk of Honduran coffee was transshipped through larger-volume export merchants in neighboring countries, much like the previous indigo and tobacco trade. In 1889, more than half of Honduran coffee (56 percent), primarily from the western towns of Copán, Gracias, and La Esperanza, was being shipped to merchants in San Salvador, and another 8 percent was shipped to merchants in Guatemala or Belize. Merchants in Puerto Cortés handled 14 percent of coffee exports and, following the brisk trade in bananas, was shipped directly to the U.S. market, while merchants from the southern port of Amapala by 1889 had established direct ties with importers in France, England, and Germany, who bought 12, 8, and 2 percent of Honduran coffee exports that year. For the country as a whole, however, only 36 percent of the commerce in coffee had direct links with the capital-rich markets of Europe and North America.[86]

Capital did penetrate the Honduran coffee sector but in a limited fashion with credits almost exclusively short-term in nature and attached to crops, not land, as collateral. Capitalist-sized farms with twenty *manzanas* or more of coffee were established in Honduras, but they represented the smallest portion of total land area in coffee of any country in Central America. In 1914–15, there were eighty-three farms in Honduras with twenty *manzanas* (thirty-five acres) or more of coffee, comprising only one-third of the coffee area in the country. Only twenty-eight of these farms were privately titled, the rest being *ejidal* lands or in one case national lands.

The area of the country where capital penetration was more advanced and private titles were more prevalent was in southeastern Honduras in the departments of Choluteca and Paraíso, where three of the five large capitalist coffee farms (100 *manzanas* of coffee or more) were located. All three of these large capitalist enterprises were privately owned by 1914–15, and only one of the fourteen capitalist-sized coffee farms in this zone remained under the *ejidal* form of land tenure. The largest coffee farm in the country was a plantation by the standards of Guatemala, El Salvador, and Nicaragua, with 500 *manzanas* (865 acres) of coffee and 520 acres of other crops, located in the department of Choluteca. It was owned by Pedro Abadíe, whose family had an import business in 1889 and who in 1914 owned retail shops in the town of Choluteca and warehouses in Choluteca and at the Pacific port of Amapala. Nearby was the third largest coffee farm in Honduras with 140 *manzanas* (242 acres) of coffee owned by the German merchant Enrique Köhncke, who, in addition to running an import-export business, also owned a soft drink factory; the Köhncke family operated an import-export business in southern Honduras in 1889. Other merchant families from Choluteca, including the Agasses and the Molinas, invested in coffee at higher elevations, with groves of 50 and 140 acres respectively. In neighboring Paraíso, the largest coffee grower was an absentee owner from Tegucigalpa, who had a coffee farm with 140 acres in groves. This operation tied with the Molina holding for sixth place in Honduras, and it was owned by the wealthy widow Isabel de Agurcia, who was listed in 1916 as the individual capitalist in Honduras who paid the largest amount in road taxes.[87] The Agurcias were late nineteenth century export-import merchants, who in 1915 also owned a cattle ranch, an ice factory, a soft drink bottling plant, a sugar mill, and a rum factory.[88]

Honduras received some of the spin-off of German capital that entered Central America through Guatemala. The main commercial attractions were gold, hides, silver, and coffee. By 1899, nine of the twenty-four export houses involved in the Honduran coffee trade were owned by individuals with German surnames, and the numbers increased until World War I, when exports were diverted to the United States.[89] A few of these merchants invested in coffee farms, but they were more likely to invest in soap factories, breweries, bottling plants, or other businesses that produced for the domestic market. Perhaps because of the unfavorable conditions for large-scale coffee production, the Germans in Honduras never gained control over the cultivation phase as their compatriots did in neighboring Guatemala and to a lesser degree in Nicaragua, but by the early twentieth century, more than half of Honduras's coffee exports went to Germany, and the rest were shipped to the United States.[90] After World War I, exports to Germany never fully recovered, but German businessmen continued to own enterprises in Honduras. Even after expropriation of German businesses during World War II, several important German coffee exporters revived their businesses, and they continue today as exporters, *beneficio* owners, and commercial lenders to the coffee sector.[91]

Although a commercial top to the coffee hierarchy can be identified, it was feeble by Central American standards, and financial and marketing connections between the top and the bottom were not nearly as strong as in Costa Rica. The larger farms had better access to processing plants and commercial credit, and their coffee was more likely to make its way into the export trade than that of the smaller farms. Even up to World War II, only one-third of annual coffee production in Honduras was released for sale on the world market, the great bulk being consumed nationally, where standards of quality were not nearly so demanding as in the world market. Some of the smaller producers of high-quality coffee must have been tied into commercial contracts with larger growers and *beneficio* owners, but at this early stage many of the smaller producers used the dry method of processing on dirt patios, and they sold coffee in excess of home consumption on local markets.

After World War II, the lower rungs of the coffee hierarchy were increasingly linked with larger-scale commercial producers and processors. In the 1950s, coffee released for export exceeded half of total production for the first time in Honduran history, and this proportion of exports to total production climbed to 62 percent in 1960, 78 percent in 1970, and 94 percent in 1987. During the same period, Honduras went from the position of a minor exporter representing 2 percent of Central America's coffee exports in 1948 to an exporter representing 15 percent of the area's exports in 1987, vying with Costa Rica as Central America's third most important exporter. When the Honduran export boom finally arrived after World War II, it produced changes in structures of land tenure, commerce, and finance.

Similar to what happened almost a century earlier in the other Central American countries, the Honduran coffee export boom after World War II was associated with a shift toward private landholdings. In 1952, only 23 percent of Honduran coffee acreage was on privately titled farms and 45 percent of the area in coffee was on purely *ejidal* holdings.[92] By the mid-1960s, 58 percent of the census area in Honduras's top ten coffee *municipios* was privately held, and only 11 percent of this area remained in *ejidal* holdings.[93] Unlike the transformation to private property in sections of Guatemala, El Salvador, and Nicaragua, however, the Honduran case did not involve the transfer of land to large holders at the expense of the peasantry. Rather, the outcome was more like that of Costa Rica, where those at the top of the commercial hierarchy relied on small and medium-sized producers to provide them with mature berries at harvest time. The rich did invest in larger holdings, but these holdings rarely exceeded one hundred acres. The bulk of the elite's profits came not from commanding large acreages and large numbers of workers but from buying cheaply from small and medium-sized producers and controlling the processing and export of the product.

By the time the export boom hit, Honduras already had a commercial banking system, and in the early 1960s, government development banks formed that provided finance for the coffee economy. The Honduran system of finance was thus less dependent on annual advances from importers in the industrialized countries than the other countries were when they experienced their export booms nearly a century earlier so that the export houses of Honduras did not come to monopolize financial channels. Rather, banks would lend to *beneficios* or to the medium-sized and large farmers who could provide land as collateral and who would serve as intermediaries, lending to higher-risk small farmers who would pledge coffee at harvest time at prices set before the season. The most favored of the intermediaries were those with coffee *beneficios* who were able to buy from smaller producers at low prices, process the coffee to the *pergamino* stage, and then store it until the export houses offered more favorable prices.[94]

Although export houses did not dominate coffee finance, sizable corporations came to control its export, making profits both from the ownership of large, centralized complexes for the drying, hulling, and grading of coffee and from the differential between the export price and the price paid to coffee farmers. Thus, though the coffee farmers were many in number and, by standards of the other countries, predominantly small producers, the export houses were as centralized or more so than in the other countries. In 1972–73, there were seventeen export houses for all of Honduras, and the largest, EXCAHO, accounted for 36.5 percent of Honduran exports; the top five together controlled 80 percent of coffee exports that year. As exports more than doubled in volume during the 1970s, other export houses participated in the boom, but still in 1977–78 the top five export houses maintained more than half of the export trade in coffee.[95]

The export houses began to invest in large, technically advanced coffee farms, but the bulk of their profits came from dealing with independent coffee farmers. Therefore, it was in the interest of the export houses for the Honduran government to stimulate the development of the coffee sector. In 1970, the Instituto Hondureño del Café (IHCAFE) was set up to encourage private farmers to expand their acreage in coffee and to upgrade existing coffee farms so that higher yields of export-quality coffee could be achieved. The government development bank, Banco Nacional de Fomento (BANAFOM), whose lending to the agricultural sector came under a separate government bank called BANADESA in 1980, extended loans to the coffee sector and encouraged private banks to do the same.[96] Producer cooperatives were favored by government programs, and by 1977 there were some twenty-six coffee cooperatives with a membership of 6,123 producers within the national federation of coffee cooperatives, FEHCOCAL, which also owned a large dry *beneficio* and export house.[97]

The government programs of the 1970s were aimed primarily toward the medium-sized coffee producers, which were deemed more likely to introduce modern methods of cultivation than the small producers. Indeed, from 1970, when IHCAFE began its work, and 1980, yields per acre rose 40 percent. In the early 1980s, when coffee rust (*la roya*) began to spread through Honduran groves, small producers who had not received government assistance or bank finance during the 1970s came to be seen as a threat to the whole coffee sector because they were more likely to have groves with poor shade management, inferior pruning practices, and fewer resources to combat the spread of the fungus. At this time, USAID joined with IHCAFE in a small farmer coffee improvement project that devoted approximately $10 million over a five-year period (1981–86) to renovate coffee groves of some forty-six hundred small producers and to connect them with private credit facilities and teach them cultivation practices that would raise yields and reduce coffee rust infestation. This project proved highly successful and was extended with an additional $10 million for another five years.[98]

Ironically, the policies of the U.S. security state in aiding the Nicaraguan Contras during the 1980s resulted in the displacement of thousands of small farmers from the eastern sections of the departments of El Paraíso and Choluteca, some of whom were recipients of the small farmer coffee improvement project supported by USAID The accumulated losses from inability to harvest coffee in this area were estimated at $3.3 million as of October 1986, and the Contras continued to occupy this territory, preventing the displaced from returning to their coffee groves until the late 1980s. The coffee area affected by the Contra war was estimated at 2,908 acres or slightly less than 10 percent of the country's total coffee area.[99]

In addition to the disruptions of production from the Contra war, the Honduran export business experienced financial upheaval in the 1980s. In 1987, one large private export house, EXCAHO, bankrupted with a net outstanding debt in excess of $15 million. Moreover, the cooperative movement suffered a financial blow in the last months of 1986, when it was revealed that the upper-level management of FEHCOCAL had misappropriated funds. The bankruptcy of FEHCOCAL's export house, which had a net outstanding debt of $17.5 million, called into question the financial viability of IHCAFE, BANADESA, and BANHCAFE, all of which had lent money to FEHCOCAL. These setbacks were somewhat counterbalanced by increased yields in areas not affected by the Contra war and by recent investments by Salvadorans, especially in coffee processing.[100]

Capital shallowly penetrated the Honduran coffee sector during the late nineteenth and early twentieth centuries, when two-thirds of the area under cultivation remained in peasant and family-sized farms, the *ejidal* form of land tenure dominated, and only one-third of production was exported. After World War II, lending to the coffee sector picked up, lands were privately titled, and capitalists invested in modern processing facilities and export houses. Nevertheless, the nineteenth-century pattern of peasant and family-sized farms producing the majority of the coffee continued despite the changes in processing, commercialization, and land tenure.

Conclusion

High potential rates of profit in the Central American coffee business attracted capital from Central America, Europe, and South and North America, but because profitability conditions were unevenly distributed in time and space, investment did not flow smoothly into all phases of the coffee business at once. In addition to economic conditions, political conditions influenced perceived profitability and risk. How governments acted (or failed to act) to remove obstacles to the flow of capital greatly affected when and where investments were made, influencing the diffusion of technology in cultivation and processing, the rate of growth of coffee exports, and the resulting social relations of production and exchange.

In the cultivation phase, the highest rates of profit were achieved in El Salvador, Guatemala, and Nicaragua, where labor costs were kept relatively low. Following the takeover of Indian lands in El Salvador during the 1880s, a flexible labor market emerged with an abundant supply of people willing and able to work at low wages. In Guatemala and Nicaragua, the cost of labor was low, but because of the ungovernable agricultural frontier and the strength of Indian communities, growers faced the uncertainty at harvest time that laborers who had signed debt agreements would evade their contracts; in both of these countries, capital did not fully penetrate the growing phase until governments (in Guatemala in the 1870s and in Nicaragua in the 1890s) effectively intervened in the labor supply process and reduced the uncertainty of securing labor at harvest time. In addition to intervening on behalf of capitalist growers to provide access to labor, Guatemalan and, later, Nicaraguan governments offered tax concessions and easy access to land to foreigners who had capital, expertise, and international business contacts. By 1900, capitalist-sized farms deominated the cultivation of coffee in all three countries.

A labor market developed in Costa Rica, but the small population, easy access to land for small farmers, and higher customary standards of living at the lower rungs of the social hierarchy led to high wage rates relative to elsewhere in Central America. Peasant and family-sized farms that were not as dependent on wage labor came to dominate the cultivation of coffee, while elites concentrated their investments in processing coffee. Because the shortage of labor limited the number of trees peasant and family-sized farms could plant at one time, Costa Rica's coffee boom was gradual compared to that of Guatemala, El Salvador, and Nicaragua, where expansion was rapid once conditions were right for capitalist investment. Members of Costa Rica's coffee elite owned coffee groves as a means of establishing a high-quality base for supplying berries to their processing plants, but because higher rates of profit could be gained from processing, Costa Rican elites plowed back most of their earnings into improved processing facilities. By the turn of the twentieth century, practically all of Costa Rican coffee exports were processed by the wet method, and Costa Rican coffee sold at more favorable prices than elsewhere in the region, where substantial amounts were still being processed by the primitive dry method. Because growing coffee yielded relatively low rates of profit, by 1900 yields per acre in Costa Rica were much lower than in El Salvador, where the combination of lower wage rates and a limited supply of land suitable for growing coffee led growers to plow capital back into techniques that would raise yields, permitting El Salvador to achieve the highest yields per acre in the region and, on the large capitalist estates, some of the highest yields in the world.

In Honduras, rates of profit in cultivation were the lowest in the region, not only because of inadequate supplies of wage labor, but also because the transport problem was the worst in Central America. Uncertainty of investing in a coffee plantation was further heightened in Honduras by a peasant-based land tenure system throughout most of the coffee region that resisted the move to privately titled holdings and favored the maintenance of *ejidal* rights to land. Furthermore, the national government of Honduras was unable to get international loans to solve the transport problem and was both unwilling and unable to confront the communities of peasants and other small farmers who controlled much of the land suitable for growing coffee. Before World War II, most of Honduras's coffee was grown on *ejidal* lands, processed on dirt patios, and sold in village markets. The only place where capital did penetrate the growing phase was in southern Honduras, where wage labor, privately titled estates, transport, and commercial connections with the world market were better developed than in other coffee-growing areas. After World War II, private titling of farms, the development of a wage labor force, state road-building programs, and government-assisted finance helped stimulate a coffee export boom that by the 1980s pushed Honduras into the ranks with Costa Rica as a coffee producer. Despite the more thorough penetration of capital after World War II, Honduran structures of coffee cultivation continued to be dominated by small and medium-sized farms, while elites invested in processing mills and heavily centralized export houses.

Because of the long period between initial investment in coffee cultivation and the time revenue began to come in, a niche emerged for commercial banks to pool local and foreign sources of liquidity and make long-term loans to growers. The founding of commercial banks closely followed the extension of coffee cultivation. The first country to have a commercial bank was Costa Rica, also the first to enter the coffee boom, followed by Guatemala, El Salvador, and Nicaragua; the last to have a commercial bank was Honduras, the latecomer to coffee cultivation. Throughout the region, long-term lending was channeled into large capitalist plantations, not peasant or family-sized farms, which were perceived as a greater credit risk. Small growers everywhere had to be content with short-term crop loans, often at exorbitant interest rates, from owners of larger plantations, owners of *beneficios*, and merchants who had access to cheaper sources of finance. Therefore, mortgage finance more thoroughly stimulated coffee cultivation in Guatemala, El Salvador, and Nicaragua, where the large plantation became the dominant model, than in Costa Rica or Honduras, where peasant and family-sized farms prevailed. Only after World War II did long-term lending to the average grower occur in Costa Rica (1950s) and Honduras (1970s), and in both cases this was the result of government direction in bank lending policies; in both instances yields per acre improved dramatically as noncapitalist and small capitalist farms responded to better access to long-term credit. Improvements in cultivation practices were so dramatic that by the late 1950s, average yields in Costa Rica had surpassed those of El Salvador as the highest in Central America, and by the late 1970s average yields per acre in Honduras paralleled those of Guatemala.[101]

The industrializing countries of Europe and North America were an important source of capital for the expanding coffee economy. At first, capital flows were short term and closely attached to the commodity trade. Importers of hardware and capital equipment would extend short-term credit to coffee growers who purchased those items, and coffee exporters would advance crop loans to coffee processors and growers. Thus capital would be borrowed from Europe and North America for nine or ten months of the year, to be paid back at the end of the harvest season. Some of the merchant middlemen were native Central Americans who over the years proved their credit ratings with commercial houses in the industrializing countries, but many were immigrants who brought with them expertise, capital, and personal connections with coffee importers and manufacturers in Europe and North America. As commercial relations matured, coffee exporters acquired processing mills and coffee plantations, sometimes taking long-term loans from commercial houses or banks in Europe and North America. As news of the coffee bonanza spread, more foreigners immigrated to Central America to invest directly in coffee *beneficios* and plantations. What had begun as strictly short-term flows diversified to include long-term investments.

Immigrants came to Central America from Britain, France, Germany, Italy, Spain, the United States, and other places. At first, there was a close connection between the destination of coffee exports and the sources of immigration. In Guatemala, trade ties with Germany were inherited from the days of cochineal, and a German community was already established there before coffee. As German immigration expanded with coffee, this earlier group of immigrants formed the nucleus of a rapidly growing German enclave with its own institutions. The German presence was so strong in Guatemala that it heavily influenced the cultural inclinations of the native elite as well as the policies of the Guatemalan state. In contrast, in El Salvador the direction of coffee exports was more diversified and no single group of foreigners tended to colonize during the coffee boom. Immigrants to El Salvador were more likely to use Spanish as the everyday language, and they were more likely to mix with native Salvadorans, thereby forming an integrated Salvadoran oligarchy with more diverse international connections than in Guatemala. In Costa Rica and Nicaragua, trade was more heavily oriented toward England so a greater number of British investors were among the early coffee exporters and processors. In Costa Rica, the orientation toward the British market led to a decided Anglophilia within the elite that was reoriented toward the United States when markets shifted to North America after World War I.

Of all the foreign investors in Central America, the most noticeable were the Germans, who were highly successful in sensing local differences and investing accordingly. In Guatemala, German plantation owners quickly adapted to the local custom of using the state to help them draft Indian labor. In Honduras, German merchants did not try, for the most part, to establish large coffee plantations as they did in Guatemala; rather, they understood the limits of Honduran capitalism and remained as merchants or manufacturers of items for the domestic market. Despite the dominance of British trade links with Costa Rica, German immigrants were able to secure a firmer hold over the ownership of *beneficios* than their British counterparts. Throughout the region, German trading firms were flexible in shifting export markets depending on the direction of the trade winds. German export houses in Costa Rica affiliated with and sometimes owned import houses in Britain, thereby capturing a portion of the British coffee market. When World War I disrupted trade patterns with Europe, German trading companies throughout the region established import houses in North America or affiliated with U.S. import companies already in the business.

The way the state intervened influenced the flow of foreign investment, the depth of capital penetration in the coffee economy, and the pace of coffee expansion. It also influenced the stability of the elite. At first blush, it might be thought that heavy state intervention on behalf of large capitalists might lead to a more firmly entrenched elite. This proposition is not supported by evidence from Central America. The countries where the national state most actively promoted the large plantation model generally experienced higher turnover among the elite than in Costa Rica, where more egalitarian land and labor policies were adopted.

One reason for this difference is economic: elites whose investments were more concentrated in large plantations reaped windfall profits during periods of high coffee prices but were more subject to losses during periods of depression, whereas elites who concentrated their investments in processing mills and export houses could quickly adjust to a downturn by lowering the prices paid to growers for their crops. During periods of depression, the large plantations of Guatemala and Nicaragua were more likely to change owners than were the large processing mills of Costa Rica.

The economic vulnerability of the large plantation was exacerbated by its political vulnerability. To the agricultural work force, the large plantation became a symbol of expropriation of peasant lands and ongoing exploitation of labor by the elite; when governments have become open to pressures from below, as in Guatemala from 1944 to 1954 and in Nicaragua after 1979, large plantations, especially those containing idle lands, were subject to land invasion by peasants and expropriation by populist governments. To groups of elites who were excluded from a land grab during one period, the large plantations represented the cronyism of parvenus of a particular period, setting a precedent for expropriation and redistribution to another group of elites later on. The Nicaraguan state provided spoils to Conservatives during one period and Liberals during another, a pattern that was established long before it became the instrument of personal accumulation for the Somoza family and its friends in the 1930s. Similarly, the highly centralized state of Guatemala was used by Liberals (1829–39) and then Conservatives (1839–70) to expropriate and redistribute land and wealth until the 1870s, when the Liberal state began to hand out potential coffee lands to foreigners and close political supporters. The single group in Guatemala that was most successful in acquiring properties was the Germans, who formed an enclave with political clout during the Liberal era. They became vulnerable to seizure of their properties, however, when political pressures were brought to bear from the United States. German holdings were expropriated by the state during World War I, returned when the political climate changed after World War I, expropriated during World War II, and gradually sold to new owners after World War II. In contrast to Nicaragua and Guatemala, Salvadoran coffee properties during the late nineteenth century were distributed more by municipal authorities than by the national state, allowing for a greater mix of medium-sized coffee farms than in Guatemala and Nicaragua. Because foreigners came to El Salvador from diverse places and mixed readily with Salvadoran elites, they were less visible and less vulnerable to outside pressures for expropriation. Furthermore, once the coffee growers' state was established in El Salvador, it ruled not for one tiny fraction of the elite versus another but for the oligarchy as a whole. This meant that in times of severe pressure from below, the coffee elite formed a more united front against workers and peasants, allowing for a lower rate of elite turnover than was true in Guatemala or Nicaragua, where the elite was more divided.

Chapter 6

Coffee, Class, and the Creation of National States

The building of national governments in Central America has a stormy history that began with independence from Spain in the early 1820s and lasted to the end of the nineteenth century. What became independent, legitimate states by the end of the century evolved from colonial institutions that were unevenly distributed over the isthmus. From this motley colonial base, national states were constructed during a period when industrial capitalism was spreading through Europe and North America, changing the demand for tropical products and revolutionizing world transport with the building of railroads and steamboats. These developments in the world system conditioned economic opportunities in Central America and unleashed conflicts among elites over how public institutions should respond to changes in the world system.

It became clear as the century progressed that the greatest economic opportunity in the region lay in the cultivation of high-grade coffee, which could be produced at a low cost because of special conditions of soil and climate. After the easiest places had been pulled into coffee cultivation, growers faced obstacles that were difficult to surmount on an individual basis and began pressuring public institutions to assist them in the acquisition of land, capital, labor, and infrastructure needed for further expansion of coffee production. The availability of productive factors and the nature of existing public institutions varied considerably from one place to the next, influencing the dynamics of struggles and the character of the national institutions that congealed when and where the coffee elite finally emerged victorious by the end of the century. Thus coffee cultivation and the social classes that formed around it shaped the evolution of national governments in the region, leaving lasting differences in the disposition of governments toward the governed.

Precoffee State Institutions
and Philosophies of Governance

The Spanish withdrawal from Central America in the early 1820s
undermined a network of central state institutions that had governed
the five-province area through its regional headquarters in Guatemala City. Some Guatemala City merchants and other established
elites who feared a chaotic and ungovernable situation attempted to
prop up the old central structure by replacing Spain with Mexico
as the higher authority, but Mexican institutions were too weak
and separationist sentiments too strong to permit such a modification; in 1823 the region cut loose from outside support structures.
For almost two decades, an umbrella government calling itself the
United Provinces of Central America officially represented the five
provinces, but its abilities to tax, supply public goods, and maintain public order were severely limited. Social tensions that had long
smoldered under Spanish rule broke into open flame with the collapse of central authority, and by 1825 civil wars had erupted that
were not curtailed until several years following the breakdown of
the United Provinces of Central America in 1838–40. Although the
idea of a federal republic composed of five provinces continued in
the public mind, it was gradually replaced between 1850 and 1900 by
the idea of five separate nations, which had officially declared themselves independent nations by the late 1840s but which developed
their actual abilities to govern at an uneven pace for the remainder
of the century.

Tensions inherited from the colonial period were many and complex, but at least two became significant in shaping the formation of
national institutions. One conflict that continued to rage after independence was between provincial elites and Guatemala City's merchant elite, which had so successfully tapped economic surplus because of its favored position in intraregional and extraregional trade
during the colonial period; this old antagonism played an important
role in trade and taxation policies and secessionist thrusts after independence. A second pervasive conflict was over basic philosophy
of governance. One perspective, which Miles Wortman has traced
to the years of Hapsburg rule in the sixteenth and seventeenth centuries, limited the role of the central state to the collection of tribute
and the establishment of a coercive apparatus for maintaining public
order and safety. From this perspective, the provision of public goods

such as roads, ports, hospitals, and schools, and even tribunals for mediating social conflicts, were better left to nonstate institutions—the church, local charitable organizations, *fueros* (groups with local representation empowered to settle certain classes of disputes), and business groups—all of which were permitted considerable local autonomy in return for loyalty to the central authority. A second perspective of governance, often associated with the Bourbon reforms of the last half of the eighteenth and the early nineteenth centuries, advocated a more interventionist role for the state in channeling capital, land, and labor to stimulate economic development and to provide public goods that would serve that higher purpose, sometimes to the detriment of the church and local institutions that may have been involved previously in such work. After independence, the elite camp was fiercely divided over the proper role of the state and quasi-public institutions in the provision of public goods and management of economic activity. The Hapsburg vision of slow adaptations under the guidance of the church and other quasi-public institutions came to be associated with the Conservative party, and the more interventionist stance came to be associated with the Liberal party, though this link between philosophy of governance and political party weakened with distance from Guatemala City and as the century progressed.[1]

Because central state institutions under the United Provinces (1823–40) could not be built to match the central power structures of the colonial period and national state institutions were constructed slowly over a lengthy period (1840–1900) does not mean that nineteenth-century Central America had no effective and continuous state structures. Although there was little continuity in centralized state institutions, local governments, centered in the major townships of the region with origins dating to the early colonial period, continued to function effectively throughout the turbulent nineteenth century, spanning the Bourbon reforms and the reaction to them during the last two decades of the colonial period, the attempts at union and civil wars of the first two decades of independence, and the nation-building process during the last half of the century. It is to these local structures of power that one must look to understand the evolution of national structures.

During the colonial period, the *ayuntamientos* (councils) of the major townships were selected and staffed by local citizens, not by the central authority. These councils were granted some limited powers to tax, to form their own local militias, to undertake public works, to set up tribunals for settling disputes, and to allocate land surrounding the township. Over the years, the *ayuntamientos* gained considerable public legitimacy in administering day-to-day affairs of a local nature, but the ultimate authority on matters of a higher order rested in the bureaucratic representatives of the Crown, who in the late colonial period attended their posts in Guatemala City (capital of the kingdom of Guatemala), Ciudad Real (the intendancy of Chiapas), San Salvador (an intendancy covering much of El Salvador except Sonsonate), Comayagua (the intendancy of Honduras), León (the intendancy of Nicaragua), and Cartago (the *Gobierno* of Costa Rica).[2] When central authority collapsed following independence, the relative power of the town councils increased, a situation that lasted for decades. When the Liberal Francisco Morazán took Guatemala in 1829, he made sure that he defeated and gained control over the *ayuntamiento* of Guatemala City, the most venerable state institution in all of Central America, which at the time was controlled by a Conservative faction of Guatemala's traditional merchant elite.[3]

The *ayuntamientos* were the most significant political institutions through which the various social conflicts of the first two decades of independence were fought, and they acted as a destabilizing force, with local *caudillos* using their positions in the townships to muster troops loyal to them in order to launch national or federal campaigns. Within every province there were at least two rival townships, each with its own power structure and memories of grievances from times past; a threatened township would occasionally forge an alliance with a more powerful township in a neighboring province to bolster its position against the dominant rival. The Liberal bastion of Los Altos (Quezaltenango) fought an ongoing battle with the Conservative stronghold in Guatemala City, Conservatives of San Miguel (El Salvador) on occasion linked up with the Guatemala City elite to counter actions by the Liberal-dominated and powerful *ayuntamiento* of San Salvador, Tegucigalpa elites cooperated with Guatemala City in opposition to the Comayagua power structure, *caudillos* of León attempted to extend their powers after independence but were resisted by the merchant elite of Granada, which allied itself with the Guatemala City elite, as did at one point the *ayuntamiento* of San José to counter its rival in Cartago and preempt the expansionary moves of León (Map 6-1).[4] Lesser townships were pulled into the fray through alliances with the major rivals,

"Quezaltenango—Guatemala," 1875. Housed in buildings like the one at the center of this photograph, *ayuntamientos* handled affairs of a local nature and distributed lands around major townships during the colonial period and after independence, providing institutional continuity at times when central state structures and the power of the church were in a state of flux. On the left in the background is the cathedral of San Juan de Dios, and in the plaza is the Indian market. (Department of Special Collections, Stanford University Libraries)

thereby enhancing the financial resources and fighting power of the various sides.

In the context of feuding city-states with shifting alliances, the thin layer of central government, which was won militarily by Liberal forces in 1829, had great difficulty collecting taxes and carrying out reforms at the federal level. The greatest success in implementing reforms at the state level during the years 1829 to 1838 was achieved by Gálvez in Guatemala, where the population was more accustomed to a centralized state whose institutions remained some-

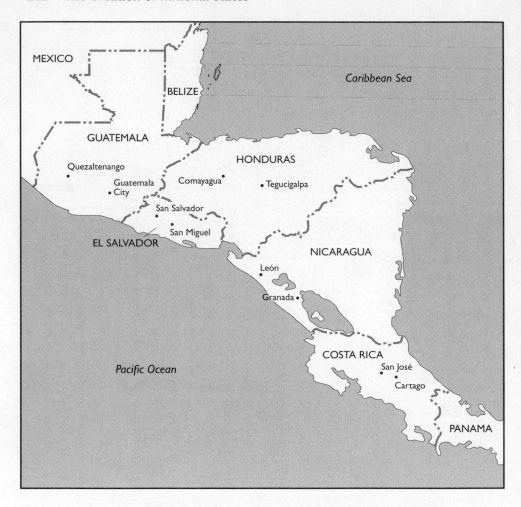

Map 6-1. Major *Ayuntamientos* in Central America, 1820s–1830s

what intact after independence. Gálvez used the state government to expropriate large landholdings of the church (and some of the landholdings of Conservatives), and he introduced land and labor legislation intended to stimulate commercial agriculture and social legislation to overturn paternalistic colonial arrangements between the state and Indian communities. A limited tax base and inadequate military forces, however, could not withstand the peasant reaction to Liberal reforms, and in 1838 a peasant uprising led by Rafael Carrera ousted the Liberals, permitting the Conservative elite and the church to regain some of their former privileges. During the three decades of Conservative rule that followed in Guatemala, the Hapsburg tradition was partially restored. Private sector organizations and the church expanded their powers to supply public goods, local communities increased their autonomy over land and labor, and the central state concentrated its efforts on strengthening the military.

Elsewhere on the isthmus, central state institutions were far more difficult to develop owing to provincial inexperience with central governance and ongoing fighting among elites, who continued to use their power in the townships as a basis for securing hold over newly forming national institutions, only to be overturned by another group that was able to get support from outside the country. Between 1841 and 1861 the Salvadoran presidency changed hands forty-two times, a term lasting on the average less than six months, with Liberals (such as Doroteo Vasconcelos and Gerardo Barrios) getting support from allies in Honduras and Nicaragua and Conservatives (such as Francisco Malespín and Francisco Dueñas) getting official recognition and occasional military assistance from the Carrera regime in Guatemala. Salvadoran rivalries continued to operate on a national level at least until the end of the nineteenth century, but patriarchs increasingly worked through the national armed forces, which gained greater coherence after 1861, and were able to hold office for longer terms. In Honduras, Conservatives such as Francisco Ferrera and Santos Guardiola held onto national office with help from Carrera in Guatemala and Mora in Costa Rica, while Liberals such as Trinidad Cabañas, who had been an ally of Morazán in the days of the federation, received tactical support from Liberals in neighboring countries. In Nicaragua, rivalries erupted between the power structures of León and Granada, and for the first decade of the national period it was not unusual for the country to have two governments operating simultaneously from the two traditional centers of power. Political instability culminated in the Filibuster War (1855–57), when the Liberals from León, who had a long-established hostile relationship with the Conservatives of Guatemala City, colluded with the North American William Walker to crush the Conservatives in Granada, which was sacked and burned to the ground. Walker was finally ousted by an army led by Costa Rican Conservative Juan Rafael Mora, who had political backing from Carrera and military equipment from the British.[5] After the defeat of Walker, the merchant-landowner elite of Granada finally brought some stability of governance to Nicaragua by moving the capital to the more neutral location of Managua and retaining hold of the presidency of the country for three decades.

Wars and political instability during the years of federation and the first decades of the national period had a devastating effect on economic development. Able-bodied men were conscripted, thereby diverting the most valuable agricultural input away from productive activity. Marauding armies slaughtered cattle and sequestered draft animals, torched buildings and destroyed farm equipment, burned crops and expropriated merchandise, depleting the capital base of the agrarian economy. Military expenditures drained public treasuries and triggered defaults on public debts, creating an unstable financial environment for public borrowing for more worthwhile pursuits like the provision of public goods.[6] Moreover, the threat of expropriation and destruction of private property discouraged long-term investments by both foreigners and local elites.

Costa Rica best avoided the ravages of war. It was the poorest province at the time of independence, the farthest from the center of power in Guatemala City, and the least dependent on central authority for social cohesion during the colonial period. From 1824 through 1842, Costa Rica experienced only five battles with an estimated total of 144 casualties, the lowest in the region by a large margin.[7] Costa Rica was able to enter the coffee trade first because colonial policy had prohibited this province from entering the dye trade, which after independence continued to tie up capital, land and labor in Nicaragua, El Salvador, and Guatemala. In addition to a more flexible international market connection, Costa Rican coffee cultivation was favored by a relatively peaceful transition following independence, whereas destruction of property and expropriations in Nicaragua, El Salvador, and Guatemala inhibited long-term investments there. Interestingly, it was in Costa Rica where the process of nation building from the bottom up began, a process repeated as coffee cultivation spread north.

Coffee and the Building of National States

The influence of the coffee boom on the construction of national states did not begin as overt pressures on central state institutions. During the early phases of coffee expansion, the key focus of collective activity by growers was not at a national level but at the level of municipal government. The most appropriate lands for the early development of coffee were near commercial townships in suitable ecological zones. In these townships a labor force could be found to plant and maintain the groves and harvest the ripe berries. Land farther away from population centers that fell within the domain of central state institutions was of little commercial value during the early days of the coffee boom. It was in the commercial townships where wealthier individuals lived who could finance coffee investments and where institutions with wealth holdings (private commercial establishments, community chests, charitable organizations of various sorts, and religious orders) were located. The major townships also hosted the state institutions that carried the greatest public legitimacy during a period when central institutions were in disarray, and the *ayuntamientos* had long-standing jurisdictional powers over land from one to ten miles from the center of town. In the more commercialized townships, a local economic elite composed of merchants, professionals, and large landowners had long held sway over town hall so that when coffee became a viable investment, this elite began using its influence in municipal government to activate the resources at hand (land, labor, capital, and public funds) to facilitate the expansion of coffee cultivation. Thus throughout the isthmus the first state actions to promote coffee were taken by municipal governments, not national state institutions.

Coffee townships prospered as profits were reinvested, municipal tax bases were deepened, and local police forces were strengthened. All of this expanded the power of coffee townships relative to those where coffee could not be grown. As the limits of accumulation within the coffee townships were approached, however, the focus of political action shifted from the municipal level to higher-order state institutions. Coffee growers began to use their positions of power in the coffee *municipios* as a springboard for pressuring national institutions to assist them in building roads, bridges, and ports and in harnessing land, labor, capital, and other resources that were beyond the jurisdictions and capabilities of their own town governments. Sometimes the interests of coffee elites in one township coincided with those in another, encouraging elites to dampen traditional rivalries to achieve a common national goal. Examples of collusive behavior across the coffee townships abounded as local limits to land, labor, and capital were realized, but when the Honduran default in the early 1870s made international investors more wary, there was a regionwide effort to present an external facade of national political stability to attract the capital necessary to build railways into the coffee districts and to undertake other major infrastructure projects that were beyond the financial means of town governments.[8] Hence the development of the coffee economy created a material incentive to suppress age-old rivalries, but the transition from chaos to order was fraught with controversy, depending on social and political dynamics that varied across the region.

Costa Rica was the first to build coherent national institutions from a base in the coffee townships. Before the collapse of the federation, the *municipio* of San José had established its commercial dominance over the other townships, and after winning the battle of the League in 1835, San José became the permanent capital of the province over the colonial capital of Cartago, a political dominance that was retained after separation from the federation. The most dynamic group of investors resided in San José, where very early on they privatized municipal lands and provided municipal subsidies to stimulate coffee cultivation. Success in San José was repeated in the other larger commercial townships of the Central Valley, and by the late 1840s national legislation was passed to project the same policies onto those municipalities that had not yet adopted the San José measures.[9] Similarly, road building and other infrastructure projects were initiated by the elite of San José with the help of the municipal government during the 1840s, but by the 1850s the national state had begun to take an active role in large projects that overstretched the boundaries of individual municipalities and their fiscal capabilities. In this way, by midcentury a centralized state structure had begun to emerge from the town governments of the highlands, and the capital was located in the center of coffee accumulation, San José.

During the late colonial period, San Salvador was the second largest town in Central America, and its *ayuntamiento* continued to exert dominance over other townships after independence and following the breakdown of the federation. Nevertheless, the proximity to Guatemala allowed elites from other townships or those with minority views from San Salvador to link up with the more powerful state in Guatemala to gain control over national institutions. The coffee boom began later in El Salvador than in Costa Rica, but once it began, a very similar political process got under way. Commercial interests worked first through the town councils to pass ordinances favorable for coffee cultivation, and once those efforts had taken hold, they moved to the national level to generalize over the entire country the measures that had proven successful in their own districts. This process came at least two decades later in El Salvador than in Costa Rica, and even by the 1890s, much of the implementation of national-level legislation was left up to the authorities in the townships.[10] The Costa Rican national state achieved greater stability in the 1870s, but the Salvadoran state continued to be weakened by *caudillo* rivalries into the 1890s, hastening turnover in the office of the president. When a Salvadoran president instituted some unpopular measure, local strongmen, who were frequently both coffee growers and generals, would seize the opportunity to take over the presidency. Although the Liberal president Rafael Zaldívar (1876–84) pushed through a sweeping land reform supported by coffee growers across the country, when he instituted a coffee export tax, coffee growers from the western districts became alarmed. General Francisco Menéndez, who was a prominent coffee grower and former mayor of Ahuachapán, allied himself with Guatemalan general Justo Rufino Barrios and forced Zaldívar from office, serving from 1885 to 1890. Similarly, when President Carlos Ezeta (1890–94) imposed a $2.25 per quintal tax on coffee exports, General Tomás Regalado, a prominent grower from Santa Ana, staged a coup from the Santa Ana barracks, enabling Rafael Gutiérrez (1894–98) to take over the presidency.[11] In summary, El Salvador experienced the building of a centralized state during the latter half of the nineteenth century, but the forward thrust of national policy continued from the local foundation of power in the prospering coffee townships. It was not until the end of the century that traditional rivalries were dampened and rule by a unified planter class, with regular four-year transitions was instituted that lasted until the crisis years of the 1930s.[12]

In Guatemala, which retained its centralized state inherited from the colonial period, town councils were significant in activating resources within their jurisdictions, but department governments became a central focus of collective action for influencing change outside of the jurisdiction of townships. Department capitals were invariably located in the most important commercial centers of a department. Even though department governors were officially appointed by the chief executive in Guatemala City, local elites came to exercise influence over them. Guatemala's coffee boom began under the Conservative rule of Rafael Carrera, who adopted an official policy of protecting Indian communities from encroachment by commercial interests. In the coffee districts, however, growers came to wield influence over department government officials, who helped growers secure labor for building roads into plantation areas. Furthermore, growers formed lobbying groups that successfully pressured the national government to reduce the *diezmo* and to give agricultural awards to growers who developed new export crops. In the early 1860s, the Carrera regime passed a law encouraging communities to rent land to commercial interests, though the communities retained the right to refuse access to outsiders. Thus pressures from the bottom up worked through department governors, gradually eroding national protections from the excesses of commercial expansionism, an erosion that increased after Carrera died in 1865 and was replaced by Cerna, who had been a departmental governor sympathetic to large landowners in eastern Guatemala. Despite relaxation of some of the Conservative brakes on accumulation, Liberal coffee growers, especially from the western district with its dominant township of Quezaltenango, desired more forceful state actions and finally seized control of the Guatemalan state in the early 1870s.

After William Walker's defeat brought the civil war in Nicaragua to an end, the León Liberals, who had colluded with Walker at the beginning of the war, lost the possibility of controlling national politics, and power shifted decidedly toward Granada. Between 1859 and 1889, all of the presidents of Nicaragua were from the merchant-landowner elite of Granada, which had identified itself early on as a Conservative stronghold in opposition to León.[13] Although Conservative in name, these leaders were from families who had a vested interest in promoting new exports, and many of the actions taken during their rule more resembled Liberal policies than those associated with Guatemalan or Salvadoran Conservatives. The first president of this period, Tomás Martínez (1859–67), placated the León Liberals by establishing the capital in Managua instead of Granada. It has been said that Martínez took measures to stimulate coffee cultivation around Managua to encourage the growth of a new group of elites separate from the traditional groups in Granada and León.[14] Martínez may or may not have intended it, but by 1867 some twenty-six coffee estates had been established in the Sierras de Managua south of the new capital, and none of the owners of these estates were from the Granada elite, which concentrated its coffee holdings and lending operations in the Carazo Plateau, closer to merchant headquarters in Granada.[15] During his eight-year rule, Martínez used funds of the national state to improve port facilities at Corinto near León, to assist in rebuilding Granada, and to construct roads that would stimulate coffee and commerce in general. The Conservative governments that followed continued to improve roads and ports, to build railroads, and to pass land laws favorable to the development of coffee. While the Granada elite controlled the presidency, coffee cultivation flourished both in the Carazo Plateau, where the Granada elite's major coffee investments were located, and in the Sierras de Managua, where local elites from Managua and foreign investors came to dominate production. In 1875, the department of Managua was carved from the larger department of Granada, possibly reflecting both the expanding population of Managua and the greater political clout of the Managua group. By the 1880s a new Liberal Unionist Club, centered in Managua, had formed that sought to link Nicaragua with the more forceful Liberal movements of Guatemala and El Salvador, and political activity in the capital became imbued with what one writer described as "an exaggerated local egoism" surrounding the "coffee aristocracy," as the Managua planters had come to be known.[16] The most difficult problem for capitalist growers in Nicaragua was securing an adequate labor supply. Frequently workers would accept money in advance for harvest labor, but at harvest time they would flee the jurisdiction of the coffee municipalities, where growers controlled the local police. Growers appealed to the national government to establish a national system to apprehend fugitive workers. Between 1862 and 1891, a new labor law was passed every three years, but the national institutions were too weak to implement these laws so that by the end of three decades of Conservative rule, coffee growers who wanted a more rapid development of coffee were ready for a shift to a leader promising a stronger national state.[17] In 1893, General José Santos Zelaya, the son of a capitalist coffee grower from Managua and a Liberal who had earlier served as adjutant to Justo Rufino Barrios in Guatemala, rose to power. During Zelaya's sixteen-year rule, he strengthened and modernized the military, enabling better enforcement of labor contracts and allowing growers to secure access to lands that had not yet been claimed by commercial agriculture. Before Zelaya's term, most of Nicaragua's coffee was cultivated in the Southern Uplands, where land and labor were already under the control of commercial interests with assistance from their municipal governments, but with the support of a stronger national military, growers were enticed to invest in plantations in the north central region around Matagalpa and Jinotega, which soon rivaled the more established Southern Uplands as a coffee producer.[18]

Unlike the other countries, Honduras did not develop a national class of coffee growers capable of building a national state. In 1876, when a Liberal state was transplanted into Honduras from Guatemala, Marco Aurelio Soto, who had served Barrios's government as vice-minister of external relations, and Soto's second in command, Ramón Rosa, who had served as Barrios's treasury secretary, began a series of reforms that imitated the Liberal reforms carried out by Barrios in Guatemala. The *diezmo* was abolished, new civil codes and a new constitution were written, and an agricultural law was designed to stimulate capitalist agriculture. Although Soto (1876–83) and his successor, Luís Bográn (1883–91), had Liberal convictions equally as firm as those of their counterparts elsewhere in Central America, the situation in which they governed could not have been more different. Without an active class of agricultural entrepreneurs to push the reforms from below, the actions of the Liberal state scarcely penetrated beyond the capital city. Although legislation was passed giving the facade of a liberal, secular state, the Honduran government continued the colonial tradition of living off concessions to *aguardiente* producers and foreign companies. Later in the nineteenth century, renewed investment in the mines brought in foreign capital and international connections for the political elite of Tegucigalpa, who sometimes secured executive positions abroad for themselves or their sons in return for "legal" services rendered in Tegucigalpa. Others used the international connection to send their children to school in the United States or to marry them to the offspring of mining company executives.[19] The Honduran state was strong enough to marshal its resources to defend a concession if it came under attack by local communities, but it was too weak to intervene in day-to-day affairs of communities that were dispersed over difficult terrain.[20] The Honduran agricultural development law and labor codes were implemented by municipal authorities, who were influenced by whatever power structure existed in that locality. Most of Honduras's potential coffee land was located in mountainous areas where peasants held sway over local governments. Thus at a time when everywhere else in Central America *ejidal* and municipal lands were being privatized for coffee production, in Honduras peasants protected themselves by having their townships petition for the registration of larger areas under municipal and *ejidal* control. Coffee was eventually grown in Honduras, but it was cultivated predominantly by peasants on *ejidal* lands and grown not for export but for sale in local markets, a situation that lasted until the 1950s. In southern Honduras, merchants and landowners had sufficient clout in the commercial township of Choluteca to secure the land at higher elevations suitable for coffee, but they did not have colleagues in a similar position in other towns to form a lobbying force at a national level.[21] It was not until the 1930s under Tiburcio Carías Andino (1932–48) that national-level institutions reached down through department and municipal governments, giving greater coherence and effectiveness to national policies in Honduras.[22]

Coffee Elites and the Holding of Public Office

To forge national institutions that could effectively promote coffee, the Central American coffee elite directly participated in government. In Costa Rica, where coffee became an important export shortly after independence, of the seventeen governors and presidents between 1824 and 1863, only five were not coffee growers, exporters, or both, and three of those five were close relatives of either growers or important import merchants (see Table 6-1). In Guatemala coffee exports more than tripled in volume between 1873 and 1892, a period of heavy state intervention to build a coffee economy. The Liberal rulers of Guatemala during this period of consolidation were Justo Rufino Barrios (1873–85), who began his term in office as a modest but enthusiastic grower and owned the largest coffee plantation in Guatemala when he died in battle, and Manuel L. Barillas (1885–92), who was the most important grower in Guatemala in 1890, when the coffee census lists him as owning five coffee plantations including the third and sixth largest in the country.[23]

In El Salvador, consecutive rule by large growers did not begin until 1898, but between 1856 and 1898 men who were either growers or later became growers served sporadically as president of the country for a total of seventeen of the forty-two years. These men were Francisco Dueñas, Gerardo Barrios, Angel Guirola, and Francisco Menéndez. Direct rule by growers was stabilized after Tomás Re-

Table 6-1. Central American Chiefs of State Who Invested in Coffee

Chief of state	Term of office	Coffee holdings
Guatemala		
Carrera, José Rafael	1844–48	
Martínez, Juan Antonio	1848	
Escobar, José Bernardo	1848	
Paredes, Mariano	1849–51	
Carrera, José Rafael	1852–65	
Aycinena, Pedro de	1865	P
Cerna, Vicente	1865–71	
García Granados, Miguel	1871–72	
Barrios, Justo Rufino	1873–85	P,B
Sinibaldi, Alejandro	1885	P,B
Barillas, Manuel Lisandro	1885–92	P,B
Reyna Barrios, José María	1892–98	
Estrada Cabrera, Manuel	1898–1920	
Herrera, Carlos	1920–21	P,B,X
Orellano, José María	1921–26	
Chacón, Lázaro	1926–30	
Palma, Baudilio	1930	
Orellana, Manuel	1930–31	
Reyna Andrada, José María	1931	
Ubico y Castañeda, Jorge	1931–44	
Ponce Vaides, Federico	1944	
Francisco Arana, Jaocobo Arbenz, Jorge Toriello Garrido	1944–45	
Arévalo Bermejo, Juan José	1945–51	
Arbenz Guzmán, Jacobo	1951–54	
Castillo Armas, Carlos	1954–57	
González, Luis Arturo	1957	
Flores Avendano, Guillermo	1957–58	
Ydígoras Fuentes, Miguel	1958–63	
Peralta Azurdia, Alfredo Enrique	1963–66	
Méndez Montenegro, Julio César	1966–70	
Arana Osorio, Carlos	1970	
El Salvador		
Lindo y Zelaya, Juan	1841–42	
Marín, Escolástico	1842	

Table 6-1. Continued

Chief of state	Term of office	Coffee holdings
Guzmán, Juan José	1842	
Villacorta, Dionisio	1842	
Guzmán, Juan José	1842–43	
Arce, Pedro	1843	
Palacios, Fermín	1844	
Malespín, Francisco	1844	
Guzmán, Joaquín Eufrasio	1844	
Malespín, Francisco	1844	
Guzmán, Joaquín Eufrasio	1844–45	
Palacios, Fermín	1845	
Guzmán, Joaquín Eufrasio	1845–46	
Palacios, Fermín	1846	
Aguilar, Eugenio	1846	
Palacios, Fermín	1846	
Aguilar, Eugenio	1846–48	
Medina, Tomás	1848	
Quiroz, Félix	1848	
Vasconcelos, Doroteo	1848–50	
Rodríguez, Ramón	1850	
Santín del Castillo, Miguel	1850	
Vasconcelos, Doroteo	1850–51	
Dueñas, Francisco	1851	P,B,X
Quiroz, Félix	1851	
Dueñas, Francisco	1851–54	P,B,X
Gómez, Vicente	1854	
Hernández, Mariano	1854	
San Martín, José María	1854–1856	
Dueñas, Francisco	1856	P,B,X
Campo, Rafael	1856	
Dueñas, Francisco	1856	P,B,X
Campo, Rafael	1856–58	
Zepeda, Lorenzo	1858	
Santín del Castillo, Miguel	1858	
Barrios Espinosa, Gerardo	1858	P
Santín del Castillo, Miguel	1858–59	

Continued

Table 6-1. Continued

Chief of state	Term of office	Coffee holdings
Guzmán, Joaquín Eufrasio	1859	
Peralta, José María	1859	
Barrios Espinosa, Gerardo	1859–60	P
Peralta, José María	1860–61	
Barrios Espinosa, Gerardo	1861–63	P
Dueñas, Francisco	1863–71	P,B,X
González, Santiago	1871–72	
Méndez, Manuel	1872	
González, Santiago	1872–76	
Valle, Andrés	1876	
Zaldívar, Rafael	1876–84	
Guirola, Angel	1884	P,B,X
Zaldívar, Rafael	1884–85	
Figueroa, Fernando	1885	
Rosales, José	1885	
Menéndez, Francisco	1885–90	P
Ezeta, Carlos	1890–94	
Gutiérrez, Rafael Antonio	1894–98	
Regalado, Tomás	1898–1903	P,B,X
Escalón, Pedro José	1898–1907	P,B,X
Figueroa, Fernando	1907–11	
Araujo, Manuel Enrique	1911–13	
Meléndez, Carlos	1913–14	P,B
Quiñonez Molina, Alfonso	1914–15	P,B,X
Meléndez, Carlos	1915–18	P,B
Quiñonez Molina, Alfonso	1918–19	P,B,X
Quiñonez Molina, Alfonso	1923–27	P,B,X
Romero Bosque, Pío	1927–31	
Araujo, Arturo	1931	
Directorio Militar	1931	
Hernández Martínez, Maximiliano	1931–34	
Menéndez, Andrés I.	1934–35	
Hernández Martínez, Maximiliano	1935–44	
Menéndez, Andrés I.	1944	
Aguirre y Salinas, Osmín	1944–45	
Castañeda Castro, Salvador	1945–48	
Consejo de Gobierno Revolucionario	1948–50	

Table 6-1. Continued

Chief of state	Term of office	Coffee holdings
Osorio, Oscar	1950–56	
Lemus, José María	1956–60	
Junta de Gobierno Cívico Militar	1961–62	
Directorio Cívico Militar	1961–62	
Cordon Cea, Ekusebio Rodolfo	1962	
Rivera, Julio Adalberto	1962–67	
Sánchez Hernández, Fidel	1967–72	
Honduras		
Ferrera, Francisco (General)	1841–45	
Chavez, Coronado	1845–47	
Lindo, Juan	1847–52	
Cabañas, Trinidad (General)	1852–56	
Guardiola, Santos	1856–62	
Montes, Francisco	1862–63	
Medina, José María (General)	1863–72	
Arias, Celeo	1872–74	
Leiva, Ponciano (General)	1874–75	
Medina, José María	1875–76	
Soto, Marco Aurelio (Lawyer)	1876–83	
Bográn, Luis	1883–91	P
Leiva, Ponciano (General)	1891–93	
Argüero, Francisco	1893	
Vasquez, Domingo (General)	1893–94	
Bonilla, Policarpo (Lawyer)	1894–99	
Sierra, Terencio (General)	1899–1903	
Arias, Juan	1903	
Bonilla, Manuel (General)	1903–07	
Dávila, Miguel (General)	1907–11	
Bertrand, Francisco	1911–12	
Bonilla, Manuel (General)	1912–13	
Bertrand, Francisco	1913–1915	
Membreno, Alberto	1915–16	
Bertrand, Francisco	1916–19	
Bográn, Francisco	1919–1920	
López Gutierrez, Rafael	1920–24	
Tosta, Vicente	1924–25	

Continued

Table 6-1. Continued

Chief of state	Term of office	Coffee holdings
Paz Barahona, Miguel	1925–29	
Mejía Colindres, Vicente	1929–33	
Carías Andino, Tiburcio	1933–49	
Gálvez, Juan Manuel	1949–54	
Lozano Díaz, Julio	1954–56	
Junta de Gobierno	1956–57	
Villeda Morales, Ramón	1957–63	
Junta de Gobierno Militar	1963–65	
López Arellano, Oswaldo	1965–71	
Cruz, Ramón Ernesto	1971–72	
López Arellano, Oswaldo	1972–75	
Melgar Castro, Juan	1975–78	
Paz García, Policarpo	1978–82	
Suazo Córdova, Roberto	1982–86	
Nicaragua		
Chamorro, Fruto	1853–54	P
Estrada, José María	1855–59	
Martínez, Tomás	1859–67	X
Guzmán, Fernando	1867–71	
Cuadra, Vicente	1871–75	P,X
Chamorro, Pedro Joaquín	1875–79	P,X
Zavala, Joaquín	1879–83	X
Cárdenas, Adán	1883–87	X
Carazo, Evaristo	1887–89	P
Sacasa, Roberto	1889–93	
Zelaya, José Santos	1893–1909	P
Madriz, José	1909–10	
Estrada, Juan José	1911	
Díaz, Adolfo	1911–16	
Chamorro, Emiliano	1917–20	P,X
Chamorro, Diego M.	1921–23	P,X
Martínez, Bartolomé	1923–24	
Solórzano, Carlos	1925–26	P,B,X
Moncada, José María	1929–32	
Sacasa, Juan Bautista	1933–36	
Brenes, J. Carlos	1936	

Table 6-1. Continued

Chief of state	Term of office	Coffee holdings
Somoza García, Anastasio	1937–47	P,B,X
Argüello, Leonardo	1947	X
Lacayo Sacasa, Benjamín	1947	X
Román y Reyes, Víctor M.	1948–50	
Somoza García, Anastasio	1951–56	P,B,X
Somoza DeBayle, Luis	1957–63	P,B,X
Schick Gutiérrez, René	1963–67	
Somoza DeBayle, Anastasio	1967–79	P,B,X
Costa Rica		
Mora Fernández, Juan	1824–33	
Gallegos, José Rafael	1833–35	P
Lara, Juan José	1835	P
Fernández, Manuel	1835	P
Carrillo, Braulio	1835–37, 1838–42	P
Mora, Joaquín	1837	P
Aguilar, Manuel	1837–38	P,X
Bonilla, Manuel	1842	
Morazán, Francisco	1842	
Pinto Suárez, Antonio	1842, 1872–73	
Alfaro, José María	1842–44, 1846–47	X,B
Oreamuno, Francisco María	1844	P
Moya Murillo, Rafael	1844–45	P
Castro Madriz, José María	1847–49	P,X
Mora Porras, Juan Rafael	1848, 1849–59	P,B,X
Mora Porras, Miguel	1849	P
Montealegre, José María	1859–60, 1860–63	P,B,X
de Jiménez, Jesús	1863–66, 1868–70	
Figueroa, Eusebio	1870	
Caranza, Bruno	1870	P
Guardia, Tomás	1870–76, 1877–82	X
Esquivel, Aniceto	1886	B,X
Herrera, Vicente	1876–77	X
Lara Zamora, Salvador	1881–83	B
Lizano, Saturnino	1882	P,X
Fernández, Próspero	1882–85	P,X
Soto, Bernardo	1885–89	

Continued

Table 6-1. Continued

Chief of state	Term of office	Coffee holdings
Durán, Carlos	1889–90	B,X
Rodríguez, José Joaquín	1890–94	
Yglesias, Rafael	1894–98, 1898–1902	
Esquivel, Ascensión	1902–06	X
González Víquez, Cleto	1906–10, 1928–32	P
Jiménez Oreamuno, Ricardo	1910–14, 1924–28, 1932–36	X,B
González Flores, Alfredo	1914–17	P
Tinoco, Federico	1917–19	
Quirós, Juan Bautista	1919	P
Aguilar Barquero, Francisco	1919–20	
Acosta, Julio	1920–24	
Cortés Castro, León	1936–40	P
Calderón Guardia, Rafael A.	1940–44	P,B
Picado, Teodoro	1944–48	
León Herrera, Santos	1948	
Figueres Ferrer, José	1948–49, 1953–58, 1970–74	(P,B after second term)
Ulate Blanco, Otilio	1949–53	
Echandi Jiménez, Mario	1958–62	P,B
Orlich Bolmarcich, Francisco J.	1962–66	P,B,X
Trejos Fernández, José Joaquín	1966–70	
Oduber Quirós, Daniel	1974–78	
Carazo Odio, R.	1978–82	
Monge Alvarez, Luís A.	1982–86	
Arias Sánchez, Oscar	1986–90	P,B
Calderón Fournier, Rafael A.	1990–94	P,B

Key: P = coffee planter
       B = *beneficio* owner
       X = coffee exporter

Sources:
Guatemala: Moore, *Historical Dictionary of Guatemala,* pp. 162–63; Quiñonez, *Directorio general de la republica de Guatemala*; Alvarado, *Tratado de caficultura*; Secretaria de Estado de Guatemala, *Memoria de fomento, 1891,* pp. 5–153.

Table 6-1. Continued

El Salvador: Flemion, *Historical Dictionary of El Salvador*, pp. 105–8; Browning, *El Salvador*, pp. 145–47; Wilson, "Crisis of National Integration," p. 134; Republica de El Salvador, *Anuario estadístico de 1921*, p. 241; Colindres, *Fundamentos económicos*, pp. 257–58; Aubey, "Entrepreneurial Formation," pp. 272–76.

Honduras: Brand, "Background of Capitalistic Underdevelopment," pp. 191–92; Peckenham and Street, *Honduras*, p. 335; República de Honduras, *Memoria de fomento, 1914–15*.

Nicaragua: Meyer, *Historical Dictionary of Nicaragua*, p. 345; Lanuza, Vázquez, Barahona, and Chamorro, *Economía y sociedad*, pp. 173, 76, 77, 79, 82, 118, 124; Bureau of the American Republics, *Commercial Directory of Nicaragua*, pp. 167–77; República de Nicaragua, "Censo cafetalero de 1909," pp. 646–72; Lang, *Business Directory of Nicaragua, 1957–58*.

Costa Rica: Creedman, *Historical Dictionary of Costa Rica*, pp. 161–63; Vega Carballo, "El nacimiento," pt. II, pp. 100–102; Oficina del Café, *Informe de labores—1973*, pp. 90–93; Dirección General de Estadística, *Boletín de exportación de café 1939–40*, pp. 15–19; Stone, "Los cafetaleros," pp. 185–88.

galado (1898–1903), a prominent grower from Santa Ana, became president and peacefully transferred power in 1903 to Pedro Escalón, another important grower and coffee exporter. Between 1913 and 1927, members of the sugar- and coffee-growing Meléndez and Quiñonez families regularly alternated in ruling the country.[24]

In Nicaragua during the three decades of Conservative rule (1859–89), the presidency was occupied by merchants and landowners from Granada; three of the seven rulers over this period were listed as major coffee exporters in an 1892 business directory, and one other president had close relatives who were growers and exporters by 1892.[25] The consolidation of a strong national state in Nicaragua was achieved under the rule of José Santos Zelaya (1893–1909), whose father, Santos Francisco Zelaya, was listed as a Managua coffee planter in 1892.

In contrast, Honduras retained a state that lived off concessions, the government was run by a succession of generals and lawyers, and only one president, Luis Bográn (1883–91), became a coffee planter.[26] After 1876 a spate of Liberal laws was passed, but there was no critical mass of entrepreneurs in the townships to reinforce and implement national legislation. The Honduran state was further crippled by its inability to borrow in international markets. Thus when states elsewhere were attracting foreign capital to build railroads to serve the coffee districts, the Honduran state was surviving off traditional concessions and exerting very little influence over affairs outside of the capital city.

The Institutionalization of the Coffee State

With the direct participation of coffee barons, national state institutions were erected that promoted coffee, but once those institutions were firmly in place, coffee growers no longer needed to occupy high office for the state to continue to operate in their interest. Government institutions in all but Honduras came to rely on coffee for their livelihood. The most important sources of tax revenue for governments without a sophisticated collection apparatus were taxes on international trade, which could be collected at the docks by a relatively small staff of customs officials, and taxes on liquor and tobacco, which were collected by private businesses that were granted local monopolies. As foreign exchange flowed into Central America from the coffee trade, so too did imports, which greatly stimulated customs collections. Similarly, as peasants received money incomes from wage work on coffee plantations, some of that income was naturally diverted toward vice, increasing the taxes collected from liquor and tobacco. Additionally, with a larger inflow of foreign exchange and tax revenues, the coffee boom expanded the borrowing base of governments. During years of abundant crops and favorable coffee prices, governments' spending power increased, while the opposite occurred during unfavorable periods. As Figures 6-1 and 6-2 reveal, during the latter half of the nineteenth century, government officials did not need regression analysis to understand the connection between the health of the coffee economy and the amount of public funds at their disposal. Once coffee became the primary source of foreign exchange, it was suicidal for governments to endanger the coffee sector. Furthermore, educational institutions and militaries, strengthened by the growth of the coffee state, trained a professional class of bureaucrats willing and able to serve the state, making it possible for coffee elites to return to the affairs of private business. The overall pattern of direct rule by cof-

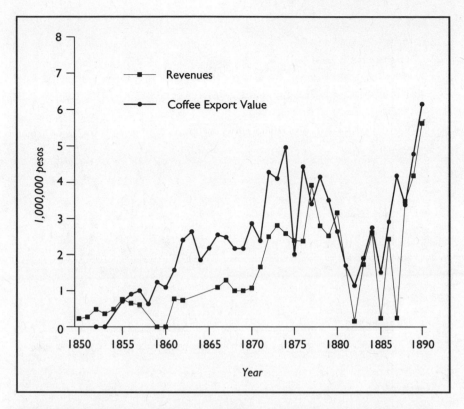

Figure 6-1. Total Revenues of the Costa Rican State and Coffee Export Revenues, 1850–1890.
Source: Vega Carballo, *Orden y Progreso*, pp. 271–72.

fee barons exhibits a crescendo of direct participation in national governance from the 1850s to a peak during the 1880s—precisely during the period of state building.

In Costa Rica direct rule by oligarchs came to be seen by the oligarchy itself as disruptive because members of the economic elite openly competed with each other in the political arena, often using military force to solve national crises or to oust opponents. National institutions received some credibility at the beginning from the four-year rule of coffee grower Braulio Carrillo (1838–42), but intrigues between coffee elites resulted in nine presidential changes during the period from 1842 through 1849 weakening the ability of national state institutions to intervene effectively. During the following decade (1849–59), national institutions were strengthened under the

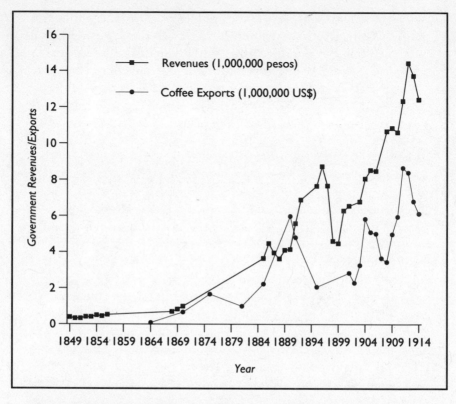

Figure 6-2. Salvadoran Government Revenues and Salvadoran Coffee Export Revenues, 1849–1914.
Source: Walter, "Trade and Development," pp. 21, 81.

leadership of Juan Rafael Mora, who received support from Carrera in Guatemala and Conservatives in other states as a counterforce to intrigues by rival coffee elites, who with popular support finally ousted Mora in 1859 and later executed him. Intrigues continued during the 1860s against coffee grower and exporter José Montealegre, but stability returned with the rule of cattle baron and general Tomás Guardia, who greatly strengthened the national state during his twelve-year rule. After the death of Tomás Guardia in 1882, coffee growers competed for the presidency until 1885, when there began what José Luís Vega Carballo calls a "strategic retreat" from direct rule by members of the coffee elite, permitting members of a growing intellectual and political elite to hold high public office.[27] Between 1885 and 1902, there was only one year (1889–90) when a member of the coffee elite actually held the presidency, and it was during this period that regular four-year terms were established, a pattern that continued through the twentieth century with disruptions in 1914–20 and 1948–49. Although open elections with broad participation, secret ballots, and effective checks against fraud were not the rule until after 1949,[28] regular four-year terms of office occurred twenty times between 1902 and 1994, during which time thirteen presidential terms were served by members of the coffee elite.[29] In addition to being involved in national politics, the Costa Rican coffee elite has exerted strong ideological pressure on the national state through its ownership and control over the media. The regularity of transfer of power after four-year terms and the increasingly broad popular participation in elections has allowed the Costa Rican government to legitimate its actions internally without resort to military force in most instances and to project to the rest of the world an image of stability, which has been advantageous in attracting foreign capital.

In Guatemala, coffee barons retreated from direct rule after the assassination of Manuel L. Barillas in 1892. Barillas's successor, General José María Reyna Barrios (1892–98), does not appear on the 1890 list of owners of farms with more than three thousand coffee trees.[30] Reyna Barrios's name does appear in a section titled "Estadística Intelectual," on a list of "officials who have completed their studies in the Escuela Politécnica de Guatemala," a college that was set up by Justo Rufino Barrios to prepare military officers for government service.[31] After the fall of Barillas, only one president of Guatemala, Carlos Herrera (1920–21), has been from a major coffee-growing family.[32]

In El Salvador, a period of direct rule by oligarchs lasted from 1898 until the late 1920s, with only two presidential terms out of ten occupied by persons who were not coffee barons. A groundswell of popular opposition to oligarchic rule during the 1920s coupled with the crash of the coffee market in 1929–31 forced the retreat of direct oligarchic rule in favor of the military in 1931, though members of the coffee elite continued to hold economic posts such as minister of agriculture or president of the central bank. This division of labor, with military officers controlling the presidency and coffee elites participating in economic affairs, lasted until 1979, when the insertion of U.S. military and economic aid to suppress a popular revolution enabled Christian Democrats, who were not backed by the coffee elite, to take over the executive branch of government. From 1979 to 1989, heavy United States aid financed a war against the revolutionary movement and oversaw the expropriation by the Christian Democrats of export houses, financial institutions, large agricultural properties, and some of the other assets owned by members of the oligarchy. Finally, in March 1989, the Christian Democrats were defeated in a national election, and for the first time in more than half a century a member of the coffee elite, Alfredo Cristiani, became president and began a program of returning nationalized assets to former owners.

After the fall of Zelaya in 1909 in Nicaragua, coffee exporters, processors, and growers occasionally occupied the presidency—Emiliano Chamorro (1917–20), Diego Chamorro (1921–23), and Carlos Solórzano (1925–26)—but a primary influence over Nicaraguan affairs was the United States, which controlled the customs receipts for a portion of the period and stationed marines in the country from 1912 to 1915 and 1927 to 1933, when the National Guard was sufficiently developed to permit U.S. withdrawal. Through his position as commander of the National Guard, Anastasio Somoza García took over the presidency in 1937, beginning a four-decade period of direct or indirect rule by the Somozas. Somoza García's father, Anastasio Somoza Reyes, was a capitalist coffee grower, but Somoza García and his two sons used their position in the government to acquire stakes in practically every sector of the Nicaraguan economy. During the 1930s, when growers were under duress, Somoza acquired some important *fincas* and *beneficios*, a process that accelerated with the expropriation of German assets during World War II. By the time of the overthrow of the Somoza regime in 1979, 29 of the 112 *beneficios* in Nicaragua and approximately 18 percent of the lands in coffee were owned by the Somozas or their close associates.[33]

The Coffee State and the Nature of Public Policy

By 1900, all five Central American countries save Honduras had a coffee state that was either directly run by members of the coffee elite or had become institutionalized under its guidance. But the nature of the coffee state and its posture toward small farmers and laborers differed substantially from one nation to the next, reflecting the practical experiences of coffee elites in the early coffee-growing districts and the problems encountered in projecting national policy into new areas of development.

As we have seen, throughout Central America coffee was first successfully cultivated where the social, economic, and biological environments were most favorable for its introduction. Early experiments outside of the most favorable growing areas failed, and local knowledge accumulated with regard to the best places to plant, the best ways to use shade, the best processing techniques, and the most practical methods of harnessing labor and organizing the work process. Once profits began pouring in, capital was reinvested in ways that had the highest probability of success based on previous experiments. Thus when new areas were opened up for coffee cultivation, there was a tendency to find the conditions where success was most likely, and if those conditions did not exist already, there was an attempt, whenever possible, either to recreate those conditions or to adapt practices to the conditions that could not be changed. One condition that could be changed was accessibility to markets, and coffee growers pressured government institutions to build roads, railroads, and port facilities for the benefit of the coffee economy.

Other conditions that growers attempted to transplant from the earlier coffee areas to the newly developing zones were land tenure and labor relations. Because these conditions varied considerably from one zone to the next, growers' perceptions of appropriate government actions to assist the further expansion of coffee depended on their prior experiences. Furthermore, the social obstacles faced by coffee growers outside of their own areas of control differed in degree and character, calling for distinct national policies to harness land, labor, and capital for the coffee sector.

Chapters 3 and 4 showed that there was no single national model of land tenure and labor relations in coffee production in any of the Central American countries. Within jurisdictions of national states, pockets of coffee production emerged with highly distinct structural arrangements, which were greatly influenced by precoffee social relations in those locales. Within the older coffee-growing region of Nicaragua, there emerged structural relations in coffee ranging from extremely high peasant participation with few capitalist-sized farms around the town of Masaya to extremely low peasant participation with an unusually high density of large capitalist plantations in the coffee district of Managua and a mixture of the two extremes emerging in what later became the department of Carazo. Within Costa

Rica, high participation by peasant and family-sized farms predominated in the districts surrounding San José, Heredia, and Alajuela, while sections to the east of Cartago, where sugar and cattle haciendas preceded coffee, there developed, albeit late in the century, a high concentration of large capitalist coffee plantations. In El Salvador, peasant farmers produced the bulk of the coffee in the northern sections of the country, but capitalist farms of various sizes predominated in the older coffee districts of San Salvador and Santa Ana. In Guatemala, small coffee farms had a relatively high participation rate in the previous cochineal districts of Antigua and Amatitlán, but in Pacific piedmont areas, where cattle and sugar haciendas preceded coffee, there evolved large-scale capitalist enterprises that came to control most of the coffee grown there.

With so many different models to choose from, why did states eventually favor one over the others? In particular, why did the governments of Guatemala, El Salvador, and Nicaragua enact national land, labor, and capital laws that reinforced the large plantation model, while the national government of Costa Rica encouraged the formation of family-sized farms in the new coffee districts?

One explanation that seems to fit for the Liberal period is that those who seized state power attempted to project the social relations they were most familiar with to new areas. The San José elite dominated national politics after winning the battle of the League in 1835, which established San José as the permanent capital of the country; as coffee developed in San José, the coffee elite naturally attempted to extend to new areas the solutions that had worked in San José, where family coffee farms and small capitalist farms had conveniently expanded the fortunes of merchants. In Nicaragua, Zelaya was from a coffee-growing family in Managua, where the large capitalist plantation was the favored mode, so that after he seized national power, this model was projected onto the north central zone. Justo Rufino Barrios was from a hacienda-owning family from the Pacific piedmont of San Marcos and was connected with Liberals from Quezaltenango (not Antigua), who perceived from their own experiences that the large plantation model was the quickest way to develop the coffee economy. Gerardo Barrios and other Salvadoran Liberals were not from peasant-controlled northern areas but from major coffee-growing townships, where the benefits of capitalist farms were proving successful, and therefore they pushed for the policy that would project that mode into new areas.

Although this explanation of projection of the proven mode onto new territory may fit for the Liberal politicians of the late nineteenth century, it does not neatly fit for some of the Conservative politicians before the Liberals took over. For example, President Dueñas of San Salvador was an owner of large haciendas who frequently sided with peasant communities in disputes over land, much like his Conservative colleague, President Rafael Carrera, the peasant leader of Guatemala. Similarly loose is the fit for the Conservatives of Nicaragua, who with one exception (Roberto Sacasa from León) were from the merchant-landowner elite of Granada, where they accumulated riches from large haciendas (later, large capitalist coffee farms) and from loans and merchant connections with small farmer clients on the Carazo Plateau and around Masaya. The Granada elite had direct experience with both modes of accumulation simultaneously, yet when it came to directing state policy toward the north central zone, this group decidedly favored the large plantation model.

An explanation supported by the investigations of land and labor suggests that ethnic struggles played a key role in the formation of national states. Indeed, one reason that the large plantation was not a widespread phenomenon in Costa Rica during the early phases of the coffee boom was that Costa Rica lacked an Indian population large enough to serve as a labor force. Scarce labor gave an advantage to family-sized coffee farms that could use kinship and friendship ties to secure a wage labor force at harvest. The coffee elite of San José quickly learned the commercial advantages of lending money to and buying mature berries from numerous small growers, and they projected that model onto other areas of the Central Valley through national land legislation during the 1850s and 1860s. In the 1880s, when the coffee boom spread into the hacienda zones to the east of Cartago, *ladino* growers met resistance when they attempted to intrude on the rich lands of the Indian community of Orósi. Although both sides appealed to the national state, the government in San José declined to intervene, and the *ladinos* succeeded in taking the lands by enlisting the powers of the *ladino*-controlled municipality of Paraíso. Thus because of the Costa Rican Indians' small numbers and limited ability to resist, ethnic struggles played a minimal role in the shaping of the national state.

In Guatemala, El Salvador, and Nicaragua, Indian communities offered a much greater potential for large-scale plantation agriculture, but they were also a more formidable obstacle than in Costa

Rica. The *ladinoized* towns of Guatemala, El Salvador, and Nicaragua developed commercial coffee production first, but when the limits of the *ladino* population were reached, growers sought ways to tap the labor and to intrude on the lands of Indian communities. Indian communities resisted advances of individual growers, who in turn called on state institutions at various levels to assist them. When national officials held firmly to colonial protections of Indian communities as was the case with some of the Conservative presidents of Guatemala and El Salvador, growers used lower-level state institutions to assist them, bypassing the national state and eroding its paternalistic stance toward the Indian communities. In Nicaragua and El Salvador, Indian communities occupied some of the finest potential coffee lands, and when these communities resisted state actions, the community structures came under attack. Ideologically, elites who maintained paternalistic attitudes toward the communities were increasingly viewed as backward-looking and nostalgic, and the dominant elites in Nicaragua and El Salvador came to perceive Indian communities and the Indian culture itself as obstacles to progress. The casting of this attitude in ethnic terms incorporated support of lower-class *ladinos*, enabling the national state to take crippling actions against Indian political structures without a backlash from the *ladino* population.[34]

In Guatemala, there was no frontal attack on Indian community structures, in part because Indian communities did not directly occupy lands in the coffee belt. The Barrios government strengthened the forces of coercion and avoided uprisings by granting land guarantees to communities in the highlands in exchange for their relinquishing looser claims on lands in the piedmont. Barrios resurrected colonial labor drafts but used existing community hierarchies to assist in the labor supply process. Although the strategies differed, the harnessing of Indian labor and land resources required the strengthening of national forces of repression, and with effective intervention (which took years to achieve in Nicaragua and El Salvador) the lever of capital could be applied to coffee production. In the zones of Guatemala, El Salvador, and Nicaragua where Indian labor and lands were taken, the stamp of the national state was remarkable. While other coffee zones reflected precoffee structures of landholding, the Indian zones reflected the opposite, switching from systems that provided widespread access to land by small producers into systems that became dominated by large capitalist plantations. Perhaps more important, the Indian communities' resistance left an indelible stamp on national states, and the governments of Guatemala, El Salvador, and Nicaragua developed stronger militaries and a more regular habit of resolving conflicts with force than in Costa Rica.

Conclusion

The nature of state institutions and the political cultures within which they operated were shaped by the formation of the coffee economy and the conflicts associated with its formation. In contrast

"City Prison—City of Guatemala," 1875. The Liberals in Guatemala inherited the best-developed repressive apparatus in Central America, but they proceeded to strengthen it after 1873. (Department of Special Collections, Stanford University Libraries)

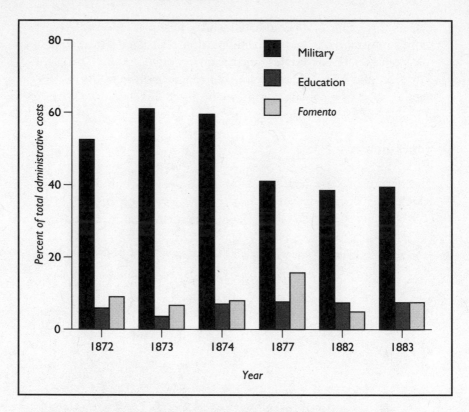

Figure 6-3. Guatemalan Government Expenditures, 1872–1883.
Source: Herrick, "Economic and Political Development," Appendix 1, pp. 273–89.

to the other countries, Costa Rican national institutions developed in the context of family-sized farms providing the bulk of the coffee crop while elites channeled their capital into higher-return endeavors such as coffee processing, finance, and trade. When the forested areas in the western sections of the Central Valley were opened up for coffee cultivation, the national government passed colonization laws that favored the formation of nucleated settlements of small farmers, the social organization that had proved so successful in providing the processing mills with an abundant supply of ripe berries in the older coffee towns of San José, Alajuela, and Heredia. Once the coffee economy was established, small and medium-sized growers became a political force in their own right. These growers purchased supplies and services from merchants, professionals, and petty commodity

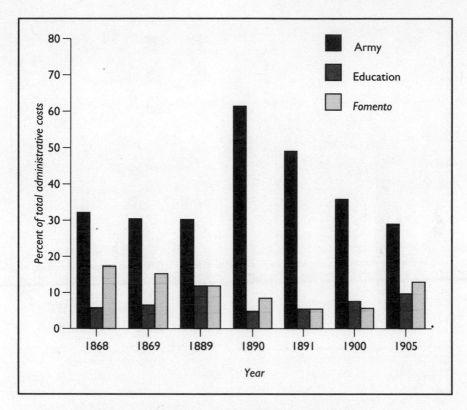

Figure 6-4. Salvadoran Government Expenditures, 1868–1905.
Source: Walter, "Trade and Development," p. 82.

producers in the towns, stimulating the growth of a prosperous but
by no means wealthy class of townspeople, who, in turn, pressured
the state for improvements in education, hospitals, roads, and other
public facilities that served their interests. Although instruments of
coercion were needed to maintain public order, reinforce the legal
system, and protect against foreign invasion, these institutions did
not have to preside over explosively antagonistic social relations of
coffee production. By the end of the nineteenth century, the Costa
Rican state expended its resources in a much more balanced fashion
between military, public education, and provision of infrastructure
(*Fomento*) than was true elsewhere in the region (see Figures 6-3,
6-4, and 6-5).

Guatemala, El Salvador, and Nicaragua, had a stronger overall
pattern than Costa Rica of hacienda agriculture in the areas suitable

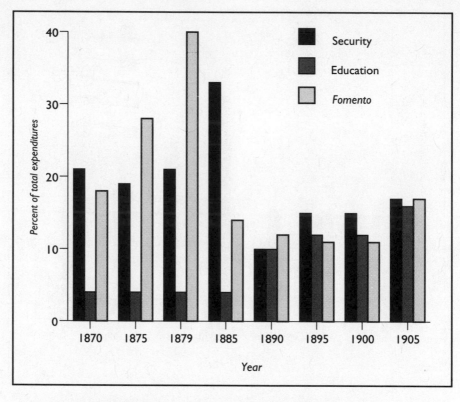

Figure 6-5. Costa Rican Government Expenditures, 1870–1905.
Source: Román, "Metodología y fuentes de las finanzas," Table 2.2, pp. 78–96.

for coffee cultivation, though pockets similar to the Central Valley of Costa Rica existed in the other countries. The adoption of national policies that favored large plantations was reinforced by the existence of a potential Indian labor force. Because of the power of Indian community structures, coffee growers needed a strong counterforce to help them pry labor and land from those communities. The Indian question was at the heart of the struggle over the national state in all three countries, and coffee growers used their economic clout and their political experience in their own townships to seize national power. Thus the creation of effective instruments of coercion took on additional importance in Guatemala, El Salvador, and Nicaragua compared to Costa Rica. Once the coffee economy and public institutions to support it were established, governments had a vested interest in preserving them, and coffee elites began to retire from holding high public office and returned to managing their economic fortunes. In Guatemala, El Salvador, and Nicaragua, this meant the maintenance of a land policy that was generally antagonistic toward small farmers and a labor policy that held wages to a minimum, both of which required strong militaries to back them up.

Chapter 7

States and Social Evolution: Lessons from the Nineteenth Century

The nineteenth century opened with a vulnerable Spanish Empire, which by the 1820s had retreated from the mainland areas of Latin America to the heavily fortified islands of Cuba and Puerto Rico. In Central America and elsewhere on the mainland, central state institutions that had been connected with the empire collapsed, and age-old struggles that had long smoldered under the mediation and repression of Crown institutions broke into open flame. Attempts to recreate a federation of five republics along colonial lines with Guatemala at its center failed because there were no outside resources to fortify the juvenile central institutions, and civil wars raged across the isthmus. When the federation finally broke down in the late 1830s and early 1840s, five self-declared republics emerged that roughly corresponded to the previous provinces of the federation and to those areas claimed by the five national states of the region during the twentieth century. Without strong central state structures and coherent national ideologies, however, the new republics of the 1840s were nations in name only. The remainder of the century was spent building national state structures and ideologies, or as Steven Palmer has put it, "inventing" nations.[1]

By 1900, four of the five Central American republics had developed national state structures with considerable public legitimacy and greatly improved powers to tax, to borrow locally and internationally, to provide public goods, to mediate third-party disputes, to coerce those acting outside the law, and to maintain diplomatic relations with other states. Between 1850 and 1900, the four republics with the greatest success at building national states (Guatemala, El Salvador, Nicaragua, and Costa Rica) became increasingly linked to the international division of labor through the production of coffee

235

as a major export crop. The first to develop a coherent national state was Costa Rica, the first to enter the coffee trade.

What lessons can be extracted from this examination of coffee and the rise of national governments in Central America, and what questions does this reading of the late nineteenth century raise with respect to states and social evolution during the twentieth century?

Reassessing the Role of World System Forces

One result of this study is clear: world system forces did not transplant into Central America any particular mode of economic or political organization. Indeed, if international pressures had been endowed with such powers, very similar structures of land tenure, labor relations, and public institutions would have developed across the region. Close examination of the historical record of the coffee sector has revealed an amazing diversity of economic and political structures, a heterogeneity that pushes one to look to local causes for explanation. Imperialist actors, whether seen as powerful outside states or international investors, cannot be viewed as the ones who determined the economic and political structures that emerged; rather, local subjects and local institutions played the decisive role in shaping the outcomes.

Nevertheless, world system forces significantly altered the environment within which local structures evolved. Over the period studied here, European and North American industrialization changed the demand for traded commodities, revolutionized transport technology, and generated capital, which sought outlets for investment around the globe. Chapter 2 showed how by midcentury, expanding world demand for coffee and new technologies that cheapened transport from Central America raised the profitability of growing coffee on the isthmus and resources began to be committed to the crop. Depending on previous connections with the global economy, changes in the center affected adaptations in Central America in different ways. In one example, areas previously connected with the dye trade continued to allocate scarce resources to dye production, postponing the full development of the coffee economy until international markets for dyestuffs (first cochineal and later indigo) collapsed. Thus the timing of coffee's advance across Central America was partially explained by previous connections with the world system and by forces of change spinning outward from the center of that system. But relative intensities of the coffee boom, the geographical spread of coffee cultivation within countries, and the nature of the structures that emerged cannot be explained by world system forces.

Some Patterns of Economic Evolution

If a single economic transformation was associated with the development of the coffee economy it was toward privately titled properties with much more clearly delineated boundaries than was true before coffee's introduction. Chapter 3 argued that the connection between coffee cultivation and private property stems from the unusually large amount of labor required to establish a mature coffee grove and the long lag time (three to five years) between planting seedlings to reaping the financial rewards of regular harvests. Whether a grower was a peasant family planting a few trees at a time with family labor or a capitalist hiring large numbers of workers to do the job, before expending the effort or cash, or both, the grower wanted to make sure that after the investment was made, the land on which the grove was planted would not be claimed by someone else. Hence, although noncoffee areas may have remained under a variety of other land tenure arrangements, the coffee zones of Central America tended to be converted into private holdings. Public registration of holdings began in the major coffee townships, and later national land registries were established. Once privatization was under way, coffee finance reinforced the tendency as growers who held secure claims to lands had greater success in obtaining loans from a financial system that was rapidly responding to the long-term capital needs of coffee by developing new credit instruments and new institutions of financial intermediation.

Although there was a general tendency toward privatization, the process of conversion into private holdings was by no means homogeneous throughout Central America, nor were the resulting structures of coffee production once the conversion was achieved. In some places, the adaptation was smooth, peaceful, and relatively easy; in others, it was accompanied by social strife. In some areas, the resulting structure consisted of many small coffee producers with few capitalist-sized plantations, whereas in other areas there emerged a more even mixture of peasant producers, family-sized coffee farms, and capitalist enterprises of various sizes, and in still other areas large capitalist enterprises came to monopolize the cultivation of the crop with very little participation by small producers. Comparing these pockets across the isthmus, the variable that best explains the diversity of resulting structures was the customary land use and land access patterns in an area before coffee was introduced. Coffee cultivation may have introduced a powerful incentive to privatize and, therefore, to override previously recognized forms of land tenure, but the particular adaptations that occurred were heavily conditioned by preexisting customs of land access and land use.

Some Patterns of Political Evolution

Because of the remarkable diversity of social formations before coffee, there did not develop a single "national" structure of coffee production anywhere in Central America; rather, various structures formed in different locations within what became the jurisdictional boundaries of national states. Therefore, a direct application of Barrington Moore's thesis at the national level does not yield results because it cannot explain why national states ended up reinforcing one model of agrarian structure when and where there were other viable ones available.

If the experience of nineteenth-century Central America teaches anything, it is a sensitivity to levels of the state. During most of the period under study, national-level institutions had far less clout than the municipal governments of the most important commercial townships, which had a long experience of home rule during the colonial period that increased in relative importance when the central authority collapsed at independence. Applied to the municipal level of government, Moore's thesis has considerable validity. The particular agrarian social formation of an area strongly influenced the behavior of town hall. During the first several decades after independence, the pulsing network of competing city-states favored instability as local *caudillos* used their power at the municipal level to muster troops to attack enemies in a rival township and, later, to overthrow an enemy who might be laying claim to incipient national institutions. Frequently, local *caudillos* could bolster their position by calling on support from a stronger force outside of the province, a pattern of shifting alliances and meddling that continued into the national period and well into the twentieth century. With the development of the coffee economy, the instability factor of competing townships was diverted, over time, into a unifying force.

Chapter 6 argued that national level institutions and the policies they ultimately adopted evolved from institutions and experiences of governance at the level of the municipality. The introduction of coffee cultivation took place first within the jurisdictions of major commercial townships that happened to be located in areas suitable for coffee cultivation. In these townships land, labor, and capital all came together in a single place. Furthermore, the governments of these townships since colonial days had exercised authority over distribution of land (and in some cases labor) within a radius of one to ten miles from the town center. In what became coffee townships, merchants, professionals, and owners of nearby haciendas had already gained control over the town councils. As early investors in coffee achieved success and learned about coffee's peculiar needs, it was only natural to call for public policies that would lower transaction costs, reduce risks of investment, provide for public goods, and directly stimulate further development of the coffee trade. Chapter 6 found that long before national institutions intervened on behalf of the coffee interests, commercially controlled town councils were privatizing town lands, granting subsidies to growers and merchants, providing infrastructure to promote commerce, providing free coffee seedlings to growers, and building up their police forces to enforce the new laws. Hence political adaptations took place first at the level of the coffee township, not the national government. Prosperity from coffee enabled town governments to expand their powers of taxation and intervention and increase their authority over outlying areas, thereby allowing the most successful coffee townships to exercise greater influence at a national level than townships that were bypassed by the coffee boom.

As the limits to accumulation within the boundaries of the townships were reached, coffee elites pressured for higher levels of government to intervene on their behalf. On a certain range of policy issues, the obstacles faced by coffee elites from one district were similar to those of another, generating similar perspectives on the correct actions to be taken by the national state. This convergence of interests created an incentive to dampen traditional rivalries for a higher-order gain, and coffee elites became an increasingly effective lobbying force at the national level. When those in control of the national state failed to respond to appeals, local elites circumvented the national level by coordinating actions of two or more townships simultaneously, by building their own paramilitary forces from the militias of several townships, by directly participating in district units of the national military, or by gaining influence over national government appointees in their districts, eroding from below what they perceived as national impediments to progress.

As the coffee boom progressed and barriers to further accumulation were reached, the coffee interests became frustrated with the unwillingness or inability of national institutions to respond to their needs. Using their own districts as a springboard, coffee elites seized control over the national state, maneuvering within existing political frameworks, calling on connections with neighboring states for reinforcement, and sometimes using military force to oust presidents or political parties that were viewed as barriers to progress. Chapter 6 documented how coffee barons came to control the office of the presidency, a pattern that began first in Costa Rica and later spread to Guatemala, El Salvador, and Nicaragua. Through direct rule by coffee elites, the latter half of the nineteenth century witnessed a decisive reorientation of government policy toward the promotion of export activity in general and coffee culture in particular. The development of coffee preceded and promoted the development of state institutions by creating the class that would forge those institutions. Even when the reoriented national state institutions were too weak to intervene effectively, in most of the countries there was a powerful vested interest of coffee growers who kept the development momentum going from their local bases of power.

The one anomaly to the regional pattern of local to national state formation was Honduras, where the productive forces suitable for coffee were scattered over a large area dominated by peasant communities; coffee was introduced slowly in these communities but as a sideline cash crop, not one to specialize in. The few capitalist-sized farms that were established throughout most of Honduras existed within the confines of peasant-based economic and political structures, renting *ejidal* lands from peasant townships and getting labor without the help of local police forces. In all of Honduras, only one pocket of capitalist coffee development was found that happened to be located in an area where commercial agriculture had already been established before coffee. Like their counterparts elsewhere in

Central America, merchants, professionals, and hacienda owners worked through their commercial township (Choluteca) to acquire as private holdings the lands in the hills outside of town that were most suitable for growing coffee. Because this was the only pocket of capitalist coffee farms in the country, Choluteca's enterprising growers had no group of growers from another district to link up with in a national thrust for power. Furthermore, Choluteca was located far from the capital city of Tegucigalpa, making it difficult for its business elite to become an effective lobbying force in the national bureaucracy. Even in the late 1870s, when Guatemalan influence brought about a reorientation of Honduran policy through the support of Marco Aurelio Soto (whose development ideas had formed while serving in Barrios's cabinet in Guatemala) the government in Tegucigalpa had no national class of capitalist planters to support the new development thrust in the provinces. Nor was Honduras's only coffee-grower president, Luis Bográn, able to make much more of an impact during his term as president between 1883 and 1891.

Contradictions of the Construction Process

From their previous struggles for change, coffee elites came to power with relatively clear agendas of what they wished to accomplish, though the agendas were by no means uniform because their experiences varied so widely. They proceeded to reorient the existing bureaucratic machinery, which in most cases was inadequately trained and understaffed to overcome the forces resisting new programs. Chapter 6 argued that the nature of the stronger state institutions that finally emerged from the process was shaped not merely by the policy ideas of coffee elites but by the dynamic interplay between state institutions charged with carrying out those ideas and the social obstacles in the way during the consolidation.

National land and labor policies developed, but the process was fraught with ambiguity and conflict. One source of ambiguity lay in the highly diverse solutions to land and labor that had already proved successful at a local level before national states began to intervene. Because these arrangements were so diverse, there was usually no single model of landholding and labor relations for the national state to project when it was called on to do so. Chapter 6 argued that which model was applied at a particular time depended, in part, upon which district's elites exercised the greatest control over the national state at the time. The least ambiguous case in the region was Costa Rica, where the early dominance of San José led to the projection to other areas of the Central Valley the model of land access and labor relations developed earlier in San José, a model that had no serious competitor in coffee production until three decades after the national land and labor laws had been established. It would have been highly unlikely for the same land policy, which set upper limits on the size of private acquisitions of national land and easy access to unclaimed land by smallholders (effectively squatters' rights), to have been designed by Cartago's elite, whose primary wealth holdings included haciendas outside of town. In Guatemala under the Conservative Carrera government, coffee growers by the 1860s were able to pressure for national laws allowing access to lands of Indian communities, but the model projected at that time was based on the one that had proved successful in the cochineal districts, where rentals of communal or municipal lands were permitted at the discretion of community leaders. For capitalist growers, this arrangement was better than no access at all, but it stopped short of private ownership by leaving future lease rights open to the whims of Indian community leaders. When General Justo Rufino Barrios came to power in 1873, national land and labor laws were reoriented with the social conditions of Barrios's own district of San Marcos in mind, where hacienda agriculture dominated; the new laws were replete with sales of state lands in large lots and the resurrection of labor drafts for plantation work.[2] In El Salvador, leaders from the coffee townships of San Salvador, Ahuachapán, and Santa Ana were able to pressure for national land and labor laws that had already proved successful in their own districts; these laws tended to favor large and medium-sized capitalist holdings, not the small peasant farmer model of the economically and politically weak districts of Chalatenango. In Nicaragua, the merchant-landholding elite of Granada was simultaneously involved in large-scale plantation agriculture and commercial and lending relationships with small producer clients, though when the Granada group was in power, it tended to project the large plantation model into new districts, a model that the Managua elite, with a more singular experience with large-scale coffee production, continued to project when Zelaya came to power in the 1890s.

The new land and labor policies enacted by the coffee elite had varying degrees of success in their implementation because of differing levels of social resistance and the uneven capacities of existing state machinery to carry them out. The policies of Costa Rica were the least contradictory with respect to tradition in that they continued to allow small farmers access to land, albeit in unsettled areas. Displacement of people through privatization of township lands could be compensated for by moving to the forest's edge and staking a claim. This procedure directly benefited smallholders and indirectly benefited elites, whose profits from trade and processing would grow with the coffee supplied by the colonists. Therefore, new land laws required little in the way of building up the forces of coercion, though the state bureaucracy had to expand and improve in competence to handle the increased volume of land transactions. The economic development policies of Guatemala, El Salvador, and Nicaragua were more laden with contradictions than Costa Rica's in that they favored the formation of capitalist plantations, which intruded on the land and labor of Indian communities who, in turn, resisted.

Regardless of the country where commercial coffee growers intruded on Indian communities, a very similar buildup of tensions was found. Struggles began as individual acts by outsiders, who would sometimes pry their way into a community's domain by paying off a member of the community for access rights. As the number of intruders increased, other members of the community became alarmed and would seek retribution against those within the community who had received bribes or against the intruders themselves. When hostile actions against the intruders occurred, the outsiders would first call on forces of the closest commercial township to support them. If community resistance was strong enough, growers would call on higher levels of the state for assistance, and in this manner, what began as acts between individual agents developed into collective conflicts between state institutions and community structures. In Costa Rica, one case was examined in which an Indian community (Orósi) finally lost its lands to coffee growers after a protracted struggle, but the community was small enough that growers could receive ample assistance from the closest municipality, while national state officials washed their hands of the affair, claiming it should be left up to local judges to decide. Thus in Costa Rica, ethnic struggles may have influenced government institutions in certain localities, but they did not significantly shape the institutions of the national state. In contrast, Indian communities in Guatemala, El Salvador, and Nicaragua presented a more enticing opportunity for growers and, at the same time, a more formidable force of resistance. The struggles over the incorporation of Indian land and labor were found to be the key reason why militaries came to occupy such an important place within the national states of Guatemala, El Salvador, and Nicaragua. More subtly, the relative strengths of central institutions when reforms were implemented, the nature of the resistance to reforms, and the way the different struggles unfolded left lasting impressions on states in their relations with both peasant communities and elites.

When Liberal reforms were implemented in Guatemala, the Barrios government inherited the strongest military apparatus in the region, the largest indigenous population with the fullest tradition of dialogue with central authority, and a potential coffee area that was not, for the most part, directly occupied by Indian communities. Furthermore, Barrios learned from the failure of earlier Liberal reforms; he strengthened the military before introducing reforms, and he did not attempt a frontal assault on Indian values, community structures, or ways of life. Rather, he traded loose claims in the coffee piedmont for firmer claims on lands closer to highland villages, skillfully playing one Indian group off against another while strengthening highland militias. Certain traditional paternalistic relations between Indian communities and the state were actually strengthened under Barrios, and existing community hierarchies served (in a contradictory manner) as a mediating device between the state and the community on matters of labor drafts and taxation. The Guatemalan reforms were carried out with no major Indian uprisings, though in several instances, when Indian communities went outside of established channels, troops were immediately dispatched to the area and the movement brutally crushed. The transformation to the coffee economy had negative consequences for Guatemala's highland Indian population because the highland formation lost access to piedmont lands and became a labor supply zone for the piedmont plantations, but Indian communities survived as communities and increased in population.

In contrast to Guatemala, national militaries were poorly developed when reforms were introduced in El Salvador and Nicaragua, Indian communities had a weaker tradition of interaction with central authorities, and they occupied some of the best potential coffee lands. In both countries, intrusions on Indian land or labor were met with strong and violent acts of resistance, which were, in turn, responded to by official acts of violence. The escalation of the conflict in both countries led to a direct attack by state institutions on community power structures and Indian ways of life. In El Salvador, the national state declared traditional Indian forms of land tenure to be illegal, and the Nicaraguan state went so far as to project a Nicaragua composed only of *ladinos*, an ideological way of defining Indians out of existence and delegitimizing the Indian community as an acceptable conduit for discourse with the state.[3] By the end of the nineteenth century, paternalistic features of the state toward indigenous communities were all but destroyed in El Salvador and Nicaragua, while in Guatemala they were strengthened.

With respect to state-elite relations, in Guatemala and Nicaragua, capitalist enterprises came to rely on central state institutions to gain access to land and to solve their labor supply problems; in both countries, the competition between enterprises for state favors led to the state taking on a power over and above that of particular individuals or corporations. In both countries but especially in Nicaragua, this overarching power of the state was used by dictators to further their own personal fortunes and the fortunes of their closest friends, thereby widening traditional splits within the ranks of the economic elite. In El Salvador, the labor supply problem was essentially solved when Indian lands were expropriated, and local elites continued to work through their own municipalities in carrying out the nationally decreed land reform. As national military forces were strengthened in El Salvador, local units were called on by local elites to evict squatters or to jail workers who were viewed as troublemakers; this tradition put Salvadoran public institutions at the service of individual economic elites for no other reason than their elite status, whereas in Guatemala and Nicaragua local elites became more beholden to centrally commanded institutions.

There was also ambiguity and conflict in the formation of national policy regarding capital and the proper role of the state in providing public goods. The key problem in both areas had to do with the restoration in the 1840s of both the church, which had played an important role in finance during the colonial period, and quasi-public institutions such as Guatemala's Sociedad Económica and its Consulado de Comercio, which had initiated economic development and infrastructure projects during the colonial period. During the early phases of the coffee boom, growers were able to work through the church and quasi-public institutions (just as they worked through existing municipal governments) to expand their access to capital and initiate public works projects, but as the boom progressed these colonial institutions came to be seen as either inadequate or, as in the case of the church, an impediment to further accumulation, and moves were taken for national state institutions to intervene directly in those areas. Liberal and Conservative policy differences, which had always been stronger in the north where the colonial church and state had been centered, had begun to dissolve by the 1860s even in Conservative-controlled Guatemala, and by the 1870s and 1880s, states, with varying degrees of success, expropriated properties of the church, abolished the church's right to collect tithes (which was seen as a drain on active capital), chartered credit institutions to replace the former lending role of the church, and established state development agencies to supersede quasi-public development societies. The interventionist stance of the state was a heralded philosophy of the Liberal party, and after Barrios came to power in Guatemala in the 1870s the philosophy was certainly reinforced elsewhere on the isthmus through connections with the Guatemalan state, but even when Conservatives ruled, the former space of the church and other quasi-public institutions began to be squeezed, suggesting a deeper process of structural change at work. The structural explanation offered by this study was that coffee's enormous needs for capital and infrastructure could not be solved by the old institutional framework; as coffee elites ran up against capital and infrastructure constraints, they sought new ways to solve the problem, and ideological attachments to the old way of doing things began to be seen as nostalgic even by members of the Conservative party.

By the last three decades of the century, the region was swept up by a Liberal frenzy, even when elites calling themselves Conservatives held high office. In addition to the policies already mentioned, laws favorable to immigration and foreign investment were passed to attract foreign capital, technology, and expertise to the region. As the zones to which access was easier were taken for coffee groves, growers called for more ambitious infrastructure projects to connect potential coffee areas, commercial centers, and ports. The larger projects were beyond the immediate capacity of states to finance, and international capital markets were unwilling to lend to governments that were perceived as unstable. Thus there was indirect pressure from the international system for coffee elites to reduce traditional rivalries with each other and establish some orderly transition procedure from one regime to the next.

In addition to economic pressures from the international system, elites began to see other long-term gains to regularizing government, and there were pressures from within public bureaucracies to establish principles of orderly transition. Throughout the region, there was a tendency to institutionalize the bureaucracy, to establish training schools, and to set educational standards for state functionaries. The institutionalization of the state proceeded in the context of the development of the coffee economy in every country except Honduras, where state functionaries continued to live off the proceeds of concessions to foreign mining and lumber companies and to local recipients of liquor, tobacco, and sugar licenses.

How States Influenced Economic Change

The development of the coffee economy preceded the consolidation of coherent national states, but once policies were reoriented and institutions selectively strengthened, actions by governments promoted the extension and deepening of the coffee economy. Coffee exports surged following national state interventions. In Costa Rica, coffee export levels quadrupled between the decade of the 1840s, when national government efforts to promote coffee began, and the late 1880s, when the coffee state had been institutionalized, though annual rates of growth in production did not equal those of countries to the north, where the large plantation model was promoted. The grandest effort of all was undertaken by the Liberal government of General Barrios of Guatemala; between 1873, when Barrios took over, and 1885, when he died in battle, Guatemalan coffee exports expanded three and a half times and average annual growth rates were in excess of 20 percent. In El Salvador, coffee exports tripled in volume between 1881, when national land laws began to be passed, and 1901, when the last stretch of the railroad system serving the coffee belt was completed, an average annual growth rate of 10 percent. The Salvadoran coffee economy continued to expand at an average rate of 6 percent for the next thirty years of direct rule by the coffee oligarchy, and export levels reached and occasionally exceeded those of Guatemala during that period. In Nicaragua, promotional efforts by Conservative governments helped coffee growers achieve export levels by 1890 that were equivalent to those reached by Costa Rica in the 1860s, and during the Zelaya period the Matagalpa region was opened up to capitalist investors, and export levels doubled. Even though attempts were made by the Honduran government to promote coffee and other commercial agriculture after 1876, the obstacles to capitalist expansion were greater and the capacities of the Honduran state to intervene effectively were lower, so that a takeoff of the coffee economy was delayed until after World War II, when the Honduran state and commercial relations in the countryside were more fully developed.

States did more than influence the rate of expansion of the export sector; they reached deeply into the patterns of everyday life. By limiting the rights of traditional institutions such as the church and peasant communities, national state institutions became a more significant mediating force between members of the broader society. New laws altered the formal rules regarding land rights, labor contracts, and civil conduct. By developing national court systems, federal agencies, and forces of coercion, states influenced informal patterns of conflict resolution between private individuals, even in situations when state institutions were not directly involved, because once it became known that the forces of the state were likely to intervene if called upon, bounds were set within which private settlements could take place. In addition, the channels were established through which various social groups could interact with state institutions, thereby conditioning the nature of public participation in the state and the patterns of social protest over state actions.

The degree to which national states projected beyond the seats of government power and penetrated the countryside was highly uneven. One lesson from the nineteenth century is that the limited resources available to the state were not scattered randomly over the national terrain but were concentrated in particular areas. Especially affected were areas targeted by states as potential export zones or labor supply areas. The nature of the projection was highly specific, namely, taking patterns of land tenure and labor relations that had proven successful in one area of the country and using the legal, administrative, and coercive forces of the state to overcome tradition in the targeted zone and reproduce the preferred mode of land tenure and labor relations there. Thus a national standard of land tenure and labor relations was stamped onto what otherwise would have been a more heterogeneous landscape. Whereas other coffee zones throughout the region tended to reflect precoffee structures of land-holding, the Indian zones targeted by the state came to reflect the opposite, switching from systems that provided widespread access to land by small producers into systems that became dominated by large capitalist plantations.

In Guatemala, El Salvador, and Nicaragua, the procedure of in-corporation of new territory provided a lever for large capitalist enterprises to displace peasants, while in Costa Rica small farmers continued to be allowed access, at least by national state institutions, when a new area was opened up for settlement. In Honduras, the national state, by default, allowed local power structures to deter-mine the outcome in the incorporation of new areas, thereby enabling a patchwork quilt of land tenure and labor relations to spread over the Honduran countryside. Although the procedures of incorpora-tion of new territory and states' roles in the labor supply process were established by the end of the nineteenth century, areas of little eco-nomic interest and zones outside the network of roads and telegraph lines continued to harbor local structures of power and tradition well into the twentieth century.

Chapter 8

Reflections on the Twentieth Century in the Light of the Nineteenth

Central America began the nineteenth century with the disintegration of an established political order (1800–1821), proceeded through a period of political chaos and civil wars (1820s–1830s), entered an era of state construction (1840s–1900), and closed with a new political order. The twentieth century began with an established political order that weathered some major disruptions (the Great Depression and World War II) only to be greeted late in the century (late 1970s and 1980s) by revolutions from below of enormous magnitude. What questions does the period of nation building in the late nineteenth century raise with respect to states and social evolution during the twentieth?

On Reading the Impact of World Economic Changes

The twentieth century has brought changes in the world economic system that have altered the opportunities for enrichment and the conditions of survival for people within Central America. Increasingly the land, labor, and capital of the region have become more closely integrated into the international system of production and exchange. Exports from the region increased during the twentieth century as more land and people were pulled into the cultivation of coffee, and a series of other economic activities came to harness the region's resources. Some of the most notable were the development of the banana industry during the first three decades of the century, the expansion of cotton, beef, sugar, and other agricultural exports during three decades following World War II, the creation of domestic and regional markets for manufactured goods in the 1950s and 1960s, and the formation of export zones for labor-intensive manufactures during the early 1990s. The greater degree of openness of the economies of the region has stimulated rapid growth of overall market activity during periods when world demand and prices have remained favorable (e.g., World War I to the mid-1920s and the two decades following World War II), only to be followed by collapse of the market and economic disruptions when world demand and terms of trade have turned sour (the Great Depression, the inflationary crises of the 1970s, and the disinflation of the 1980s, which most recently struck the coffee market between 1989 and 1994).

In reading the social evolutionary implications of world economic changes during the twentieth century, the experience of the late nineteenth century may be instructive. World system forces during the late nineteenth century were found to have significantly changed social formations on the isthmus, but these forces did not work like an architectural blueprint for a construction project. Rather, they operated as a grand environmental shift to which local social organisms adapted, whereby a considerable part of the genetic material present beforehand was preserved and sometimes enhanced during the transition while social forms that were less viable relative to the new conditions withered. Because of the unusually wide range of social organizational modes possible for successful coffee cultivation, in conducting this study I was forced to examine how conditions at a local level influenced outcomes. A strong result was that pre-coffee land tenure and labor relations had a profound impact on the way coffee production came to be organized. This result raises the question of the degree to which social customs and geography at a local level have continued to express themselves in twentieth-century adaptations to world system changes.[1]

In understanding the relationships between states and agrarian structures, this close look at the late nineteenth century underscores the importance of viewing states at many levels, not just the national level. This book's theory of state formation centers on the significance of local governments, which were found to be both highly responsive to local agrarian structures and influential in the building of national governments. Although national state institutions have increased their intervention powers in the twentieth century, it would be foolhardy to overlook the roles played by local and departmental state institutions in the dynamics of agrarian change and national politics. New economic activities rarely take place evenly in geographical space but tend to concentrate in particular zones within countries, creating their own social and ecological tensions in those zones. In cases in which new activities have been introduced, the question should be asked, How have local political structures mediated or aggravated these tensions, and how have these local adjustments interacted with politics at a national level?

On Reading the Impact of Geopolitical Changes

The late nineteenth century has been aptly called the Age of Imperialism, but for Central Americans that imperialism was more commercial than political. The rise of the United States as a global power in the early twentieth century brought an additional force for institutional change into the picture. Indeed, direct interventions by the U.S. government have overturned presidents, U.S. troops have been stationed in the region for sometimes lengthy occupations, U.S. military and economic aid has been deployed to bolster unpopular regimes, and economic aid has been applied in more subtle ways to shape the behavior of national governments. It has been said that imperialist powers attempt to reproduce their own images in the societies they seek to dominate. Although the Central American experience in the nineteenth century gives us little to work with regarding state-state interactions, the nineteenth-century experience of outside economic forces does raise the question, Can a powerful outside state imprint itself, recreating a social formation in its own image, or do outside political pressures work in a parallel fashion to outside economic pressures, namely, as environmental shifts that local actors and institutions adapt to?

Although a closer examination may disprove the hypothesis, a few examples from the twentieth century suggest that geopolitical pressures operate in a manner similar to world economic forces, as sometimes grand and abrupt environmental shifts that local social formations respond to and alter, significantly modifying the outcomes. Because Central America's strategic location is of greater significance to the U.S. government than the region's limited economic potential, U.S. interventions since the early 1900s have not been steady and unidirectional but have vacillated wildly depending upon strategic perceptions in Washington and changing geopolitical connections between the United States and major world powers. In periods when no strategic threat has been visible, Central America has received little attention from Washington, and meager resources have been provided to influence national governments in the region, allowing greater room for play of local forces. When it appears that a hostile state has the opportunity to make political inroads in the region, however, an alarm is sounded in Washington, strategic manpower is mobilized, and resources far beyond the absorptive capacity of states are pumped into the region.

These periodic bursts of activity have quickly altered political space for competing groups within Central America, often leading to swift changes in behavior of national states, but the long-term outcomes of U.S. actions have rarely been accurately envisioned or understood by U.S. policymakers. One of the most forceful U.S. interventions, which was outlined in some detail in Chapter 5, was the order from Washington during World War II for national governments to expropriate the assets of Axis nationals and deport those suspected of being supporters of falangist political parties.[2] The expropriation unsettled the coffee elite, permanently breaking the dominance of the largest foreign enclave in Central America's coffee economy and disrupting the management of farms, processing companies, export businesses, and financial houses. Furthermore, repressive dictatorships that had ruled since the early years of the Depression had ideological and political ties with falangist parties that had sprung up during the 1930s. Expropriations and deportations removed some of the strongest allies of Depression-era dictatorships. These actions combined with a pervasive antitotalitarian bias in Washington to create an opening for wage laborers, peasants, artisans, intellectuals, and professionals, who had chafed under the dictators, to pressure for change. For Central America as a whole, the antitotalitarian thrust of U.S. policy made conditions favorable for the ouster of Depression-era dictators, who were overthrown in every country except Nicaragua, where General Somoza showed greater dexterity than the other dictators by courting organized labor and peasant groups with populist rhetoric and conciliatory acts.

Long-term structural repercussions varied considerably, depending upon the concentration of Axis holdings and the way governments handled expropriated estates. In El Salvador, Germans (and Italians) had more thoroughly married into elite Salvadoran families, thus escaping expropriation and deportation. In Honduras and Nicaragua, German holdings were significant, but disruption from expropriation was minimized by the rapid auction of assets to other owners who kept the estates intact and in working order. The disruption was greatest in Guatemala, where German ownership was most highly concentrated and where the U.S. security state intervened most forcefully; the same year German properties were expropriated, the dictatorship of Jorge Ubico was overthrown. The nationalized properties remained in the hands of the Guatemalan government, whose appointees managed the farms poorly and slowly decapitalized them, making them targets for land reform as peasants moved onto idle portions of these estates. For Guatemala, U.S. actions during World War II unleashed a revolutionary decade of labor struggles and land redistribution that was far removed from the original intentions of U.S. policymakers.

Even when U.S. interventions have been prolonged, it appears from a glance that the results have rarely been those intended by Washington. One needs only to point to the case of Nicaragua, which because of its natural isthmian crossing has suffered most from strategic fears in Washington. Throughout the century, the U.S. government has played on traditional rivalries within the economic elite of the country, propping up officials who projected a loyal image to Washington. Earlier in the century the U.S. government went so far as to occupy Nicaragua militarily for approximately two decades. The attempt by the U.S. state to control Nicaragua strategically, however, created conditions for an opposition movement against U.S. presence to form. Nicaraguan dictators continued the nineteenth-century practice of using their position in the state to expand personal fortunes, provoking a backlash from other elites. Blatant abuses of power and the obvious security connection with Washington stimulated a popular anti-imperialist movement led by General Sandino during the 1920s and 1930s that was resurrected by the Sandinistas during the 1960s and 1970s. Rather than implanting North American institutions on Central American soil, it appears that U.S. interventions have penetrated the region only to be digested by Central American institutions and turned into something quite different.

On the Question of Path Dependence

Changing geopolitical and economic forces have altered the environments within which national states operate, and during the twentieth century national states have changed in response to these environmental shifts.Despite these changes, however, certain patterns of governance present at the end of the nineteenth century have resurfaced repeatedly during the twentieth century, suggesting an institutional inertia at work, or what Douglass North has called path dependence. During periods of economic expansion, when new areas have been opened for development, states have exhibited the same promotional patterns as those of the late nineteenth century, and during periods of crisis, when economic structures have been threatened, states have systematically revealed their nineteenth-century origins. State institutions have evolved considerably over the century, but they have resiliently held onto some modes of behavior that were present at the creation.

When new areas have been targeted for economic development in the twentieth century, national governments have tended to promote the same land tenure and labor relations patterns that they projected to new coffee zones during the late nineteenth century. For example, during the 1950s and 1960s, when the Pacific coastal plain was being opened for commercial development, national state institutions in Guatemala, El Salvador, and Nicaragua unmercifully favored the formation of large cotton, cattle, and sugar operations, sometimes at the expense of peasant communities in the area. When peasant resistance mounted, national military units were dispatched to the area to reinforce the claims of large commercial enterprises. A similar projection occurred during the late 1960s and early 1970s, when the governments of Nicaragua and Guatemala targeted the agricultural frontier towards the Atlantic as an economic development zone. In both cases, peasants who had lost land in other areas or who were squeezed by population growth in older peasant settlements moved onto national land in the tropical forests toward the Atlantic to continue swidden agriculture. The governments of Nicaragua and Guatemala received outside financing to build roads into these zones and used military force to evict peasant settlers, carving out vast estates for military officers and others close to the dictators in power.[3]

In contrast, the Honduran state made no clear national policy on land tenure in newly developed areas but tended to allow patterns already dominant in an area to be extended. When the coffee boom finally reached Honduras during the 1960s and 1970s, the Honduran state granted land titles, loans, and technical assistance to family-sized farms, reflecting the dominance of peasant holdings in those areas before coffee. Simultaneously, large cattle ranchers were granted loans and titles to extend their operations in eastern Honduras, though when conflicts between peasant settlers and cattle ranchers reached national level institutions, which side would win the judgment was not predetermined.[4]

In Costa Rica, the land and colonization agency of the national government settled disputes between ranchers and peasants in the expanding cattle zones, sometimes paying ranchers for properties that peasants had settled on. In areas opened toward the Atlantic, the Costa Rican government continued to sell land and grant loans to small farmers from the Central Valley who were willing to settle in targeted areas, thereby repeating the nineteenth-century pattern of colonization.[5] A recent example of projection of Central Valley social relations onto an unlikely landscape is the Tempisque River Irrigation Project, which during the 1970s and 1980s promoted small and medium-sized commercial farms in the province of Guanacaste, which had been dominated for more than a century by large cattle haciendas. Marc Edelman has neatly documented how cattle barons in the region attempted to sabotage the intrusion from San José and how once irrigation was available, a classic conflict between peasants and cattlemen over land was converted into a conflict over water, when large landowners channeled water into their holding ponds for cattle, while peasants, "operating under the cover of darkness, broke padlocks on sluices and pumps to irrigate their fields." After a decade of heavy investments by the national state and conflictual adjustments in the targeted district (which included complaints by laborers of losing their traditional afternoon *faena* or work break), the irrigation project seemed to have worked in permitting a "rapid intensification of traditional hacienda enterprises into highly capitalized plantations" and the formation of a "new stratum of sophisticated smallholders" producing melons and other commercial crops, but as Edelman noted, the irrigation district is but a small pocket within a much larger area where local power structures are still dominated by traditional cattle barons.[6]

During periods of economic crisis, such as the 1930s and 1970s, when shocks from the world system have disrupted economic structures of the region, states have responded in ways reminiscent of the late nineteenth century. Both periods of economic crisis were preceded by booms in agricultural export activity. While export prices and government revenues were rising, economic elites and government officials could allow some concessions to trade unions and other popular-based organizations so that the 1920s and the 1960s were periods of relative opening of states to popular pressures. When world market conditions squeezed export sector profits, however, the space for political participation collapsed.

The worldwide depression of the 1930s blasted the coffee economies of Central America. Between 1929 and 1933, world coffee prices dropped from approximately twenty-two cents per pound to nine cents per pound, and prices for some Central American coffees dropped even more precipitously.[7] With world prices falling, the crop lien system that growers had become so dependent upon for cash advances dried up, and many plantation owners who had mortgaged their lands when coffee and land prices were high could not make payments. With long-term and short-term credit lines broken and banks folding, there was a premium on holding cash. Where the large plantation had become the model of production, the system of labor relations was severely disrupted as plantation owners became unwilling and unable to come forth with customary payments for labor. In Nicaragua and Guatemala, where a system of debt servitude had emerged as a way for growers to lasso laborers from the agricultural frontier, plantation owners suspended cash advances and called on the state to intervene directly on their behalf. In the north central region of Nicaragua marginal coffee estates were abandoned, and peasants invaded those properties; when the owners called in the National Guard to reclaim the lands, Sandino's army repelled the attacks, and it was not until the National Guard swept through the area after Sandino's assassination in 1936 that coffee production was restored on these estates. In Guatemala, the military government of Jorge Ubico (1931–44) enacted a national decree prohibiting growers from paying cash advances to workers and resurrecting a vagrancy law requiring those without profession or adequate property to work 100 to 150 days per year on the plantations or on the road gang, with payments to be made only after work was completed.[8] In El Salvador, where a purer system of wage labor had developed, growers responded to the crisis by cutting harvest wages from fifty centavos per day to twenty and by evicting permanent workers living on the plantations.[9] When a mass uprising in the western coffee districts broke out in January 1932, the Salvadoran military intervened brutally on behalf of the growers, terrorizing peasants and workers with a massacre that lasted several months.[10] In all three countries where the large plantation was the model, adjustments to the crisis were made through direct military repression of rural workers, repeating the practices perfected during the late nineteenth century.

In the coffee highlands of Costa Rica, social conflict during the 1930s erupted less over wages or land than over the price of ripe berries. During periods of rising world prices, *beneficio* owners could collect excess profits from small producers by granting cash advances on a crop that would be purchased at preset prices; if the world price rose in the meantime the *beneficio* collected the premium. During periods of falling prices, advance contracts with preset prices were disadvantageous to the *beneficio* owners. Late in 1929, when world coffee prices began to drop, owners of *beneficios* responded by suspending cash advances to growers and pressuring small producers to liquidate outstanding debts. Between 1929 and 1932, *beneficio* owners apparently overcompensated for falling world prices by setting prices of mature berries artificially low; one source estimated that the rate of deflation of the price of mature berries was one-third again as great as the rate of deflation of world coffee prices.[11] In essence, wealthy processors and exporters were pushing the burden of the crisis onto the backs of the small and medium-sized growers. Small producers, who were the most vulnerable to price gouging, began forming local associations to protect their interests against the *beneficio* owners and exporters, who in 1929 formed the Asociación Nacíonal de Cafetaleros. Finally, in 1932, smaller coffee growers formed their own national organization, the Asociación Nacíonal de Productores de Café, which became an effective lobbying force for the small producers.[12] Throughout the crisis years, conflict between the two social groups was heated, but instead of resorting to violence to reach a solution, they fought their battles in the arena of public opinion and legislative action.[13] Thus, although the nation's coffee elite exerted a powerful force in national politics, the Costa Rican state did not intervene in a violent fashion to crush the less powerful small farmers but served as a mediator (though not a completely neutral one) of conflict between the two sides.

During the 1970s, not only did export prices soften, but interest rates on loans and prices of imported inputs, which the economy had become dependent upon, escalated dramatically, creating a double squeeze on profits of elites. Simultaneously, living standards of the poor deteriorated as food and transportation prices soared. Following world economic shocks, workers struck for higher wages and peasants invaded idle lands. Elites throughout the region resisted pressures from the poor, but states elicited their own peculiar responses. The three states that had been constructed a century earlier to support capitalist plantation agriculture responded to peasant land invasions and worker strikes with brutality, making a wide sweep of society that included anyone who might be suspected of sympathizing with workers or peasants, while the Costa Rican state took efforts to resolve conflicts using dialogue instead of military force; ranchers in Guanacaste and San Carlos used local forces to repress the peasant movement, but when national state institutions were appealed to, they did not invariably back up the large landowners. In sections of Honduras dominated by large cattle ranches (Olancho), departmental representatives of the national military operated in much the same way as their counterparts in Guatemala, Nicaragua, and El Salvador by torturing and murdering those associated with the peasant movement, but the national peasant and worker movements were successful in pressuring the military dictatorship to decide numerous cases in their favor, resulting in land reform and minimum wage adjustments that prevented an escalation of the conflict there.

It appears that at least for the 1960s and 1970s, social formations evolved at a faster pace than states. With the mechanization of agriculture and the eviction of permanent workers from large estates, the takeover of traditional peasant strongholds by commercial interests, the heightened conflict over land at the forest's edge, and the associated movement of populations both from the countryside to the city and from one country to the next, class, gender, and ethnic relations along with belief systems were rapidly transformed. Numerous studies of this period have pointed to how creatively workers, slum dwellers, and peasants drew both from their collective pasts and from organizing experiences of others to develop new strategies for coping with a hostile and changing world. The tendency of national states to respond to social tensions in a habitual way produced different results depending on the particular customs of governance established almost a century earlier. The Costa Rican mode of governance provided a flexibility that absorbed intense shocks. In Guatemala, El Salvador, and Nicaragua, the habits of projection onto outlying areas and response to pressures from below proved brittle in the face of rapid social change, resulting in social revolutions. In Honduras, the ability of local power structures to influence the national state provided a fortuitous flexibility toward workers and peasants at a critical juncture (1973–75), though U.S. intervention and the anti-communist thrust in the 1980s created more room for cattle barons (of Olancho) and large plantation owners (from Choluteca) to re-assert their influence over national state institutions, making those institutions less flexible to pressures from below.

As the twentieth century comes to a close, the signature of the nineteenth remains visible. Honduran public officials continue to col-lect benefits from concessions to foreign companies, the Guatemalan state continues rule by terror over labor and peasant groups, and the Costa Rican state continues to promote dialogue between conflictual parties. Even in El Salvador and Nicaragua, where state institutions were most thoroughly shaken by civil wars and outside intervention during the 1980s, nineteenth-century patterns have reappeared in the reconstruction of those states during the 1990s. In both coun-tries the descendants of nineteenth-century oligarchs have returned to direct rule, and though the repressive apparatus at their disposal is in disarray, businessmen with surnames of nineteenth-century cof-fee barons have flown back from Miami seeking to reclaim assets taken during the 1980s. Meanwhile, peasants, who have become much more sophisticated in their organizational capabilities, move onto idle lands as the rich attempt to reestablish rights to properties titled a century ago. The Nicaraguan elite remains as politically di-vided as it was in the 1890s, and the Salvadoran tendency to resolve class conflicts through violent means smolders under the supervi-sion of United Nations peacekeepers. Much has changed in Central America, but aspects of political culture peculiar to each state have somehow survived.

Statistical Appendix

Table A-I. Central American Coffee Exports and World Coffee Prices, 1832–1987

(export volumes = quintals oro; world price = US¢/lb. Brazil Santos #4)

Year	Guatemala	El Salvador	Honduras	Nicaragua	Costa Rica	Central America	Price/lb.
1832					500		
1833					978		
1843					25,276		7.3
1844					50,000		6.5
1845					66,808		6.8
1846					83,074		7.1
1847							7.0
1848							6.1
1849							6.9
1850							10.6
1851							9
1852					67,776		8.5
1853					80,000		8.75
1854							10.1
1855					71,707		9.9
1856					84,172		10.8
1857					91,270		11.0
1858					61,207		10.4

Continued

Table A-1. Continued

Year	Guatemala	El Salvador	Honduras	Nicaragua	Costa Rica	Central America	Price/lb.
1859					110,116		11.3
1860					91,219		12.0
1861					114,528		13.8
1862					109,426		22.0
1863					87,671		30.1
1864		4,930			114,178		16.3
1865					136,524		16.0
1866					183,957		13.9
1867					202,823		12.3
1868					206,880		10.5
1869					206,880		10.5
1870		58,964			254,797		11.3
1871					183,731		13.0
1872					255,557		16.8
1873	149,069				202,823		20.3
1874	159,980				237,656		20.9
1875	161,959	88,061			106,616		18.9
1876	205,346				246,379		18.0
1877	207,885				184,219		18.5

Table A-1. Continued

Year	Guatemala	El Salvador	Honduras	Nicaragua	Costa Rica	Central America	Price/lb.
1878	207,285				255,451		16.3
1879	249,521				235,932		14.9
1880	286,893			45,283	174,915		15.1
1881	257,794	145,200			247,789		6.9
1882	309,179				163,323		7.0
1883	400,068				202,883		9.4
1884	367,630				366,614		7.5
1885	515,167	297,000		70,525	201,740	1,084,433	7.5
1886	524,506				199,230		14.6
1887	473,951				288,404		14.5
1888	362,770				227,362		14.9
1889	546,920				285,442		16.8
1890	503,563	330,000		113,820	339,389	1,286,772	18.1
1891	519,302	320,428			311,778		15.0
1892	486,774				238,053		15.6
1893	592,478				252,251		17.1
1894	614,000				237,584		15.9
1895	692,000	132,000			244,479		15.6
1896	684,000				258,286		12.6

Continued

Table A-I. Continued

Year	Guatemala	El Salvador	Honduras	Nicaragua	Costa Rica	Central America	Price/lb.
1897	755,000				305,808		7.8
1898	826,000				429,591		6.3
1899	841,000				338,773		6.1
1900	730,000				354,960		8.3
1901	676,213	437,326			365,390		6.5
1902	774,023	416,191			303,112		5.5
1903	578,973	580,972			382,114		5.6
1904	647,633	753,140		216,000	277,303		7.8
1905	810,817	618,222		201,000	397,876		8.3
1906	684,410	626,856		194,000	303,667		8.0
1907	1,101,997	563,292		187,000	381,958		6.5
1908	560,719	552,151		206,000	197,918		6.3
1909	881,628	633,301		185,700	265,215		7.9
1910	664,551	618,351		261,489	317,394	1,861,785	9.6
1911	774,573	647,195		166,257	278,686	1,866,711	13.4
1912	723,045	583,983	6,992	133,972	269,796	1,717,789	14.4
1913	875,337	625,943	5,280	260,715	287,018	2,054,293	10.9
1914	831,341	753,609	11,880	225,016	390,590	2,212,436	8.1

Table A-1. Continued

Year	Guatemala	El Salvador	Honduras	Nicaragua	Costa Rica	Central America	Price/lb.
1915	775,631	662,343	2,640	198,533	269,101	1,908,248	7.5
1916	874,696	777,320	5,280	227,235	371,338	2,255,869	9.4
1917	903,878	788,105	7,920	183,223	270,442	2,153,568	6.1
1918	782,520	783,707	2,640	252,045	252,464	2,073,376	9.0
1919	896,670	718,541	18,480	332,193	307,838	2,273,722	17.9
1920	939,539	817,112	10,560	151,317	308,603	2,227,131	11.9
1921	935,261	615,487	2,640	295,211	294,013	2,142,612	7.1
1922	935,367	936,496	7,920	192,911	410,426	2,483,120	10.3
1923	956,748	912,916	19,800	298,103	244,454	2,432,021	14.8
1924	888,004	1,062,062	18,480	391,246	401,474	2,761,266	21.8
1925	968,630	697,049	17,160	235,265	338,469	2,256,573	24.6
1926	932,552	1,100,573	26,400	384,166	402,318	2,846,009	22.5
1927	1,146,921	787,017	31,680	222,937	356,130	2,544,685	18.1
1928	959,800	1,154,535	51,480	387,053	415,386	2,968,254	23.5
1929	954,680	1,017,013	35,274	288,002	433,779	2,728,748	22.2
1930	1,232,824	1,274,378	39,683	332,667	518,888	3,398,440	13.0
1931	784,722	1,187,627	24,251	344,476	507,381	2,848,457	8.6
1932	984,731	862,063	35,273	176,684	407,829	2,466,581	10.6

Continued

Table A-1. Continued

Year	Guatemala	El Salvador	Honduras	Nicaragua	Costa Rica	Central America	Price/lb.
1933	765,605	1,221,506	41,887	297,911	612,392	2,939,301	9.1
1934	1,052,014	1,084,050	41,887	319,068	420,255	2,917,274	11.1
1935	887,227	1,088,418	24,251	402,721	534,362	2,936,979	8.9
1936	1,105,436	1,074,111	33,069	284,937	470,156	2,967,709	9.5
1937	1,024,267	1,469,955	55,115	343,233	584,659	3,477,229	11.1
1938	1,065,455	1,169,661	26,455	310,015	550,734	3,122,320	7.8
1939	954,253	1,212,864	41,887	378,618	446,310	3,033,933	7.5
1940	902,878	1,229,334	30,864	332,589	412,351	2,908,016	7.2
1941	908,162	907,923	19,841	275,381	460,962	2,572,269	11.4
1942	1,080,597	1,154,314	48,501	276,656	443,162	3,003,230	13.4
1943	1,030,001	1,225,765	44,092	260,160	495,121	3,055,139	13.4
1944	1,049,604	1,371,789	41,887	284,142	411,838	3,159,260	13.4
1945	1,166,597	1,254,755	59,524	266,351	514,900	3,262,127	13.6
1946	1,081,472	1,046,901	83,775	256,008	283,528	2,751,684	18.7
1947	1,213,576	1,360,995	57,320	218,422	395,133	3,245,446	26.4
1948	1,054,959	1,310,047	70,547	315,016	506,241	3,256,810	26.8
1949	1,191,748	1,621,275	136,685	148,689	359,492	3,457,889	31.8
1950	1,192,231	1,528,229	132,276	456,170	433,014	3,741,920	50.9

Table A-1. Continued

Year	Guatemala	El Salvador	Honduras	Nicaragua	Costa Rica	Central America	Price/lb.
1951	1,086,742	1,452,296	180,777	349,960	362,851	3,432,627	54.3
1952	1,310,131	1,475,344	182,982	411,129	385,553	3,765,139	54.1
1953	1,230,710	1,452,831	246,915	408,131	622,914	3,961,501	58.5
1954	1,131,801	1,371,472	205,028	371,156	437,679	3,517,136	78.3
1955	1,270,250	1,582,850	196,209	494,888	662,108	4,206,305	57.0
1956	1,358,007	1,421,976	262,347	368,319	452,379	3,863,028	58.3
1957	1,344,276	1,834,783	209,206	479,020	638,390	4,505,675	57.3
1958	1,551,120	1,774,386	222,995	498,097	901,501	4,948,100	48.9
1959	1,797,469	1,829,473	312,260	354,549	1,002,654	5,296,406	37.6
1960	1,737,321	1,973,144	313,273	479,941	1,002,552	5,506,232	36.9
1961	1,717,602	1,908,586	254,785	462,194	1,096,260	5,439,428	36.3
1962	1,791,216	2,305,219	351,214	453,067	1,262,982	6,163,699	34.4
1963	2,135,596	2,228,675	448,944	530,691	1,089,070	6,432,977	34.6
1964	1,653,291	2,410,521	419,226	454,610	1,205,766	6,143,415	47.9
1965	2,071,348	2,201,608	549,187	603,288	899,806	6,325,239	45.1
1966	2,374,630	2,138,182	506,264	511,797	1,172,477	6,703,351	41.4
1967	1,767,280	2,678,417	489,531	569,205	1,379,061	6,883,495	38.4
1968	2,049,844	2,605,386	589,135	627,605	1,550,742	7,422,713	37.6

Continued

Table A-1. Continued

Year	Guatemala	El Salvador	Honduras	Nicaragua	Costa Rica	Central America	Price/lb.
1969	2,202,395	2,469,152	542,904	585,277	1,402,717	7,202,446	40.8
1970	2,096,575	2,447,106	562,173	659,021	1,665,486	7,430,360	55.7
1971	2,204,600	2,158,303	555,559	714,290	1,446,458	7,079,211	46.1
1972	2,528,676	2,303,807	701,063	723,109	1,813,557	8,070,212	54.4
1973	2,530,881	2,682,998	828,930	822,316	1,538,899	8,404,023	67.6
1974	2,669,771	3,174,624	676,812	714,290	1,986,345	9,221,842	70.2
1975	2,991,642	3,137,146	1,071,436	892,863	1,697,542	9,790,629	67.8
1976	2,625,679	3,375,243	965,615	1,159,620	1,417,558	9,543,713	122.8
1977	2,925,504	2,956,369	800,270	1,091,277	1,490,310	9,263,729	
1978	2,901,254	3,284,160	1,269,850	1,203,717	1,869,501	10,528,476	148.4
1979	3,394,818	4,462,920	1,387,320	1,263,240	2,022,240	12,530,538	176.3
1980	2,843,127	3,833,280	1,293,600	1,102,200	1,749,000	10,821,207	206.6
1981	2,476,656	3,018,840	1,359,600	1,111,440	2,065,800	10,032,336	159.4
1982	3,196,368	2,855,160	1,202,520	1,086,360	2,092,200	10,432,608	142.0
1983	2,655,261	3,564,000	1,512,720	1,420,320	2,027,520	11,179,821	140.0
1984	2,616,894	3,828,000	1,386,000	1,036,200	2,352,240	11,219,334	143.0
1985	4,118,499	3,248,520	1,690,920	904,200	2,791,800	12,753,939	
1986	3,044,223	3,513,840	1,954,920	976,800	1,848,000	11,337,783	

Table A-1. Continued

Year	Guatemala	El Salvador	Honduras	Nicaragua	Costa Rica	Central America	Price/lb.
1987	3,594,591	3,284,160	1,805,760	877,800	2,376,000	11,938,311	

Export Volume Data

Guatemala: 1873–1934, Jones, *Guatemala*, p. 210; 1935–68, Dirección General de Estadística y Censo, *Censo agropecuario de 1964*, Table 51, p. 249; 1969–78, SIECA, *Compendio estadístico de 1981*, Table 125, pp. 190–91; 1979–87, Agricultural Attaché to Guatemala, "Central American Coffee Statistics."

El Salvador: 1864–75, 1891, Browning, *El Salvador*, p. 162; 1881–90, 1895, *Commodity Yearbook 1942*, p. 52; 1901–49, Dirección General de Estadística, *Anuario estadístico de 1949*, 2:51; 1950–68, Dirección General de Estadísticos y Censos, *Anuario estadístico de 1969*, Table 4, p. 5; 1968–77, SIECA, *Compendio estadístico de 1981*, Table 125, pp. 190–91; 1978–87, Agricultural Attaché to Guatemala, "Central American Coffee Statistics."

Honduras: 1912, Mendioróz, *Pequeño atlas de Centroamérica*, p. 31; 1913–28, Bynum, *World's Coffee Exports*, Table 1; 1929–56, Food and Agriculture Organization, *The World's Coffee*, Table 3a; 1957–59, Dirección General de Censos y Estadísticas, *Honduras en cifras*, Table 5; 1960–69, SIECA, *Desarrollo integrado*, Table 15; 1970–78, SIECA, *Compendio estadístico*, Table 125, pp. 190–91; 1979–87, Agricultural Attaché to Guatemala, "Central American Coffee Statistics."

Continued

Table A-1. Continued

Nicaragua: 1880–90, 1910–59, Dirección General de Estadísticos y Censos, *El café en Nicaragua;* 1904–9, Playter, "Report on Nicaraguan Coffee," p. 10; 1960–69, SIECA, *Desarrollo integrado,* Table 15; 1970–78, SIECA, *Compendio estadístico de 1981,* Table 125, pp. 190–91; 1979–87, U.S. Department of Agriculture, "Coffee Statistics," p. 3.

Costa Rica: 1832–53, Vega Carballo, "El nacimiento," pt. II, Appendix 5 (questionable data for 1847–50); 1855–1940, Dirección General de Estadistica y Censos, *Boletín de exportación,* p. 14; 1941–73, Oficina del Café, *Informe de labores—1973,* Tables 21, 51; 1974–78, SIECA, *Compendio estadístico,* Table 125, pp. 190–91; 1979–87, U.S. Department of Agriculture, "Coffee Statistics," p. 3.

World Price Data

1840–1941, *Commodity Yearbook 1942;* 1942–49, *Commodity Yearbook 1950;* 1950–62, *Commodity Yearbook 1963;* 1963–74, *Commodity Yearbook 1975;* 1975–84, *Commodity Yearbook 1985;* 1840–95, "Fair to Prime Rio"; 1898–1922, "Rio No. 7s"; 1923–84, "Santos No. 4s."

Table A-2. The Guatemalan Coffee Elite, 1890

Name of owner	Number of trees (100s)	1934	1930	1794– 1871	1820
Acuña, Luís	100				
Aguirre, Juan Francisco	150			C	
Aguña, Guillermo	200				
Anguiano, M. de G.	325				
Aparicio, Francisco	100		X	C	
Aparicio, Juan e hijos	400		X	C	
Arroyo, Julio R.	150				
Arseyuz, Gonzalo	180				
Augéner, Andrés	130				
Auyón, Familia	300				
Avila, Emeterio	300				
Avila, Familia	400				
Ayau, Rafael y Manuel	128				
Barillas, Manuel L.	1,300				
Barillas, Mercedes	400				
Beltranena, R. y Miguel	250			C	A
Boy, Gustavo	445				
Brammá, Jorge	370				
Bruny, Pedro A.	100				
Campanias, Enrique	150				
Carrera, Antonio	300				
Cerda, Nicolás de la	140				
Chacón V., F.	102				
Cía Hamburguesa de Plantaciones	1,025	G	X	C	A
Díaz, A. Rafael	100				
Durán, C.	600				
Escobar, Cornelio	150				
Escobar, Narciso J.	125				
Felice, Antonio	180				
Felice, E.	100				
Fernández, M. e hijos	230	G			
Figueroa, Mariano	128				
Flores A., Alejandro	102				
Flores, Alberto	634				
Fournier, Pablo	200				
Fuentes, Micaela de	100				

Continued

Table A-2. Continued

Name of owner	Number of trees (100s)	1934	1930	1794– 1871	1820
García, Pedro	135				
Gesellschaft, H.	600				
González, Rafael	105			C	
Goubaud, Emilio	130				
Gómez, Santiago	100				
Guardiola, José	500				
Hanseatische Plantagen	—				
Harris, La familia	268				
Herrarte, Rosalío	120				
Herrera, Francisco	200	G	X		
Herrera y Cía.	900	G	X		
Hockmeyer, Ernesto	100				
Jacoby, Luis	100				
James, Santiago	100				
Javalois y Lusbielles	179				
Leger, Jorge y Cía.	250				
de León, Socorro	278	G			
Llerandi, David	100				
López, Hdos. de Pedro	115	G			
Luttmann, Juan	250	G			
Machado, M.	500			C	
Makepeace y Trampé	240				
Martínez, Maury A.	140				
Matheu, Víctor	400			C	
Maury, Pedro	125				
Mejicanos, Manuel	100				
Meyer Boy, H.R.	485				
Molina, R. G.	295	G			
Morales, Rafael	130				
Navarro, Bonifacio	126				
Nelson, Guillermo	200	G			
Neutze, Enrique	120				
Norrel, Alejandro	126				
Nostitz y Dieseldorff	110				
Onaye, F. é hijos	120				
Oribe, Marcelo	200				

Table A-2. Continued

Name of owner	Number of trees (100s)	1934	1930	1794–1871	1820
Orosco, Marcelino	100	G			
Perusma, Antonio	128				
Portillo, Miguel	100				
Posadas, T. S.	250				
Potter, Antonio	240				
Rodríguez, Eugenio	100	G			
Rodríguez, Juan	150	G			
Rodríguez, Mauricio	119	G			
Rodríguez Hermanos	108	G			
Sablá, Eugenio de	300				
Salas, Marcial G.	100				
Samayoa, José María	810	G		C	
Samayoa, Manuel	100	G		C	
Saravia, Ignacio G.	215				A
Saravia, José E.	150				A
Sánchez, P.	110				
Schlesinger y Jacophsen	1,000				
Sinibaldi, Dolores de	200				
Sinibaldi, Salvador	150				
Sosa, Tadeo	130				
Suárez, Asencio	200				
Traivitz, Carlos	100				
Urruela, Gándara	150			C	A
Urruela, Indalencio	100			C	A
Valle, Félix	100				
Valle, Luis	150				
Vásquez, Juan Bautista	600				

Note: Only surnames were matched.
Key: G=coffee grower
      X=coffee exporter
      C=Consulado de Comercio, prior or consul, 1794–1871
      A=Aristocracy, 1820

Sources:
    1. Coffee growers (112 farms, 99 growers) with 100,000 trees or more: 1890, Secretaria de estado, República de Guatemala, *Memoria de fomento,* 1891, pp. 5–143.

Continued

Table A-2. Continued

2. Coffee growers (125 farms, 98 growers) producing 2,000 quintals or more in 1933–34: Alvarado, *Tratado de caficultura*, pp. 557–66.

3. Coffee exporters (19 firms), 1930: Quiñonez, *Directorio general de la republica de Guatemala*, pp. 247–48.

4. Priors and consuls of the Consulado de Comercio, 1794–1871: list of 60 surnames taken from Woodward, *Class Privilege*, pp. 130–33.

5. 1820 list of José Cecilio del Valle of 60 individuals (23 surnames) of Aycinena family related by blood or marriage: Strobeck, "Political Activities of Some Members of the Aristocratic Families of Guatemala," p. 5.

Table A-3. The Salvadoran Coffee Elite, 1921

Coffee exporter, 1921	1922	1930	1970–71	1973–74	1974	1970s
Aguilar y Co., E.		B				L
Alvarez L., Rafael	B	B	G	X	X/B	L
Alvarez L., Roberto	B	B	G	X	X/B	L
Araujo, Eugenio						L
Arguello, J. Leopoldo						
Arguello, José						
Ayala, Federico						L
Baires, Filadelfo H.						L
Barrios y Co.						
Block Hermanos	B					L
Bloom y Co., David						
Boillat y Aeschbacher					X/B	
Borghi, B. Daglio y Co.			G	X	X/B	L
Bunneli, Mare						
Bunting y Co., Ltd.						
Canessa, Amadeo					X/B	
Canessa, E. Colombo					X/B	
Cohn, M. y R.						
Davidson Hermanos	B	B				
Deininger, A.		B	G	X	X/B	L
Deininger, W.		B	G	X	X/B	L
Del'pech, Mauricio						L
de Sola y Co., H.	B	B	G	X	X/B	L
Dreyfus Hermanos						
Dreyfus May y Co.						
Dueñas, Miguel			G	X	X/B	L
Escalón, Pedro					X/B	
Gallegos R., Salvador						
Goldtree Liebes y Co.	B	B	G		X/B	L
Grace & Co.						
Guirola, Angel		B	G			L
Guirola, Claudia de		B	G			L
Haltmayer, Max						
Hard y Rand						
Hill, J.	B	B	G	X	X/B	L
Huber y Co., E.E.						
Larín, J.S.					X/B	L

Continued

Table A-3. Continued

Coffee exporter, 1921	1922	1930	1970–71	1973–74	1974	1970s
León Dreyfus y Co						L
León Umberton						L
LLach, Prudencio			G	X	X/B	L
López y Duke	B	B	G	X		L
Martínez, Joaquina v. de						L
Matheu, Pablo						
McAllister y Co., Otis						
Meardi y Co., M.			G	X	X/B	
Meardi y Gavio			G	X	X/B	
Mugdan, S.	B	B				
Nicolás, Ernesto						
Olcovich y Oppenheimer						
Petersen, P. Carl						
Prieto, Federico G.				X	X/B	L
Regalado, Concha G. v. de			G	X	X/B	L
Reyneri, José						
Risso, Luis					X/B	
Ruggiero, Alberto						
Ruggiero Hermanos						
Savage y Co., Arturo						
Sawerbrey, G.A.						
Sol, Lidia de		B	G		X/B	
Sol M., Benjamín		B	G		X/B	
Sol M., Salvador		B	G		X/B	
Sol, Vicente		B	G		X/B	
Soundy, A.T.	B	B	G			L
Ulloa M., Francisco						
Ulmo y Co.						
Vidri Hermanos						
Vilanova, Cristina K. v. de			G	X	X/B	L
Vinutolo, Antonio						
Wieser, D.						

Key:　B=*beneficio* owner
　　　G=coffee grower
　　　X=coffee exporter
　　　X/B=*beneficio* owner and/or exporter
　　　L=landowner with more than 250 acres

Table A-3. Continued

Sources:

1. 1921 coffee exporters (72): República de El Salvador, *Anuario estadístico de 1921*, p. 241.

2. *Beneficio* owners 1922 (list of 13) and 1930 (list of 21): Wilson, "Crisis of National Integration," p. 134.

3. Lists of growers, exporters, *beneficio* owners, and large landowners (with 250 acres or more) in seven western departments during the early 1970s: Colindres, *Fundamentos económicos.*

Table A-4. The Salvadoran Coffee Elite, Early 1970s

Family name	Production 1970–71	Exports 1973–74
Quiñonez	14,500	
Meza Ayau	41,100	53,500
Sol Meza	6,000	
Alvarez Lemus	42,000	22,500
Alvarez Drews	16,000	24,000
Otros Alvarez	33,000	
Alvarez Meza	8,000	
Hill/LLach Hill	49,500	37,000
Garcia Prieto (Miguel A. Salaverría)	20,000	168,500
Henriquez	7,500	
Llach-Schonenberg	50,000	93,000
De Sola	13,500	497,000
Suc. Walter Deinenger	22,000	119,500
Regalado Dueñas		
Mathies Regalado	85,000	84,000
Dueñas	45,500	76,000
Bustamante	8,000	
Bonilla	10,000	85,000
Cohen		12,000
Salaverría	31,500	152,500
Eduardo Salaverría	12,000	41,500
Cristiani	12,500	57,500
Belismelis	5,500	
Battle	18,000	124,000
Lopez-Harrison		7,000
Alfaro Castillo	22,000	
Alfaro Vilanova		
Alfaro Lievano		
Dalton	21,500	11,000
Daglio	35,500	231,000
Lima	20,000	
Liebes	18,000	
Guirola	72,107	
Soler	7,500	
Borgonovo		119,000

Table A-4. Continued

Family name	Production 1970–71	Exports 1973–74
Kriete	13,000	13,000
Duke	5,500	7,000
Homberger	6,000	48,000
Avila Meardi	19,000	23,500
Meardi Palomo		
Totals	**791,207**	**2,107,000**

Total production, 1970–71: 2,711,280 qq.*oro*; Total exports, 1973–74: 3,174,624 qq.*oro*

Source: Colindres, *Fundamentos económicos*, Table 67.

Table A-5. The Nicaraguan Coffee Elite, 1909

Name of owner, 1909	Number of trees (100s)	1892	1873	1867	1958
Aguirre, Rosa v. de	100				
Arana, Saturnino	155				B
Arceyut, Pedro J.	215				
Balke, Julio C.	950				
Baltodano, Igno.	180				B
Benard, Adolfo	319				
Bermúdez, Ester v. de	280	G X		G	
Bonilla, Julio	120		X		
Cabrera, Rafael	171	G			B
Calif. Commercial Co.	100				
Caligaris, Angel	325				
Castrillo, Salvador y hjos	400	G X			
Chamorro, Fernando	210	G X	X	G	B
Cia.Cafe.Ticuantepe	171				
Espinosa R., Adolfo	100	X		G	B
Franember, Agusíu	150				B
Frixione, Daniel	190	G X			
Fuentes, Alcibíades	100				
Giusto, Bernadino	200	X			
González, José E.	257				B
González, José Igno.	160				B
Hecho, Teodoro E.	135				
Knoeffer, Pablo	135				B
Lugo T., Juan J.	118				
Marín, Basilio	230				
Martínez, Gabriel	110	X		G	
Michilles, Gebruders	163				
Mierisch y Wiest	170				
Morales, Nicolasa de	110				
Navas, A. M. de	300	G			
Padilla, Gregorio	110				
Pasos, Juan	150				
Peper, E.	125				
Potters Hermanos	336				
Rappaccioli, Vic. y Hnos	299				B
Raunk, Guy E.	120				

Table A-5. Continued

Name of owner, 1909	Number of trees (100s)	1892	1873	1867	1958
Reñasco, Francisco	100			G	B
Rodríguez, Vicente	383	X		G	B
Sáenz, Ramón	158	G X			
Sequiera, Fernando	130				
Solís, Juan Ig.	100				B
Solís, Marcial E.	105				B
Solórzano, Federino y Hno	155	G X			
Solórzano, Mercedes de	100	G X			
Sullivan, Alejo	116				B
Tefel, Teodoro	800				
The Minn. y Nic. Cia.	180				
Vaughan, Arturo L.	222	G X			B
Vita, José	130				B
Wheelock, Carlos	254				B
Zelaya, Carlos	100	G		G	B
Zelaya R., Feliz P.	105	G		G	B

Note: Only surnames were matched.
Key: G = coffee grower
X = coffee exporter
B = *beneficio* owner

Sources:
1. 52 coffee growers in 1909 with 100,000 trees or more: República de Nicaragua, "Censo cafetalero de 1909," pp. 646–72.
2. 35 coffee growers, 63 coffee exporters in 1892: Bureau of the American Republics, *Commercial Directory of Nicaragua*, pp. 167–77.
3. 18 coffee exporters who received export subsidies in 1873: compiled from *La gaceta oficial* by Alberto Lanuza, "La formación del estado nacional en Nicaragua: las bases económicas, comerciales, y financieras entre 1821 y 1873," in Lanuza, Vázquez, Barahona, and Chamorro, *Economía y sociedad*, p. 82.
4. 25 Managua coffee growers and 7 Rivas coffee growers in 1867: lists compiled from *La gaceta oficial* by Lanuza, "La formación," pp. 77, 79.
5. 100 coffee *beneficio* owners in 1957–58: Lang, *Business Directory of Nicaragua, 1957–58*.

Table A-6. Honduran Coffee Growers with Capitalist-Sized Farms, 1914–1915
(20 manzanas *of coffee or more)*

Name	Mz. coffee	Mz. cultivated	Tenure	1889
Tegucigalpa				
Dávila, Pablo P.	25	35	*ejidal*	
Reina, Pedro	32	332	*ejidal*	
Rodríguez, Petrona v. de	30	30	private	
El Paraíso				
Agurcia, Isabel v. de	80	81	private	X, M
de Dios Sauceda, Juan	25	55	private	
Gamero, Luís	20	20	private	
Gutierrez, Eligio	30	36	national	
Zamora, Máximo	50	90	private	
Choluteca				
Abadíe, Pedro	500	800	private	M
Agasse, Hipólito	30	50	private	
Kohnke, Enrique	140	188	private	M, X
Maradiaga, Jesús	30	206	private	M, X
Molina, Esteban	80	80	private	
Pérez, Ceferino	25	175	private	
Rosales, Máximo	40	631	private	
Sánchez, Rubén	25	50	*ejidal*	
Vicente, Antolín de	130	139	private	
Comayagua				
Aguilar, Cruz y otros	26	27	*ejidal*	
Bonilla, Ignacio y otros	22	23	*ejidal*	
Bueso, Antonio	36	48	*ejidal*	
Cruz, Tomás	20	24	*ejidal*	
Echever, C. y otros	34	37	*ejidal*	
Flores, Raimundo y otros	39	57	*ejidal*	
Gross, José	20	75	private	
Martínez, B. y otros	41	41	*ejidal*	
Mejía, Martín	25	55	*ejidal*	
Mejía, Paz y otros	26	39	*ejidal*	
Mencía, Fermín y otros	40	41	*ejidal*	
Molina, Antonio	25	114	private	
Morales, Ildefonsa v. de	34	68	*ejidal*	
Ortega, Eduvigis	40	52	*ejidal*	

Table A-6. Continued

Name	Mz. coffee	Mz. cultivated	Tenure	1889
Oviedo, Atanasio	21	43	private	
Ramos, Claudio y otros	32	46	*ejidal*	
Rittenhausen, Martín	20	147	private	
Robles, Diego	38	109	private	
Rubí, Jesús	30	30	*ejidal*	
Ulloa, José María y otros	46	61	*ejidal*	
Zavala, Vicente	26	30	private	
Santa Barbara				
Bográn, Luis	66	450	private	M
Castellanos, Casimiro	20	80	private	
Enamorado, Felipe	50	50	*ejidal*	X
Fajardo, Bertilio	26	46	*ejidal*	
Fajardo, Pablo	20	28	*ejidal*	
Fajardo S., Pedro	20	24	*ejidal*	
Fajardo, Victor	30	33	*ejidal*	
Fernández, Néstor	23	35	private	
Guzmán, Juan J.	40	120	*ejidal*	
Herrera, José María	20	20	*ejidal*	
Howard, Herbert	150	150	*ejidal*	
León Madrid, J.	22	55	*ejidal*	
Muñoz, Audato	20	402	private	
Paredes, Enrique	50	70	*ejidal*	
Paredes, J. Antonio	45	117	*ejidal*	
Paredes, Jesús M.	20	44	*ejidal*	
Paredes, Pedro B.	20	24	*ejidal*	
Perdomo, Jesús	20	26	*ejidal*	
Pineda, Amadeo	20	24	*ejidal*	
Pineda, Guillermo	35	50	*ejidal*	
Regalado, Jesús	36	74	*ejidal*	
Rivera P., Antonio	20	31	*ejidal*	
Rivera, Procopio	20	43	*ejidal*	
Rivera, Santos	20	50	*ejidal*	
Rivera, Santos	32	39	*ejidal*	
Rodríguez, Manuel	60	67	private	
Savillón, Santos	20	36	*ejidal*	

Continued

Table A-6. Continued

Name	Mz. coffee	Mz. cultivated	Tenure	1889
Savillón, Tiburcio	32	32	*ejidal*	
Tobias Rosa, J. M.	20	20	*ejidal*	
Turcios, Natividad	22	28	*ejidal*	
Cortes				
López, Fidel	20	20	*ejidal*	
Olancho				
Durón, Pedro	20	20	private	
Ruiz Torres, Agaqito	100	100	private	
Yoro				
Devauz, Pedro	25	25	*ejidal*	
Martínez, Rosendo	40	83	private	
Murillo, Ezekiel	25	25	*ejidal*	
Palma, Concepcion	76	135	*ejidal*	
Ramírez, Zenón	30	32	*ejidal*	
Vaquedano, Antonio	52	54	*ejidal*	
Varela, Olegario	20	20	*ejidal*	
Velásquez, Mortual	24	24	*ejidal*	

Key: X=Coffee exporter
          M=Import merchant

Sources:
   1. List of growers 1914–15: República de Honduras, *Memoria de fomento, 1914–1915.*
   2. Export-import merchant lists for 1888–89: República de Honduras, *Primer anuario estadístico de 1888–89,* pp. 268–89.

Table A-7. The Costa Rican Coffee Elite, 1907

Beneficio owners, 1907	1910	pre-1850	1820–50	1981
Aguilar, Alejo		M	G	B
Aguilar F., José	X	M	G	B
Aguilar, Pedro J.	X	M	G	B
Aguilar, Ramón		M	G	B
Aguilar, Rosa Soto de		M	G	B
Alfaro, Feliciano		M		B
Alfaro, Maurilio		M		B
Alvarado, Manuel		M	G	B
Alvarado, Santiago	X	M	G	B
Aqueche, Fco. Jinesta				
Arana, Procopio				
Arce V., Pilar				
Arce V., Rafael				
Ardón, Paulino				
Arias, A. Macario			G	B
Arroyo, Yanuario	X			
Atirro Coffee Estates	X			
Azofeifa, Ramón				
Badilla, Pedro Ant.				B
Barrantes, Francisco				
Barrantes, Ramón				
Bastos, Juan	X			
Beer, Guillermo				
Benavides, Macedonio				
Blanco, Ramón	X		G	B
Bogantes, Laura				
Bonilla, Clara v. de		M	G	
Bonilla, Genaro		M	G	
Brealey, Guillermo	X	M		
Brenes, Roberto				B
Camacho & Roldán	X	M		
Campos, Rafael				B
Campos, Tranquilino				B
Carballo, Miguel M.				
Castro, Florentino	X		G	B
Castro, Teodosio	X		G	B
Chacón, Juan R.	X	M	G	

Continued

Table A-7. Continued

Beneficio owners, 1907	1910	pre-1850	1820–50	1981
Challe, Emilio E.	X			
Chavarría, Nicolás				
Chaverri V., Alberto				
Chaves, Santos				B
Colibá, Nicolás				
Coronado, José A.	X			
Costa Rica Coffee Estates	X			
Cox & Co.	X			
Cox, Federico				
Crespi, Alberto			G	
Dent, Teresa de	X	M		B
Dewis, Luis K.				
Durán, Carlos				
Durán, José				
Durán, Mariano				
Echeverría & Co.				B
Echeverría, Guillermo	X			B
Echeverría, Juana de	X			B
Ernst, Santiago				
Espinach, Hermanos		M	G	
Esquivel, Aniceto	X		G	B
Esquivel, Fabián	X		G	B
Esquivel, José	X		G	B
Esquivel, Narciso	X		G	B
Esquivel y Iglesias			G	B
Field, Walter J.				
Flores, Manuel J.				
Flores, Paula v. de				
Ford, Mr.				
Fortoso, Francisco				
González, Domingo		M		B
González, Federico		M		B
González, Higinio		M		B
González, Pablo & Co.		M		B
González, Ramón Vte.		M		B
González Soto, Ramón	X	M		B
Gutiérrez, Dolores		M	G	B

Table A-7. Continued

Beneficio owners, 1907	1910	pre-1850	1820–50	1981
Gutiérrez, Ezequiel	X	M	G	B
Gutiérrez, Filomena		M	G	B
Gutiérrez, M.A.		M	G	B
Hernández, Gerardo				B
Hernández, Juan				B
Hernández, Patrocinio	X			B
Herrera, Felipe				B
Herrera, José María	X			B
Herrer, Juan Bautista				
Hidalgo, Juan G.				
Hube, Otto		M		
Inksetter, George				
Inksetter & Inksetter				
Jara, Javier				
Jara, Laura v. de				
Jiménez O., Ricardo		M	G	B
Jiménez, Señor		M	G	B
Jiménez, Señora viuda de		M	G	B
Jiménez, Vicente		M	G	B
Jongh, Juan de				
Keith, Minor C.	X			
Koberg, Maximiliano	X			
Lara, Salvador			G	B
Lindo Bros	X			
Lobo, Juan				
Lohrengel, Carlos	X			
López Castillo, Dr.			G	
López García, Francisco			G	
Madrigal, Manuel	X		G	
Mata, J.R.	X			
Millet, F.N.	X	M	G	
Monestel, Cleto	X			
Montealegre, Edmundo	X		G	B
Montealegre, Juan	X		G	B
Montealegre, Mariano			G	B
Montealegre, Ricardo	X		G	B
Montenegro, Mercedes de				

Continued

Table A-7. Continued

Beneficio owners, 1907	1910	pre-1850	1820–50	1981
Morales, Esmeralda de	X	M		
Morales, Lucila de		M		
Morera, Antonio	X			
Murillo, Zacarías				
Niehaus, Guillermo	X			
Nuñez, Julia A. de	X			
Núñez, Daniel				
Núñez, Jesús				
Ocampo, Malaquías				
Orlich & Co.				B
Orlich, Francisco & Cia.	X			B
Ortuño, Gaspar	X			
Pinto, Alberto		M		
Pinto, Jesús		M		
Pirie & Co.				
Pirie & Pacheco	X			
Piza, Benjamín	X			
Prendas, José				
Quesada, Concepción			G	B
Quesada, Elías			G	B
Quesada, Francisco			G	B
Quesada, Gregorio			G	B
Quiros, Silverio		M	G	B
Ramirez, Joaquín	X		G	B
Ramírez, Toribio			G	B
Rivera, Aurelio A. de	X			
Rivera, Pedro				
Rodríguez, José Manuel			G	B
Rodríguez, Juan	X		G	B
Rodríguez, María			G	B
Rohrmoser Hnos.	X			B
Rohrmoser, Oscar				B
Rojas, Antonio			G	B
Rojas, Isaías			G	B
Rojas, José			G	B
Rojas, Ramón			G	B
Romero, Manuel	X			

Table A-7. Continued

Beneficio owners, 1907	1910	pre-1850	1820–50	1981
Rosabal, Amado				B
Ross, Roberto sucesión				
Ruvacado, Ricardo				
Saborío, Nicolas				B
Saborío R., José	X			B
Salas, Inocente				B
Salas, Tranquilino				B
Salazar Ch., Francisco	X		G	
Sandoval, Manuel				
Sánchez, Julio				B
Sánchez, J. y Vega, r.				B
Sánchez, Rosario				B
Scriba, Guillermo				
Sobrado, Federico				
Solera, Juan María	X	M		B
Solis, Bernardino	X			
Solis, Gregorio				
Solís, Leonardo				
Soto, Apolinar de J.				
Soto, Jesús				
Soto, Mechora				
Soto, Ronulfo				
Soto, Rufino				
Starke & Lindo				
Tournon & Co.	X	M		
Ulate, Estanislao				
Umaña, J. Carlos			G	B
Urrutia, Ramona de				
Valenciano, Maria				
Valerio, Santiago				
Valiente, Francisco	X			
Vargas, Jesús M.				B
Víquez A., Manuel				
Víquez, Cipriano				
Volio, Enrique				B
von Schroter, Guido	X	M		B
von Schroter, Otto	X	M		B

Continued

Table A-7. Continued

Beneficio owners, 1907	1910	pre-1850	1820–50	1981
Von Storren, Jorge				
Wathen, Burton	X			
Zamora, Delfina				B
Zamora, Juan J.	X			B
Zamora O., Manuel				B
Zamora, Santiago	X			B
Zeledón, Juan	X		G	B

Key: X = Coffee exporter 1910, individuals matched
M = Import merchant, pre-1850, family name matched
B = Board member of 1981 *beneficio*, family name matched
G = Early San José grower, 1820–50, family name matched

Sources:
1. *Beneficio* owners 1907 (221 *beneficios*, 200 owners): Oficina del Café, *Informe de labores—1973*, pp. 90–93.
2. Coffee exporters 1910, individuals and companies matched (93 principal coffee exporters, 1909–10 crop year): República de Costa Rica, *Anuario estadístico de 1910*, pp. 154–55.
3. Import merchants before 1850 (79): Vega Carballo, "El nacimiento," pt. II, pp. 100–102.
4. San José coffee growers 1820–50 (103 persons): Stone, "Los cafetaleros," pp. 185–88.
5. Family names that appear on list of 303 managers and board members of 107 coffee *beneficios* in 1981: Oficina del Café, "Registro de beneficiadores."

Notes

Chapter 1

1. Human rights groups claim that Honduran security forces were responsible for 150 political assassinations and approximately 300 disappearances during the 1980s. The majority of the violations reportedly occurred when security forces were under the control of General Gustavo Alvarez (1980–84).

2. This rough description of size distributions of coffee farms will be developed more sharply in later chapters and will be tested with agricultural census data.

3. Moore, *Social Origins of Dictatorship and Democracy*, p. 421; see generally pp. 413–432. For a survey of the literature applying the Moore thesis to Central America see Gudmundson, "Lord and Peasant." Also see the comparative essay by Paige, "Coffee and Politics."

4. North, *Institutions, Institutional Change, and Economic Performance*, p. 99.

5. Theda Skocpol has formulated a corollary to the Moore thesis that reverses the causation, allowing for state behavior to reinforce broader social patterns of interaction, enabling path dependence despite changes in economic structures. Skocpol's thesis is that the behavior of states toward the various social classes conditions the nature of social protest and the nature of interactions between social classes, including general patterns of conflict resolution (Skocpol, "Bringing the State Back In," pp. 3–37, in Evans, Rueschemeyer, and Skocpol, *Bringing the State Back In*).

6. Skocpol, *States and Social Revolutions*, pp. 4, 33, 161–281.

7. Burns, *Poverty of Progress*, p. 16; Wortman, *Government and Society*, p. 276.

8. Palmer, "Liberal Discipline."

9. The methodology adopted in this book is consciously economic, asking the question Fernand Braudel posed in his studies of the rise of capitalism in Europe: How were the day-to-day material lives of people being changed at the time? Once this question is brought into focus, the major causes and consequences of the economic transformation can be sought, including the role of state institutions in promoting the change and the way the eco-

nomic transformation itself may have shaped the development of the state. See Braudel's three-volume series *Civilization and Capitalism, 15th–18th Century* (New York: Harper & Row, 1979–84).

10. As Robert Brenner has shown in his studies of the development of capitalism in northern Europe, the promotion of the same export, grain, had uneven rates of expansion and greatly differing social consequences, leading to enhanced peasant control in northwestern Germany and enhanced landlord power in northeastern Germany and the Baltic; Brenner correctly stresses the importance of seeking explanations that go beyond the forces of the world market to the structures of production and balances of class power as they evolve in specific locations ("Agrarian Class Structure and Economic Development," in Aston and Philpin, eds., *Brenner Debate*, pp. 37–38).

11. Roseberry, "La Falta de Brazos," pp. 351–82.

12. Douglass North has shown that when the neoclassical assumption of zero transactions costs is relaxed, one can then understand the necessity of public institutions in the market process, especially in the area of reducing private transaction costs (*Institutions, Institutional Change, and Economic Performance*). I extend the analysis to include transformation costs and risks associated with both market transactions and nonmarket transformations of productive inputs into marketable outputs.

Chapter 2

1. Coffee is thought to have originated in Abyssinia (Ethiopia), where it grew wild. By the end of the sixth century A.D. it was being cultivated in Yemen, from whence it came to be traded throughout the Muslim world. For centuries the Arabs maintained a monopoly on production by parching the beans before export, thereby destroying germination capabilities, but this monopoly over genetic material was circumvented shortly after coffee was introduced into the European trading system in the seventeenth century. See Ukers, *All About Coffee*, pp. 1–6.

2. In 1711 the Dutch East India Company, which had been buying coffee from the port of Mocha in Yemen since 1640, began trading coffee from Java, where cultivation was initiated in 1699; later plantations were established in other Dutch colonies of Sumatra, Celebes, Timor, and Bali (Braudel, *Structures of Everyday Life*, p. 260).

3. For example, in 1692 the king of France granted a single merchant, Damame Francois, a ten-year monopoly on the domestic trade in coffee and tea. Germany at that time remained split into numerous principalities, each with its own tariffs and none great enough to underwrite a great trading company. The English penetrated the fragmented German market, setting up coffee houses in Hamburg (1679–80), Regensburg (1689), Leipzig (1694), Nuremberg (1696), Stuttgart (1712), Augsburg (1713), and Berlin (1721). As kings, princes, and dukes noticed the drainage of bullion caused by imports of coffee, they applied bans on the beverage to restrict its consumption by

all but the very wealthy. These bans proved difficult to enforce. In Prussia, Frederick the Great abolished the ban and created a royal monopoly on coffee imports in 1781, granting costly licenses to roasters. In Württemberg, the duke sold the rights to maintain coffee houses to a single financier, who, in turn, sold individual licenses to the highest bidder (Ukers, *All About Coffee*, pp. 30, 41–43).

4. Braudel, *Structures of Everyday Life*, p. 258.

5. Henderson, *Zollverein*.

6. Ukers, *All About Coffee*, p. 527.

7. Ibid., p. 529.

8. Commodity Research Bureau, *Commodity Yearbook 1939*, p. 313.

9. Ukers, *All About Coffee*, pp. 2, 4, 5, 503, 527, 529, 39, 734, 735.

10. The Brazilian government had been aware of its market dominance for some time and as early as 1906 began buying up surplus coffee during bumper years and selling coffee from stockpiles in lean years in an attempt to diminish international price fluctuations. During the Great Depression the coffee glut was so great that the Brazilian government destroyed millions of bags of excess coffee per year. In 1937, when the price support policy was temporarily abandoned, international coffee prices dropped by one-third (Wickizer, *Coffee, Tea, and Cocoa*, pp. 81–84). Following World War II, Colombia's production spurted, allowing that country's producers to maintain a 15 to 20 percent share of world output, while Brazil's relative share declined to the 20 to 30 percent range, thereby giving both producers some influence over prices.

11. The other two species are *coffea liberica*, which has almost no commercial value except as a source of caffeine, and *coffea robusta*, which has a thin taste but can be grown at lower altitudes and is resistant to funguses and other coffee pests; Brazilian coffee is primarily *robusta*.

12. For the technical conditions best suited for *coffea arabica* see Wickizer, *Coffee, Tea, and Cocoa*, pp. 42–44, and Ukers, *All About Coffee*, pp. 134–35.

13. Domínguez, "Desarrollo de los aspectos tecnológicos," p. 98.

14. Alvarado, *Tratado de caficultura*, p. 526.

15. The Jesuits could well have been cultivating coffee before 1767 when they were expelled from Guatemala. Alvarez de Asturias is thought to have planted the seeds on his hacienda in the last two decades of the eighteenth century (ibid., p. 525).

16. Woodward, *Class Privilege*, p. 130.

17. Bureau of the American Republics, "Costa Rica," p. 32.

18. Hall, *El café de Costa Rica*, p. 33.

19. Fowler, "Cacao, Indigo, and Coffee," pp. 149–51.

20. José Antonio Fernández documents one hacienda in Baja Verapaz that in 1793 produced 5,064 pounds of indigo, and anecdotal evidence points to some smaller growers in eastern Guatemala ("Colouring the World in Blue," p. 17). Fernández and other sources claim that Salvadoran and Nicaraguan production was more important than Guatemalan throughout the colonial period. One Guatemala City merchant family, the Aycinenas, also

owned large indigo estates, though many of them were located in the province of El Salvador. In 1819, the Aycinena family owned seven indigo estates, whose production amounted to one-sixth of the export trade calculated through Guatemala City (Robert Smith, "Indigo Production and Trade," p. 197).

21. Smith, "Indigo Production and Trade," p. 183; Fernández, "Colouring the World in Blue," pp. 404–74.

22. Mosk, "Coffee Economy of Guatemala," p. 7. It is interesting that during the colonial period production of cochineal was said to be an Indian-controlled process that required a long apprenticeship. MacLeod notes that non-Indians experienced difficulty breaking into the production or even supervision of this crop ("Ethnic Relations and Indian Society," in Macleod and Wasserstrom, *Spaniards and Indians*, p. 199). Nevertheless, in the 1830s and 1840s, a significant portion of the cochineal crop was being produced in districts where *castas* (those who were not part of Indian cultural communities) lived, and there is good evidence that although small producers continued to exist, production came to be dominated by medium-sized producers who were better connected with the merchant/credit mechanism. Michael Fry argues that this process of outsiders entering areas suitable for cochineal production and taking over lands previously used by peasants led to the Carrera revolt in 1838 ("Liberal Land Reform in Guatemala," p. 38).

23. Wortman, *Government and Society*, pp. 219, 241–45, 258–59.

24. Acuña and Molina, *Historia económica y social de Costa Rica*, p. 72.

25. Gudmundson, *Costa Rica before Coffee*.

26. Vega Carballo, "El nacimiento," pt. I, pp. 171–83, casts serious doubt on the wealth generated by mining, but Araya, "La minería y sus relaciones," pp. 49–63, argues that this was a great fountain of early accumulation in the postcolonial period.

27. Vega Carballo, "El nacimiento," pt. II, p. 85.

28. Hall, *El café de Costa Rica*, pp. 38–39.

29. Araya, "La minería y sus relaciones," p. 51.

30. Susan Strobeck's list of aristocratic families includes the names Aycinena, Arriaga, Asturias, Arrivillaga, Barrundia, Barrutia, Batres, Beltranena, Castilla, Croquer, Echeverría, García Granados, Irisarri, Larrave, Larrazábal, Montúfar, Olaverri, Palomo, Pavón, Piñol, Saravia, Urruela, Valenzuela ("Political Activities," p. 5).

31. Rubio, "Breve historia," p. 192.

32. Solís, *Memorias*, p. 931.

33. The first coffee trees in El Salvador are believed to have been brought over to the department of Ahuachapán in western El Salvador from the Asturias' hacienda Soyate in neighboring Jutiapa, Guatemala. In 1837–38 two *finca* owners from Santa Ana acquired offspring of these first trees from two Indians in Ahuachapán who had several trees in their garden. In 1840, a Brazilian merchant named Coelho introduced coffee as a commercial venture on his small farm La Esperanza near San Salvador. Others followed these early examples, but it was not until 1855–56 that enough coffee was produced for export. In that year some eighty-seven thousand pounds were

exported, primarily to Guatemala (Alvarado, *Tratado de caficultura*, pp. 579–80).

34. Ibid., pp. 585–86.

35. Ibid., pp. 540, 572, 579–81.

36. Solís, *Memorias*, p. 916.

37. Castellanos Cambranes, *Café y campesinos*, pp. 52–54.

38. Solís, *Memorias*, p. 933. Rubio Sánchez sets the initial coffee export date at 1855, when fifty-five hundred pounds were exported through the Pacific port of San José. ("Breve historia," p. 203). Juan Antonio Alvarado sets first exports to Europe, probably England, in 1855 at ninety-five hundred pounds (*Tratado de caficultura*, p. 528).

39. Woodward, *Class Privilege*, p. 48.

40. Browning, *El Salvador*, p. 159.

41. Alvarado, *Tratado de caficultura*, pp. 585–86.

42. Regarding passenger traffic see Lanuza, Vázquez, Barahona, and Chamorro, *Economía y sociedad*, p. 43.

43. Coffee exports in 1851 reached 3 percent of total exports (ibid., p. 52; Woodward, *Central America*, pp. 138–39).

44. Levy, *Notas geográficas*, p. 465.

45. Squier, *States of Central America*, p. 205; Alvarado, *Tratado de caficultura*, p. 540.

46. Guevara-Escudero, "Nineteenth Century Honduras," pp. 258, 240–41.

47. Out of a total of $4.1 million in exports in 1889, $3.1 million were destined for the U.S. market, while regional markets absorbed $838,000 and northern Europe $166,000 (República de Honduras, *Primer anuario estadístico de 1888–89*, p. 293).

48. República de Honduras, *Memoria al Congreso Nacional, 1914–1915*, pp. 3–145.

49. SIECA, *Compendio estadístico centroamericano*, pp. 194–95.

Chapter 3

1. Martínez Peláez, *La patria del criollo*, pp. 144–72.

2. Cardoso, "Formation of the Coffee Estate," p. 170.

3. Hall, *El café de Costa Rica*, p. 35.

4. Castro Sánchez, "Estado, privatización de la tierra," p. 210.

5. Some of the pertinent articles in National Decree 39 were Article 1, which stipulated rights to purchase lands that had been worked for several years if there were some permanent delineation of boundaries; Article 2, which stipulated the procedure of presenting the request to the authorities; Article 3, which outlined the procedures for examining the case, surveying the area, and classifying the land according to quality and required the township to appoint a nationally approved surveyor and a local team of assistants to carry out the survey; Article 4, which fixed base prices on the different quality classes of land but left it up to the local authorities to alter

the price off that base; Article 7, which required the buyer to pay the fees for the survey and processing; Article 10, which set the term of five years to pay off the principal and a monthly payment of interest at an annual rate of 6 percent, which would be doubled if the buyer made a payment more than thirty days late; Article 16, which provided for public use of municipal woodlands; Article 17, which provided for public use of grazing lands; Article 18, which provided for short-term leases of one or two *manzanas* of municipal cropland for those who held no land; Article 19, which prevented the private transfer of public lands. These articles are reprinted in Castro Sánchez, "Estado, privatización de la tierra," pp. 210, 211, 219.

6. Salas Víquez, "La privatización de los baldíos nacionales," pp. 68–73.

7. Unoccupied lands not suitable for coffee cultivation could be obtained very cheaply by having the land surveyed, notifying the appropriate authorities, and acquiring the land at public auction (Cardoso, "Formation of the Coffee Estate," pp. 170–73; Hall, *El café de Costa Rica*, p. 35). From fragmentary documentation of deeding of public lands between Santo Domingo and San Isidro in Heredia in the 1850s and 1860s, Gudmundson found that most grants were in small lots of a few *manzanas* rather than large ones in *caballerías* ("Peasant, Farmer, Proletarian," p. 229).

8. Hall, *El café de Costa Rica*, p. 61; Vega Carballo, "El nacimiento," pt. II, pp. 94–96.

9. Between 1844 and 1864, the population of Alajuela Province almost tripled, making it the fastest-growing province in Costa Rica during this period (Ministerio de Economía y Hacienda, *Censo de la república de Costa-Rica, 1864*, p. 3). For an excellent analysis of the settlement of this area see Samper, *Generations of Settlers*.

10. Hall, *El café de Costa Rica*, pp. 71–95. Samper argues that earlier settlers to this area were as much influenced by "pull" as by "push" factors; one attraction was to evade government taxes and controls on *aguardiente* and tobacco production, a more general one was to acquire a larger land area at a much lower cost than in the commercial centers (*Generations of Settlers*, p. 58).

11. Dirección General de Estadística y Censos, "Estadística agrícola de 1883–84," in Oficina del Café, *Informe de Labores—1973*, pp. 78–79. This area is represented by the *cantones* Grecia, Naranjo, and San Ramón, all in Alajuela Province.

12. Hall, *El café de Costa Rica*, pp. 64–68.

13. In the 1883–84 harvest, only 18 percent of Cartago Province's coffee production came from the *cantón* of Paraíso to the east of Cartago. Later, new *cantones* (Jiménez, Turrialba, and Alvarado) were created out of Paraíso as population and commercial development spread to the east (Oficina del Café, "Estadística agrícola, 1883–84," p. 78). In 1914, 50 percent of the coffee acreage of Cartago Province was in Paraíso, Jiménez, Turrialba, and Alvarado (Dirección General de Estadística de Costa Rica, *Censo Agrícola de 1914*, pp. 169–72).

14. Hall, *El café de Costa Rica*, p. 85.

15. Gudmundson, *Costa Rica before Coffee*, p. 75.

16. Castro Sánchez, "Estado, privatización de la tierra," pp. 215–16.

17. Cardoso, "Formation of the Coffee Estate," p. 173.

18. José Antonio Salas Víquez collected and published the petitions, counterpetitions, and other correspondence relating to the case of Orósi; this collection constitutes an invaluable source for understanding not only the way different levels of the state were involved in the privatization process but also the conflictual ideologies of the parties involved. See Salas Víquez, "El liberalismo positivista en Costa Rica," pp. 187–217. According to the census of 1864, Orósi, whose population was counted with that of Cachí, had 406 persons of "pura raza india," consisting of 211 men and 195 women, out of a total population of 518. It is curious why Orósi was counted in the same unit as Cachí, which is located ten kilometers down the Río Grande de Orosi to the east. See Ministerio de Economía y Hacienda, *Censo de la república de Costa-Rica, 1864*, p. 4.

19. Oficina del Café, "Estadística agrícola, 1883–84," p. 78. The average number of trees per farm was 10,230 in Paraíso compared with the national average of 3,131.

20. Thanks to Mario Samper for sharing with me tables derived from the 1935 Costa Rican coffee census ("Coffee Households," Table 2).

21. Cardoso, "Formation of the Coffee Estate," p. 173; Stone, "Los cafetaleros," pp. 191–95.

22. Gudmundson, *Costa Rica before Coffee*, p. 82.

23. Hall, *El café de Costa Rica*, p. 87.

24. Samper, "Coffee Households," Table 2.

25. Official recognition by a municipality or the national government that a land area was privately owned became a more formal process of actually registering deeds during the latter half of the nineteenth century, especially after the establishment in 1864 of the Public Property Registry. Thus land may have been treated as private property (and recognized as such by the authorities) without an officially registered deed, though by the 1880s and 1890s older forms of proof of ownership were being brought to the registry for inscription, especially for prime coffee lands. By looking at probate inventories in Santo Domingo de Heredia for the period 1860–80, Gudmundson found that the property registry accepted the highly informal evidence of "peaceful occupation of the deceased" as a basis for inscribing titles to inherited lands ("Peasant, Farmer, Proletarian," p. 229).

26. The 1845 manual is reprinted in Fernández, "Formación de una hacienda cafetalera," pp. 199–214.

27. In an 1889 agricultural survey, Trapiche Grande, owned by Ismael Larraondo in the *municipio* of Cuoyotenango, Suchitepéquez was listed as the largest hacienda in the area with an extension of seventeen hundred *caballerías*, which is probably a misprint (Secretaria de Fomento, *Memoria*, p. 38).

28. Solís, *Memorias*, p. 936. As Chapter 5 will indicate, some of the other early growers along the Pacific piedmont were not nationals but immigrants who brought capital and expertise from Germany, England, Belgium, Costa Rica, Colombia, and other countries.

29. Solís reports the departmental data for 1859 (*Memorias*, p. 937). Rubio Sánchez, "Breve historia," p. 205, reports the same data for the year 1862. Municipio data reported by Rubio Sánchez show that the total under Suchitepéquez includes some coffee *municipioas* of Retalhuleu as well. Petapa, Amatitlán, an important cochineal district in the 1850s, had the largest number of coffee trees of any *municipio* reported in the 1862 data. Strict comparisons of percentages are not possible because Alta Verapaz, San Marcos, and Quezaltenango are left out of this survey.

30. Castellanos Cambranes, *Café y campesinos*, p. 471.

31. Woodward, *Class Privilege*, pp. 35–54.

32. Woodward, *Rafael Carrera*, p. 359.

33. The largest holdings were those of the Dominicans, followed by the Order of La Merced, followed by the Franciscans. Sales of these properties are recorded in Archivos General de Guatemala, *Protócolos de hacienda del supremo gobierno 1831–37*. The following are rural properties auctioned during these years:

1832
La Chácara, Dominicans, sold to Antonio Batres January 2
Huerta de San Francisco, Franciscans, sold to Basilio Porras, January 16
La Provincia, Order of La Merced, sold to Manuel Larrave, February 11
La Chácara, *municipio* de Antigua, Dominicans, sold to Leocadio Asturias, February 15
Potrero de Borges, in Antigua, Doroteo Vasconcelos, September 29
Potrero de Santo Domingo, Dominicans, sold to Juan Antonio Albures, December 27

1833
Hacienda Cacabal o Tuluche, Dominicans in Sololá, sold to Lucas Vever?, March 15
Lands of Chicoyó, Verapáz, Dominicans, sold to Presbitero Estevan Lorenrana?, November 11

1834
Hacienda de San Nicolas (sitio de Cachil), Dominicans, sold to Placido Flores, February 4
Hacienda San José Buenavista, Dominicans, sold to José Nájera, February 28
Hacienda de Palencia, Dominicans, sold to Leocadio Asturias, November 18

1835
Hacienda San Gerónimo, Dominicans in Baja Verapaz, sold to Mr. Bennet and Mr. Meany, March 27

The following list of sales of rural properties is provided in Holleran, *Church and State in Guatemala*, pp. 58–59:

Date	Property	Belonging to	Amount paid
August 8, 1831	Hacienda San José	Dominicans	$5,226
September 25	Cerro Redondo	Dominicans	$12,416
January 16, 1832	Farm of San Francisco	Franciscans	
February 11	Ranch	Order of La Merced	$4,010
September 29	Ranch of Borges	Franciscans	$2,005
December 17	Ranch of Santo Domingo	Dominicans	$10,500
March 15, 1833	Cacabal and Tuluché (182 caballerías), other plots in Tecpán, Plantation Choacorral		
November 11, 1833	Plantation of Chicozo	Dominicans	$86
November 18, 1833	Estate of La Palencia (96¾ caballerías)	Dominicans	$28,075
March 27, 1835	Hacienda and Mill of San Jerónimo	Dominicans	$253,528
July 2, 1835	Hacienda of Pacayita	Dominicans	$1,012
December 18, 1835	Hacienda of San Andrés	Order of La Merced	$400

34. Despite the Carrera regime's close ties with the church, in 1857 merchants and commercial farmers successfully pressured the national government to reduce *diezmos* to 1 percent on coffee and sugar, in an effort to stimulate alternatives to cochineal (Rubio Sánchez, "Breve historia," p. 204).

35. Secretaria de Estado de Guatemala, *Memoria*, "Estadísticas de café, 1890," pp. 43–44, 47–54. San Andrés Osuna was bought by José Longino Estradas in October 1835 and the Order of La Merced did not recover it during the Conservative period (Archivo General de Centroamérica, "Protócolos de hacienda 1891"). Cerro Redondo was returned to the Dominicans during the Carrera regime (see Archivo General de Centroamérica, Archivo de la escribanía del gobierno y sección de tierras, "Indice de los expedientes," p. 207, which shows a request for measurement by the Dominicans in the period 1841–58) but was in the possession of a Costa Rican coffee grower named Saturnino Tinoco in the 1860s (Solís, *Memoria*, p. 943).

36. Castellanos Cambranes estimates that 70 percent of the best lands were controlled by one thousand Indian communities (*Café y campesinos*, p. 122).

37. Fry, "Liberal Land Reform," pp. 13–14, 40–41.

38. McCreery, "Coffee and Class," p. 441.

39. Cazali Avila, "El desarrollo," p. 49.

40. Ibid., p. 45.

41. Because of excessive issue for expenditures on a war, the National Bank failed in 1876 (McCreery, "Coffee and Class," p. 442).

42. McCreery has shown that assistance from Fomento was not always forthcoming, even when promised. For example, the bridge over the Polochíc River in Alta Verapaz was finally completed without the help of Fomento (*Desarrollo económico*, p. 66).

43. Castellanos Cambranes, *Café y campesinos*, p. 516. By 1884 the port of Champerico had surpassed San José in value of exports.

44. Cazali Avila, "El desarrollo," p. 49.

45. Castellanos Cambranes, *Café y campesinos*, pp. 528–29.

46. By 1897, 135 miles of track had been laid between Puerto Barrios and Rancho de San Augustín, but track was lacking over 60 miles of the roughest terrain to reach the capital (ibid., p. 539).

47. David J. McCreery, "State Power, Indigenous Communities, and Land in Nineteenth Century Guatemala, 1820–1920," in Carol Smith, ed., *Guatemala Indians and the State*, p. 100.

48. Woodward, *Rafael Carrera*, p. 428.

49. Although Carrera frequently intervened on behalf of Indian communities when their appeals reached the presidential office, in one case Carrera expropriated some six thousand acres from the village of Santa Lucía Cotzumalguapa and sold it to the wealthy Creole Manuel Herrera (ibid.).

50. McCreery, "Rural Guatemala," chap. 6. McCreery has carefully documented the intrusion of *ladino* growers through rentals of municipal lands and resistance by the Indian communities of San Felipe, San Francisco Zapotitlán, and El Palmar in the *boca costa* sections of the departments of Retalhuleu and Quezaltenango. In 1864, the *corregidor* of Retalhuleu, fearing a repetition of the Carrera Uprising of 1839, sent two hundred militia into the town of San Sebastián, where Indians had burned several houses and the *aguardiente* monopoly, killing seven people, in protest over the intrusion of *ladino* coffee growers onto their traditional landholdings.

51. Woodward, *Rafael Carrera*, p. 429.

52. McCreery, "State Power," p. 106.

53. Castellanos Cambranes, *Café y campesinos*, p. 341.

54. Cazali Avila, "El desarrollo," p. 46.

55. Herrick, "Economic and Political Development," p. 275.

56. Handy, *Gift of the Devil*, p. 69.

57. Castellanos Cambranes, *Café y campesinos*, pp. 368–69.

58. For examples of redistribution of lands between villages in the highlands see Mendez Montenegro, *444 años de legislación*, which records the following cases: one hundred *caballerías* of land to Sololá for division among its inhabitants, July 22, 1873, p. 124; adjudication of "terrenos baldíos" of San Antonio to inhabitants of San Rafael Chilasco, May 20, 1874, p. 132; adjudication of lands to the community of San Pedro Sacatepéquez, San Marcos, February 8, 1884, p. 183. See also Castellanos Cambranes, *Café y campesinos*, p. 370; Garlant, "Developmental Aspects," pp. 26–27.

59. This was the third largest coffee *finca* in the department. When I visited El Capetillo on the outskirts of Alotenango in 1987, the manager

explained that the *finca* was almost entirely devoted to sugar before coffee. The water wheel that was used to run the coffee *beneficio* in 1987 had been used to run the sugar mill a century before; the wheel was produced by Mirless and Tart in Glasgow in 1865.

60. The upper limit of five thousand trees for "peasant" holdings was based on the reasoning that a family of five could care for and pick the fruit from five thousand trees (0.6 pounds *oro* per tree and a six-week picking period with an average of one quintal oro [one hundred pounds] picked per family member per week) without being forced to hire outside labor. The upper limit of twenty thousand trees for a family farm was based on the assumption that a family of five would not have to hire outside labor for the weeding, pruning, fertilizing, ditch digging, and other permanent labor needs of the farm but would have to obtain outside labor for peak labor needs at picking time. A farm with twenty thousand or more trees, under normal conditions, must hire additional labor both for permanent care of the grove and for picking. Naturally some farms with more than twenty thousand trees would use family labor, and some farms with fewer than five thousand trees might be owned by rich townspeople, who might operate the farm as a capitalistic enterprise, hiring labor for all the care of the farm. See note 112 below for empirical justification for the choice of these size classes.

61. The one Indian department that remains an anomaly is Alta Verapaz, where small, mostly *ladino* owners had 36 percent of the trees by the time of the 1890 census; more research on precoffee land tenure patterns and the way municipal lands were converted into coffee farms needs to be done to explain this apparent anomaly. This was not a real estate development zone targeted by the Barrios government but was developing as a center of coffee production before the Conservatives were ousted from power.

62. The *municipios* of the Pacific piedmont where identifiably Indian surnames appear on the lists as small coffee growers are Tajumulco (San Marcos), Santo Tomás Perdido (Suchitepéquez), San Pablo (Suchitepéquez), Samayac (Suchitepéquez), Mazatenango (Suchitepéquez), San Miguel Panán (Suchitepéquez), San Gabriel (Suchitepéquez), and San Sebastián (Retalhuleu).

63. Upper piedmont *municipios* of Retalhuleu and Suchitepéquez were also part of the real estate development zone, though lower piedmont haciendas began coffee cultivation on a large scale much earlier. The coffee district listed in the 1890 census as part of Sololá was later annexed to the department of Suchitepéquez.

64. The first major road after independence was built in 1845–47 between the indigo market town of San Miguel and the port of La Union. See Browning, *El Salvador*, pp. 164–65.

65. Kerr, "Role of the Coffee Industry," p. 65.

66. Ibid., p. 104.

67. In 1807, 21 percent of the country's indigo production was grown in the district of San Vicente; San Miguel was the second most important indigo district with 19 percent of the country's production. The rest was

spread about the country, all other districts growing less than 10 percent of the country's output. Indigo tithes in 1804 suggest that the larger holdings were found in the Pacific piedmont and coastal plain, while smaller holdings were in the north. The Aycinena family's colonial period holdings in El Salvador consisted of sixteen haciendas located around Zacatecoluca (La Paz), San Vicente, and San Miguel (Lindo-Fuentes, *Weak Foundations*, pp. 25, 26, 54).

68. When Santa Tecla was rebuilt by the national government in 1854, the original intention was to distribute the *ejidal* lands surrounding the town equitably in ten- to twenty-acre lots, but only a year later the government was giving preference to those who promised to plant coffee (Browning, *El Salvador*, p. 177). Browning notes that "grain" was also given preference which may have been *grana*, or cochineal in the original document.

69. In those municipalities, insiders often paid no rent for the use of village lands although outsiders were required to pay a yearly fee (ibid., pp. 194–95).

70. Lindo-Fuentes, *Weak Foundations*, pp. 90, 133.

71. Browning, *El Salvador*, pp. 181–82.

72. Ibid., p. 184.

73. In the eighteenth century, the Indian community of Coatepeque secured communal control over these lands following a protracted struggle. By the time of the 1950 census all traces of communal holdings had been removed and Coatepeque was the fifth most important coffee *municipio* in El Salvador (ibid., p. 193; Dirección General de Estadísticos y Censos, *Censo agropecuario de 1950*, pp. 209–16).

74. Browning, *El Salvador*, pp. 205, 208.

75. Walter, "Trade and Development," p. 28.

76. Dunkerley, *Long War*, p. 12.

77. Lindo-Fuentes, *Weak Foundations*, p. 133.

78. Kerr, "Role of the Coffee Industry," pp. 93–94.

79. Browning, *El Salvador*, p. 218.

80. Kerr, "Role of the Coffee Industry," pp. 44, 86, 109.

81. Browning, *El Salvador*, pp. 210–11.

82. Further confusion was created in 1889, when the national land registry was burned to the ground (Kerr, "Role of the Coffee Industry," p. 98).

83. In a fine study of the political economy of indigo, José Antonio Fernández shows how indigo haciendas and *poquiteros* (small peasant producers) along with peasant corn and bean producers coevolved into an interdependent system in which the haciendas purchased *mostaza* (indigo seed) from the *poquiteros* and corn and beans and a seasonal work force from the small peasant farmers, while the haciendas supplied cheese and beef to both the *poquiteros* and the peasant corn producers. The population of workers, *poquiteros*, and peasant corn producers that developed in this commercial matrix were made up of what were called *mulattos* during the colonial period, a term that meant generically of mixed blood and of hispanicized, non-Indian culture. The *mulatto* population as a work force on indigo haciendas was given a peculiar economic niche stemming from

a colonial ban on the use of Indian labor in the indigo *obrajes* that lasted until 1736 ("Colouring the World in Blue," pp. 79–143).

84. Although coffee is planted at different densities, on average in nineteenth-century Central America coffee was planted at approximately one thousand trees per *manzana*, making the two censuses roughly comparable. Farms with fewer than ten *manzanas* of coffee accounted for 19 percent of the land area in coffee in El Salvador in 1939, whereas farms with fewer than twenty thousand trees accounted for 19 percent of Guatemalan coffee trees in 1890. The Salvadoran census does not have a size class of five to nineteen *manzanas*, making comparisons of family-sized farms difficult between the two censuses. See Asociación Cafetalera de El Salvador, "Primer censo nacional del café."

85. Less high-quality coffee land was available in the north, allowing peasants to maintain access to those lands.

86. Asociación Cafetalera de El Salvador, "Primer censo nacional del café."

87. The departments of San Vicente and La Paz, strong indigo producers, had lower than average participation rates by large capitalist enterprises and much higher than the national average participation rates by farms with less than ten *manzanas* of coffee; similarly, San Miguel shows a lower than national average participation rate by large capitalist farms (27 percent).

88. Precisely how the process of takeover of Indian lands unfolded in geographical space is not well understood for El Salvador, and it would make a fascinating study if some other sources (for example, municipal documents), in addition to the widely used 1879 survey, could be unearthed. Some Indian communities, for example, on the southeastern slope of the San Salvador volcano and in the Nonualcos area south of Lake Ilopango, appear to have been more successful in retaining access to lands than the communities in the departments of Sonsonate and La Libertad. Was it simply a matter of Izalco (in Sonsonate) possessing greater concentrations of prime land that led to the consolidation of large holdings there, or did the conflictual process itself influence the division of community lands into large capitalist plantations? Did the Nonualcos and the Volcán San Salvador groups have less attractive lands for large plantations, or had they developed a more successful political discourse with the municipal authorities of the closest commercial townships when coffee expansion occurred? The first coffee census (1939), which is inconclusive in that it could reflect a gradual consolidation of holdings since the original 1875 Izalco uprising and/or a more abrupt consolidation following the 1932 Izalco uprising, shows an extremely high participation rate (53 percent of the *municipio*'s coffee land as compared to the country average of 37 percent) in large capitalist farms with more than one hundred *manzanas* of coffee. Also, the heiress to General Regalado's fortune is listed in the 1939 document as owning a first-class *beneficio* in Izalco; this may or may not have been the outcome of an earlier primitive accumulation of Indian lands through the use of military force in Izalco. At the department level, the 1939 coffee census reveals that farms with more than one hundred *manzanas* of coffee claimed 58 percent of the coffee land in La Libertad and

42 percent in Sonsonate, compared with the national average of 37 percent for that group. Of the departments that became major coffee producers by 1939, the ones with the highest concentrations of coffee lands in large capitalist farms (La Libertad, 58 percent; Usulután, 46 percent; and Sonsonate, 42 percent) were listed in the 1879 survey as having large *ejidal* holdings. It is unclear in the 1879 survey whether communal lands are lumped in with *ejidal* lands, as Browning suggests, or whether communal lands were left out of the survey, as Rafael Menjívar suggests. We do know that La Libertad and Sonsonate had a heavy concentration of Indian communities at the time of the survey, and these two show up as having the largest *ejidal* holdings in the 1879 survey, which omits La Paz and Ahuachapán. One wonders as well what the process of conversion was in Usulután to have produced the higher than average concentration of holdings in large capitalist enterprises. For a discussion of some of the drawbacks of using the 1879 land survey, see Lindo-Fuentes, *Weak Foundations*, pp. 128–30.

89. Radell, "Historical Geography," p. 14.

90. Juarros, *Statistical and Commercial History*, pp. 65, 68–69.

91. Lanuza, Vázquez, Barahona, and Chamorro, estimate that the cattle population of Nicaragua in 1870 was approximately four hundred thousand head and that Chontales was the largest cattle-raising department (*Economía y sociedad*, pp. 90–91).

92. Squier, *Nicaragua*, p. 415.

93. During the three decades after independence, there were times when two separate governments existed simultaneously, one in León, the seat of colonial government and the church, and the other in Granada, the commercial center, where contraband trade flourished during the late colonial period.

94. Radell, "Historical Geography," p. 188.

95. Walker first entered Nicaragua in 1854 and was killed in 1860. See Bermann, *Under the Big Stick*, pp. 51–72, 123–25; Alvarado, *Tratado de caficultura*, p. 585.

96. Lanuza, Vázquez, Barahona, and Chamorro, *Economía y sociedad*, p. 78.

97. In 1855, the Río San Juan changed course, and the port of San Juan del Norte was stopped up by a sandbar, which was not dredged out until the early 1890s.

98. Radell, "Historical Geography," pp. 191–95.

99. Levy, *Notas geográficas*, pp. 441–42.

100. Lanuza, Vázquez, Barahona, and Chamorro, *Economía y sociedad*, pp. 124, 76.

101. Radell, "Historical Geography," chap. 8.

102. Wheelock, *Imperialismo y dictadura*, p. 77.

103. Radell, "Historical Geography," p. 202; Gould, "El trabajo forzoso."

104. Gould says that 532,453 "pies de café" had been planted in Matagalpa by 1881, only 18,215 of which were mature. At one thousand trees per

manzana, this would translate into 921 acres planted and only 31.5 acres in production ("El trabajo forzoso," p. 7).

105. The communities were divided along colonial lines into four political groupings or *cañadas,* each with a designated section of the town of Matagalpa along with lands and smaller villages outside of the city. Each grouping had a council of elders that elected a mayor, who represented the group on the community board. In addition, each *cañada* had its own military and religious organizations.

106. Gould, "El trabajo forzoso," p. 16. Wheelock estimates that five thousand Indians were killed (*Imperialismo y dictadura,* p. 77).

107. Bureau of the American Republics, *Commercial Directory of Nicaragua,* p. 29. Gould estimates that 5,100 of the 8,000 *manzanas* taken in the 1889–90 distribution were located within Indian jurisdictions ("El trabajo forzoso," p. 20).

108. Santos Francisco Zelaya is listed as one of twenty-five "planters of coffee" in Managua in Bureau of the American Republics, *Commercial Directory of Nicaragua,* p. 174.

109. Gould, "El trabajo forzoso," pp. 24, 27, 39; Teplitz, "Political and Economic Foundations," pp. 197–230.

110. The 1909 census was taken during an abnormally low production year. It covers 95 percent of Nicaraguan exports that year and 87 percent of production. It lists by department the name of the owner, the name of the farm, the total land area of the farm in *manzanas* (including all land, not just the coffee area), the number of coffee trees (newly planted and mature), the number of quintals (one hundred pounds *oro*) of production, the types and number of machines on each farm, and the estimated value of the farm (República de Nicaragua, "Censo cafetalero de 1909," pp. 646–72). This is a very rare, important document that is not available in North American library collections (the Library of Congress has only parts of the *Boletín de estadística* series that does not include 1911). My thanks to Richard Grossman, who took a portable copier (and paper!) to Nicaragua; he copied the manuscript from the collection of the Instituto Histórico in Managua and was kind enough to send me a photocopy.

111. This assumes planting at a density of one thousand trees per *manzana.*

112. The assumptions behind the size class analysis were based on labor input requirements taken from a 1925–26 survey of Nicaraguan coffee farms undertaken by the U.S. Consulate in Corinto. The permanent labor input requirements, which would normally be spread over a nine-month period, were estimated at sixty-eight days of labor per thousand trees, and it was estimated that the average laborer (including men, women, and children) could pick one hundred pounds (one quintal) of clean coffee per week when the harvest on a farm was spread over six weeks. It was further assumed that the average workweek was five and a half days, and the average yield per tree was 0.6 pounds of clean coffee. Under these assumptions the maximum number of trees a family of five could care for and harvest without using

outside labor would be fewer than five thousand (the binding constraint being the harvest); for lack of a better term I have labeled this a "peasant" farm. The maximum number of trees a family of five could take care of on a permanent basis would be fewer than twenty thousand, and outside labor equivalent to fifteen persons working for six weeks each would have to supplement the labor of the family of five to complete the harvest on a farm approaching twenty thousand trees; I call these "family-sized" coffee farms. Any farm in excess of twenty thousand trees would have to hire outside labor for both permanent care of the groves and picking; these are called "capitalist" farms, and this group was divided, somewhat arbitrarily, into small capitalist farms with twenty to forty-nine thousand trees, medium-sized capitalist farms with fifty to ninety-nine thousand trees, and large capitalist farms with one hundred thousand or more trees. These are admittedly rough categorizations and subject to variability owing to changes in yields per tree, technologies available for permanent care of groves, and so forth. It is also clear that some very small peasant-sized coffee farms and some farms in the family size class might actually be operated on a pure wage labor basis for some absentee owner living in the city. It is interesting that the assumption of one quintal clean coffee per harvest worker per week fits post–World War II estimates and was the rule of thumb used by coffee growers in Central America when I did fieldwork there in 1988 (Playter, "Report on Nicaraguan Coffee"). For a careful survey of labor inputs on Salvadoran coffee farms in the mid-1950s see United Nations Food and Agriculture Organization, *Coffee in Latin America*. This survey shows a wide range of labor inputs, the averages for permanent care of groves in El Salvador in the mid-1950s being somewhat higher than the estimates for Nicaragua in 1926, as might be expected in a country with a greater relative abundance of labor. The labor estimates for the harvest, however, are suprisingly similar in the two studies.

113. Radell, "Historical Geography," pp. 214–15.

114. Ibid., p. 213.

115. Gould, *To Lead as Equals*.

116. Incer, *Geografía básica de Nicaragua*, p. 99.

117. Radell, "Historical Geography," p. 236.

118. One name that is known to be *ladino* is Gregorio Sandino, who had eighteen thousand trees on a seventy-acre farm. Gregorio Sandino, who was from the town of Niquinohomo, had an illegitimate son by an Indian woman; he was named Augusto César Sandino.

119. In 1912, there was a movement against the U.S. occupation by "El Indio" Zeledón; that year Zeledón was killed and his body was paraded in public. It is said that Sandino saw the procession as it passed through his hometown, Niquinohomo, leaving a strong impression on him (Black, *Triumph of the People*, p. 15).

120. The department of León registered the highest percentage of small farm participation but was a marginal producer with only eight coffee farms.

121. In Boaco 36 percent of the land in farms was listed as *ejidal*; in Chontales 20 percent was *ejidal*.

122. Dirección General de Estadísticos y Censos, *Censo agropecuario de 1962–63*, Table 2, p. 4. In the departments of Matagalpa and Jinotega 38 percent and 31 percent of the land was occupied without title, and 4 percent and 6 percent was still in *ejidal* form.

123. Luciano Mendioróz, *Atlas de Centro-América*; Peckenham and Street, *Honduras*, p. 25.

124. Molina Chocano, *Estado liberal*, pp. 39–41.

125. República de Honduras, *Memoria de fomento, 1914–1915*, p. 145.

126. Pérez Brignoli, "Economía y sociedad en Honduras," p. 66.

127. Guevara-Escudero, "Nineteenth Century Honduras," pp. 226–27.

128. República de Honduras, *Memoria de fomento, 1914–15*, "Commercial and Industrial Directory," pp. 65–87.

129. This was a natural extension of the colonial principle that improvements made on land were the property of the individual who made them, but improvements made for coffee cultivation were generally more permanent and more valuable than those made for previous commercial crops.

Chapter 4

1. SIECA, *Desarrollo integrado*, p. 74. These are average labor requirements in 1970 on Central American capitalist farms in excess of eighty-six acres. The two export crops that exceeded coffee's labor requirements in this sample were bananas (202.4 man-days per acre) and tobacco (166 man-days per acre). The estimates for the various crops are as follows: coffee (68.4 man-days per acre), sugar (38.5 man-days per acre), cotton (29.6 man-days per acre), corn (23.9 man-days per acre), and beans (14.6 man-days per acre). Of course, these averages were estimated a century after the coffee boom. Labor inputs and yields vary considerably from one farm to the next; an input-output study of El Salvador in 1954 showed a variation of man-days of labor per acre per year from 11 on abnormally low labor-intensive farms to 139.4 on abnormally high labor-intensive farms, with a weighted average of all farms equal to 77.6 man-days per acre, which was probably higher than in other Central American countries because of the greater availability of labor in El Salvador (United Nations Food and Agriculture Organization, *Coffee in Latin America*, Table 16, p. 122). A 1926 study of Nicaraguan coffee farms estimated 72.6 man-days per acre for a mature coffee farm (43.6 man-days per acre permanent care and 29 man-days per acre seasonal labor for picking) (Playter, "Report on Nicaraguan Coffee," p. 41). With these caveats in mind, the 1970 estimate of 68.4 man-days per acre for coffee is not unreasonable.

2. United Nations Food and Agriculture Organization, *Coffee in Latin America*, p. 110. This estimate is for El Salvador in 1954–55. Where labor is not as abundant and trees are not planted so thickly (809 trees per acre), less labor is expended, and in areas where trees are more densely planted, more labor is required.

3. Labor intensity in El Salvador is higher than the average for Central

America because there is a relative abundance of labor and a relative scarcity of land there.

4. In wetter zones toward the Atlantic, the picking season is more extended.

5. República de Honduras, *Primer anuario estadístico 1889*. Population statistics for the other countries during the nineteenth and twentieth centuries are compiled in Cardoso and Pérez Brignoli, *Centroamérica y la economía occidental*, pp. 225, 226, 230, 232.

6. Roseberry, "La Falta de Brazos," pp. 351–82.

7. Castellanos Cambranes, *Café y campesinos*, p. 411.

8. Ibid., p. 143. For an excellent treatment of the ethnic differences of wage laborers in Antigua and Amatitlán see McCreery, "Rural Guatemala," chap. 4, p. 11.

9. McCreery, "Rural Guatemala," chap. 6, pp. 5, 6.

10. Cazali, "El desarrollo," p. 68; Castellanos Cambranes, *Café y campesinos*, pp. 77–79.

11. McCreery, "Odious Feudalism," p. 103.

12. Castellanos Cambranes, *Café y campesinos*, p. 186.

13. Woodward, *Rafael Carrera*, p. 431.

14. Cazali, "El desarrollo," p. 68.

15. Decree 177, "Reglamento de Jornaleros," reprinted in full in Castellanos Cambranes, *Café y campesinos*, Annex 1, pp. 581–94.

16. Decree 177, Article 6, ibid., p. 584.

17. McCreery, "Odious Feudalism," p. 109.

18. Decree 177, Article 4, Section 10, in Castellanos Cambranes, *Café y campesinos*, pp. 583–84.

19. McCreery, "Debt Servitude," p. 758.

20. Decree 177, Article 7, in Cambranes, *Café y campesinos*, p. 584.

21. For a list of growers and number of trees see Secretaria de Estado de Guatemala, "Estadística de café de 1890," *Memoria que la secretaría de estado de 1891*, pp. 5–153. For a listing of *fincas* in 1889 see Secretaria de Fomento, "Memoria de Fomento, 1889." Choacorral was an hacienda owned by the church during the colonial period and sold at auction in 1831.

22. Nañez, "Erwin Paul Dieseldorff." The farms purchased for securing and maintaining labor were Chiachal (123 adult males), Secac-Ulpán and Río Frío (200 adult males together) (p. 210); Cantaloc, Sarruj Jucub, and Sacchicagua (p. 118); El Salto and Panzal (p. 115). In addition, two farms, Cubilguitz and Yaxcabnal, were bought for growing corn and beans to supply *colonos* on other estates (p. 118).

23. Quiñonez, *Directorio general*, pp. 145–220.

24. In the 1890 coffee census, one or more distinctly Indian surnames appear as coffee growers in the following *municipios*: Barahona (Sacatepéquez), San Sebastián (Retalhuleu), Nuevo San Carlos (Quezaltenango), Tajumulco (San Marcos), Santo Tomás Perdido (Suchitepéquez), San Pablo (Suchitepéquez), Samayac (Suchitepéquez), Mazatenango (Suchitepéquez), San Miguel Panán (Suchitepéquez), San Gabriel (Suchitepéquez), Carchá (Alta Verapaz), San Cristóbal (Alta Verapaz), and Purulhá (Baja Verapaz). Indian coffee growers listed in the 1890 census rarely had more than a thou-

sand trees, which could be easily cared for and picked using only family labor. The largest number of Indian growers listed were in the department of Suchitepéquez, which suggests that Indians in that department may have acquired private holdings along with *ladinos* during the scramble for village and communal lands in previous decades.

25. Handy, *Gift of the Devil*, pp. 70–71.

26. Castellanos Cambranes, *Café y campesinos*, pp. 321–23. On occasion, the worst dreams of elites were fulfilled. On July 17, 1898, the Indians of the peripheral village of San Juan Ixcoy in Huehuetenango province murdered the local *habilitador* of Helvetia, a plantation in the Pacific piedmont. In an attempt to prevent information of the murder from reaching the government, the Indians proceeded to murder all but one of the thirty remaining *ladinos* in the town (McCreery, "Debt Servitude," p. 756).

27. Castellanos Cambranes, *Coffee and Peasants*, pp. 317–18.

28. Decree 177, Articles 4, 7–10, in Castellanos Cambranes, *Café y campesinos*, pp. 583–85.

29. McCreery, "Odious Feudalism," p. 110.

30. The upper limit of five thousand trees for peasant holdings was based on the reasoning that a family of five could care for and pick the fruit from five thousand trees (0.6 pounds *oro* per tree and a six-week picking period with an average of 1 quintal *oro* [100 pounds of clean, dry, hulled coffee] picked per family member per week) without being forced to hire outside labor. The upper limit of twenty thousand trees for a family farm was based on the assumption that a family of five would not have to hire outside labor for the weeding, pruning, fertilizing, ditch digging, and other permanent labor needs of the farm but would have to obtain outside labor for peak labor needs at picking time. A farm with twenty thousand trees or more, under normal conditions, must hire additional labor both for permanent care of the grove and for picking. Naturally, some farms with more than twenty thousand trees would use family labor, and some farms with fewer than five thousand trees might be owned by rich townspeople who would hire labor for all the care of the farm.

31. For Guatemala as a whole, only 19 percent of the trees were on farms with fewer than twenty thousand trees.

32. Upper piedmont *municipios* of Retalhuleu and Suchitepéquez were also part of the real estate development zone, though haciendas in the lower piedmont began large-scale coffee cultivation much earlier. The coffee district listed in the 1890 census as part of Sololá was later annexed to the department of Suchitepéquez.

33. Farms using family labor for permanent tasks and supplemental wage labor for picking (those with between five and fewer than twenty thousand trees) came to represent approximately 7 percent of the trees listed in the 1890 census, and even smaller peasant operations of fewer than five thousand trees had approximately 12 percent of the trees in the country, according to the census.

34. Lindo-Fuentes has estimated that per capita corn consumption went up 3.5 times from 1807 to 1858 (*Weak Foundations*, p. 87).

35. Ibid., p. 84.

36. Kerr, "Role of the Coffee Industry," p. 93; Browning, *El Salvador*, p. 217.

37. Browning, *El Salvador*, pp. 169–71.

38. Lindo-Fuentes estimates that corn sold for 1.86 pesos per *fanega* (approximately one hundred pounds) in 1858 and rose to 5 pesos per *fanega* in 1885 although the money wage remained at 2 reales (20 cents). This collapse of real wages was cushioned somewhat because the growers provided workers with tortillas and beans for one or two meals a day (*Weak Foundations*, pp. 156–57).

39. Cardoso, "Formation of the Coffee Estate," p. 178.

40. Cholera was reportedly brought back to Costa Rica from Nicaragua by troops who were sent to fight the army of William Walker. Some six thousand persons were estimated to have died in the epidemic (Hall, *El café de Costa Rica*, p. 54).

41. Ibid., pp. 55–56.

42. Gudmundson, *Costa Rica before Coffee*, pp. 74–77. Gudmundson documents kinship labor recruitment and its ideological implications in Santo Domingo de Heredia in "Peasant, Farmer, Proletarian," pp. 231–34.

43. Cardoso, "Formation of the Coffee Estate," p. 179.

44. Hall, *El café de Costa Rica*, p. 57.

45. The *cantones* of Jiménez and Turrialba, where most of these large farms are located, represented about 10 percent of Costa Rica's coffee production in 1973 (Dirección General de Estadística y Censos, *Censo agropecuario de 1973*, Table 17).

46. These figures are for 1973 and represent total farm size, not the acreage in coffee (Aguilar, Barboza, and León, *Desarrollo tecnológico*, pp. 4–16).

47. See Gudmundson, "Peasant, Farmer, Proletarian," pp. 231–48, and Acuña, "La ideología de los pequeños y medianos productores," pp. 137–54.

48. Morales Fonseca, *Nicaragua*, chap. 3.

49. In 1902–3, when the national government registered some 44,344 workers nationwide, the towns of Somoto and Pueblo Nuevo were able to register only 83 and 126 workers respectively. Most of the inscriptions were achieved in the departments of Managua, Granada, Matagalpa, Diriamba (Carazo), and León (ibid., p. 112).

50. "El café de la montaña era de los pobres" (ibid., p. 119).

51. Nueva Segovia also included what is today the department of Madriz (República de Nicaragua, "Censo cafetalero de 1909").

52. Gould, "El trabajo forzoso," pp. 20–21.

53. In the 1960s, it was estimated that 40 percent of the picking force was made up of women and 10–25 percent was children (Wheelock, *Imperialismo y dictadura*, p. 99).

54. Wheelock estimates that 70 to 90 percent of salaries were recouped by commissaries on large farms in Nicaragua in the 1960s (ibid., pp. 91–93).

55. Levy, *Notas geográficas*, p. 463. Coffee growers in the early 1900s who owned stores calculated a normal 25 percent loss from bad debts and legal charges from prosecution of defaulters (Palmer, *Through Unknown Nicaragua*, p. 65).

56. Teplitz, "Political and Economic Foundations," pp. 182–89.

57. In the department of Matagalpa alone, the Indian population in 1880 was approximately thirty to thirty-five thousand.

58. Gould describes how Indian leaders were able to play one Conservative faction against another to gain political space; he also shows how threats of another armed rebellion held the actions of the state in check ("El trabajo forzoso," pp. 7, 19).

59. Teplitz, "Political and Economic Foundations," pp. 195–99.

60. Ibid., pp. 201, 203.

61. República de Honduras, *Memoria de fomento, 1914–1915*.

62. República de Honduras, *Primer anuario estadístico de 1889*, p. 151.

63. Squier, *States of Central America*, p. 205.

64. There was also a surge in private and communal claims to land during the 1850 to 1900 period (Pérez Brignoli, "Economía y sociedad en Honduras," p. 66).

65. República de Honduras, *Primer anuario estadístico de 1889*, pp. 144–45.

66. República de Honduras, *Memoria de fomento, 1914–1915*.

67. Also, Choluteca, a geographical extension of the Salvadoran coastal plain, had easier access than other areas of Honduras to the pool of landless laborers in El Salvador.

68. Dirección General de Censos y Estadísticas, *Censo agropecuario de 1952*, p. 56.

69. Williams, *Export Agriculture*, pp. 55–72, 124–28.

70. Del Cid, *Formas de organización*, p. 172.

71. U.S. Agency for International Development, "Honduras Small Farmer Coffee Improvement," Annex G, p. 6. A USAID-IHCAFE survey in 1988 estimated that only 16 percent of Honduran coffee production was on capitalist farms of twenty *manzanas* or more, 53 percent was on family farms with five to twenty *manzanas*, and 31 percent was from peasant holdings of one to less than five *manzanas*. See Baumeister, "La situación de la producción cafetalera en Honduras," p. 12.

72. The study estimated that 48.3 percent of Honduran farms required wage labor for 25 percent or less of their total labor needs, and only 20.6 percent of the farms used wage labor for more than half their total labor needs (U.S. Agency for International Development, "Honduras Small Farmer Coffee Improvement," Annex G, p. 9).

Chapter 5

1. The United Nations Food and Agriculture Organization's study of coffee in El Salvador in the 1950s estimated that a typical coffee *beneficio* required 6.9 man-hours per one hundred kilograms to get the beans to the dry stage using the wet method, whereas farm-drying required 25 man-hours (*Coffee in Latin America*, p. 131).

2. By 1938, 31 percent of Salvadoran coffee exports and 48 percent of Nicaraguan coffee exports were still being processed by the dry method

(United Nations Food and Agriculture Organization, *The World's Coffee*, pp. 32, 164).

3. It is unclear from the data presented who the sellers or providers of long-term finance were; it would be especially interesting to know what portion of the zero-interest seller financing was conducted by municipalities as part of the privatization of municipal lands taking place over the time period in question. Of 133 transactions in which the maturity periods were known, 110 involved installment periods exceeding one year, though more than half (76) had terms of three years or less (Rodríguez Saenz and Molina Jiménez, "Compraventas de cafetales"; also see Molina Jiménez, *Costa Rica*, pp. 220–35, 258–65). Early actions by the young national government also stimulated the mobilization of capital for coffee production. In 1825, the national government passed a law exempting coffee and other commercial crops from taxes and tithes, and in 1831, the National Assembly followed the lead of the townships and passed a law permitting private individuals to claim national lands free if they grew coffee on those lands for five years (Cardoso, "Formation of the Coffee Estate," pp. 170–73; Hall, *El café de Costa Rica*, p. 35).

4. Oficina del Café, *Informe de labores—1973*, Table 44, pp. 100–104. Direction of trade figures is in Dirección General de Estadística y Censos, *Boletín de exportación de café*, pp. 20–23.

5. In 1846, Juan Mora was the fourth largest coffee exporter in Costa Rica, taking 8 percent of the coffee trade, and Crisanto Medina was the sixth largest with 7 percent of the trade (Stone, "Los cafetaleros," pp. 216–17).

6. One of the first directors of this bank was Alan Wallis, the British consul to Costa Rica (Hall, *El café de Costa Rica*, p. 45).

7. Young, *Central American Currency and Finance*, p. 211.

8. Hall, *El café de Costa Rica*, p. 46. In probate records in Santo Domingo de Heredia, Gudmundson found a small class of relatively prosperous growers (with twenty to fifty *manzanas* of coffee) who did not become indebted to rich processors and who lent to smaller growers in the area during the latter half of the nineteenth century. Gudmundson, "Peasant, Farmer, Proletarian," pp. 234–37).

9. Samper, "El significado social," p. 39.

10. These differential yields were maintained until after World War II.

11. Oficina del Café, *Informe de labores—1965*, p. 9.

12. Oficina del Café, *Leyes y reglamentos*, Appendix 4, pp. 267–304.

13. Nine persons on Stone's list did not buy or sell large coffee properties in San José Province over this period; they either held lands before coffee or held lands in other provinces (Stone, "Los cafetaleros," pp. 185–88). This list of early growers is only partial because it primarily focuses on land purchases and sales in San José Province, but because of San José's early importance as a coffee center, the list does give a picture of the process of elite formation at this time.

14. Araya, "La minería," p. 53.

15. The list of 80 important import merchants before 1850 was collected in Vega Carballo, "El nacimiento," pt. II, pp. 83–120. The 27 coffee export-

ers in 1846 are listed in Stone, "Los cafetaleros," pp. 216–17. The list of 221 *beneficios* in 1907 is found in Oficina del Café, *Informe de labores—1973*, Table 35, pp. 90–93.

16. Gudmundson, *Costa Rica before Coffee*, pp. 78–79.

17. Araya, "La minería," p. 51; Hall, *El café de Costa Rica*, pp. 49–50; Stone, "Los cafetaleros," pp. 216–17; Vega Carballo, "El nacimiento," pt. II, pp. 100–101.

18. Stone, "Los cafetaleros," pp. 216–17.

19. Hall, *El café de Costa Rica*, p. 52.

20. Oficina del Café, *Informe de labores—1973*, pp. 90–93. The 1915 list of coffee exporters is in Ministerio de Fomento, *Informe de la dirección general de estadística*, pp. 213–15.

21. Ministerio de Fomento, *Informe de la dirreción general de estadística*, pp. 212–15. Many of the German import houses adjusted to the dislocations caused by World War I by setting up branches in the United States and Great Britain.

22. Hall, *El café de Costa Rica*, pp. 52–53.

23. Ibid., p. 53; Oficina del Café, *Informe de labores—1973*, pp. 90, 92; Ministerio de Fomento, *Informe de la dirección general de estadística*, pp. 213–14; Echeverria Morales, *Breve historia del café*, p. 81.

24. Carcanholo, "Las relaciones de producción," pp. 125–26.

25. In 1965–66 there were sixty small *beneficios* processing less than five thousand *fanegas* of coffee. By 1976–77, the number of small *beneficios* had been reduced to twenty-two, and the number of large mills (processing more than twenty thousand *fanegas*) had risen from seventeen to thirty-one (ibid., p. 123).

26. Small growers are defined by Carcanholo as those producing fewer than fifty *fanegas* of coffee, medium-sized producers between fifty and five hundred *fanegas*, and large growers in excess of five hundred *fanegas* per year ("Las relaciones de producción," p. 124). One *fanega* equals approximately four hundred liters.

27. In 1960, Costa Rican growers were producing 14.9 quintals of finished coffee (oro) per *manzana* of land, compared to 10.2 in El Salvador, 9.3 in Guatemala, 5.1 in Nicaragua, and 4.5 in Honduras. By 1986 Costa Rican yields had increased to 23.7 quintals per *manzana*, compared with 13.5 in El Salvador, 10.3 in Guatemala and Honduras, and 7.1 in Nicaragua, which suffered from decapitalization of war and revolution (U.S. Department of Agriculture, "Coffee," p. 3).

28. Oficina del Café, *Leyes y reglamentos*, Appendix 4, pp. 267–304. The coincidence of names does not necessarily indicate descendance. For example, some of the names on the earlier and later lists are such common Spanish surnames as Fernández, Jiménez, and Rodríguez, which gives an upward bias to the family name analysis. In the opposite direction, some descendants of earlier elites are lost in the analysis because female descendants married out of this small circle so that after two generations the original surname is lost. For example, if a daughter of Mariano Montealegre married a man named Alvarez, their daughter would be an Alvarez Montealegre, but

she would lose the Montealegre appendage when she married, though her cousins of patrilineal descent would still be Montealegres; this factor gives a downward bias to the name-matching mode of analysis, somewhat counter-balancing the upward bias from the common surname factor. Of course, blood descendance from the early coffee elite did not ensure elite status for later generations. Because of partible inheritance and poor management of opportunities, more descendants fell from elite status than retained it.

29. Oficina del Café, *Leyes y reglamentos*, Appendix 3, pp. 260–66.

30. McCreery, *Desarrollo económico*, pp. 57–59.

31. One year after the Banco Agrícola-Hipotecario was founded, Barrios expanded its powers to include government finance, renaming it the Banco Nacional, but financing the war with El Salvador led to bankruptcy in 1876, after which remaining assets were transferred to the privately owned Banco Internacional, formed in 1877 (Garlant, "Developmental Aspects," pp. 53–55).

32. McCreery, *Desarrollo económico*, p. 59.

33. These banks with their founding dates are Banco Internacional, 1877; Banco Colombiano, 1878; Banco del Occidente, 1881; Banco Agrícola-Hipotecario, 1894; Banco de Guatemala, 1895; and Banco Americano, 1895 (Young, *Central American Currency and Finance*, p. 28).

34. Garlant, "Developmental Aspects," pp. 59–60.

35. Ibid., p. 61.

36. Alvarado, *Tratado de caficultura*, pp. 545, 572.

37. Secretaria de Estado de Guatemala, *Memoria de fomento de 1891*, "Estadísticas de café, 1890."

38. David McCreery searched the *protócolos* and found José María Samayoa, José Tomás Larraondo (an early coffee grower), and Manuel María Herrera to be heavy lenders to cochineal; J. M. Samayoa, M. M. Herrera, and Juan Matheu show up in an 1855 list of large cochineal growers who rented municipal lands in Antigua ("Rural Guatemala," chap. 4, pp. 5, 10). In 1890 the Herreras, who were nineteenth-century newcomers to the Guatemalan elite, owned the second largest coffee farm in Guatemala, San Andrés Osuna, with 900,000 trees.

39. By 1890, Barrios's widow had sold El Porvenir to the German consortium Compañía Hamburguesa de Plantaciones. A check of property records reveals that General Justo Rufino Barrios owned the property in 1879 (Secretaria de Estado de Guatemala, *Memoria de fomento de 1891*, "Estadísticas de café, 1890"; Archivos Generales de Centroamérica, "Protócolos de hacienda," 1891).

40. Castellanos Cambranes, *Café y campesinos*, p. 341.

41. Secretaria de Estado de Guatemala, *Memorias de fomento de 1891*, "Estadísticas de café, 1890," pp. 5–142.

42. Ibid., p. 153.

43. Nañez, "German Contributions," pp. 39–45.

44. Brazilian plantings increased considerably in the early 1890s, and by 1896 these new trees began yielding crops. In 1896 the Brazilian harvest was 792 million pounds, rising to 1,231 million pounds in 1897 and 1,483 mil-

lion pounds in 1898. This represented some two-thirds of world output and exerted a significant effect on the world price. Even after recovery from the recession, these supplies weighed down prices on the international coffee market (Mosk, "Coffee Economy of Guatemala," p. 16).

45. Commodity Research Bureau, *Commodity Yearbook 1942*, p. 53.

46. Nañez, "German Contributions," pp. 39, 51. For a map of holdings by nationality in Alta Verapaz in 1900, see Sapper, "Die Alta Verapaz," pp. 78–224.

47. Wagner, "Actividades empresariales," pp. 100–103.

48. Del Cid Fernández, "Llegada de los primeros alemanes," pp. 13–18.

49. For a list of expropriated assets of the Nottebohm family see International Court of Justice, *Pleadings, Oral Arguments, Documents*, Annex 20.

50. For an idea of the scale and breadth of the Dieseldorff empire and how it evolved, see the account books housed in the Dieseldorff Collection in the Tulane University Library. For an outstanding analysis of the Dieseldorff enterprise see Nañez, "Erwin Paul Dieseldorff."

51. Guatemala's eight most important coffee firms in 1932–33, as cited in Alvarado, *Tratado de caficulturo*, p. 557, were as follows:

Name of firm	Number of farms	Number (quintals oro)
C. A. Plantation Corporation of New York (CAPCO owned by Schlubach, Sapper & Co.)	9	65,000
Nottebohm Hermanos	11	34,000
Gordon Smith and Co.	7	21,000
Sapper and Co.	15	11,000
Guillermo Luttmann	2	11,000
C. C. J. Mohr	3	10,000
M. H. Hempstead	8	9,000
Ovidio Pivaral	6	8,000

The largest Guatemalan coffee farms with production greater than 10,000 quintals oro in 1933–34, according to Alvarado, *Tratado de caficultura*, p. 566, were

Concepción, Cía. Plantaciones Concepción, Escuintla, Escuintla
San Andrés Osuna, Central America Plantation Corporation of New York (CAPCO-Schlubach, Sapper & Co.), Escuintla, Escuintla
Cerro Redondo, Sociedad Agrícola Viñas Zapote, Barberena, S.R.
El Rosario, Buhl and Hochmeister, Tumbador, San Marcos
El Porvenir, CAPCO, San Pablo, San Marcos
La Libertad, Federico Moesller, Colomba, Quezaltenango
Helvetia, Gordon Smith and Co., El Palmar, Quezaltenango
Santa Margarita, Wyld Hermanos, Acatenango, Chimaltenango
El Pacayal, D. B. Hodgsdon, Pochuta, Chimaltenango

52. Including all Axis nationals, a total of 208 farms were listed (Archivos General de Centroamerica, "Lista de fincas productoras de café que son propiedades de ciudadanos o compañías alemanes," 1942, B/Legajo 4156).

53. Not all persons of German descent lost their lands during World War II. Some had married Guatemalans or had become naturalized citizens of Guatemala. Others, like the Dieseldorffs, could claim Jewish ancestry and escape expropriation. A 1952 directory of coffee farms reveals the following names of those with probable German ancestry who still had farms (some of these names may have been misspelled in the directory): Dieseldorff, Koester, Schleehauf, Thomae, Wyld Hermanos, Luttmann, Merck, Kong, Wahl, Schwendener, Mittelstaedt, Rosenthal, Esser, Pieters, Stahl, Weissenberg, Bornhauser, Widmann, Mohr, Lowenthal, Lippmann, Hauesler, Neuhaus, Buhl, Rosengarten, Hochsteter, Steinberg, Boppel, Klee, Rodeman, Hoffens, Kaufman, Seeman, Moller, Bruderer, Straub, and Brol (Rubio Sánchez, "Historia del cultivo del café," pp. 587–624).

54. Instituto Nacional de Transformación Agraria, *Monografía de las fincas nacionales*, 1981.

55. Dirección General de Estadística, *Censo agropecuario de 1979*, Vol. 2, Book 1, p. 251. In the 1970s and 1980s ANACAFE and USAID pushed for credit and cooperative ventures to assist small and medium-sized coffee producers. This help, combined with favorable coffee prices, encouraged the participation of small and medium-sized farms in the coffee sector (Asociación Nacional del Café, *Proyecto del desarrollo tecnológico*).

56. Plant tour and interviews with general adminstrator don Miguel Angel León Aviles and technical administrator Willy López, Amate Blanco *beneficio*, Santa Rosa Department, December 8, 1987.

57. In 1987, San Lázaro had four hulling machines, nine Guardiola dryers, two vertical drying machines, and thirteen laser sorters, and it hired fifty-two women to assist in sorting; the holding company also has its own export house (interview with don Adrián Solares, general adminstrator, San Lázaro *beneficio*, Antigua, Guatemala, December 19, 1987). Don Adrián said that large producers were phasing out of coffee processing in part because of the high risk of theft of dried coffee. Thieves will not steal mature coffee berries, but they will steal sacks of *pergamino*; it is much easier to guard the large centralized *beneficio* than smaller *beneficios* in the countryside, and many thefts occur each year from trucks shipping dry coffee from the *beneficio* to the export house.

58. The ANACAFE list includes 3,978 farms, representing most of the coffee farms with more than one hundred acres of land (*Directorio*).

59. Lists of coffee, indigo, cacao growers, hacienda owners, and merchants in 1867 were taken from the official publication *Gaceta nacional* and compiled by Lanuza, Vázquez, Barahona, and Chamorro, *Economía y sociedad*, pp. 173, 76, 77, 79, 82, 118, 124.

60. The three are César Costiglio, Pablo Eisentuck, and L. E. Degener (ibid., p. 82).

61. The 1871 estimate is from ibid., p. 80. The 1890 estimate is from the series in Dirección General de Estadísticos y Censos, *El café en Nicaragua*.

62. These lists are in Bureau of the American Republics, *Commercial Directory of Nicaragua*, pp. 167–77.

63. Charlip, "Coffee and Class," p. 22.

64. Bureau of the American Republics, *Commercial Directory of Nicaragua*, pp. 167–77; Charlip, "Coffee and Class," pp. 22–23.

65. Gould, "El trabajo forzoso," p. 19.

66. The 1909 census showed that forty-five of the country's forty-seven water-powered *beneficios* were located in Matagalpa or Jinotega (República de Nicaragua, "Censo cafetalero de 1909," p. 672).

67. In the Sierras de Managua, of twenty-five large capitalist enterprises, only eight had wet *beneficios*, six of which were run by steam and two with animal or manpower.

68. Eighteen surnames on the 1909 large grower list also appeared as import-export merchants in 1892; seven of these were not listed as growers or coffee exporters in 1892.

69. Teplitz suggests that these individuals had probably converted to Liberalism ("Political and Economic Foundations," pp. 229–31).

70. Young, *Central American Currency and Finance*, pp. 135–36.

71. In 1926, 85 percent of the coffee from Matagalpa and Jinotega was water-processed, compared with 36 percent nationwide (Playter, "Report on Nicaraguan Coffee," p. 32). By 1938, 52 percent of national exports were water-processed and hulled, and another 23 percent were exported in the hull, which usually implies water processing (United Nations Food and Agriculture Organization, *World's Coffee*, p. 164).

72. Wheelock, *Imperialismo y dictadura*, pp. 140–41.

73. North American Congress on Latin America, "Nicaragua," pp. 4–12. Wheelock, *Imperialismo y dictadura*, p. 160.

74. Instituto Nacional de Estadísticas y Censos, *Directorio de establecimientos de la industria manufacturera*, pp. 4–9.

75. Colburn, *Post-Revolutionary Nicaragua*, p. 69.

76. Young, *Central American Currency and Finance*, pp. 70–71. In 1892 the Banco Particular was renamed the Banco Salvadoreño. In 1893 the Banco de Nicaragua (later called London Bank of Central America, Ltd.) was permitted to establish a branch bank in El Salvador; in 1902, this business was taken over by the Banco Salvadoreño. In 1898, following the crisis in the international coffee market, the Banco Salvadoreño and the Banco Internacional were merged.

77. In 1913, Salvadoran exports were divided as follows: United States, 28 percent; France, 20 percent; Germany, 17 percent; Italy, 12 percent; and the United Kingdom, 7 percent (Pan American Union, *General Descriptive Data on El Salvador*).

78. Ward, *Blue Book of El Salvador*, p. 305. Colindres, *Fundamentos económicos*, Table 67.

79. Ward, *Blue Book of El Salvador*, p. 246.

80. Kerr, "Role of the Coffee Industry," p. 107.

81. United Nations Food and Agriculture Organization, *World's Coffee*, p. 177.

82. Samper, "El significado social," p. 42.

83. United Nations Food and Agriculture Organization, *Coffee in Latin America*, p. 130.

84. Colindres, *Fundamentos económicos*, Table 67.

85. Molina Chocano, *Estado liberal*, p. 102.

86. República de Honduras, *Primer anuario estadístico, 1889*, pp. 290–92.

87. In 1916 Isabel viuda de Agurcia paid 135 *lempiras* in road tax, while the New York and Honduras Rosario Mining Company paid 355 *lempiras*, the Bank of Honduras 175, the Banco de Comercio 105, and Santos Soto and Co. 175. Below these top five were approximately eight thousand companies and individuals who paid lesser amounts (República de Honduras, "Lista general de los capitalistas de la república obligados a contribuir en el presente año al fondo de caminos," *Memoria de fomento 1916–17*, p. 3).

88. República de Honduras, *Memoria de fomento, 1914–15*.

89. The 1899 exporters were Bahr, Gerbal, Gost, Koenemann, Maier, Rossner, Scheyer, Streber, and Wittkugel (Perry, *Directorio nacional de Honduras*, p. 214). By 1914–15, the Uhlers, Sierckes, Drechsels, Waisses, Werlings, and Fritzgartners had joined the earlier immigrants (República de Honduras, *Memoria de fomento, 1914–15*).

90. In 1913, 56 percent of Honduran coffee exports went to Germany, and the United States bought 41 percent (Pan American Union, *Honduras*, p. 25).

91. The Uhlers and Sierckes are examples of earlier German immigrants who continue to participate in the Honduran coffee business.

92. Dirección General de Censos y Estadísticas, *Censo agropecuario de 1952*, Table 19, p. 56.

93. In the area covered by the census 26 percent in these *municipios* was national land and 5 percent was rented (Dirección General de Censos y Estadísticas, *Censo agropecuario de 1965–66*, Tables 5 and 19b, pp. 28–38, 162m–162y).

94. Rafael del Cid's study in the early 1980s reveals a normal margin of 35 percent between purchase price and sales price by intermediaries ("Formas de organización," pp. 176–77). USAID data from 1978–79 reveals that 84 percent of the small and medium-sized farmers of its project target group received less than 60 percent of the export value of their coffee, and 38 percent of the target group received less than 44 percent of the export value equivalent of their coffee, implying significant gouging by intermediaries, export houses, or both (USAID, "Honduras Small Farmer Coffee Improvement," p. 9).

95. Del Cid, "Formas de organización," Appendix Table, "Volumen y tanto por ciento de las exportaciones clasificadas por exportador," p. 62.

96. In 1980, a private sector bank, BANHCAFE, was established to concentrate on financing the coffee sector (USAID, "Honduras Small Farmer Coffee Improvement," p. 49).

97. Instituto Hondureño del Café, *Manual de recomendaciones*; del Cid, "Formas de organización," p. 170.

98. USAID, "Honduras Small Farmer Coffee Improvement," Amendment 2.

99. These estimates are from the eastern sections of El Paraíso, where Contra occupation was heavy (AHPROCAFE, "Informe sobre desplazados de guerra," Table 2).

100. U.S. Department of Agriculture, Foreign Agricultural Service, "Honduras—Coffee Annual Report."

101. U.S. Department of Agriculture, "Coffee," p. 3.

Chapter 6

1. Wortman, *Government and Society*, p. 276; Woodward, *Rafael Carrera*, pp. 26–27.

2. Rodríguez, *Cádiz Experiment*, p. 16.

3. Woodward, *Rafael Carrera*, pp. 31–39.

4. Rodríguez, *Cádiz Experiment*, pp. 236–37.

5. Pérez Brignoli, *Brief History of Central America*, pp. 48, 82.

6. For an excellent analysis of the impact of war on economic development of El Salvador in the nineteenth century see Lindo-Fuentes, *Weak Foundations*, pp. 35–61.

7. For the early independence period, the following statistics on battles and war casualties, 1824–42, have been compiled by Lindo-Fuentes (*Weak Foundations*, p. 50) from information in Marure, *Efemérides*, pp. 141 and 154:

Country	Number of battles	Men killed
Guatemala	51	2,291
El Salvador	40	2,546
Honduras	27	682
Nicaragua	17	1,203
Costa Rica	5	144

8. Molina Chocano, *Estado liberal*, pp. 106–54. In 1872, the Guatemalan government was turned down when it tried to float an international bond issue to construct the railroad between Guatemala City and the Pacific port of San José (McCreery, *Desarrollo económico*, pp. 61–62). Even with an external facade of stability, venture capitalists often required government guarantees, cash advances, land concessions, and in some cases forced labor, in return for railroad construction.

9. Castro Sánchez, "Privatización de la tierra," pp. 207–30.

10. Browning, *El Salvador*, pp. 210–11.

11. Gutiérrez was deposed by General Regalado in 1898 (Kerr, "Role of the Coffee Industry," pp. 80–113).

12. Walter, "Trade and Development," p. 63.

13. Wheelock, *Imperialismo y dictadura*, p. 105. The last of the

nineteenth-century Conservative presidents was Roberto Sacasa (1889–93) from León, who was said to have been mistrusted by the elite from Granada.

14. Bermann, *Under the Big Stick*, p. 124.

15. Lanuza, Vázquez, Barahona, and Chamorro, *Economía y sociedad*, pp. 79, 124. It would be very interesting to examine actions taken by the *ayuntamiento* of Managua during the period of early Conservative rule to verify which level of the state was actively promoting coffee in the Sierras de Managua south of town. What is commonly attributed to the president of the country may have really been actions taken by the local Managua elite, which we know from property records possessed some 133 cattle haciendas outside of town.

16. Lanuza quotes from Don José Madriz, ibid., p. 84.

17. Teplitz, "Political and Economic Foundations," pp. 182–89.

18. Despite the strengthening of national state institutions under Zelaya, enforcement of labor contracts continued to be a serious problem for coffee growers.

19. Brand, "Background of Capitalistic Underdevelopment," p. 125.

20. Finney documents how the executive branch in Tegucigalpa not only overrode *municipio* and department governments in defense of the Rosario Mining Company, but it also overturned decisions of the national judiciary (*In Quest of El Dorado*, pp. 392–413).

21. It remains unclear how the merchant class of Choluteca was able to secure privately titled lands in a highland area that was practically dominated by peasant agriculture. To answer the question, a more careful study of land documents would have to be done. In particular, were the large coffee farms reported in the 1914–15 survey on the lands previously occupied by haciendas that had supplied the mines of El Corpus? In this case, the merchants could have simply purchased these lands from the former owners. Or was there a political struggle to turn *ejidal* lands into private property? Indeed, this would fit the more general pattern of coffee expansion in El Salvador, Nicaragua, and Guatemala. One bit of evidence that suggests political maneuvering is that in 1907, Concepción de María, an area that was still *ejidal* in the survey, and El Corpus, a capitalist *municipio* by 1914–15, were split into two separate *municipios*. See Boyer, "Simple Commodity Production," p. 70.

22. From the available records it is clear that in Honduras a national coffee elite did not emerge to influence the formation of the national state during the late nineteenth and early twentieth centuries. The empirical focus on coffee alone, however, prevents this study from uncovering the forces that did shape the evolution of the Honduran state. The theory of state formation developed here might shed light on what occurred in Honduras during the first three decades of the twentieth century. To apply this theory to the Honduran case, one would have to examine the municipal records of commercial townships located in zones other than the peasant-dominated coffee areas. It would be interesting to see to what extent local elites in the North Coast, cattle barons in Olancho, and mining company officials or merchants in the major mining centers may have played a positive role in the development of national state institutions in Tegucigalpa, using their local

townships as a springboard for national action. I look forward to seeing the results of Honduran historian Dario Euraque's inquiries, which appear on the verge of solving this question.

23. After Justo Rufino Barrios died, his widow sold El Porvenir to the German consortium Compañia Hamburguesa de Plantaciones; in 1890, El Porvenir had 1,025,000 trees, the largest number of any *finca* in the country. Alejandro Sinibaldi, who served as interim president for five days in 1885, was from an important grower family that had large plantations in the department of Sololá in 1890 (Secretario de Estado de Guatemala, *Memoria de fomento, 1891*, "Estadística de café, 1890," pp. 5–153).

24. The Meléndez family owned the largest sugar operation in El Salvador along with coffee farms and a *beneficio*, and the Quiñonez family owned coffee farms. Alfonso Quiñonez was a brother-in-law of Carlos Meléndez.

25. The 1892 directory listed Tomás Martínez (1859–67) as a coffee exporter and importer of general merchandise, Pedro Joaquín Chamorro (1875–79) as an export-import merchant, and Adán Cárdenas (1883–87) as a coffee exporter. Apparent relatives of Vicente Cuadra (1871–75) appear in the directory with Virginia Cuadra & Sons as coffee exporters and Asunción Cuadra and José de la Paz Cuadra are listed as coffee growers (Bureau of the American Republics, *Commercial Directory of Nicaragua*, pp. 167–77).

26. In 1915 Luís Bográn is listed as growing 114 acres of coffee in the department of Santa Barbara. República de Honduras, *Memoria de fomento 1914–15*.

27. Vega Carballo, *Poder político*, p. 47.

28. For a critical overview of the sometimes stormy evolution of electoral politics in Costa Rica and a choice-theoretical analysis of why politicians opted for more inclusive electoral procedures and divisions of power after the 1948 civil war, see Lehoucq, "Origins of Democracy in Costa Rica."

29. Although José Figueres was not from Costa Rica's coffee elite, he acquired a large coffee farm and *beneficio* in Turrialba after his first term in office. If his elected terms of office are counted, it could be said that coffee barons have held the presidency for fifteen out of twenty regular terms during this century, though frequently coffee elite presidents have had primary professions other than directly managing their family's coffee estates, *beneficios*, or export businesses.

30. Two Reynas, who may or may not have been related to the general, appear as owners of coffee *fincas* in the department of San Marcos, Mariano B. Reyna, who had a *finca* with 7,704 trees, and Eugenio Reyna M., who had a *finca* with 16,000 trees (Secretario de Estado de Guatemala, *Memoria de fomento 1892*, "Estadística de café").

31. Ibid., p. 31.

32. With the notable exception of 1950–54, when the coffee elite lost control over the national government, Guatemala has been ruled indirectly, usually with military officers occupying the presidential palace.

33. These are estimates of coffee properties in the hands of Sandinista government in 1982 (Gariazzo, "El subsistema del café," Tables 5 and 16).

34. Jeffrey Gould has charted the development of what he calls the

"myth of *ladino* Nicaragua," which he suggests was forged into a dominant attitude during the late nineteenth century. Lawyers, who assisted coffee growers in the takeover of Matagalpa Indian lands, used the argument that the people of Nicaragua were "naturally *ladino*" to delegitimize traditional Indian claims on territory. Later the view became generally accepted or "hegemonic." By individualizing the peasantry, it stripped that class of a strategy of community resistance rooted in the Indian past ("The Limits of Ladinoization").

Chapter 7

1. Palmer examines the ideological creation of the nation through the manipulation of symbols. For example, he shows how during the late nineteenth century national heroes were created from real historical figures whose public images became national through newspaper articles, novels, public monuments, national holidays, and the like, providing citizens of diverse backgrounds and experiences who lived within the jurisdictional boundaries claimed by a state the identity of belonging to a single nation, thereby empowering and legitimating institutions of the national state. Palmer also demonstrates how politicians used the railroad as a symbol of national progress ("Liberal Discipline").

2. That the model adopted as the "national" one was not inevitable but contingent upon which group of growers was able to take command of the state in its formative phase is supported for the Guatemalan case by an essay written for the Sociedad Económica in 1887 by Luis Wolfram, who served as an agricultural surveyor for Guatemalan governments from 1861 until the late 1880s. Wolfram praises the slower development of the coffee economy under the Carrera government, which allowed smaller-scale producers to participate, and he attacks the forced labor and large plantation model developed under Barrios, which according to Wolfram worked to the detriment of personal liberty and against the incentive to contribute one's greatest effort to improving production, undermining the long-run viability of Guatemalan coffee production. Thanks to Lowell Gudmundson for sending me this document, Wolfram, *Principios elementales*.

3. See Gould, "Limits of Ladinoization."

Chapter 8

1. Twentieth-century Central America provides numerous cases for comparative study that would shed further light on social evolutionary processes. An extreme test of the hypothesis that local social formations matter would be to reexamine the history of banana cultivation, which is normally viewed as an implantation from outside the region of an alien technology controlled by powerful international corporations. Such a comparative study of bananas would broaden the analysis beyond the typical national

state/banana company observations and include the role of noncompany banana producers, agrarian structures surrounding banana enclaves, the social origins of workers on the banana plantations, and local governments' interplay with banana companies. Dario Euraque has proven the importance of local structures in the North Coast of Honduras, but parallel work on the banana zones of Guatemala, Costa Rica, and, even, Nicaragua should be undertaken for comparative analysis with the Honduras case. See Euraque, "Merchants and Industrialists in Northern Honduras."

2. As Chapter 5 pointed out, similar action was taken during World War I, but the repercussions were much less notable because of the late entry of the United States in the conflict and the quick return of assets to former owners after the war.

3. The process has been best documented for the Northern Transversal Strip of Guatemala, where infrastructure was put in to develop oil fields and the roads opened the possibility of cattle ranching and logging, which were taken advantage of by those close to the Lucas García regime. Also, eastern Matagalpa was developed by the Somoza government for cattle ranching, and outside funds were used to build roads and carry out evictions in the area (Williams, *Export Agriculture*, pp. 129–51).

4. During certain periods, Honduran ranchers had an edge in winning the disputes; in other periods, peasants were in a more favorable position to pressure the national land agency (ibid., pp. 124–29, 179–82).

5. This policy of the Costa Rican government has sometimes led to disputes with previous inhabitants of a zone. When I visited the Huetar Norte of Costa Rica in 1985, peasants who had lived for many years in an area outside of the town of San Rafael de Guatuso in Alajuela Province complained that the national government gave priority to settlers from the Central Valley and tended to overlook locals when they applied for tracts of land or loans.

6. Edelman, *Logic of the Latifundio*, pp. 348–50.

7. World prices are yearly average New York spot prices for Santos number 4s taken from Commodity Research Bureau, *Commodity Yearbook*, 1942. Nicaraguan prices are from Dirección General de Estadísticos y Censos, *El café en Nicaragua*, p. 52. Costa Rican prices are from Dirección General de Estadísticos y Censos, *Boletín de exportación de café*, Table 11, p. 13.

8. McCreery, "Odious Feudalism," p. 110.

9. Anderson, *Matanza*, p. 12. For a comparative analysis of ethnicity and community in three uprisings in El Salvador, 1833 (Nonualco), 1932 (Izalco), and 1970s (Aguilares), see Kincaid, "Peasants into Rebels."

10. McClintock, *American Connection*, 1:110.

11. Acuña Ortega, "Clases sociales," p. 187.

12. Coffee processors and exporters tried to preempt the organization of coffee growers by inviting small producers to become members of the Cámara de Cafetaleros and by proposing legislation in 1930 that would regulate relations between growers and processors (ibid., pp. 188–89).

13. In 1933 growers pressured lawmakers into creating the Instituto de Defensa del Café and a state board for fixing the prices paid for mature

berries and regulating the profit margins of *beneficios*; in addition, the International Bank was instructed to build state-owned *beneficios* that would provide an alternative for small producers. The coffee elite reacted to the legislation and later was successful in watering it down with amendments and in gaining influence in the Instituto de Defensa del Café and the National Marketing Board.

Bibliography

This list of articles, books, pamphlets, and documentary sources is organized according to geographical area, beginning with the Central American region as a whole and then proceeding to each of the separate countries from north to south. Other works not dealing with a specific geographic area are listed separately at the end of the bibliography.

Central America

Alvarado, Juan Antonio. *Tratado de caficultura práctica*. Vol. 2. Guatemala: Gobierno Nacional de Guatemala, 1936.

Arbingast, Stanley, et al. *Atlas of Central America*. Austin, Tex.: Bureau of Business Research, 1979.

Brockett, Charles. *Land, Power, and Poverty*. Boston: Unwyn Hyman, 1988.

Bulmer-Thomas, Victor. *The Political Economy of Central America since 1920*. Cambridge: Cambridge University Press, 1987.

Bynum, Mary. *The World's Coffee Exports*. Washington, D.C.: U.S. Government Printing Office, 1930.

Cardoso, C. F. S., and Héctor Pérez Brignoli. *Centroamérica y la economía occidental (1520–1930)*. San José: Editorial de la Universidad de Costa Rica, 1977.

Childs, James. *The Memorias of the Republics of Central America and of the Antilles*. Washington, D.C.: U.S. Government Printing Office, 1932.

Dunkerley, James. *Power in the Isthmus*. London: Verso, 1988.

Fernández Molina, José Antonio. "Colouring the World in Blue: The Indigo Boom and the Central American Market, 1750–1810." Ph.D. dissertation, University of Texas at Austin, 1992.

————. "El poder del mercado y el mercado del poder: Comerciantes y cabildos provinciales en la Centroamérica del siglo xviii." Heredia: Escuela de Historia de la Universidad Nacional de Costa Rica, 1993.

Flemion, Philip F. *Historical Dictionary of El Salvador*. Metuchen, N.J.: Scarecrow Press, 1972.

Griffin, Keith. *Land Concentration and Rural Poverty*. New York: Holmes and Meier, 1976.

Griffith, William. "The Historiography of Central America Since 1830." *Hispanic American Historical Review* 40 (Nov. 1960): 548–69.

Gudmundson, Lowell. "Lord and Peasant in the Making of Modern Central America." In A. E. Huber and Frank Safford, eds., *Agrarian Structures and Political Power in Latin America*. Pittsburgh: University of Pittsburgh Press, forthcoming.

Juarros, Domingo. *Statistical and Commercial History of the Kingdom of Guatemala*. London: John Hearne, 1823.

Macleod, Murdo, and Robert Wasserstrom. *Spaniards and Indians in Southeastern Mesoamerica: Essays on the History of Ethnic Relations*. Lincoln: University of Nebraska Press, 1983.

Martínez Peláez, Severo. *La patria del criollo*. San José: Editorial Universitaria Centroamericana, 1985.

Marure, Alejandro. *Efemérides de los hechos notables acaecidos en la República de Centro América*. Guatemala: Tipografía Nacional, 1895.

Mendioróz, Luciano. *Atlas de Centro-América*. N.p.: N.p., 1912.

Monroe, Dana. *The Five Republics of Central America*. New York: Oxford University Press, 1918.

Paige, Jeffery. "Coffee and Politics in Central America." Ann Arbor: Center for Research on Social Organization, 1985.

Parker, Franklin. *The Central American Republics*. London: Royal Institute of International Affairs, 1964.

Pelupessy, Wim, ed. *Perspectives on the Agro-Export Economy in Central America*. Pittsburgh: University of Pittsburgh Press, 1991.

Pérez Brignoli, Héctor. *A Brief History of Central America*. Berkeley: University of California Press, 1989.

———. "Reckoning with the Central American Past: Economic Growth and Political Issues." Working Paper 160. Washington, D.C.: Wilson Center, 1984.

Rodríguez, Mario. *The Cádiz Experiment in Central America, 1808 to 1826*. Berkeley: University of California Press, 1978.

SIECA. *Compendio estadístico Centroamericano*, Guatemala: Secretaría de Integración Económico Centroamericano, 1981.

———. *Desarrollo integrado de Centroamérica en la presente década*. Buenos Aires: Banco Interamericano de Desarrollo, 1973.

Solano, Francisco. "Tierra, comercio, y sociedad: Un análisis de la estructura social agraria Centroamericana durante el siglo XVIII." *Revista de Indias* 31 (July–Dec. 1971): 311–65.

Squier, Ephraim George. *The States of Central America*. New York: Harper & Brothers, 1858.

Stone, Samuel Z. *The Heritage of the Conquistadors*. Lincoln: University of Nebraska Press, 1990.

Torres Rivas, Edelberto. *Interpretación del desarrollo social Centroamericano*. 7th ed. San José: EDUCA, 1981.

U. S. Department of Agriculture. "Coffee." *Foreign Agricultural Circular*, Sept. 1986.

Williams, Robert G. *Export Agriculture and the Crisis in Central America*. Chapel Hill: University of North Carolina Press, 1986.

Woodward, Ralph Lee, Jr. *Central America: A Nation Divided*. Oxford: Oxford University Press, 1985.

Wortman, Miles. *Government and Society in Central America, 1680–1840*. New York: Columbia University Press, 1982.

Young, John Parke. *Central American Currency and Finance*. Princeton: Princeton University Press, 1925.

Guatemala

ANACAFE. *Directorio de productores de café*. Guatemala: ANACAFE, 1984.

———. *Leyes vigentes sobre café*. Guatemala: ANACAFE, 1984.

Archivo General de Centroamérica. "Lista de fincas productoras de café que son propiedades de ciudadanos o compañías alemanes." B/Legajo 4156, 1942.

———. "Protócolos de hacienda." 1891.

———. "Protócolos de hacienda del supremo gobierno 1831–37."

Asociación Nacional del Café. *Proyecto del desarrollo tecnológico del pequeño productor*. Guatemala: ANACAFE, 1984.

Bataillon, Claude, and Ivan Lebot. "Migración interna y empleo agrícola temporal en Guatemala." *Estudios sociales Centroamericanos* 13 (Jan.–Apr. 1976): 35–67.

Biechler, Michael J. "The Regionalization of Coffee Culture in Guatemala." *Revista geográfica* 77 (Dec. 1972): 33–55.

Carmack, Robert, John Early, and Chris Lutz, eds. *The Historical Demography of Highland Guatemala*. Albany: State University of New York Press, 1982.

Castellanos Cambranes, Julio. *Agrarismo en Guatemala*. Guatemala: Serviprensa, 1986.

———. *Café y campesinos en Guatemala, 1853–1897*. Guatemala City: Editorial Universitaria de Guatemala, 1985.

———. *Coffee and Peasants: The Origins of the Modern Plantation Economy in Guatemala, 1853–1897*. Stockholm: Tryckop, 1985.

———. "Los empresarios agrarios modernos y el estado." *Mesoamérica* 10 (Dec. 1985): 243–91.

———. *El imperialismo alemán en Guatemala*. Guatemala: Instituto de Investigaciones Económicas y Sociales de la Universidad de San Carlos, 1977.

———. *Introducción a la historia agraria de Guatemala 1500–1900*. Guatemala: Serviprensa Centroamericana, 1986.

———. "Sistemas de producción agrícola latifundio-minifundio: el cultivo del café en Guatemala." *Mesoamérica* 1 (Jan.–June 1980): 186–95.

Castillo Cordero, Clemente, and Juan Alfredo García. *Atlas político-administrativo de la república de Guatemala*. Guatemala: Ministerio de Educación Pública, 1953.

Cazali Avila, Augusto. "El desarrollo del cultivo del café y su influencia en el regimen del trabajo agricola epoca de la reforma liberal (1871–1885)."

Anuario de estudios Centroamericanos, 1st ed. San José: Universidad de Costa Rica, 1976.

Chandler, David. "Juan José Aycinena, 19th Century Guatemalan Conservative." Master's thesis, Tulane University, 1965.

Cifuentes Medina, Edelberto. "De la producción de grana a la producción cafetalera." *Economía* 79(Jan.–Mar. 1984): 1–14.

Contreras Marín, Bayron. "Evaluación y perspectivas agro-socioeconómicas del sector cafetalero." Master's thesis, Universidad de San Carlos, Guatemala, 1987.

Del Cid Fernandez, Enrique. "Llegada de los primeros alemanes a Guatemala." Typescript. Guatemala City, 1969.

de León, Carlos Umberto. *Mi defensa de café*. Guatemala: Asociación General de Agricultores, 1982.

Dessaint, Alain. "Effects of the Hacienda and Plantation Systems on Guatemala's Indians." *América Indígena* 22 (Oct. 1962): 323–54.

Dirección General de Estadística. *Censo agropecuario de 1950*. Guatemala: DGEG, 1954.

———. *Censo agropecuario de 1979*. Guatemala: DGEG, 1983.

———. *Informe en el ramo de agricultura 1945*. Guatemala: DGEG, 1951.

Dirección General de Estadístico y Censos. *Censo agropecuario de 1964*. Guatemala: DGECG, 1966.

Dominguez, Mauricio. "Desarrollo de los aspectos tecnológicos y científicos de la industria del café en Guatemala, 1830–1930." *Estudios Centroamericanos* 3 (1977): 97–114.

Estrada Monroy, Augustín. *Datos para la historia de la iglesia en Guatemala*. Guatemala: Sociedad de Geografía e Historia de Guatemala, 1974.

Estrada Paniagua, Felipe. *Recopilación de las leyes de la república de Guatemala*. Guatemala: Tipografía de Arturo Signere y Co., 1909.

Federal Bureau of Investigation. *Totalitarian Activities: Guatemala . . . Today*. Washington, D.C., July 1944. (Declassified Sept. 21, 1972)

Fernández Molina, José Antonio. "La formación de una hacienda cafetalera en 1845: Un intento de trasmisión de tecnología agrícola." *Revista de historia* 14 (July–Dec. 1986): 199–214.

Fry, Michael G. "Liberal Land Reform in Guatemala and Peasant Reaction in La Montaña, 1821–1838." Master's thesis, Tulane University, 1980.

Gall, Francis. *Diccionario geográfico de Guatemala*. Guatemala: Instituto Geográfico Nacional, 1980.

Garlant, Julia V. "Developmental Aspects of Barrios' Agrarian Program, Guatemala, 1871–1885." M.A. thesis, Tulane University, 1968.

Gobierno de Guatemala. *Anuario estadístico de 1894*. Guatemala: Tipografía Nacional, 1895.

———. *Guía de forasteros de Guatemala para el año 1853*. Guatemala: Government Printing Office, 1853.

———. *Memoria de la secretaria de fomento de 1885*. Guatemala: Tipografía Nacional, 1886.

———. *Memoria que la sección de estadística presenta á la secretaría de fomento 1892*. Guatemala: Encuadernación y Tipografía Nacional, 1893.

Griffin, Keith B. *Land Concentration and Rural Poverty.* New York: Holmes and Meier, 1976.

Handy, Jim. *Gift of the Devil: A History of Guatemala.* Boston: South End Press, 1984.

Herrick, Thomas R. "Economic and Political Development in Guatemala during the Barrios Period—1871 to 1885." Ph.D. dissertation, University of Chicago, 1967.

Holleran, Mary. *Church and State in Guatemala.* New York: Columbia University Press, 1949.

Immerman, Richard H. *The CIA in Guatemala: The Foreign Policy of Intervention.* Austin: University of Texas Press, 1982.

Instituto Nacional de Estadística. *Anuario estadístico 1985.* Guatemala: INEG, 1987.

———. *Directorio nacional de establecimientos industriales 1986.* Guatemala: INEG, 1987.

———. *Estadísticas agropecuarias continuas 1985.* Guatemala: INEG, 1986.

Instituto Nacional de Transformación Agraria. *Monografía de las fincas nacionales.* Guatemala: INTA, 1981.

International Court of Justice. *Pleadings, Oral Arguments, Documents: The Nottebohm Case, Lichtenstein v. Guatemala.* The Hague: International Court of Justice, 1956.

Jonas, Susanne. *The Battle for Guatemala.* Boulder: Westview Press, 1991.

Jonas, Susanne, and David Tobis. *Guatemala.* Berkeley: North American Congress for Latin America, 1974.

Jones, Chester Lloyd. *Guatemala: Past and Present.* New York: Russell & Russell, 1940.

La Guardia, García. *El pensamiento liberal de Guatemala.* San José: EDUCA, 1977.

López de León, Edgar. *Situación del cultivo del café en Guatemala.* Guatemala: ANACAFE, 1987.

Lovell, George. *Conquest and Survival in Colonial Guatemala: A Historical Geography of the Chuchumatán Highlands, 1500–1821.* Montreal: McGill-Queen's University Press, 1985.

McBryde, Felix. *Cultural and Historical Geography of Southwest Guatemala.* Washington, D.C.: Smithsonian Institution, 1948.

Mariscal Ordóñez, Emilio. "Desarrollo del cultivo del café en Guatemala." *Revista cafetalera,* June 1986, pp. 7–19.

Martínez Peláez, Severo. *La patria del criollo.* San José: EDUCA, 1985.

McCreery, David J. "Coffee and Class: The Structure of Development in Liberal Guatemala." *Hispanic American Historical Review* 56 (1976): 438–60.

———. "Debt Servitude in Rural Guatemala, 1876–1936." *Hispanic-American Historical Review* 63 (1983): 735–59.

———. *Desarrollo económico y política nacional: el ministerio de fomento de Guatemala, 1871–1885.* Monograph Series No. 1, Centro de Investigaciones Regionales de Mesoamérica, Guatemala: Serviprensa Centroamericana, 1981.

————. "An Odious Feudalism: Mandamiento Labor and Commercial Agriculture in Guatemala, 1858–1920." *Latin American Perspectives* 48 (Winter 1986): 99–117.

————. "Rural Guatemala, 1760–1940." Manuscript, History Department, Georgia State University, 1991.

Méndez Montenegro, Julio Cesar. *444 años de legislación agraria 1513–1957*. Guatemala: Imprenta Universitaria, 1958.

Ministerio de Fomento. *Boletín de la dirección general de estadística*. Guatemala: Tipografía Nacional, 1922.

Moore, Richard E. *Historical Dictionary of Guatemala*. Metuchen, N.J.: Scarecrow Press, 1973.

Mosk, Sanford. "The Coffee Economy of Guatemala, 1850–1918: Development and Signs of Instability." *Inter-American Economic Affairs* 9 (Winter 1955): 6–20.

Nañez Falcon, Guillermo. "Erwin Paul Dieseldorff, German Entrepreneur in the Alta Verapaz of Guatemala, 1889–1937." Ph.D. dissertation, Tulane University, 1970.

————. "German Contributions to the Economic Development of the Alta Verapaz of Guatemala, 1865–1900." Masters thesis, Tulane University, 1961.

Orellana, Rene A., et al. "Migraciones internas y estructura agraria: El caso de Guatemala." *Estudios sociales Centroamericanos* 12 (Sept.–Dec. 1975): 41–91.

Pan American Union. *Guatemala: General Descriptive Data*. Washington, D.C.: Pan American Union, 1919.

Quiñonez, José A. *Directorio general de la república de Guatemala*. Guatemala: Tipografía Nacional, 1930.

República de Guatemala. *Estadística Nacional*. Guatemala: Dirección General de Estadística, 1927.

Rodríguez, Mario. *The Cádiz Experiment in Central America, 1808 to 1826*. Berkeley: University of California Press, 1978.

Rubio Sanchez, Manuel. "Breve historia del café en Guatemala." *Anales de la sociedad de geografía e historia de Guatemala* 27 (Mar. 1953–Dec. 1954): 169–238.

————. "Historia del cultivo del café en Guatemala." Vol. 3. Typescript, Guatemala, 1968.

Sapper, Karl. "Die Alta Verapaz." *Mittheilungen der geographischen gesellschaft in Hamburg* 17 (1901): 78–224.

Schmid, Lester. "The Role of Migratory Labor in the Economic Development of Guatemala." Ph.D. dissertation, University of Wisconsin, 1967.

Schmit, Patricia. "Guatemalan Political Parties: Development of Interest Groups, 1820–1822." Ph.D. dissertation, Tulane University, 1977.

Secretaria de Estado de Guatemala. *Memoria que la secretaria de estado en el despacho de fomento presenta a la asamblea legislativa de la republica de Guatemala en sus sesiones ordinarias de 1891*. "Estadísticas de café, 1890," pp. 5–153. Guatemala: Fomento, 1891.

Secretaria de Fomento. *Memoria de la secretaria de fomento de la república de Guatemala presentada a la asamblea legislativa en 1889.* Guatemala: Tipografía la Union, 1889.

Smith, Carol A., ed. *Guatemalan Indians and the State, 1540 to 1988.* Austin: University of Texas Press, 1990.

Smith, Robert S. "Indigo Production and Trade in Colonial Guatemala." *Hispanic American Historical Review* 39 (May 1959): 181–210.

Solano, Francisco. "La economía agraria de Guatemala 1768–72." *Revista de indias* 33 (Jan.–June 1971): 285–327.

Solís, Ignacio. *Memorias de la casa de moneda de Guatemala y del desarrollo económico del país.* Vol. 3B. Guatemala: Impresos Industriales, 1979.

Strobeck, Susan. "The Political Activities of Some Members of the Aristocratic Families of Guatemala, 1821–1839." Master's thesis, Tulane University, 1958.

U.S. Agency for International Development. *Guatemalan Agricultural Sector Review.* Guatemala: USAID, 1987.

Van Oss, Adriann C. *Catholic Colonialism: A Parish History of Guatemala, 1524–1821.* Cambridge: Cambridge University Press, 1986.

Villedas Rodas, Miguel. *Mi lucha por el café de Guatemala.* Guatemala: Tipografía Nacional de Guatemala, 1965.

Wagner, Regina. "Actividades empresariales de los alemanes en Guatemala, 1850–1920." *Mesoamerica* 13 (June 1987): 87–123.

Watanabe, John. "Cambios económicos en Santiago Chimaltenango, Guatemala." *Mesoamérica* 2 (1981): 20–41.

Wolfram, Luis. *Principios elementales de la economía social sobre la civilización de los pueblos y los progresos de la agricultura.* Guatemala: Tipografía la Estrella, 1887.

Woodward, Ralph Lee, Jr. *Class Privilege and Economic Development: the Consulado de Comercio of Guatemala, 1793–1871.* Chapel Hill: University of North Carolina Press, 1966.

———. *Rafael Carrera and the Emergence of the Republic of Guatemala, 1821–1871.* Athens: University of Georgia Press, 1993.

El Salvador

Anderson, Thomas. *Matanza: El Salvador's Communist Revolt of 1932.* Lincoln: University of Nebraska Press, 1971.

Asociación Cafetalera de El Salvador. "Primer censo nacional del café." San Salvador: Asociación Cafetalera de El Salvador, 1940.

Aubey, Robert T. "Entrepreneurial Formation in El Salvador." *Explorations in Entrepreneurial History* 2d ser., 6 (1969): 268–85.

Baloyra, Enrique. *El Salvador in Transition.* Chapel Hill: University of North Carolina Press, 1982.

Browning, David. *El Salvador: Landscape and Society.* Oxford: Clarendon Press, 1971.

Burke, Melvin. "El sistema de plantación y la proletarización de trabajo agrícola en El Salvador." *Estudios Centroamericanos* 31 (Sept.–Oct. 1976): 473–86.

Burns, E. Bradford. "The Modernization of Underdevelopment: El Salvador, 1858–1931." *Journal of Developing Areas* 18 (Apr. 1984): 293–316.

Colindres, Eduardo. *Fundamentos económicos de la burguesía salvadoreña.* San Salvador: Universidad Centroamericana, 1977.

――――. "La tenencia de la tierra en El Salvador." *Estudios Centroamericanos* 31 (Sept.–Oct. 1976): 463–72.

Dirección General de Estadística. *Anuario estadístico de 1912.* San Salvador: Tipografía la Unión, 1913.

――――. *Anuario estadístico de la república de El Salvador correspondiente a 1949.* San Salvador: DGES, 1950.

Dirección General de Estadísticos y Censos. *Anuario estadístico de 1969.* San Salvador: DGECS, 1970.

――――. *Censo agropecuario de 1950.* San Salvador: DGECS, 1954.

――――. *Compendio del segundo censo nacional de café.* San Salvador: DGECS, 1961.

――――. *Segundo censo agropecuario 1961.* San Salvador: DGECS, 1967.

――――. *Tercer censo nacional agropecuario 1971.* San Salvador: DGECS, 1974.

Dunkerley, James. *The Long War.* London: Verso, 1982.

Federal Bureau of Investigation. *El Salvador . . . Today.* Washington, D.C.: FBI, 1943.

Fowler, William R., Jr. "Cacao, Indigo, and Coffee: Cash Crops in the History of El Salvador." *Research in Economic Anthropology* 8 (1987): 139–67.

Hewson, David C. "Agrarian Reform in El Salvador: Causes and Consequences." Unpublished paper, Guilford College, Dec. 1988.

Hill, A. J. *Report on Economic and Commercial Conditions in the Republic of El Salvador.* London: His Majesty's Stationery Office, 1939.

Kerr, Derek. "The Role of the Coffee Industry in the History of El Salvador, 1840–1906." Master's thesis, University of Calgary, 1977.

Kincaid, Douglas. "Peasants into Rebels: Community and Class in Rural El Salvador." *Society for the Comparative Study of Society and History* 1987, pp. 466–94.

Leitch, Adelaide. "Farming the Volcanoes of El Salvador." *Canadian Geographical Journal* 60 (Jan. 1960): 34–37.

Lindo-Fuentes, Héctor. *Weak Foundations.* Berkeley: University of California Press, 1991.

López, Lorenzo. *Estadística general de la república de El Salvador.* San Salvador: Ministerio de Educación, 1858.

López, Roberto. *The Nationalization of Foreign Trade in El Salvador: The Myths and Realities of Coffee.* Occasional Papers of the Latin American and Caribbean Center of Florida International University 16 (Mar. 1986).

Marroquín, Alejandro D. "Estudio sobre la crisis de los años treinta en El Salvador." *Anuario de estudios Centroamericanos* 3 (1977): 115–60.

McClintock, Michael. *The American Connection: State Terror and Popular Resistance in El Salvador*. London: Zed Books, 1985.

Meléndez, D. Pedro. *Memoria de los actos del poder ejecutivo*. San Salvador: Imprenta Nacional, 1884.

Menjívar, Rafael. *Acumulación originaria y el desarrollo del capitalismo en El Salvador*. San José: EDUCA, 1980.

Pan American Union. *General Descriptive Data on El Salvador*. Washington, D.C.: Pan American Union, 1917.

República de El Salvador. *Anuario estadístico de 1915*. San Salvador: Imprenta Nacional, 1915.

——— . *Anuario estadístico de 1921*. San Salvador: Imprenta Rafael Reyes, 1922.

Ruiz Granadino, Santiago. "Modernización agrícola en El Salvador." *Estudios Sociales Centroamericanos* 22 (Jan.–Apr. 1979): 71–95.

Simon, Laurence, and James Stephens. *El Salvador Land Reform, 1980–81*. Boston: Oxfam America, 1981.

Slutzky, Daniel, and Ester Slutzky. "El Salvador: Estructura de la explotación cafetalera." *Estudios Sociales Centroamericanos* (May–Aug. 1972): 101–25.

Smith, R. H. Tottenham. *Economic and Commercial Conditions in El Salvador*. London: Her Majesty's Printing Office, 1951.

Suay, José E. *Memoria de hacienda y crédito público*. San Salvador: Imprenta Nacional, 1915.

——— . *Memoria de hacienda y crédito público*. San Salvador: Imprenta Nacional, 1919.

United Nations Food and Agriculture Organization. *Coffee in Latin America: Colombia and El Salvador*. New York: United Nations, 1958.

Walter, Knut. "Trade and Development in an Export Economy: the Case of El Salvador, 1870–1914." Master's thesis, University of North Carolina–Chapel Hill, 1977.

Ward, L. A. *Blue Book of El Salvador, 1866–1912*. San Salvador: Latin American Publicity Bureau, 1916.

White, Alistair. *El Salvador*. New York: Praeger, 1973.

Willig, Richard Lee. "Urban Organization and Urban Rural Relations: A Case Study of Polarized Development in El Salvador." Ph.D. dissertation, University of California–Berkeley, 1974.

Wilson, Everett Alan. "The Crisis of National Integration in El Salvador, 1919–1935." Ph.D. dissertation, Stanford University, 1970.

Wise, Michael L. *Agrarian Reform in El Salvador: Process and Progress*. San Salvador: USAID, 1986.

Honduras

AHPROCAFE. "Informe sobre desplazados de guerra." Tegucigalpa: Asociación Hondureña de Productores de Café, 1987.

Arancibia C., Juan. *Honduras: Un estado nacional?* Tegucigalpa: Guaymuras, 1984.

Arias, Marco, ed. *Ramón Rosa: obra escogida.* Tegucigalpa: Guaymuras,
1980.

Baumeister, Eduardo. "La situación de la producción cafetalera en Honduras." Madison, Wisc.: Land Tenure Center, 1990.

Board of Trade. *Review of Commercial Conditions.* London: His Majesty's
Stationery Office, 1948.

Boyer, Jefferson. "Charisma, Martyrdom and Liberation in Southern Honduras." In Terence Evens and James Peacock, eds. *Transcendence and
Utopia,* pp. 115–58. London: JAI Press, 1990.

———. "Simple Commodity Production, Agrarian Capitalism, and Economic Rationality in Southern Honduras." Ph.D. dissertation, University
of North Carolina–Chapel Hill, 1982.

Brand, Charles. "The Background of Capitalistic Underdevelopment: Honduras to 1913." Ph.D. dissertation, University of Pittsburgh, 1972.

Coghill, J. P. *Honduras: Economic and Commercial Conditions.* London:
His Majesty's Stationery Office, 1954.

Del Cid, Rafael. *Formas de organización productiva en el agro Hondureño: La economía campesina y las empresas capitalistas.* San José:
CSUCA, 1982.

Dirección General de Censos y Estadísticas. *Anuario estadístico 1954.*
Tegucigalpa: Talleres Ariston, 1956.

———. *Censo agropecuario de 1952.* Tegucigalpa: DGCEH, 1954.

———. *Censo agropecuario de 1965–66.* Tegucigalpa: DGCEH, 1967.

———. *Censo agropecuario de 1974.* Tegucigalpa: DGCEH, 1978.

———. *Honduras en cifras.* Tegucigalpa: DGCEH, 1964.

Euraque, Dario. "Merchants and Industrialists in Northern Honduras: The
Making of a National Bourgeoisie in Peripheral Capitalism." Ph.D. dissertation, University of Wisconsin–Madison, 1990.

———. " 'Reforma liberal' en Honduras y la hipótesis de la 'oligarquía
ausente': 1870–1930." *Revista de historia* 23 (Jan.–June 1991): 7–56.

Finney, Kenneth V. *In Quest of El Dorado: Precious Metal Mining and the
Modernization of Honduras (1880–1900).* New York: Garland, 1987.

Gómez, Ena, et al. "Reforma liberal: Relaciones iglesia-estado 1887–1901."
B.A. thesis, Universidad Nacional Autónoma de Honduras, 1982.

Guevara-Escudero, José. "Nineteenth Century Honduras: A Regional Approach to the Economic History of Central America, 1839–1914." Ph.D.
dissertation, New York University, 1983.

Instituto Hondureño del Café. *Boletín estadístico 1976–1981.* Tegucigalpa:
IHCAFE, 1982.

———. *Manual de recomendaciones para cultivar café: Décimo aniversa-
rio 1970–1980.* Tegucigalpa: IHCAFE, 1980.

Latin America Bureau. *Honduras: State for Sale.* Birmingham, England:
Latin America Bureau, 1985.

Mendioróz, Luciano. Pequeño atlas de Centroamérica. San Salvador: Librería Salesiana, 1928.

Meza, Victor. *Antología del movimiento obrero Hondureño*. Tegucigalpa: Editorial Universitaria, 1981.

———. *Historia del movimiento obrero Hondureño*. Tegucigalpa: Guaymuras, 1980.

———. *Política y sociedad en Honduras*. Tegucigalpa: Guaymuras, 1981.

Molina Chocano, Guillermo. *Estado liberal y desarrollo capitalista en Honduras*. Tegucigalpa: Editorial Universitaria, 1982.

———. "La formación del estado y el origen minero-mercantil de la burguesía Hondureña." *Estudios Sociales Centroamericanos* 25 (1980): 55–89.

———. "Población, estructura productiva, y migraciones internas en Honduras (1950–1960)." *Estudios Sociales Centroamericanos* 12 (Sept.–Dec. 1975): 9–39.

Newson, Linda. *The Cost of Conquest: Indian Decline in Honduras under Spanish Rule*. Boulder: Westview Press, 1986.

Pan American Union. *Honduras: General Descriptive Data*. Washington, D.C.: Pan American Union, 1919.

Peckenham, Nancy, and Annie Street, eds. *Honduras: Portrait of a Captive Nation*. New York: Praeger, 1985.

Pérez Brignoli, Hector. "Economía y sociedad en Honduras durante el siglo XIX." *Estudios Sociales Centroamericanos* 11 (Sept.–Dec. 1973): 51–82.

Perry, G. R. *Directorio nacional de Honduras*. New York: Spanish-American Directories Co., 1899.

Posas, Mario. *Conflictos agrarios y organización campesina: Sobre los orígenes de las primeras organizaciones campesinas de Honduras*. Tegucigalpa: Editorial Universitaria, 1981.

———. *El movimiento campesino Hondureño*. Tegucigalpa: Guaymuras, 1981.

———. "Política estatal y estructura agraria en Honduras (1950–1978)." *Estudios Sociales Centroamericanos* 24 (Sept.–Dec. 1979): 37–116.

Posas, Mario, and Rafael del Cid. *La construcción del sector público y del estado nacional de Honduras, 1876–1979*. San José: Instituto Centroamericano de Administración Pública, 1981.

República de Honduras. "Lista general de los capitalistas de la república obligados a contribuir en el presente año al fondo de caminos." In *Memoria de fomento 1916–17*. Tegucigalpa: Tipo Litografía y Fotograbado Nacionales, 1918.

———. *Memoria de hacienda y crédito público*. Tegucigalpa: Tipo Litografía y Fotograbado Nacionales, 1937.

———. *Memoria del secretario del estado en el despacho de fomento, obras públicas, y agricultura presentada al congreso nacional, 1914–1915*. Tegucigalpa: Tipo Litografía y Fotograbado Nacionales, 1916.

———. *Primer anuario estadístico de 1888–89*. Tegucigalpa: Tipografía Nacional, 1893.

Rydings, D. G. *Report on Economic and Commercial Conditions in the Republic of Honduras*. London: His Majesty's Stationery Office, 1938.

Salomon, Leticia. *Militarismo y reformismo en Honduras*. Tegucigalpa: Guaymuras, 1982.

Seligson, Mitchell, and Edgar Nesman. "Land Titling in Honduras: An Impact Study in the Comayagua Region." Washington, D.C.: USAID, 1989.

Stockley, G. E. *Honduras: Economic and Commercial Conditions*. London: His Majesty's Stationery Office, 1951.

U.S. Agency for International Development. "Honduras Small Farmer Coffee Improvement." Project Number 522–0176. Washington, D.C.: 1981.

U.S. Department of Agriculture, Foreign Agricultural Service. "Honduras—Coffee Annual Report." Guatemala: Agricultural Attaché, 1987.

Nicaragua

Bermann, Karl. *Under the Big Stick*. Boston: South End Press, 1986.

Black, George. *Triumph of the People*. London: Zed Press, 1981.

Blandón, Alfonso. "Land Tenure in Nicaragua." Master's thesis, University of Florida, 1962.

Bureau of the American Republics. *Commercial Directory of Nicaragua*. Bulletin 51. Washington, D.C.: Bureau of the American Republics, 1892.

Charlip, Julie. "Coffee and Class in Pre-Revolutionary Nicaragua." Paper presented at the Latin American Studies Association, Los Angeles, Sept. 1992.

Colburn, Forrest. "Class, State, and Revolution in Rural Nicaragua: The Case of Los Cafeteleros." *Journal of Developing Areas* 18 (July 1984): 501–18.

———. *Post-Revolutionary Nicaragua: State, Class, and the Dilemmas of Agrarian Policy*. Berkeley: University of California Press, 1986.

Dirección General de Estadísticos y Censos. *El café en Nicaragua*. Managua: DGECN, 1961.

———. *Censo agropecuario de 1962–63*. Managua: DGECN, 1966.

Enríquez, Laura. *Harvesting Change: Labor and Agrarian Reform in Nicaragua, 1979–1990*. Chapel Hill: University of North Carolina Press, 1991.

Federal Bureau of Investigation. *Axis Penetration in Nicaragua*. Washington, D.C.: FBI, March 1942.

Gariazzo, Alicia. "El subsistema del café." Mimeo. Managua: INIES, 1982.

Gould, Jeffrey L. "The Limits of Ladinoization in Central America: A View from the Nicaraguan Highlands." Paper presented at the Latin American Studies Association meetings, Los Angeles, Sept. 1992.

———. *To Lead as Equals*. Chapel Hill: University of North Carolina Press, 1991.

———. "El trabajo forzoso y las comunidades indígenas Nicaragüenses." In Hector Pérez Brignoli and Mario Samper, eds. *El café en la historia de Centroamérica*. FLACSO, 1993.

Grossman, Richard. "Patria y Libertad: Sandino and the Development of Peasant Nationalism in Northern Nicaragua." Paper prepared for the

Seventeenth Latin American Studies Association International Congress, Los Angeles, 1992.

———. "Rural Rebellion in Northern Nicaragua: The Sandino Movement, 1927–33." Ph.D. proposal, University of Chicago, 1989.

Hill, Roscoe. *Fiscal Intervention in Nicaragua*. New York: Former Member of Nicaraguan High Commission, 1933.

Incer Barquero, Jaime. *Geografía básica de Nicaragua*. Managua: Librería y Editorial Recalde, 1972.

———. *Nueva geografía de Nicaragua*. Managua: Editorial Recalde, 1970.

Instituto Nacional de Estadísticas y Censos. *Directorio de establecimientos de la industria manufacturera*. Managua: República de Nicaragua, 1980.

Kaimowitz, David. "Nicaraguan Debates on Agrarian Structure and Their Implications for Agricultural Policy and the Rural Poor." *Journal of Peasant Studies* 14 (Oct. 1986): 100–117.

Lang, Guillermo. *Business Directory of Nicaragua, 1957–58*. New York: Consul General, 1958.

Lanuza, Alberto, Juan Vázquez, Amaru Barahona, and Amalia Chamorro. *Economía y sociedad en la construcción del estado en Nicaragua*. San José: Instituto Centroamericano de Administración Pública, 1983.

Levy, Paul. *Notas geográficas y económicas de la república de Nicaragua*. Paris: Librería Española de E. Denné Schmitz, 1873.

Meyer, Harvey K. *Historical Dictionary of Nicaragua*. Metuchen, N.J.: Scarecrow Press, 1972.

MIDINRA. *Diagnóstico socioeconómico del sector agropecuario*. Managua: CIERA, 1980.

Millett, Richard. *Guardians of the Dynasty*. Maryknoll, N.Y.: Orbis Books, 1977.

Ministerio de Economía, Industria, y Comercio. *Estadísticas del desarrollo agropecuario de Nicaragua, 1965–68*. Managua: MEIC, 1969.

Morales Fonseca, Manuel. *Nicaragua: Y por eso defendemos la revolución*. Managua: Centro de Investigaciones y Estudios de la Reforma Agraria, 1984.

Niederlein, Gustavo. *The State of Nicaragua*. Philadelphia: Philadelphia Commercial Museum, 1898.

Newson, Linda. *Indian Survival in Colonial Nicaragua*. Norman: University of Oklahoma Press, 1987.

North American Congress on Latin America. "Nicaragua." *Latin America and Empire Report*. 10 (Feb. 1976): 4–12.

Palmer, Mervyn G. *Through Unknown Nicaragua: The Adventures of a Naturalist on a Wild-Goose Chase*. London: Jarrolds, 1945.

Pan American Union. *Nicaragua: General Descriptive Data*. Washington, D.C.: Pan American Union, 1917

Playter, Harold. "Report on Nicaraguan Coffee." Corinto: American Consulate, May 26, 1926.

Radell, David. "An Historical Geography of Western Nicaragua." Ph.D. dissertation, University of California–Berkeley, 1969.

República de Nicaragua. "Censo cafetalero de 1909." *Boletín de estadística*, Mar. 1911, pp. 646–72.

―――. *Compendio estadístico 1965–1974*. Managua: Ministerio de Economía, Industria y Comercio, 1975.

Spalding, Rose. "Capitalists and Revolution: State-Private Sector Relations in Revolutionary Nicaragua (1979–1990)." Paper prepared for the Sixteenth International Conference of the Latin American Studies Association, Los Angeles, 1991.

Squier, Ephraim George. *Nicaragua: Its People, Scenery, Monuments, and the Proposed Interoceanic Canal*. New York: Appleton, 1852.

Stansifer, Charles L. "José Santos Zelaya: A New Look at Nicaragua's 'Liberal' Dictator." *Revista/Review Interamericana* 7 (Fall 1977): 468–85.

Steward, N. O. W. *Economic and Commercial Conditions in Nicaragua*. London: His Majesty's Stationery Office, 1951.

Teplitz, Benjamin I. "Political and Economic Foundations of Modernization in Nicaragua: The Administration of José Santos Zelaya, 1893–1909." Ph.D. dissertation, Howard University, 1973.

Walter, Knut. *The Regime of Anastasio Somoza, 1936–1956*. Chapel Hill: University of North Carolina Press, 1993.

Warnken, Philip F., et al. *An Analysis of Agricultural Production in Nicaragua*. Washington, D.C.: USAID, 1974.

Wheelock Román, Jaime. *Imperialismo y dictadura: Crisis de una formación social*. Mexico City: Siglo XXI, 1975.

Zalkin, Michael. "Rural Workers or Peasants: Agrarian Class Structure in Nicaragua." Paper prepared for the Fifteenth International Conference of the Latin American Studies Association, Miami, 1989.

Costa Rica

Acuña Ortega, Victor Hugo. "Clases sociales y conflicto social en la economía cafetalera Costarricense: Productores contra beneficiadores, 1932–36." *Revista de Historia: Historia, Problemas, y Perspectivas Agrarias en Costa Rica*, Special ed. Heredia: EUNA, 1985.

―――. "La ideología de los pequeños y medianos productores cafetaleros costarricenses (1900–1961)." *Revista de Historia* 16 (July–Dec. 1987): 137–59.

Acuña, Victor Hugo, and Ivan Molina. *Historia económica y social de Costa Rica (1750–1950)*, San José: Editorial Porvenir, 1991.

Aguilar, Justo, Carlos Barboza, and Jorge León. *Desarrollo tecnológico del cultivo del café*. San José: Consejo Nacional de Investigaciones Científicas y Tecnológicas, 1981.

Alvarenga Venutolo, Patricia. "Las explotaciones agropecuarias en los albores de la expansión cafetalera." *Revista de Historia* 14 (July–Dec. 1986): 115–32.

Araya Pochet, Carlos. "La minería y sus relaciones con la acumulación de capital y la clase dirigente de Costa Rica, 1821–1841." *Estudios Sociales Centroamericanos* 11 (May–Aug. 1973): 31–64.

Bourgois, Philippe. *Ethnicity at Work: Divided Labor on a Central American Plantation*. Baltimore: Johns Hopkins University Press, 1989.

Bureau of the American Republics. "Costa Rica." *Bulletin* 31 (Jan. 1892): 1–141.

Carcanholo, Reinaldo. "Las relaciones de producción en la actividad cafetalera en Costa Rica." *Revista Centroamericana de Economía* 4 (Jan.–Apr. 1981): 95–132.

Cardoso, C. F. S. "The Formation of the Coffee Estate in Nineteenth Century Costa Rica." In Kenneth Duncan and Ian Rutledge, eds., *Land and Labor in Latin America*, pp. 165–202. Cambridge: Cambridge University Press, 1977.

Castro Sánchez, Silvia. "Estado, privatización de la tierra y conflictos agrarios." *Revista de Historia* 21–22 (Jan.–Dec. 1990): 207–63.

Cooperativa Agrícola Industrial la Victoria. *Informes*. Grecia, Costa Rica: Consejo de Administración y Gerencia, Dec. 1981.

Creedman, Theodore S. *Historical Dictionary of Costa Rica*. Metuchen, N.J.: Scarecrow Press, 1977.

Dirección General de Estadística y Censos. *Atlas estadístico de Costa Rica No. 2*. San José: Instituto Nacional de Geografía, 1981.

———. *Atlas estadístico de 1950*. San José: Casa Gráfiza, 1953.

———. *Boletín de exportación de café, 1939–40*. San José: Imprenta Nacional, 1941.

———. *Censo agropecuario de 1950*. San José: Instituto Geográfico, 1953.

———. *Censo agropecuario de 1955*. San José: Instituto Geográfico, 1958.

———. *Censo agropecuario de 1963*. San José: DGECCR, 1965.

———. *Censo agropecuario de 1973*. San José: DGECCR, 1975.

———. "Estadística agrícola de 1883–84." in Oficina del Café, *Informe de Labores—1973*. San José: Oficina del Café, 1974.

———. *1864 censo de población*. San José: DGECCR, 1964.

Dirección General de Estadística de Costa Rica. *Censo agrícola de 1914*. San José: DGECR, 1915.

Dirección General de Estadística. *Informe de 1913*. San José: Tipografía Nacional, 1914.

Echeverria Morales, Guillermo. *Breve historia del café*. San José: Trejos Hermanos, 1972.

Edelman, Marc. *The Logic of the Latifundio*. Stanford: Stanford University Press, 1992.

Edelman, Marc and Joanne Kenen, eds., *The Costa Rican Reader*. New York: Grove Weidenfeld, 1989.

Federal Bureau of Investigation. *Totalitarian Activities: Costa Rica . . . Today*. Washington, D.C.: FBI, 1943.

Fernández Arias, Mario. "Evolución de la estructura de la tenencia de la tierra en Costa Rica: Café, caña de azucar, y ganadería (1950–1978)." Ph.D. dissertation, Universidad de Costa Rica, 1981.

Gudmundson, Lowell. *Costa Rica before Coffee*, New Orleans: Louisiana State University Press, 1987.

————. "La expropriación de los bienes de las obras pías en Costa Rica, 1805–1860: Un capítulo en la consolidación económica de una élite nacional." *Revista de Historia* 7 (July–Dec. 1978): 37–73.

————. "Peasant, Farmer, Proletarian: Class Formation in a Smallholder Coffee Economy, 1850–1950." *Hispanic American Historical Review* 69 (May 1989): 221–57.

Gutierrez Espeleta, Nelson. "Formación de la estructura agraria Costarricense." *Mesoamérica* 1 (Jan.–June 1980): 296–311.

Hall, Carolyn. *El café y el desarrollo histórico-geográfico de Costa Rica.* San José: Editorial Costa Rica y Universidad Nacional, 1978.

Henríquez Guerra, Pedro. "Costa Rica: el caso de café." Mimeo. San José: CSUCA, 1982.

Herrera Balharry, Eugenio. *Los alemanes y el estado cafetalero.* San José: Editorial Universidad Estatal a Distancia, 1988.

Instituto de Defensa del Café. "Censo Cafetero de 1935." *Revista del Instituto de Defensa del Café.* 4 and 5 (Dec.–Feb. 1936–37): 1–520.

Lehoucq, Fabrice Edouard. "Class Conflict, Political Crisis, and the Breakdown of Democratic Practices in Costa Rica: Reassessing the Origins of the 1948 Civil War." *Journal of Latin American Studies* 23 (Feb. 1991): 37–60.

————. "The Origins of Democracy in Costa Rica in Comparative Perspective." Ph.D. dissertation, Duke University, 1991.

Merz, Carlos. "Coyuntura y crisis en Costa Rica de 1924 a 1936." *Revista del Instituto de Defensa del Café* 5 (Jan.–Feb. 1937): 603–21.

————. "Estructura social y económica de la industria del café en Costa Rica." *Revista del Instituto de Defensa del Café* 5 (June–July 1937): 172–86.

Ministerio de Economía y Hacienda. *Atlas estadístico de Costa Rica.* San José: Casa Gráfica, 1953.

————. *Censo de la república de Costa-rica, levantado el 27 de noviembre de 1864.* San José: DGECCR, 1964.

Ministerio de Fomento. *Informe de la dirección general de estadística.* San José: Tipografía Nacional, 1916.

Molina Jiménez, Iván. *Costa Rica (1800–1850): El legado colonial y la génesis del capitalismo.* San José: Editorial de la Universidad de Costa Rica, 1991.

————. "Habilitadores y habilitados en el valle central de Costa Rica: El finaciamiento de la producción cafetalera en los inicios de su expansión (1838–1850)." *Revista de Historia* 16 (July–Dec. 1987): 85–131.

Niederlein, Gustavo. *The Republic of Costa Rica.* Philadelphia: Philadelphia Commercial Museum, 1899.

Nuhn, H. *Regionalización de Costa Rica.* San José: OFIPLAN, 1972.

Oficina del Café. *Informe de labores—1965.* San José: Oficina del Café, 1965.

————. *Informe de labores—1973.* San José: Oficina del Café, 1974.

————. *Leyes y reglamentos usuales sobre café.* San José: Oficina del Café, 1981.

————. "Registro de beneficiadores." *Circular No. 907.* San José: Oficina del Café, March 16, 1981.

Oficina Nacional de Estadística. *Anuario de 1907.* San José: Tipografía Nacional, 1909.

Palmer, Steven. "A Liberal Discipline: Inventing Nations in Guatemala and Costa Rica, 1870–1900." Ph.D. dissertation, Columbia University, 1990.

Pan American Union. *Costa Rica: General Descriptive Data.* Washington, D.C.: Pan American Union, 1919.

Peters Solórzano, Gertrud. "La formación territorial de las fincas grandes de café en la meseta central: estudio de la firma Tournon (1877–1955)." *Revista de Historia* 9–10 (Jan.–Dec. 1980): 81–159.

República de Costa Rica. *Anuario estadístico 1891.* San José: Tipografía Nacional, 1892.

————. *Anuario estadístico 1909.* San José: Tipografía Nacional, 1911.

————. *Anuario estadístico 1910.* San José: Tipografía Nacional, 1912.

————. *Informe de la dirección general de estadística año 1928.* San José: Imprenta Nacional, 1929.

————. *Resúmenes estadísticos años 1883 á 1910.* San José: Imprenta Nacional, 1912.

Rodríguez Saenz, Eugenia. "Las interpretaciones sobre la expansión de café en Costa Rica y el papel jugado por el crédito." *Revista de Historia* 18 (July–Dec. 1988): 163–86.

Rodríguez Saenz, Eugenia, and Iván Molina Jiménez. "Compraventas de cafetales y haciendas de café en el valle central de Costa Rica (1834–1850)." *Avances de investigación*, No. 52, San José: Universidad de Costa Rica, 1991.

Rojas Bolaños, Manuel. *Lucha social y guerra civil en Costa Rica 1940–48.* San José: Editorial Porvenir, 1980.

Román, Ana Cecilia. "Metodología y fuentes de las finanzas públicas de Costa Rica (1870–1948)." San José: Universidad de Costa Rica, 1992.

Rovira Mas, Jorge. *Estado y política económica en Costa Rica 1948–1970.* San José: Editorial Porvenir, 1982.

Salas Víquez, José Antonio. "El liberalismo positivista en Costa Rica: La lucha entre ladinos e indígenas en Orosi (1881–1884)." *Revista de Historia* 5 (July–Dec. 1977): 187–217.

————. "La privatización de los baldíos nacionales en Costa Rica durante el siglo XIX: Legislación y procedimientos utlilizados para su adjudicación." *Revista de Historia* 15 (Jan.–June 1987): 63–118.

Samper, Mario. "Coffee Households, and Haciendas during a Period of Crisis (1920–36): A Comparative Analysis." Paper presented at the Symposium on Coffee and Class Formation in Latin America, Bogotá, Colombia, 1988.

————. "Fuerzas sociopolíticas y procesos electorales en Costa Rica, 1921–1936." *Revista de Historia* Número Especial (1988): 157–221.

————. *Generations of Settlers: Rural Households and Markets on the Costa Rican Frontier, 1850–1935.* Boulder: Westview Press, 1990.

————. "Los productores directos en el siglo del café." *Revista de Historia* 7 (July–Dec. 1978): 123–81.

————. "El significado social de la caficultura costarricense y salvadoreña: Análisis histórico comparado a partir de los censos cafetaleros." Paper presented at the Symposium "Las sociedades agrarias centroamericanas" in Alajuela, Costa Rica, June 1990.

Seligson, Mitchell. *Agrarian Capitalism and the Transformation of Peasant Society: Coffee in Costa Rica.* Buffalo, N.Y.: Council on International Studies, 1975.

SEPSA. *Información básica del sector agropecuario y de recursos naturales renovables de Costa Rica.* San José: Ministerio de Agricultura, 1982.

Stone, Samuel Z. "Los cafetaleros: Un estudio de los cafetaleros de Costa Rica." *Revista de Ciencias Jurídicas* 13 (June 1969): 167–217.

————. *La dinastía de los conquistadores.* San José: EDUCA, 1975.

Vega Carballo, José Luís. "Estado y dominación social en Costa Rica." San José: Instituto de Investigaciones Sociales, 1980.

————. "El nacimiento de un régimen de burguesía dependiente: El caso de Costa Rica" (Part I). *Estudios Sociales Centroamericanos* 11 (May–Aug. 1973): 157–86.

————. "El nacimiento de un régimen de burguesía dependiente: El caso de Costa Rica." (Part II). *Estudios Sociales Centroamericanos* 11 (Sept.–Dec. 1973): 83–120.

————. *Orden y progreso: La formación del estado nacional en Costa Rica.* San José: ICAP, 1981.

————. *Poder político y democracia en Costa Rica.* San José: Editorial Porvenir, 1982.

Winson, Anthony. *Coffee and Democracy in Modern Costa Rica.* New York: St. Martin's Press, 1989.

Other Works

Aston, T. H. and C. H. E. Philpin, eds., *The Brenner Debate.* Cambridge: Cambridge University Press, 1985.

Braudel, Fernand. *The Structures of Everyday Life.* New York: Harper & Row, 1979.

Burns, E. Bradford. *The Poverty of Progress.* Berkeley: University of California Press, 1980.

Buzzanell, Peter J. "Coffee Production and Trade in Latin America." U.S. Department of Agriculture Food and Agriculture Service Paper M-288. Washington, D.C.: U.S. Department of Agriculture, May 1979.

Christian Science Monitor.

Commodity Research Bureau. *Commodity Yearbooks,* 1939, 1942, 1950, 1963, 1975, 1985.

Evans, Peter B., Dietrich Rueschemeyer, and Theda Skocpol, eds., *Bringing the State Back In*. Cambridge: Cambridge University Press, 1985.

Henderson, W. O. *The Zollverein*. Chicago: Quadrangle Books, 1939.

Jiménez, Michael F. "Traveling Far in Grandfather's Car: The Life Cycle of Central Colombian Coffee Estates." *Hispanic American Historical Review* 69 (May 1989): 185–220.

Los Angeles Times.

Lucier, Richard. *The International Political Economy of Coffee*. New York: Praeger, 1988.

Mesoamérica.

Moore, Barrington, Jr. *Social Origins of Dictatorship and Democracy: Lord and Peasant in the Making of the Modern World*. Boston: Beacon Press, 1966.

Mulhall, Michael. *The Dictionary of Statistics*. London: George Routledge and Sons, 1899.

North, Douglass C. *Institutions, Institutional Change, and Economic Performance*. Cambridge: Cambridge University Press, 1990.

Paige, Jeffery. *Agrarian Revolution*. New York: Free Press, 1975.

Payer, Cheryl, ed. *Commodity Trade of the Third World*. New York: Wiley, 1975.

Romero, Matías. *Cultivo del café en la costa meridional de Chiapas*. Mexico City: Oficina Tipografía de la Secretaría de Fomento, 1893.

Roseberry, William. *Coffee and Capitalism in the Venezuelan Andes*. Austin: University of Texas Press, 1983.

———. "La Falta de Brazos: Land and Labor in the Coffee Economies of Nineteenth-Century Latin America." *Theory and Society* 20 (1991): 351–82.

Rowe, J. W. F. *The World's Coffee*. London: Her Majesty's Stationery Office, 1963.

Skocpol, Theda. *States and Social Revolutions*. Cambridge: Cambridge University Press, 1979.

Ukers, William H. *All About Coffee*. New York: The Tea and Coffee Trade Journal Company, 1935.

United Nations Food and Agriculture Organization. *The World's Coffee*. Rome: Villa Borghese, 1947.

Weber, Max. *Theory of Social and Economic Organization*. London: William Hodge, 1947.

Wickizer, Vernon D. *Coffee, Tea, and Cocoa*. Stanford: Stanford University Press, 1951.

Williams, C. N. *The Agronomy of the Major Tropical Crops*. London: Oxford University Press, 1975.

Index